Hodgson called:
ofai Buy 12.6
Deivito mgr.

Corder file: CSR

Patent approved: nothing to steel (mining).

Patent attorney: Flair & Swain — wait on this.

when do we want to get into production:

Jan 6   Sawing   JB   ⟹ transfer to production Dic
           Orientation   CSR   Shown
           lapping (routine)   JT

           Crystal evaluation

Mar 3   photo etching   RNN
              routine diff NPN   GEM

Mar 17   evap & alloying   GEM

April 1   assembly NPN   R.B.

April 15   test & selection   UG

May 5   PNP Diffusion   JAH.

June 2   polish to thickness JT

June 15   PNIP   JT

supervisors for production — low tech skills in general
   ∴ we write production specs.

Jan 6   Feb   ∴ 13 more tech people by 2/1
                     2 tech
Sr. Eng. JAH.   Sr. Eng. UG.
2 tech
                                                santos now.
                                                girl   "

6   3

Makers of the Microchip

This is a joint publication of the Chemical Heritage Foundation's Center for Contemporary History and Policy and the MIT Press.

The Center's program in the Chemical History of Electronics is devoted to studying the place of materials and chemical processes in the history of electronics, particularly semiconductor electronics.

About the Chemical Heritage Foundation

The Chemical Heritage Foundation (CHF) fosters an understanding of chemistry's impact on society. An independent nonprofit organization, we strive to inspire a passion for chemistry, highlight chemistry's role in meeting current social challenges, and preserve the story of chemistry across centuries. CHF maintains major collections of instruments, fine art, photographs, papers, and books. We host conferences and lectures, support research, offer fellowships, and produce educational materials. Our museum and public programs explore subjects ranging from alchemy to nanotechnology.

Chemical Heritage Foundation
LIBRARY · MUSEUM · CENTER FOR SCHOLARS
315 Chestnut Street, Philadelphia, PA 19106
Phone: 215-925-2222 Fax 215-925-1954
www.chemheritage.org

Makers of the Microchip

A Documentary History of Fairchild Semiconductor

Christophe Lécuyer
David C. Brock

The MIT Press
Cambridge, Massachusetts
London, England

For information about special quantity discounts, email special_sales@mitpress.mit.edu.

Set in Stone Sans and Stone Serif by Graphic Composition, Inc.
Printed and bound in Canada.

Library of Congress Cataloging-in-Publication Data

Lécuyer, Christophe.
Makers of the microchip : a documentary history of Fairchild Semiconductor / Christophe Lécuyer and David C. Brock.
p. cm.
Includes facsimiles of historical documents.
Includes bibliographical references and index.
ISBN 978-0-262-01424-3 (hardcover : alk. paper) 1. Fairchild (Firm)—History. 2. Fairchild (Firm)—Archives. 3. Semiconductors—Design and construction—History. 4. Integrated circuits—Design and construction—History. I. Brock, David C. II. Title.
TK7871.85.L4167 2010
338.7'621381528097309045—dc22

2009049182

10 9 8 7 6 5 4 3 2 1

Contents

Foreword

Jay Last

This documentary history covers the period from 1957 to 1961, four years in which the co-founders of Fairchild Semiconductor established the path of technological development in semiconductor electronics that the industry has followed to this day.

In October 1957, my fellow Fairchild founders and I left the firm Shockley Semiconductor Laboratory to go into business for ourselves, with the intention of developing and producing diffused silicon transistors. At this time, most transistors were made one at a time, mainly using germanium and alloying techniques. While silicon technology was in its infancy and initially would present more technical and fabrication problems than would be the case with germanium, we felt that the future lay with silicon. Specifically, we believed that by diffusing arrays of devices on silicon wafers, we might turn transistor fabrication into a mass-production process that would eventually lead to very low-cost devices. Also, the fact that silicon devices would operate at much higher temperatures than those fabricated from germanium would open a large number of potential new markets.

The basic ideas we would use, silicon diffusion and the use of silicon oxide as a mask to delineate device structures, had been developed over the previous few years, mainly at Bell Laboratories, and were known to us from our Shockley experience. However, these approaches were far from production processes, and the road to making reproducible reliable products involved a better understanding of the basic science they were based on, and the development of a host of supporting technologies.

As the documents in this book show, the elapsed time from moving into an empty building to having the first device for sale was only ten months, and the total amount expended during this start-up was under $2 million. This was a period of intense activity for us. We were all very young (27 to 32), only a few years beyond our school days. We were a very compatible group, and spent a lot of time together outside our working hours. Most of the founders were married, busy starting their families and raising small children in addition to all the time and effort they were spending building Fairchild. Within the group we possessed the backgrounds in physics, chemistry, metallurgy, semiconductor electronics, and mechanical engineering necessary to solve the host of problems that arose. We had an important advantage: we were starting from scratch and had no products that would be outmoded by our new advances. We were all focused on the single common goal of producing our first product, a double diffused silicon mesa transistor.

The rapid acceptance of Fairchild's first products showed that we had picked a promising direction. This was a very frightening period on the world scene. The Cold War was well underway, and there was a tremendous military effort in this country directed toward the development of miniaturized airborne electronic systems. Our small, lightweight, high-performance transistors proved to be ideal for these needs. Over the next few years, our accelerating military sales enabled us to build up the volume needed to lower our production costs, thereby hastening our ability to sell our products into commercial and consumer markets.

In these early days, we could not foresee, of course, what the semiconductor electronic world would be like half a century later. With all the advances of understanding the electronic properties of a wide variety of materials from the 1950s and the 1960s on, we never envisioned that silicon would still be the basic material used, and that devices would still be fabricated in large part through extensions of the diffusion and photolithographic processes that we developed. From our viewpoint in the late 1950s, when new product developments and factories outfitted with production equipment cost a few million dollars at most, we could not imagine the vast sums that semiconductor companies throughout the world would steadily spend to improve and refine the technology, and that new product introductions today would cost a billion dollars. The complexity of today's integrated circuits, composed of millions of minuscule individual interconnected devices, and their widespread use in personal computers and other consumer products were beyond the realm of science fiction when we started Fairchild.

As I look back on what the technical world was like in the 1950s, I am struck by what a remarkable time it was and what innovative opportunities were available. The basic ideas of quantum mechanics, which led to our understanding of the electronic properties of solids, had been developed in the 1920s. However, the depression of the 1930s slowed down the utilization of these new concepts. There were enormous technological advances during the war years of the 1940s, aimed of course toward specific military goals. In the 1950s, therefore, the technology buckets were full, ready to be exploited in a host of new directions for innovative products of all sorts. Our silicon transistors and then integrated circuits were classic products of such exploitation.

In the past few years, I have been thinking about the nature of what we call invention: how inventions are nearly all based on the work of large numbers of innovators who preceded them, and how few ideas are really radically new. I have realized that the successful inventor is one who is conversant with an existing technology and the promise it holds, and who can then visualize how to make a product or product improvement that the world needs, wants, and will pay for. The successful inventor works to develop the supporting technology needed to make a particular product and then aggressively promotes the fruits of his work. In nearly all cases, a number of people are pursing the same basic ideas at the same time, and the successful innovator is the one from this number who puts all the pieces together first.

Our work at Fairchild fit into this mold. With our knowledge of existing semiconductor theory and technology, and the ways they were being used when we started Fairchild, we could envision a host of new directions to take. We were not constrained by a lack of imagination, and were able to think up new device structures with ease. Nevertheless, we constrained ourselves by focusing on the goal of using the technology we had at hand to make a family of devices that would find a ready market. A great source for our success was this ability to define in detail the problems we faced, which provided us with directions for developing missing pieces required to make a practical device. After establishing our first family of products, diffused mesa transistors, we could then visualize the new directions to pursue, for which Fairchild is now famous: the planar process and the integrated circuit. Both of these ideas were contemplated at least a year before active work was started on them, and this work commenced only when the technology had advanced enough so that it was practical to do serious development work toward actual products.

Beyond the planar process and the integrated circuit, another result from Fairchild was the onset of the venture capital industry. We were one of the first companies set up in this way. Arthur Rock, who was instrumental in providing the support for our company, moved from New York to San Francisco around 1960, and set his own venture capital firm. The promise and rewards from this new financial vehicle led to the establishment of a large number of venture capital firms, most of them located in the San Francisco Bay area. The huge amount of money they raised provided the support for the explosive growth of Silicon Valley over the coming decades.

I have been asked many times how the semiconductor industry would have evolved if we had not started Fairchild and made the technical advances we did. With the intense interest in and need for miniature electronic devices, and with the large number of companies working on the development of semiconductor technology at the same time we were, it would only have been a matter of time before the innovations were made by another firm. In all likelihood, this would have happened outside of what is now called Silicon Valley, taking place in Southern California, in Texas, or in any one of a number of locations in the eastern United States. As it happened, we speeded up the process, made a number of innovations at the right time, and firmly established Silicon Valley as a technological center.

The majority of the documents reproduced in this book came from my private collection. When I left Fairchild, I packed up a box of documents relating to our formative days. I kept this collection stored in my cellar throughout the years as I moved from place to place. I didn't look at these papers for years, but at least this benign neglect kept them safe and intact.

In the first several decades after our work of the late 1950s, there was little interest in the early Fairchild history. What little that was written about the early days was rather superficial and anecdotal. About ten years ago, as the invention of the transistor at Bell Telephone Laboratories reached its fiftieth anniversary and explosive growth in the incorporation of integrated circuits in commercial products occurred, serious historians of technology began to express an interest in the beginnings of Fairchild and how it influenced the growth of the semiconductor industry. I sorted my documents and made my holdings available to a number of researchers.

The chief document, many pages of which are reproduced here, was a notebook in which I recorded what transpired at the various meetings we held during the early Fairchild years. We worked at first as a group without strong formal leadership, and our main method of interaction was a series of weekly meetings, usually held on Monday mornings, where we would discuss the problems we were facing, and would allocate tasks and set schedules. We were novices in the business world, and many of our early discussions dealt with the steady flow of business and budgetary problems we faced. Also, the notebook contained reports of technical meetings members of the group attended, discussions of our efforts to find a market for our new devices, and the exact specifications for the initial product. I am not clear today why I kept meeting notes in this form, the only one in the group who did. Part of the reason was that I am more comfortable in a meeting if I am busy doing something, and part was because I was less than two years beyond my graduate school days and still in the habit of keeping notes of my professors' lectures.

When historians asked to use my box of documents, I looked at this notebook for the first time in many years and realized that it held a great deal of material of interest to them. A few years ago Gordon Moore and I went over the notebook, which jogged our memories about a number of points not included in the notebook. David Brock and Christophe Lécuyer recorded our discussions, which helped them to develop additional material for their commentaries here. Gordon kindly contributed a number of important historical documents from the early history of Fairchild to this book, documents he had likewise saved in his personal papers.

Another notable document reproduced here is a copy of the letter that Eugene Kleiner wrote to Hayden Stone & Company when we had decided to leave Shockley and were looking for some way to keep working as a group. In the 1970s I was curious to recall what we had said in this first prospectus. I asked Eugene if he still had a copy, and he gave me the bedraggled carbon copy reproduced here. Shortly later all of his Fairchild records were destroyed in a fire in his garage, so this is the only surviving copy.

After Jean Hoerni's death in 1997, his widow Jennifer Wilson went through his papers and was nice enough to send the ones relating to his technical history to me, asking me to be their custodian. One of the main documents reproduced in this book, Jean's disclosure of his ideas for the planar process, accurately dates the time he was working to develop this revolutionary approach.

National Semiconductor became the owners of the Fairchild archives when they acquired Fairchild in 1987. They realized the historical importance of our patent notebooks, carefully preserved them and provided access to them for this book. National Semiconductor donated other Fairchild materials, including the early monthly progress reports of the Fairchild integrated circuit development group, to Stanford University, where they are available to scholars.

So, by one means and another, this body of material has survived for half a century. I am pleased that it will be accessible in this form, helping readers of this book to better understand these important events and their contexts.

Acknowledgments

This book would not have been possible without the generous support of Jay Last, who allowed us to reproduce documents from his personal collection and assisted us at every step of this project. His help was given liberally and with no conditions attached. We are also grateful for the backing of the Chemical Heritage Foundation and the support of Arnold Thackray, Thomas Tritton, Miriam Fisher Schaefer, Ron Reynolds, and Hyungsub Choi for this project. We would like to extend special thanks to W. Bernard Carlson for his wise counsel and to Patrick Fridenson for his insightful reading of the manuscript. Philip Scranton made helpful suggestions on documentary history and two anonymous referees provided very perceptive comments on an earlier version of the manuscript. We also want to thank Marguerite Avery, Paul Bethge, and Erin Shoudy at the MIT Press for supporting our book project and shepherding it to publication.

In addition to Jay Last, the following individuals and institutions granted us permissions to reproduce documents and photographs in this volume: Gordon Moore, Lionel Kattner, Dick Schubert of National Semiconductor, Margaret Kimball at the Stanford University Archives, Patti Olson of Fairchild Semiconductor, Patrick Hindle of Horizon House, Time & Life Pictures, and the McGraw-Hill Companies. We would like to thank them for allowing us to publish these documents. We would also like to thank the cofounders and former employees of Fairchild Semiconductor who granted us numerous interviews over the last 14 years. An oral history interview with Gordon Moore and Jay Last specifically oriented to discussion of Jay Last's personal notebook—the main document reproduced in this volume—was especially helpful.

It was Christophe Lécuyer who developed the general concept for the book and much of the foundational research for it is his. David Brock and Christophe Lécuyer equally shared the writing and the development of the analysis and interpretation for this effort. The book is the result of a true collaboration—an experience that both authors enjoyed.

We would like to thank our families for their forbearance and their encouragements as we worked many long days and long nights on this manuscript. We would like to dedicate this book to our spouses and daughters, Judith Zakaria, Pascaline Lécuyer, Jennifer Stromsten, Vivian Brock, and Lucinda Brock.

Introduction

The world has changed profoundly since 1950, and one prominent aspect of the change has been digitalization. In technical parlance, digitization is the process of converting an analog signal—which varies smoothly across a range of values—into a digital signal that models the analog input as a series of discrete values of 0 or 1. The term 'digitalization' describes a larger historical development that encompasses the digitization of information but also much more. It denotes the transformation of the human-built world by its thorough saturation with digital electronics. Since 1950, industries have increasingly incorporated digital electronics into their products, their manufacturing technologies, and their infrastructures for providing services. Moreover, new industrial sectors have developed solely on the basis of digital electronics. These new sectors, including personal computing and digital telecommunications (the Internet, mobile telephony), have affected economies and cultures dramatically.[1]

The most important technological trend, one that has allowed groups to carry on the project of digitalization, has been the steady and exponential increase in the capacities of silicon integrated circuits—which have become synonymous with digital electronics—in tandem with the decrease in their cost. This technological trend in silicon integrated circuits has required the concerted efforts of hundreds of thousands of researchers, engineers, and technicians and the investment of several hundred billion dollars over five decades (and counting). The spread of digital electronics has required substantial expansion of the semiconductor industry. The digitalization of existing industries and technologies and the development of natively digital sectors (e.g. personal computing) have similarly required large-scale economic activities. Chief among these economic activities has been the venture capital funding that has been used to create new firms that pursue products and services based on new digital technologies or on the reform of established technologies, products, or services through digital electronics. This "Silicon Valley dynamic" was risk-tolerant, with the majority of start-ups failing quickly. The net result of this scattershot approach, which produced crucial successes, was the rapid expansion of digitalization.[2]

It is the argument of this volume that in the period 1957–1961—during which Fairchild Semiconductor went from a start-up firm to the creation of the first planar integrated circuit or microchip—Fairchild Semiconductor was a critical site in the establishment of the technology path for digital electronics that has continued to the present day. Fairchild was also a critical site in the initiation of important aspects of the Silicon Valley business dynamic (which, like silicon integrated circuits, spread worldwide). During that period, the founders of Fairchild Semiconductor, and the groups they assembled and worked alongside, responded to an unfolding sequence of challenges posed by three distinct contexts—each with its own dynamic or logic—as they worked to develop and manufacture silicon semiconductor devices for applications in military digital computing. These three contexts were *silicon logic*, *user logic*, and *competitive logic*. Silicon logic encompassed the characteristics and behaviors exhibited by silicon materials, and the processes for working with them. These materials and processes seldom conformed to researchers' initial hopes and intentions. Instead, they consistently presented new phenomena that created challenges for the researchers to explore, overcome, and exploit. Silicon logic led not just to resistance but also to positive contributions to researchers' goals. Indeed, the central innovations produced at Fairchild Semiconductor between 1957 and 1961—a manufacturing technology for diffused silicon devices, the planar process, and the planar integrated circuit—were fundamentally based on the specific characteristics and performances of the layers of silicon oxide that readily formed on silicon crystal.

User logic was another prime context that shaped developments at Fairchild Semiconductor. The initial aim of the founders of Fairchild Semiconductor was to create a manufacturing technology with which to produce silicon devices for use in military digital computers. Thus, the needs, demands, and interests of their intended customers—the users of their products—were, from the very earliest stage, significant factors in the decisions of the founders. The users were the producers of digital avionic systems—including computers—for the U.S. military. As the founders of Fairchild Semiconductor interacted with these users during the firm's early years, they became increasingly cognizant of and responsive to the aims and interests of these producers of military digital computers and systems—their user logic.

Four aspects of this user logic were particularly important for Fairchild Semiconductor. First, the users emphasized the reliability of semiconductor components, as they were under intense pressure from the military to provide computer and avionics systems with far lower failure rates. Second, they emphasized the miniaturization of semiconductor components and digital circuits. The military believed that the miniaturization of components and circuits was another route to reliability. It was a straightforward argument that smaller, lighter electronic systems would also reduce the cost of aerospace projects (e.g., intercontinental ballistic missiles). Third, the user logic had a constant trend toward increased speed of transistors and diodes for use in military digital computers. Faster was better for military digital computers, and the switching speeds of the transistors and diodes used in these systems were a limiting factor in the overall speed of the computers' operation. Fourth, and broadest, was the strong push within the user logic for digital systems and digital computers in military applications, particularly aerospace applications. The military was actively pursing the digitalization of its technologies, weapons, and systems as a way of increasing their effectiveness, their reliability, and their capabilities. Fairchild Semiconductor's founders responded to these pushes for reliability, miniaturization, and speed in semiconductor devices with technological innovations; they also responded to the pull of expanding digitalization by making the business decisions to rapidly expand their firm and the number and variety of their products for digital computing.

The third logic that shaped the early history of Fairchild Semiconductor was competitive logic. To enter the semiconductor business, Fairchild Semiconductor's founders set out to integrate several new approaches to the fabrication of silicon devices that had been established within a laboratory context at a variety of different organizations. Their aim was to combine diffusion, oxide masking, and photolithography to produce a diffused silicon junction transistor—something that was, at the time, not available on the market. This opportunity, the founders reasoned, represented a substantial market that they could capture if they acted quickly. This element of urgency in the early history of Fairchild Semiconductor was a response to a competitive logic: the structure of the semiconductor industry at the time, along with the relative advantages and approaches of firms.

Through the 1950s, the semiconductor industry moved with extreme rapidity, with a high turnover of players in the industry, new manufacturing approaches developed frequently, and a flurry of new device designs making it to the marketplace. Many of Fairchild Semiconductor's competitors were also responding to the same silicon and user logics, which intensified their competitive threat. In the period covered by this volume, 1957–1961, Fairchild Semiconductor was in an ongoing race with Texas Instruments. Texas Instruments, the largest semiconductor firm at the time, was the early leader in silicon semiconductors and so was focused on the same user logic as Fairchild Semiconductor. Moreover, several of the same elements of the silicon logic that Fairchild encountered were faced by Texas Instruments too. At the time of the formation of Fairchild Semiconductor, Texas Instruments was headed in the direction of diffused silicon junction transistors. From the start the two firms were engaged in a race.

Responding to these logics (silicon logic, user logic, and competitive logic), Fairchild Semiconductor's founders created technological innovations and made business decisions that brought Fairchild from a start-up to a leadership position in the semiconductor industry by 1961. The innovations that Fairchild produced in this period—the manufacturing technology for diffused silicon devices, the planar process, and the planar integrated circuit—were fundamental innovations, setting the mainline path of technological development that the semiconductor industry has pursued to this day. Further, the business actions that took place at the firm did much to set in motion a business dynamic—the Silicon Valley dynamic. In this business dynamic, risk-tolerant venture capital funding supported the creation of numerous firms aimed at new technologies, particularly technologies connected to digital electronics. Thus, Fairchild

Semiconductor's activities in the years 1957–1961 led to the tremendous growth in silicon digital electronics and to the digitalization of the world. Although several excellent treatments of the history of Fairchild Semiconductor exist in the literature, this volume is unique in addressing the roles of all three of these contexts, or logics, in the early history of Fairchild, and in providing a detailed account of how these logics simultaneously shaped fundamental innovations and business actions.[3]

The analysis developed in this book follows a *documentary history* approach. Historical documents relating to Fairchild Semiconductor are reproduced in facsimile, accompanied by interpretive discussions and a historical overview (chapter 1). From several private and archival sources, we were able to gather together a significant fraction of the surviving unpublished documents and ephemera connected with the founders of Fairchild Semiconductor from the period 1957–1961. This documentary history offers close interpretations of important historical documents, yielding detailed insights into Fairchild Semiconductor's activities and contexts, a view of its business decisions, and an examination of the fine-grain structure of technological innovations.

What is a documentary history? Such a publication, often consisting of multiple volumes, is a collection of historical documents—letters, memoranda, notes, essays, sketches, legislation, diaries, novels—accompanied by explications and interpretations. Traditionally, documentary histories have taken as their subjects literary figures, statesmen, and political institutions. For literary subjects, the traditional goal has been to produce a definitive collection, both in terms of the version of the individual works collected and the completeness of the collection itself. For political subjects, the completeness of the collection is also a goal, but in many ways explication and interpretation are the foremost concerns. That is, the central concern in such documentary histories, once the assembly of an exhaustive collection is achieved, is the manner in which the documents should be interpreted for the reader. Over time, the methodological pendulum has swung from little interpretation (save in footnotes for the identification of proper nouns and cryptic markings) to highly interpretive approaches with lengthy explanatory footnotes and interpretive essays.[4]

Two foundational aspects of traditional documentary history are easily overlooked. First, the historical importance of the subject is already established: for example, the significance of John Steinbeck, of Thomas Jefferson, or of the first Federal Congress is not at issue. Second, the completeness of traditional documentary histories conceals the inherently interpretive nature of document selection. The selection of documents to include in a documentary history is, fundamentally, an interpretive act. Selection is argument. Documentary histories that aim for completeness—presenting nearly every document attributable to or connected with its subject—are the result of a specific selection decision: inclusion of all. The interpretive stance of such a decision is simple: the historical importance of the subject is such that every document is significant, and that the effort and cost of its publication is thereby justified. Perhaps, then, it is not surprising that such comprehensive traditional documentary histories have been government-supported decades-long endeavors.

In recent decades, documentary history has expanded to include cultural figures, institutions, and historical topics beyond the traditional remit of statesmen, organizations of state, and the authors of literary canons. Recent titles from just the discipline of American History include documentary histories on such subjects as Emma Goldman; everyday life in Laredo, Texas; the experience of Jews in the California Gold Rush; and "Jim Crow New York." For such documentary histories, especially those with historical topics as their subject, selection and argument go hand in hand. Selection in these projects is of practical and often also intellectual necessity. The scale and resource constraints of these projects require a targeted approach to the acquisition and the presentation of documents. More significantly, these new documentary histories have as their aim the establishment of the importance of their subjects, or of some particular interpretive claim about them. In this way, the selection of documents for inclusion in the work reflects a deliberate process of historical interpretation. The documents are evidentiary. Within such works, other interpretive apparatus frequently appear: long explanatory notes and layers of interpretive essays.[5]

Just as the universe of subjects for documentary history has changed, along with views of the propriety of interpretation, so too have the media of publication. With the rise of desktop publishing, digital imaging and printing, many of the underlying rationales for the practices of documentary history have been revisited. In traditional documentary histories, handwritten materials were cast into typescript and, when the original language of the document was deemed obscure, translated. Transcription and typescripting raised a host of methodological options and approaches, including questions of revisions of spelling and even of grammar.[6] In these editions, facsimile reproductions of documents were rare inclusions, comparable in cost and technique to the inclusion of photographs. Recently, with the advent of lower-cost digital imaging and printing, facsimile reproductions for documentary histories have become more practical. Facsimile reproductions add a new dimension to documentary history: an experience of the materiality of the documents and the material culture of their production.[7]

This volume is an interpretive documentary history in this recent, digital mode. Its primary goal is interpretation: to provide an answer to a particular historical question. Its secondary goal, expressed through the use of facsimile reproduction, is experiential: to give readers an encounter with the raw materials from which history is produced. With these two goals, the volume is apparently unique in the history of technology literature. In its focus on the construction of an argument it does, however, share common cause with a recent work by Caroll Pursell: *A Hammer in Their Hands: A Documentary History of Technology and the African-American Experience*.

As in other historical genres, documentary history has most often taken as its subject the "early" figures, organizations, and topics associated with a particular area. In the case of American history, the focus of documentary history has been the Founding

Fathers and the early Republic. In the case of the history of technology, this same orientation appears. Some documentary histories in the traditional mold treat seminal figures such as the Wright Brothers and Thomas Edison. More recently, documentary histories of American atomic policy, genetic engineering, and of the contributions of African-Americans to American technology have been published.[8] One of the great contributions of documentary history authors and editors has been the assembly of relevant materials from widely disparate and often obscure sources: government repositories, institutional holdings, archival and library deposits, and collections in private hands.

This documentary history of Fairchild Semiconductor is the result of just such a sustained effort at collecting materials. The central document in this volume is Jay Last's personal notebook, in which he recorded notes, primarily as an *aide-mémoire*, about the fast-paced developments at the new firm in its first months and years. Last not only retained his notebook; he also gathered around it a large and organized collection of other documents from the early history of Fairchild Semiconductor. In addition, collections in the hands of National Semiconductor (which purchased Fairchild Semiconductor in the late 1980s) and of Gordon Moore (one of the founders of Fairchild Semiconductor) provided documents for this volume. The materials from these private collections are here publicly available in full for the first time. In addition to these private collections, the Special Collections of the Stanford University libraries provided an essential document.

A number of principles guided our selection of documents for this book. We were interested in presenting documents illuminating the different logics—silicon logic, user logic, and competitive logic—that shaped the organization of the firm and the development of silicon technology. Another consideration was the desire to cover the important milestones in the development of Fairchild Semiconductor's manufacturing technology and organizational structure. We also wanted to reproduce several types of documents on Fairchild Semiconductor and the development of the planar process and the integrated circuit. Among these documents are letters, business memoranda, personal notebooks, patent notebooks, patent disclosures, lecture notes, monthly reports, engineering drawings, advertisements, and several articles published in the trade press and in Fairchild Semiconductor's newsletter, *Leadwire*. These documents offer a rich picture of Fairchild's technological and business developments and their effects.

The documents reproduced either partially or in their entirety in this book represent a significant fraction of the entire corpus of known documents on Fairchild Semiconductor during this period. Few personal letters and business memoranda related to Fairchild Semiconductor have survived the last 50 years. What remains are mostly advertisements, product sheets, sales pamphlets, and application notes published by the firm. These application notes explained how customers could use Fairchild's devices and integrate them into their own circuits and systems. Stanford University's Archives and Special Collections also hold a series of monthly reports, mostly from Fairchild's research and development laboratory. Most of these reports were written in 1960 or

1961. Another important source on Fairchild Semiconductor is the collection of patent notebooks held by National Semiconductor.[9]

Our method of presentation for this documentary history is the reproduction of facsimiles of the historical materials. The reasons for this are manifold. In many cases, the original documents are typed, so transcription of handwriting was not necessary. Further, in cases where the documents are handwritten, the hands are modern, as are the spelling and the grammar; again, transcription was not necessary. On the positive side, facsimile provides the viewer with rich visual detail, providing experiential information about the material culture associated with the documents, their production, and their circulation.

Each facsimile document is explained and interpreted. This allows the reader to move through the historical narrative and the interpretations more easily than if extended footnotes were appended to the facsimiles. The interpretive essays provide explications of the details of the historical events captured by each document: who the players were, and what they did. Additionally, each essay examines the document as a historical artifact, addressing such issues as its origins, its authorship, its circulation, and its intended effects. In terms of the resources that were utilized to construct these interpretive essays, and to develop the overall interpretation, this volume is seemingly unique in the literature of documentary history in the history of technology, and perhaps in documentary history. This uniqueness is the use of extensive oral histories with the authors of the documents, and others who worked alongside them. We conducted extensive oral history interviews with more than twenty founders and early employees of Fairchild Semiconductor. We also conducted an extensive joint oral history interview with Jay Last and Gordon Moore, about Last's notebook. Through these oral histories, our interpretation of the documents is uniquely enriched by the historical actors' own recollections of the creation, meaning, and consequences of the documents and the events they reflect.

Our approach—a contextualized historical reconstruction of the fine structure of technological innovation—takes its methodological inspiration from the works of Frederic L. Holmes in the history of science, from W. Bernard Carlson and Michael E. Gorman's study of the notebooks of Thomas Edison in the tradition of sociologically informed history of technology, and from the positions articulated in several recent works in the field of science and technology studies by Andrew Pickering.[10] Holmes, Carlson, and Gorman used close examination of laboratory and experimental notebooks along with related manuscript material for reconstructions of the intellectual and physical activities of scientists and technologists—set against a number of different contexts—in their creation of new knowledge and innovations. In this, for Holmes especially, the historical reconstructions are "thick descriptions," filled with detail and contextual connections, and also possessing extensive treatments of technical subjects: the materials, instruments, machines, devices, concepts, processes, practices, and understandings that were the scientist or technologist's constant, immediate companions in his or her work. These detailed reconstructions led several critics to disparage such an approach as "internalist." Works following a similar approach in the history of technology are often criticized with the corresponding accusation of "antiquarianism." Both the charge of internalism in the history of science and that of antiquarianism in the history of technology are associated with detailed reconstructions and a high level of technical content. The common charge, in essence, is that these reconstructions miss more important features and dynamics (often social, political, and economic).

Holmes articulated a number of responses to this charge, and his answers may stand as a response for not just his work, but also the general methodological approach of basing contextualized reconstructions on notebooks and related manuscript materials in the history of science, the history of technology, and science and technology studies.

> There is no doubt that . . . social processes are centrally important to the construction of scientific knowledge; but a fixation on these processes obscures another crucial dimension of scientific activity, the sustained private encounters of the investigator with a bounded domain of nature. It is this dimension that can be best explored through such documents as laboratory notebooks. Through them, I believe, we can obtain a more balanced view of the issue of how scientific knowledge is constructed. . . . My own view is that investigative scientists are immersed simultaneously in a network of social processes and of encounters of what we identify, however vaguely or metaphorically, with nature or material reality. We still have much further to go than some of us believe before we will have sufficiently detailed pictures of the interactions. . . . We need historical reconstructions at all scales of resolution.[11]

Indeed, Holmes' position is closely aligned with the general account of scientific and technological change developed by the historian and sociologist Andrew Pickering. Pickering's view of the generative dynamic of scientific and technological change centers on his concept of reciprocal structuring. In his framework, the workspaces of scientists and technologists are the location for sustained encounters between human and material agency, between the intentions of human researchers and the performances of material systems (e.g., the material samples and instrumental tools in a laboratory). Through these open-ended, intensive interactions, researchers' intentions and the configuration and performances of material systems produce change in one another. This reciprocal structuring results in new intentions and understandings, and in new materials and physical systems with novel performance characteristics—in short, scientific and technological change. For Pickering, the historical investigations required to examine and elucidate this process are just these contextualized detailed reconstructions that engage the technical. Just as contextualization provides understanding of the structure of the intentions of the researcher, the technical details provide the essential description of the performances of the material systems.[12]

In chapter 1 we present an overview of the historical narratives and interpretive arguments, which we then develop in greater detail and length in the interpretive discussions that accompany the facsimiles of the primary documents in chapter 2. The concluding chapter is followed by an appendix that presents a technical overview of silicon technology, transistors, integrated circuits, and digital computing. Readers who have little previous exposure to semiconductor electronics may find the appendix of use in orienting them to the technical aspects of the documentary history.[13]

1 Fairchild Semiconductor, Silicon Technology, and Military Computing

The Fairchild Semiconductor Corporation was founded in September 1957 by eight scientists and engineers: Gordon Moore, Jay Last, Jean Hoerni, Robert Noyce, C. Sheldon Roberts, Victor Grinich, Eugene Kleiner, and Julius Blank. These men were very young, in their late twenties and early thirties, at the time of Fairchild Semiconductor's formation. They also had impeccable academic pedigrees. Last, Noyce, and Roberts had PhDs in the physical sciences from the Massachusetts Institute of Technology. Moore had a doctorate in chemistry and physics from the California Institute of Technology. Grinich had a PhD in electrical engineering from Stanford University. Hoerni had a doctorate in physics from Cambridge University and another from the University of Geneva. Kleiner and Blank were mechanical engineers with significant manufacturing experience at Western Electric, the production arm of the Bell Telephone system. The men in the group had a wide set of skills, ranging from glass blowing to infrared spectroscopy. They were also well versed in solid-state physics, metallurgy, optical engineering, physical chemistry, and circuit theory—all disciplines that later proved critical for the development of diffused silicon transistors. With the exception of Noyce, who had worked on high-speed germanium transistors at Philco, the founders of Fairchild Semiconductor were relatively new to the semiconductor industry. In 1956, they had joined the Shockley Semiconductor Laboratory, a small semiconductor firm located on the San Francisco Peninsula, where they had familiarized themselves with the complex techniques required to make silicon transistors.[1]

Silicon for Military Computing

Fairchild Semiconductor entered a dynamic field of technology and business—silicon transistors—that was dominated by Texas Instruments and the Bell Telephone Laboratories. Bell Labs originated much of semiconductor technology, including silicon transistors and the techniques for making them. A Bell Labs research group directed by William Shockley invented the first transistor, a point-contact germanium transistor, in 1947. Other scientists at Bell Labs later found ways of growing single crystals of germanium and silicon, the basic materials used in transistor production. Employing these crystal-growing techniques, the Bell Labs chemist Morgan Sparks made the

Figure 1.1
Fairchild Semiconductor's founders, circa 1960. Collection of Christophe Lécuyer.

first germanium junction transistor. This "grown-junction" transistor was fabricated by introducing dopants directly into the melted germanium during crystal growing.[2] That breakthrough led to the emergence of a large industry manufacturing germanium bipolar transistors. Many firms also made alloy transistors (a variant of the germanium junction transistor devised at Bell Labs; the junctions in such transistors were created by alloying a P-type material to a piece of germanium crystal). Engineers at Philco fabricated the first high-speed germanium junction transistor by creating a very thin slice of germanium crystal and alloying it on both sides with indium. As a result, the transistor had a very thin base region, which provided fast switching. Competing with Philco's approach, a group at Bell Labs made the diffused germanium transistor in 1954. Solid-state diffusion was a new technique that made possible controlled introduction of dopants into the crystal and fabrication of very thin base regions. With the new fast-switching germanium transistors, the producers of digital computers began to transistorize new products—particularly for military and government customers—thereby beginning a move away from vacuum tubes to semiconductor electronics.[3]

Starting in 1955, Bell Labs made major contributions to the art of the silicon transistor. In March, Morris Tanenbaum pioneered the use of solid-state diffusion for the fabrication of silicon transistors. By diffusing dopants into the crystal, Tanenbaum fabricated base regions thinner than had been made with other processing techniques and obtained a transistor that switched significantly faster than grown-junction devices. That transistor was called a "mesa transistor" because its profile resembled that of a mesa in the American Southwest. Other important techniques, including oxide masking, were developed at the Bell Telephone Laboratories. In oxide masking, a silicon oxide layer on top of the silicon crystal was used to control the areas in which dopants were introduced into the crystal. Tanenbaum's diffused silicon mesa transistor convinced the leaders of Bell Labs that diffused silicon transistors were the wave of the future. In March 1955, they began to reorient Bell Labs' resources toward the further development of that technology.[4]

Although Bell Labs had the largest and most productive research program in silicon transistors, it was Texas Instruments that dominated the early market for these devices. In 1952, TI's managers recruited Gordon Teal, a chemist who had developed techniques for growing single crystals of semiconductor elements at Bell Labs, to establish the firm's central research laboratory. Working with Willis Adcock and Morton Jones, Teal replicated the work he had done at Bell Labs on growing single crystals of silicon. Competing with Bell Labs, they fabricated the first grown-junction silicon transistor in May 1954. TI quickly marketed these grown-junction silicon transistors, which found a ready market in the military sector. Because silicon transistors, unlike their germanium counterparts, could operate at high temperatures, the military increasingly required that they be used in military equipment. Silicon transistors were also viewed in military circles as a way of improving the reliability and reducing the size of electronics systems. Unlike germanium transistors, silicon transistors did not require air conditioning to operate in high-temperature environments.[5]

Because the grown-junction technique yielded relatively slow-switching silicon transistors, researchers at TI looked for ways to make transistors that could operate at higher frequencies. In March 1956, a group directed by Willis Adcock combined grown-junction techniques with diffusion techniques to make faster silicon transistors. This combination approach made it possible to form thinner base regions, producing much greater speeds. The new transistors could reach frequencies of 250 megacycles. These new silicon transistors from TI were adopted for use in new military applications: airborne radars, communications, and navigation equipment. They could also be used in the logic circuitry of digital computers. The primary shortcoming of TI's silicon transistors was their high collector saturation resistance. This high resistance limited their ability to handle high power levels. Nevertheless, as a result of this wave of new products, TI became a major supplier of silicon transistors to the military sector. TI's sales of silicon transistors grew from a few hundred thousand dollars in 1954 to more than $80 million in 1960. By the late 1950s, Texas Instruments was the largest semiconductor manufacturer in the United States.[6]

In the mid 1950s, inspired by the success of Texas Instruments, other firms moved into the silicon transistor business. Transitron and some others replicated TI's grown-junction transistors. Others sought to make alloy transistors in silicon. In spite of considerable investments in this technology, no firm succeeded in fabricating viable silicon alloy transistors. Still other firms focused on bringing the diffused silicon mesa transistors pioneered by Bell Labs to the market. California was an important center of diffused silicon transistor activity. Indeed, all semiconductor firms in California focused on silicon devices (diodes and transistors). That included Hughes Semiconductor, a division of Hughes Aircraft, a large aerospace and electronics firm based in Southern California. Hughes Semiconductor was a major producer of silicon diodes and was in the process of entering the silicon transistor field in the middle 1950s. Hoffman Electronics, also based in Southern California, had an active research program in diffused silicon transistors, as did Pacific Semiconductors (a subsidiary of TRW).[7]

Notable among the silicon-oriented firms in California was the Shockley Semiconductor Laboratory, which had been established by William Shockley, the head of the group that had invented the transistor at Bell Labs. After the invention of the first transistor, Shockley played a significant role in leading the overall semiconductor research effort at the Bell Labs. In 1955, he established the Shockley Semiconductor Laboratory in Palo Alto as a subsidiary of Beckman Instruments, Inc., a chemical instrumentation company based in Southern California. Not only did Beckman Instruments rely on electronic components, but the firm was also moving into the production of both analog and digital computer systems. Shockley's initial goal was to bring the diffused silicon mesa transistors developed at Bell Labs to market and to manufacture them in significant volume. To build his research and engineering organization, Shockley hired the scientists and engineers (Moore, Last, Hoerni, Noyce, Grinich, Roberts, Kleiner, and Blank) who later would co-found Fairchild Semiconductor. At Shockley, these men conducted research on the basic technology of diffused silicon transistors. Much of their work was devoted to diffusion phenomena. They calculated diffusion-rate curves and tested these curves experimentally. They also experimented with forming mesa transistor structures.[8]

Shockley, however, reoriented his firm toward the production of another silicon device: the PNPN diode, which Shockley had conceived at Bell Labs a few years earlier.[9] The PNPN diode, directed at communication applications, was a more complex device than the transistor. It was a "functional device." In other words, it could perform a complete electronic circuit function. It was equivalent in operation to an electronic circuit made of two transistors, a diode, and a resistor. The PNPN proved much more difficult to make than Tanenbaum's mesa transistor. It required three diffusions instead of two. As a result, the engineers and scientists at Shockley Semiconductor encountered great difficulties in fabricating the PNPN device reproducibly. In addition, they thought that diffused transistors would lend themselves more easily to volume production, and that transistors had greater market potential than PNPN diodes, especially in the military sector.[10]

These differences of opinion regarding Shockley Semiconductor's technical and market orientation were compounded by the group members' increasingly tense personal relations with William Shockley. Shockley proved extremely difficult to work for. He frequently changed his opinions and his project goals. He also treated his staff poorly, staging public firings and ordering his employees to take lie-detector tests over a trifling issue. In April 1957, seven members of the senior staff (Moore, Last, Hoerni, Grinich, Roberts, Kleiner, and Blank) rebelled and asked Arnold Beckman, the president of Beckman Instruments, to remove Shockley from the day-to-day direction of the laboratory. After several meetings with the group where he considered alternative managerial arrangements, Beckman eventually sided with Shockley, and Shockley remained the leader of the organization.[11]

Feeling that they had burned their bridges with Shockley and Beckman, the rebels looked for a firm that would employ them as a group. They contacted Hayden Stone & Company, a small investment banking firm in New York with which the father of one of the rebels, Eugene Kleiner, had an account. They asked for Hayden Stone's help in finding a company that would be interested in sponsoring a group to produce diffused silicon transistors. Aware of the business opportunities in the semiconductor industry through previous deals, Alfred (Bud) Coyle (a Hayden Stone partner) and Arthur Rock (a young analyst) visited the Shockley rebels in San Francisco. Coyle and Rock, impressed by the rebels' intellects and their ability to work as a group, advised them to start their own semiconductor company. They offered to help the group of eight (Robert Noyce had now joined the original seven) to secure financing for the new venture. A difficult search for funding ensued, with only one firm, Fairchild Camera and Instrument, expressing an interest in financing the new organization. Fairchild Camera and Instrument, a military contractor based on Long Island, was keen to diversify into semiconductors in order to revive its sagging fortunes. The firm had seen its sales and its profits decline significantly since the end of the Korean War. Fairchild Camera and Instrument was also interested in entering other high-growth areas related to digital computing.[12]

In the summer of 1957, Hayden Stone and the group of Shockley employees negotiated an agreement with Fairchild Camera and Instrument. Under this agreement, Fairchild Camera and Instrument would finance the formation of a semiconductor firm. For this initial investment, it would have the option of buying the semiconductor company under certain conditions at a pre-approved price.[13] The minutes of a meeting of Fairchild Camera and Instrument's board of directors on 23 August 1957 summarized the agreement with Hayden Stone and the group of Shockley rebels as follows:

The President [John Carter] outlined a plan whereby the California group and Hayden Stone and Company of New York would organize under the laws of the state of Delaware a new corporation authorized to do business in California for the purpose of conducting research and development in the semi-conductor field and the production and sale of such semi-conductor products. The capital stock of the new corporation shall be subscribed for by the California group and Hayden Stone. The stock will immediately be placed in a voting trust with Fairchild Controls [Fairchild Camera's subsidiary on the West Coast] having the controlling interest. Fairchild Controls will then make loans to the new corporation for operating expenses, such loans to be evidenced by promissory notes of the new corporation. During the first eighteen months such advances are not to exceed $1,388,600. Fairchild Controls shall have the right at any time after the initial eighteen month period to terminate its obligation to make additional loans to the new corporation and if the stockholders do not purchase the outstanding promissory notes the assets of the new corporation will be sold to pay off the said notes. Up to the time when the average net earning of the new corporation shall exceed $300,000 per year, Fairchild Controls shall have an option to purchase all of the stock issued to the California group and Hayden Stone at a price per share determined by dividing $3,000,000 by the total number of shares theretofore issued by the new corporation.[14]

This was a very unusual financing agreement that anticipated, and indeed helped to establish, aspects of the venture capital business as it emerged on the San Francisco Peninsula in the 1960s. The agreement gave significant financial incentives to the founders to make a success of the business. But at the same time, their ownership would be limited in time, for just the first several years—a clause that had significant consequences a few years later. The majority stake that Fairchild Camera and Instrument and one of its existing West Coast subsidiaries together had in the voting trust gave them controlling representation on the semiconductor company's board. Richard Hodgson, Fairchild Camera and Instrument's executive vice-president, became the chairman of Fairchild Semiconductor. H. E. Hale, a vice-president of Fairchild Controls, was nominated to the presidency of the new corporation. Fairchild Camera and Instrument had three additional seats on the board. Representing Hayden Stone and the eight California scientists on the board were Bud Coyle and Robert Noyce.[15]

Adopting the name of its backer, the Fairchild Semiconductor Corporation opened for business in October 1957. The first task for the founders was to find a building and set up facilities suitable for semiconductor production. The founders soon located and rented a new building at 844 East Charleston Road, at the border between the towns of Palo Alto and Mountain View, only a mile from the Shockley Semiconductor Laboratory's original site. The Fairchild Semiconductor building was initially little more than a 14,000-square-foot shell without plumbing or electrical service. Over the next several months, Kleiner and Blank led an intensive push to build production, research, and office spaces. The majority of the founders set out to construct for themselves the specialized equipment required for developing a silicon transistor manufacturing technology: crystal growers, diffusion furnaces, vacuum evaporators, and optical systems for mask making and photolithography.[16]

With Hodgson's support, the founding group at Fairchild Semiconductor made fundamental decisions regarding the firm's technical orientation and business strategy in the first months of the corporation's existence. They decided to make diffused silicon mesa transistors for military computing and avionics applications. ('Avionics' refers to electronic systems used in airplanes and missiles for control, guidance, communications, and firing; many of these systems included computers.) Two members of the founding group, Noyce and Grinich, were familiar with digital computing. Noyce had worked on high-speed germanium transistors for computing at Philco, and the experience

Figure 1.2
Construction of Fairchild Semiconductor's laboratory, late 1957. Collection of Christophe Lécuyer.

Figure 1.3
Fairchild Semiconductor, late 1957. Collection of Christophe Lécuyer.

had familiarized him with digital logic circuits and military computers designed at both Philco and Bell Labs. Grinich had engineered transistor circuits for ERMA, the first digital computer for banking applications, in his previous position at the Stanford Research Institute. Through trips to aerospace firms in Southern California, the group confirmed that there was a big market for silicon transistors in digital computers for military avionics.[17]

In October 1957, as Fairchild Semiconductor got underway, the Soviet Union launched Sputnik, the first artificial satellite. This proxy demonstration of the advanced state of Soviet ballistic missile technology spurred the U.S. military to expand and accelerate a set of ballistic missile programs. By the late 1950s, the U.S. intercontinental ballistic missile (ICBM) program was enormous. It would expand to roughly the same size as the Manhattan Project. At the same time, the military was putting significant pressure on suppliers of avionics systems to move to digital computing in order to improve the reliability and capabilities of avionics systems.[18]

In 1956 the Air Force began to champion the digitalization of avionics equipment. Aircraft and missiles had been controlled by analog techniques, including analog computers. Analog systems, however, depended on failure-prone vacuum tubes and complex mechanical assemblies. As a result, analog autopilots, bombsights, and navigation systems failed, on average, once per 70 hours. This failure rate impaired the military's operational readiness and entailed enormous repair and maintenance costs. Furthermore, analog computers had a severe disadvantage relative to digital computers: to solve new problems, they had to be broken down and reconfigured. For these reasons, the Air Force encouraged firms to digitalize avionics systems and to incorporate digital computers into their equipment. As Sperry, American Bosch Arma, Hughes Aircraft, and other manufacturers of navigation and flight-control systems shifted from analog to digital techniques, they began to build high-speed digital computers. As a result, a market for high-performance components suitable for building these digital systems emerged within the military avionics industry.[19]

Another major decision that Fairchild Semiconductor's founders made very early was their tactic for competition. It would be through speed and flexibility that they would compete with Texas Instruments, Pacific Semiconductors, and the other firms moving into diffused silicon transistors. This led them to take a very particular tack for financing their research and development activity, in marked contrast to the moves made by most of their established competitors. At the time, most firms in the semiconductor industry, Texas Instruments included, depended substantially on military contracts to fund research and development. With these contracts came constraints, Fairchild Semiconductor's founders reasoned. They decided to finance their technology development internally. Fairchild Camera and Instrument's significant investments permitted them to do so. The founders believed that, if they were to achieve success, time was of the essence. With many firms actively working toward getting diffused silicon transistors to production, it was critical for the nascent venture to bring such transistors to the market soon and to respond rapidly to new opportunities. The founders viewed military contracts as an impediment to the required speed and flexibility, as the contracts would commit the firm to projects of direct and immediate interest to the military for long periods of time. Military contracts were typically for one to three years. In addition, these contract projects only occasionally matched well with the actual needs of military contractors and procurement offices.[20]

Fairchild Semiconductor's focus on the military computing and avionics markets and its insistence on funding research and development internally contrasted with the decisions made by other firms active in diffused silicon transistors. For example, Pacific Semiconductors, a firm with considerable expertise in diffusion, concentrated on the military communications market. Its leaders had come from Bell Labs and, like William Shockley, focused their start-up on electronic communications components, such as radio frequency and power silicon transistors. This different market orientation had major repercussions for the firms' commercial and technological trajectories. Fairchild Semiconductor thrived in a large and dynamic market for fast switching devices in military computing. Pacific Semiconductors focused on communication systems that required a relatively small number of transistors. The firm did not react rapidly to new opportunities for silicon transistors emerging in military digital computing and avionics.[21]

Beyond market orientation and R&D financing, the founders of Fairchild Semiconductor took another major decision very early on in the life of the start-up: the new firm would bring in management and sales expertise from the outside. Because none of the founders were interested in managing the start-up or had the necessary sales expertise, Hodgson—the most interested and supportive of the Fairchild Camera and Instrument executives—brought in some managers who had experience in related markets and industries. He hired Thomas Bay, who had worked at Fairchild Controls, as manager of sales and marketing. Hodgson also recruited Ewart Baldwin, an experienced executive from Hughes Semiconductor with a PhD in physics, as Fairchild Semiconductor's general manager, offering him a share of the company. Baldwin received an option to buy, for $500, a similar number of Fairchild Semiconductor shares as had each of the founders. However, Baldwin never exercised that option. Bay and Baldwin were important recruits. Bay had an excellent understanding of selling in a military context and knew the military avionics industry well. At Fairchild Controls, Bay had sold potentiometers (components used in analog computers) to military avionics firms. Baldwin brought significant experience in the silicon device business, especially in the mass production of silicon diodes. He knew how to organize a semiconductor firm and how to bring new products into high-volume manufacturing. In addition, he had a good sense of the military market for semiconductors, and he understood the size of the market opportunity for diffused silicon transistors.[22]

Defining Fairchild's Manufacturing Technology

In November 1957, computer engineers working in IBM's Military Systems Division contacted Fairchild Semiconductor to discuss Fairchild Semiconductor's product plans and the Military Systems Division's needs for "computer transistors." The IBM engineers had seen a report on the start-up and its plans to produce diffused silicon transistors for computer applications in *Electronic News*, a trade publication covering the electronics industry. The IBM engineers were keenly interested in using silicon transistors in the advanced digital computer they were designing for the navigational computer in the B-70 bomber. However, the silicon transistors available from Texas Instruments did not meet the engineers' requirements for use in the memory unit of their advanced computer. The TI transistors produced by a grown-junction technique or a combination of grown-junction and diffusion techniques could not handle the power required to drive the machine's core memory unit. IBM engineers also judged TI's transistors to be too unreliable. The transistor contacts had a tendency to fail when they were exposed to vibrations. These issues sparked the interest of IBM's military systems engineers in Fairchild Semiconductor.[23]

IBM invited Fairchild Semiconductor's representatives for a meeting in upstate New York to discuss the particular transistor requirements for the airborne computer. In mid December, Noyce, then head of research and development, and Bay, the sales manager, traveled to Owego, New York. At the IBM military systems facility there, they learned more about the new airborne computer project and about its needs for silicon transistors. It soon became clear to Fairchild Semiconductor's founders that one of the transistors needed by IBM, the core-memory driver, was "a vacant area in transistors." In other words, no silicon or germanium transistor then on the market was appropriate for this particular application. This realization elicited considerable interest among Fairchild Semiconductor's founders. They expected to be able to meet IBM's specifications for this transistor on the basis of their earlier work at the Shockley Semiconductor Laboratory.[24]

Within a few weeks, the group decided to go ahead with the core-driver transistor as their first product and to submit a quote to IBM. They also decided to design and fabricate two different versions of this transistor: a NPN and a PNP transistor. The IBM engineers had told them that they could use either of these forms initially, and that they would eventually want both. The founders knew that there was a broader need for complementary devices (pairs of NPN and PNP transistors with matched specifications) in digital circuitry. Having both NPN and PNP core-driver transistors would enhance their position in the silicon transistor business. In March 1958, IBM placed an order with Fairchild Semiconductor for a hundred core-driver transistors at the hefty price of $150 apiece.[25]

Gordon Moore and David Allison (a junior engineer at Shockley Semiconductor who joined Fairchild Semiconductor soon after its formation) tackled the issue of making the NPN transistor. Hoerni, who had been alerted to the market potential of PNP transistors by Grinich and who had worked on a PNP device during his last weeks at Shockley Semiconductor, took on the more difficult problem of designing a PNP transistor. PNP transistors relied more heavily on diffusions of the P-type dopant boron, which were more difficult than other diffusions. It was also harder to make good electrical contacts to the PNP structure. However, the overriding issue facing the founders was how to manufacture these transistors in quantity. What fabrication processes should they choose to make diffused silicon transistors? Which techniques would be adaptable to high-volume manufacturing? The answers to these questions were not obvious. Considerable technological uncertainty was associated with them. Research and development groups working on diffused silicon transistors at different firms explored different approaches to transform experimental devices into manufacturable products. For example, engineers at Western Electric made conservative choices, using gallium diffusion and metal masks to make diffused silicon transistors. They also employed two different metals, silver and aluminum, for making contacts to their transistors.[26]

In contrast, the Fairchild Semiconductor researchers selected what they viewed as the best and most promising techniques *for the long run* and decided to develop them by intensive trial-and-error engineering. These promising techniques had originated in other research organizations, especially Bell Labs and the Diamond Ordnance Fuze Laboratory (DOFL). Among the approaches were boron and phosphorus diffusion, oxide masking, photolithography, and aluminum evaporation. Oxide masking was developed at Bell Labs. In 1955, Carl Frosch and Lincoln Derick had found that a layer of silicon oxide could easily be grown on top of the silicon crystal, and that this oxide layer was impervious to certain dopants. In other words, one could open windows in the oxide layer to control where dopants could diffuse into the silicon crystal and where they could not. Researchers at Bell Labs pioneered the use of boron and phosphorus diffusion techniques with oxide masking: boron and phosphorus could not diffuse through the oxide layer and were thus suitable for oxide masking. The researchers at Fairchild Semiconductor closely followed Bell Labs' lead, concentrating on boron and phosphorus diffusions for their further development of the oxide masking approach.[27]

Photolithography, another important transistor fabrication technique that the founders adopted, had originated at the Diamond Ordnance Fuze Laboratory (DOFL) and at Bell Labs. James Nall and Jay Lathrop at DOFL and Jules Andrus at Bell Labs developed photomasking techniques to make transistors and other types of semiconductor components. In early 1957, Nall and Lathrop adapted photomasking techniques used in the making of printed circuit boards to the production of germanium transistors. These photolithographic techniques could also be used for patterning oxide layers on top of silicon crystal surfaces, and thus as a method to pursue oxide masking of diffusion. While at Shockley Semiconductor, the Fairchild Semiconductor founders had become aware of the photolithography work done at DOFL and Bell Labs. They thought that this technique was very promising, as it enabled the precise control of the lateral dimensions of diffused silicon transistors. (In other words, photolithography could be used to precisely control the placement and the size of the windows through the silicon oxide layer.) Photolithography thus allowed the fabrication of increasingly small silicon transistors and hence faster devices. According to former co-workers at Shockley Semiconductor, Robert

Noyce began experimenting with photolithography to make silicon transistors during his last months there. He brought these techniques to Fairchild Semiconductor.[28]

An essential aspect of the manufacturing technology that Fairchild Semiconductor's founders pursued, combining diffusion, oxide masking, and photolithography, was that it was largely batch production. That is, most of the processes involved were batch operations, acting to form a large number of devices simultaneously on silicon wafers. This batch character of silicon manufacturing technology was significant for the potential economics and for the founders' strategies of speed and flexibility. Batch production, if it could be successfully developed, held the promise of markedly lowering the manufacturing cost of silicon transistors without sacrificing flexibility. In contrast, sequential manufacturing approaches (e.g. grown junctions and alloying) required capital-intensive automation for reducing production costs. However, automation required the lock-in of manufacturing processes and thereby limited flexibility. The batch character of the founders' proposed manufacturing technology was, thus, central.[29]

Once the Fairchild researchers had settled on the principal techniques they wanted to improve for manufacturing the core-driver transistors, they divided up the process development work. Roberts grew single silicon crystals, Noyce and Last worked on photolithography. Moore and Allison focused on diffusion and metallization. Hoerni explored new diffusion technologies. Last worked on mesa etching and on assembly problems. Grinich developed the testing procedures and equipment for transistor production, and also worked on device applications.[30]

In a characteristic example of the work the group performed, Noyce and Last took up the laboratory technique of photomasking and turned it into a production process. Along with Kleiner, they designed a step-and-repeat camera to make photomasks and devised an innovative method for aligning the masks. Last and Noyce also made improvements to photoresists, the photographic emulsions used to coat the wafers of silicon single crystal in the photolithography process. Originally developed at Eastman Kodak for the manufacture of printed circuit boards, photoresists did not meet the requirements of silicon processing. They did not stick to the silicon oxide layer, so they could not be used to etch it properly. Photoresists also introduced impurities into the silicon crystal. To solve these serious problems, Last and Noyce collaborated with Eastman Kodak chemists. They transformed the photoresists' composition and purified them in order to eliminate contaminants and make them adhere to the silicon wafer.[31]

The Fairchild researchers also devoted significant efforts to diffusion, the all-important technique used to introduce dopants into the silicon crystal. They carefully engineered a phosphorus process to create the N-type transistor regions. They also worked on two different approaches to boron diffusion. Boron diffusion, used to make P-type regions, was the more delicate of the two diffusion techniques. Moore and Allison developed a process based on boron oxide powder, which had the disadvantage of rapidly ruining the furnace tubes in which the diffusions took place. In parallel, Hoerni, who was keenly interested in boron diffusion for forming the P-type regions of his PNP transistor, pursued a gaseous-diffusion approach. He was inspired by a reference that he had seen in the scientific literature to a boron trichloride-based diffusion process developed at RCA. Hoerni engineered a process whereby pressurized gases of nitrogen, oxygen, hydrogen, and boron trichloride were introduced into the diffusion tube. By carefully controlling this explosive mixture, Hoerni doped the silicon wafer in a more reproducible and controllable way than was practical with boron oxide powder. The new process had the further advantage of not requiring the furnace tubes to be replaced as often.[32]

In addition to transforming and developing semiconductor-fabrication techniques invented elsewhere, the group made an important process innovation of its own. Acting on a suggestion from Noyce, Moore developed an all-aluminum process for creating the contacts of NPN transistors. Transistor contacts were used to connect the transistor's emitter and base regions to the lead wires of the transistor package, which, in turn, would connect the transistor to a circuit. Using aluminum for both transistor contacts was a counter-intuitive move. Aluminum, a P-type element, would easily make a good contact to a P-type transistor region (such as the base in an NPN transistor). However, the metal could be expected to create a PN junction when alloyed to an N-type region (the emitter of an NPN transistor). To avoid creating such a junction for the N-type emitter contact, Moore developed a complex process in which alloying the aluminum film at 600 degrees Celsius eliminated the unwanted PN junction. He also heavily doped the emitter layer as a way of preventing the formation of a junction. Moore's innovation was an important one. It most immediately offered a good way of creating the transistor contacts for the IBM core driver. More important, aluminum became the metal of choice for making transistors, and later integrated circuits, throughout the semiconductor industry.[33]

Simultaneously with the development of manufacturing processes, the Fairchild Semiconductor group refined their NPN and PNP core-driver transistors for IBM. By late March, it was clear that Moore's NPN transistor was closer to the production stage than Hoerni's PNP transistor. The PNP effort still faced significant challenges. Hoerni had not yet found a suitable material for forming the transistor contacts. He also faced the problem of the formation of an unwanted junction when attaching the transistor to its package using a gold alloy as solder. These problems with the PNP led Moore, who was the head of device development in the research and development laboratory, to choose to bring his own transistor to pre-production. This decision led to significant tensions with Hoerni, who adamantly argued that his PNP should be the first transistor to go into manufacturing. Hoerni's competitive personality led him, nearly a year later, to make Moore's NPN transistor obsolete by developing a better version of it—an effort that led Hoerni to a major innovation, the development of the planar process.[34]

After choosing the NPN transistor as Fairchild Semiconductor's first product, Moore moved with his device and became the head of engineering, in charge of the pre-production group. The reasoning behind this move was that the engineer most responsible for the design of a new product should be closely involved in its production.

Bringing the NPN transistor to pilot production was a complex undertaking, requiring the writing of process manuals that specified a complex sequence of steps that operators had to perform in order to make the device. The preparation of these manuals was a lengthy endeavor, requiring constant rewriting because operators needed considerably more process details than did research engineers to make transistors. As head of engineering, Moore directed the work of the manufacturing and instrumentation engineers. Ewart Baldwin, Fairchild Semiconductor's general manager, had recruited many of these engineers from his former employer, Hughes Semiconductor. This influx of manufacturing talent from Hughes greatly accelerated the move of the NPN transistor to production. At Hughes, these engineers had gained significant experience in bringing silicon diodes to volume production and in creating the equipment for testing them.[35]

The NPN transistor's swift move to production also benefited from the San Francisco Peninsula's rich technical and labor resources. The Peninsula was an important center for electronics design and production by the late 1950s. It had instrumentation and testing equipment companies, including Hewlett-Packard. It also had large manufacturers of vacuum tubes: Eitel-McCullough, Varian Associates, and Litton Industries. These tube and instrumentation corporations attracted and trained an experienced labor force (especially production operators, technicians, and foremen) that Fairchild Semiconductor's managers drew on to staff the firm's first pre-production line. One source of experienced workers was a small plant, owned by Federal Telegraph which made selenium rectifiers. When that plant was closed, some of its employees found positions at Fairchild Semiconductor. The San Francisco Peninsula had many precision metal working shops and makers of vacuum equipment that served the needs of nearby makers of instruments and vacuum tubes. Julius Blank and his crew at Fairchild relied on these shops to fabricate the processing and assembly equipment that was needed to manufacture Fairchild Semiconductor's NPN transistor.[36]

In early August 1958, Fairchild Semiconductor delivered its first core driver transistors to IBM's Military Systems Division. A few weeks later, the firm's management publicly announced the NPN transistor at Wescon, the trade show of the Western Electronics Manufacturers Association, a major meeting ground of the national semiconductor industry. In the late 1950s, it was customary in the semiconductor industry to time announcements of new products to coincide with trade conventions such as Wescon and the Institute of Radio Engineers show (held in New York). At the 1958 Wescon, the founders of Fairchild Semiconductor discovered, to their great relief, that no other firm had yet succeeded in bringing diffused silicon transistors to the market. Only Western Electric produced mesa transistors, but their use was restricted to the Bell Telephone system and a few military programs.[37]

The Fairchild founders' strategy of competing through speed and focusing on the NPN and PNP transistors had succeeded. The firm had become the sole commercial supplier of diffused silicon transistors. No other firm—neither Hoffman Electronics, Pacific

Semiconductors, Texas Instruments, nor a large East Coast firm such as Philco or RCA—had yet mastered the complex techniques required for the production of silicon mesa transistors. The speed with which the group had designed the transistors while solving process and manufacturing problems gave Fairchild Semiconductor a monopoly on diffused silicon transistors for nearly a year. In this, Fairchild Semiconductor mounted the greatest challenge to Texas Instruments' silicon transistor business that TI had yet faced. Fairchild Semiconductor's NPN mesa transistor had significantly better electrical characteristics than TI's devices made by grown-junction and diffusion techniques. In particular, it could handle more power than TI's transistors. This characteristic made it attractive for engineers designing a variety of electronic circuits, ranging from logic circuits to circuits that required power transistors. As a result, Fairchild's device was a "universal transistor" of sorts—a transistor that could be used in many different military applications.[38]

The diffused silicon mesa transistor attracted considerable attention in the electronics industry and generated a large number of inquiries. In the late summer and fall of 1958 and early in 1959, Fairchild Semiconductor's sales department received hundreds of orders. These orders, mostly for small quantities, came from engineering groups at military contractors that were interested in evaluating the device for possible use in systems they were designing. Some orders were for devices that would control the hydraulics of airplanes and missiles. A large number of orders came from firms that developed avionics systems, including digital computers, for military aircraft and missiles. This was a fast-growing market, as the United States' ballistic missile programs continued to expand through 1958 and 1959. Fairchild Semiconductor received additional orders from IBM's Military Systems Division. Sperry Gyroscope's division that produced digital computers for flight control and submarine detection placed orders for the mesa transistor. Sperry's engineers were especially interested in the transistor for use with the magnetic-drum computer memory. Important customers were also found among the military electronics firms based in Southern California. The most significant order may have been one from Autonetics, the avionics division of North American Aviation. Autonetics had recently received a large contract to design the navigation and control computer for the Minuteman ICBM. This computer was to guide the Minuteman missile and its nuclear payload to targets in the Soviet Union. The Minuteman computer had unprecedented reliability specifications and required fast silicon transistors.[39]

Greatly supporting these sales to military contractors and the makers of airborne digital computers was Fairchild Semiconductor's applications engineering group. Victor Grinich, the only circuit engineer among the founders, set up an applications engineering organization in the spring of 1958. The goal of the applications group was to teach potential customers how to use and test Fairchild Semiconductor's transistors. This was extremely important because in late 1958 and early 1959 circuit designers who had a solid understanding of transistors and the ways in which they could be employed in electronic circuits were still rare. Engineers who did have experience using transistors also needed to learn how to design Fairchild Semiconductor's specific transistor in their circuits. As the only commercially available diffused silicon mesa transistor, Fairchild Semiconductor's transistor had unique characteristics. To teach circuit engineers how to use the NPN transistor, Grinich and his group of circuit engineers wrote applications notes that described the transistor's characteristics and presented schematics for the digital circuits in which the transistor could be used. Though applications engineering was not unique to Fairchild Semiconductor (most semiconductor firms produced applications notes), it was particularly emphasized at the company. This emphasis on applications engineering and the writing of applications notes became a hallmark of Fairchild Semiconductor and its spin-offs in Silicon Valley.[40]

Immediately after the NPN transistor (known in the industry as the 2N696) was announced to the market, in August 1958, the founders of Fairchild Semiconductor concentrated on expanding the firm's product line by designing new mesa transistors using variants of the manufacturing process that had been developed for the 2N696. Their goals were to solidify their foothold in transistors for digital computing applications and to build a family of mesa transistors with different speed, voltage, and power characteristics. The second device in the family was Jean Hoerni's PNP transistor. In the summer and fall of 1958, Hoerni gradually solved the manufacturing problems with the PNP. He adopted aluminum for both transistor contacts, and used diffusion to keep the contacts from forming unwanted junctions. By November 1958, the PNP transistor was in its pre-production phase. Like Moore earlier, Hoerni followed his device to production, helping the pre-production group to ready it for volume manufacturing.[41]

The PNP transistor was a very important addition to Fairchild's product line. For the next several years, the firm had a monopoly on PNP diffused silicon transistors, as no other firm succeeded in fabricating them. As a result, Fairchild Semiconductor could charge premium prices for the PNP, garnering significant profits. The other transistor that Fairchild Semiconductor's R&D group worked on starting in the summer of 1958 was a smaller version of the 2N696. This device, developed under the supervision of David Allison, was targeted at the logic circuits of military computers. The main objective was to increase the switching speed of Fairchild's first product by reducing its dimensions. This required significant improvements in photolithographic techniques.[42]

The main focus of Fairchild Semiconductor's general manager and founding group in the fall of 1959 and the winter of 1960 was, nevertheless, to increase production of the 2N696 in order to meet growing market demand (sales expanded from half a million dollars in 1958 to $2.8 million in the first eight months of 1959). Ewart Baldwin set up a massive hiring and training program. The firm's ranks boomed from 70 in August 1958 to more than 220 in March 1959. Most of the new hires were technicians and operators employed in production. Baldwin also built a new factory in nearby Mountain View at a cost of $1 million. The construction of this plant required another round of capital investment from Fairchild Camera and Instrument. (Most of the $1.38 million promised at the outset by Fairchild Camera had been spent.) Sensing that the market for Fairchild's first NPN transistor would be large, Baldwin had advocated the construction of the new manufacturing plant as early as May 1958, several months before the transistor was announced at Wescon. Fairchild Camera and Instrument's management approved the new plant "in principle" in June, and construction of the factory commenced in November.[43]

Recasting Fairchild Semiconductor's Manufacturing Technology

In late 1958 and early 1959, as production increased, it became clear that Fairchild Semiconductor's first NPN transistor (the 2N696) had significant limitations. Engineers working in IBM's Military Systems division discovered that the NPN transistors were taking longer and longer to switch off. This was problematic because these transistors were employed to drive memory cores. If the transistors did not turn off, the computer's memory would be significantly compromised. The transistors' degrading switching speeds were due to a change made in Fairchild Semiconductor's manufacturing processes. The firm had developed a new process that entailed plating the back side of the silicon wafer (that is, the side of the wafer beneath the mesa transistor structures) with nickel and doping it with phosphorus. This technique was, in industry jargon, "gettering" impurities in the bulk of the crystal—that is, the new technique caused

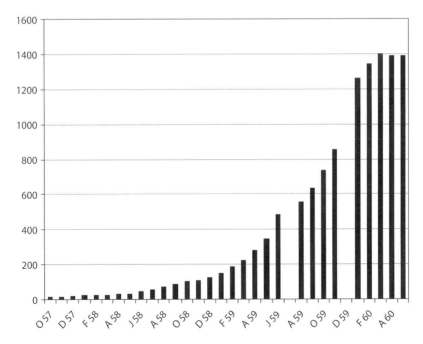

Figure 1.4
Employment at Fairchild Semiconductor, October 1957–May 1960. Source: *Leadwire*. Courtesy of Jay Last.

the impurities that negatively affected the transistor's electrical characteristics to be attracted to the back of the wafer. This "gettering" was too effective, however, as it also slowed switching speeds. This slowing switching problem affecting IBM's system was a potential problem for customers who used transistors for memory systems and in other digital applications where switching speed was of paramount importance.[44]

The second problem that Fairchild Semiconductor encountered with its first product was one of reliability. A customer, possibly Autonetics, discovered that a significant percentage of Fairchild's NPN transistors unexpectedly ceased to operate—that is, they failed completely. Other units saw their electrical characteristics deteriorate more gradually. These were fundamental problems for Fairchild Semiconductor, whose customers, especially the makers of digital computers, were very concerned about reliability. Autonetics, for example, specified an extremely high level of reliability for its component suppliers, as it sought to improve the reliability of avionics systems by two orders of magnitude. In the mid 1950s the average mean time to failure for avionics equipment was 70 hours. Autonetics' objective was to achieve mean times between failure of *7,000* hours for the guidance and control system of the Minuteman missile. In light of these requirements, it was imperative for Fairchild Semiconductor to solve the reliability problem with its transistor. The future, possibly the survival, of the firm was at stake.[45]

The founders launched a crash program to identify the cause of the reliability problem. A foreman in the manufacturing organization discovered that the problem stemmed from loose particles within the transistor package. When the package was tapped or shaken, the loose particles were attracted to the high electric fields at the transistor's junctions. The particles would then short out the junctions. This finding led Fairchild Semiconductor engineers to look for all possible sources of particles in the transistor package and to find ways of eliminating them. Manufacturing engineers also designed new tests to identify the transistors most likely to fail because of these loose particles. Despite a thorough cleaning of the manufacturing process and the establishment of new testing procedures, the failure rate of the mesa transistors remained unacceptably high. It was clear that another solution had to be found to resolve the reliability problems of Fairchild Semiconductor's transistors.[46]

In the winter of 1959, Jean Hoerni focused his attention on the reliability and performance problems of the mesa transistors. In doing so, he made two major innovations—gold doping and the planar process—that refashioned Fairchild Semiconductor's production technology and vaulted the firm to technological and business leadership of the semiconductor industry. Hoerni's innovations went against all accepted knowledge in the semiconductor community: he used materials that were widely viewed as highly detrimental to transistor performance in order to greatly improve transistor characteristics. Hoerni's invention of the planar process and gold doping led to the production of high reliability and high-speed switching transistors for military computing. But the effects of these inventions went far beyond Fairchild Semiconductor's product line. They firmly established silicon as the main material used in semiconductor electronics.

Most important, Hoerni's planar process set out a developmental path for semiconductor technology that the industry has pursued since the late 1950s.[47]

From November 1958 to January 1959, Hoerni developed his solution to the switching-speed limitations of Fairchild Semiconductor's first mesa transistor. He was inspired to do so by an article on the fabrication of high-speed silicon diodes published by some Bell Labs engineers who had diffused gold into a silicon crystal in order to improve the diode's performance characteristics. This led Hoerni to consider using gold doping to make faster-switching transistors. This was heretical. It was widely held in the semiconductor community that gold should be removed from silicon transistors at all costs. Gold was viewed as "deathnium"—as a material that destroyed the gain, or amplification, ability of transistors. Gain was primarily associated with the thickness and composition of a transistor's base region.[48]

Hoerni reasoned that if he could diffuse gold into the transistor's collector region only, he would increase the switching speed without affecting the transistor's amplification characteristics. He experimented with different techniques of diffusing gold, varying the duration and temperature of the diffusions, until he found parameters that did in fact produce faster switching without negatively affecting transistor gain. Gold doping had a dramatic effect on the switching speeds of Fairchild Semiconductor's NPN mesa transistors, increasing them by roughly an order of magnitude. Fairchild engineers soon brought this technique to the production lines. They manufactured a gold-doped version of Fairchild's first NPN transistor, and then the "small geometry" transistor developed by Allison and his group. These products were significantly faster than TI's fastest silicon transistors; more important, they approached the speed of germanium transistors. Until then, speed had been the main advantage of germanium transistors over their silicon rivals. Gold doping and the shrinking of the transistor dimensions erased that advantage and thus opened up new markets for silicon transistors in high-speed digital circuits and in the logic circuits of digital computers.[49]

Simultaneously with his development of gold doping, Hoerni engineered a revolutionary approach—the planar process—that solved the reliability problems of mesa transistors. The planar process was an idea that Hoerni initially conceived just a few months after Fairchild Semiconductor's formation. In December 1957, he jotted down ideas about a new structure and process for a PNP transistor in his patent notebook. This "planar" transistor structure was different from the mesa transistor structure pioneered by Bell Labs and used at Fairchild Semiconductor to make NPN and PNP devices. The mesa structure profile looked like a Southwestern mesa, with smaller base and emitter regions atop a larger collector. The emitter-base junction and the base-collector junction were both left exposed at the mesa's surfaces. Contacts were attached to the base and emitter on the top of the mesa and on the back to the collector.[50] In contrast, the planar transistor was flat. The surface of the transistor was covered by a layer of silicon oxide that protected the transistor junctions. Another interesting aspect of the planar structure was that all contacts could be deposited on top of the transistor. In his patent

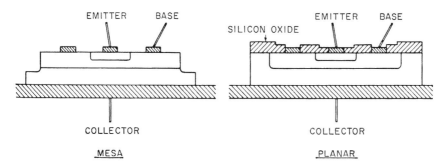

Fig. 1.   Transistor Structures

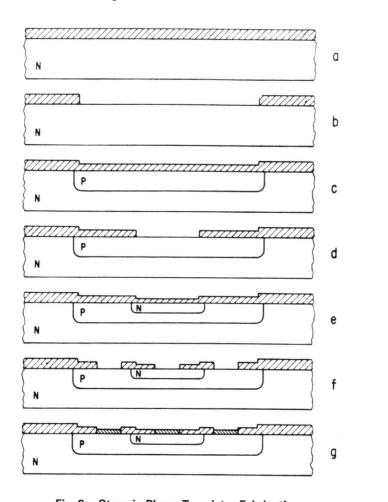

Fig. 2.   Steps in Planar Transistor Fabrication

Figure 1.5

The planar process. Source: Jean Hoerni, "Planar Silicon Transistors and Diodes," unpublished paper presented at 1960 Electron Devices Meeting, Washington, October 1960. Collection of Christophe Lécuyer.

notebook, Hoerni outlined the fabrication of a PNP planar transistor. He would first grow a silicon oxide layer on top of the silicon crystal by exposing it to water vapor. This layer of silicon oxide would be used to diffuse the base and emitter regions of the transistor. He then would leave the oxide on top of the silicon wafer and open small windows in it to create transistor contacts. Hoerni soon shared his planar PNP transistor ideas with Fairchild's founders.[51]

The planar structure and especially the idea of leaving the oxide layer on top of the wafer after multiple diffusion processes went, like gold doping, against all accepted knowledge in the semiconductor community. Semiconductor engineers and scientists considered the oxide layer that had served as a mask for diffusions to be "dirty"—that is, full of contaminants that would impair the electrical characteristics of the transistor. This idea of the "dirty" oxide seems to have originated at Bell Labs in 1955 and then spread rapidly to the entire community of semiconductor scientists and engineers. By the time Hoerni jotted down his ideas on the planar process in his patent notebook, it was widely accepted that the oxide layer that had been exposed to diffusions had to be stripped off and replaced by a "clean" re-grown oxide.[52]

Though exactly what led Hoerni to his conception of the planar process cannot be determined with absolute certainty, three different strands appear to have been central: a material strand, a communal strand, and an individual strand. On the material side is a particular characteristic of the chemical element silicon. Silicon readily forms an oxide layer, silicon dioxide, on its surfaces in the presence of oxygen. The silicon dioxide layers are stable, strongly adherent, and electrically insulating. While at Shockley Semiconductor, and during the launch of Fairchild Semiconductor, Jean Hoerni's coworkers had conducted investigations of silicon's ability to form oxide layers, and of the properties of the oxide layers that underlay the oxide masking and diffusion approaches developed at Bell Labs. The communal strand in Hoerni's conception of the planar process built on this material characteristic. Throughout the semiconductor community, researchers were studying in detail the formation, properties, and uses of silicon dioxide layers in the context of using oxide masking and diffusion for creating semiconductor devices. The semiconductor research community was discussing diffusion and oxide layers at conferences and in print at the time that Hoerni conceived the planar process.

The individual factor in Hoerni's conception of the planar process was his deep theoretical understanding of crystals and his engagement with both theoretical and experimental studies of diffusion. Hoerni had published a theoretical article on electron diffraction by crystals in the *Physical Review* before joining Shockley Semiconductor. His work on calculating and empirically measuring diffusion profiles in silicon also gave Hoerni an arguably unique intuition for this physical process. With this intuition, he was able to see that, with oxide masking of diffusion, dopants would diffuse into the silicon crystal not only vertically, down into the wafer, but also *laterally*, spreading out to the sides underneath the window in the oxide layer. Hoerni's deep understanding of diffusion allowed him to attend closely to the significance of this lateral spread, and to perceive that the junctions so formed would be protected by the overlying silicon dioxide layer.[53]

For about a year after his December 1957 notebook entry, Hoerni left his heterodox processing ideas aside as he concentrated his attention on fabricating the PNP mesa transistor and on developing techniques to increase the switching speeds of NPN transistors. Another possible reason why he did not attempt his planar transistor sooner was that, according to the conventional wisdom, it appeared to have a low probability of success. A staff meeting that Hoerni attended in May 1958 may have rekindled his interest in his planar concept. At this meeting, he heard a co-worker report on papers recently presented at the Electrochemical Society meeting. At this meeting, M. "John" Atalla, a Bell Labs researcher, had shown that silicon oxide layers "passivated" or electrically stabilized the surface of silicon crystals. This was an important finding because the electrical conditions of semiconductor surfaces were a major source of reliability problems in transistors. Atalla's findings indicated that Hoerni's early planar idea may have had some merit. Documentary evidence shows that the planar idea resurfaced at another staff meeting of Fairchild's R&D laboratory in September 1958. At that meeting, Hoerni's idea of a planar diode was discussed as worth patenting. A few months later, a Fairchild Semiconductor researcher, perhaps Hoerni himself, created a *partial* planar transistor structure. Having left the oxide layer (which had been exposed to diffusion processes) on top of the emitter-base junction, he discovered that this half-planar transistor had a higher gain and was more electrically stable than mesa transistors.[54] This finding led Hoerni to begin work on a fully planar transistor in late January 1959. Initially intending to make a planar version of his PNP mesa transistor, he asked Noyce and Last to make an additional mask for it. However, he soon ran into the usual problems with PNP transistors. He decided to re-focus his efforts on making an NPN planar transistor—a planar version of Fairchild's first product. (The masks could be used interchangeably for NPN and PNP transistors.) According to Hoerni, his primary motivation in trying to make an NPN planar transistor was to solve the vexing reliability problem that Fairchild Semiconductor had experienced with the NPN mesa transistor.[55]

By the first week of March 1959, Hoerni and his technician had succeeded in making an operational, fully planar NPN transistor. As they soon discovered, that transistor amplified signals much better than its mesa equivalent. The planar transistor was also characterized by very low leakage currents (the reverse current that appears when a transistor switches). Leakage counts were lower by three orders of magnitude than in mesa transistors. As a result, the planar transistor was an excellent computer transistor. It switched much better than mesa transistors, grown-junction silicon transistors, or germanium transistors. (Germanium transistors were notorious for their high leakage.) More important, the planar transistor that Hoerni and his technician made in early March 1959 was extremely reliable. It was not subject to the particle-caused shorting problems of mesa transistors.[56]

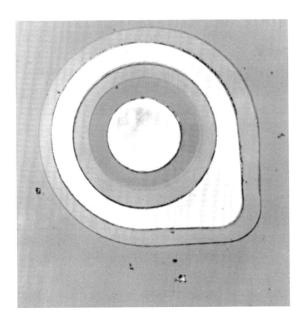

Figure 1.6
Photograph of the first planar transistor, March 1959. Collection of Christophe Lécuyer.

Hoerni shared his results on the planar transistor with Fairchild Semiconductor's other founders on 12 March 1959. He staged a dramatic demonstration emphasizing the reliability of the new devices. He banged the transistor packages with a hammer, put them in the tapping test machine, and showed that the transistors worked as well as ever. They did not fail, as mesa transistors did. Hoerni also spat on the unpackaged transistor chip. Spit was full of contaminants that were deadly for silicon devices, but the planar transistor still worked. Hoerni's showmanship convinced his colleagues that his planar transistor, which went against all orthodoxy in the semiconductor community, was very promising and should be pursued.[57]

Beyond Hoerni's persuasive demonstrations, another factor that led Noyce and Moore (who had emerged as Fairchild Semiconductor's main leaders) to invest significant resources in developing planar transistor products was Autonetics' keen interest in them. Autonetics was intent on improving the reliability of semiconductor components and saw the planar approach as a promising avenue. Moore later recalled that "the preliminary work on the planar was the principal reason [Fairchild] got a [large production] contract" from Autonetics. "They heard that the planar was coming along and it was to increase reliability dramatically."[58]

An additional impetus for "going planar" was the defection of Baldwin, Fairchild Semiconductor's general manager. One week before Hoerni showed the planar transistor to his colleagues, Baldwin left to start another semiconductor company, Rheem Semiconductor, with financing from a firm whose main product was water heaters. The objective of Rheem Semiconductor was to make diffused silicon mesa transistors and compete directly with Fairchild Semiconductor. Baldwin took with him several manufacturing and instrumentation engineers he had brought from Hughes Semiconductor; he also took manuals that documented in great detail the manufacturing processes required for making NPN and PNP mesa transistors.[59]

The loss of Baldwin and of several important staff members, and the competitive threat that Rheem Semiconductor presented, were major shocks to Fairchild Semiconductor's founders. Recognizing their business, organizational, and manufacturing inexperience, they had approved of bringing Baldwin in as general manager. Moreover, they had appreciated Baldwin's managerial insights and his aggressive plans to capitalize on the firm's technical advantages. Baldwin's departure and his direct competitive challenge caused great uncertainty within Fairchild Semiconductor. Several weeks after Baldwin's defection, Robert Noyce assumed the role of general manager and Gordon Moore assumed directorship of R&D. The business and technological fate of the firm was now in the hands of relatively inexperienced managers. Compounding the shake-up, Noyce and Moore would have to quickly develop a technological breakthrough to ensure the company's survival and success. To compete with Rheem, Fairchild Semiconductor had to introduce new and better devices. Bringing the planar transistor to market would give Fairchild a competitive edge.[60]

Fairchild Semiconductor encountered substantial difficulties in transferring the planar process to production. It took nearly a year for Hoerni and the pre-production engineering group (now headed by Harry Sello, a chemist who had worked with the founding group at Shockley Semiconductor) to bring the process to a stage where it could produce high-quality transistors in volume. "The yield [the percentage of good transistors coming out of the production line] was very low at the beginning," Hoerni later reminisced, "because the oxide was imperfect and you got some little pinholes with N+ material in the collector. So it was like putting an emitter on the collector."[61] The silicon oxide layer on top of the transistor had small holes in it. As a result, the phosphorus diffusion used to create the emitter of the planar transistors would also dope the collector and create emitter regions in it. It was not uncommon for the pre-production group to obtain only one good planar transistor per wafer.[62] To solve this "pinhole problem," Hoerni and the pre-production engineers put considerable effort into improving the oxidation process by making the oxide layer more uniform across the wafer. In conjunction with this work in pre-production engineering, the physics research section of the laboratory directed by Hoerni conducted studies on oxides and silicon-silicon oxide interfaces to better understand planar technology.[63]

In the spring and summer of 1959, in conjunction with "cleaning up" the planar process, Hoerni returned to the idea of the planar diode. In discussions with Autonetics representatives, he learned that mesa diodes had the same reliability problems as mesa transistors. Autonetics' engineers were interested in procuring fast and ultra-reliable diodes for their military digital computers. Knowing that there would be a market for high-quality, high-price diodes at Autonetics and other makers of small military computers, Hoerni and his group engineered silicon diodes using gold doping and the planar process.[64] And Hoerni went further, acting as what today would be called an "intrapreneur." He convinced Fairchild Semiconductor's head of manufacturing, Frank Grady, to agitate with him for the creation of a new division at Fairchild Semiconductor that would engineer, manufacture, and market his silicon planar diodes. Grady, in turn, secured the support of Hodgson and Carter (respectively vice president and president of Fairchild Camera and Instrument). Hoerni and Grady's proposal won the approval of the Fairchild Camera and Instrument board. In November 1959, Fairchild Semiconductor announced that it was creating a new diode division and that it would build a plant for the production of silicon diodes in San Rafael, north of San Francisco.[65]

The building of the San Rafael plant was part of a larger expansion program at Fairchild Semiconductor. In October 1959, Fairchild Camera and Instrument exercised its option to buy Fairchild Semiconductor. Under the agreement that the founders had signed with the company, Fairchild Camera and Instrument had the right to buy the semiconductor venture 18 months after its formation for $3 million. By October 1959, Fairchild Semiconductor (led by Noyce who had succeeded Baldwin as general manager) was a remarkable business success. Its new products, Hoerni's PNP mesa transistor and the "small geometry" mesa transistor designed by Allison for computer applications, sold extremely well and brought in significant profits. Fairchild Semiconductor now had 737 employees—more than three times as many as it had had six months earlier. It was also becoming increasingly clear that Fairchild Semiconductor's annual sales for 1959 would reach $7 million (versus $500,000 the previous year). Furthermore, the planar breakthrough promised even greater sales in subsequent years.[66]

Fairchild Camera and Instrument's management was interested in capitalizing on this success, and it had the resources to do so. In the second half of 1959, the stock of Fairchild Camera and Instrument was trading on the American Stock Exchange at more than $200 per share. Only a year earlier, it had traded at about $60, and in 1957, when Fairchild Semiconductor was founded, the parent company's stock had traded at about $20. Thus, in October 1959, Fairchild Camera and Instrument had an order of magnitude larger market capitalization for acquisition and investment. Fairchild Camera and Instrument exercised its option, acquired Fairchild Semiconductor, and transformed it into a wholly owned subsidiary. Fairchild Camera and Instrument's management also decided to invest more capital in the semiconductor business in order to reap the benefits of the semiconductor operation's technical innovations. This round of capital investment was Fairchild Camera and Instrument's third cash infusion into Fairchild Semiconductor, after the initial loan and the construction of the transistor plant in the fall of 1958. To realize the sales growth projected to come from planar transistors, Fairchild Camera and Instrument invested in a $750,000 extension of the transistor plant in Mountain View. It also financed the construction of the new $1 million factory for diode manufacturing in San Rafael. In addition, plans for the construction of a large building to house Fairchild Semiconductor's R&D laboratory were under development.[67]

Under Moore, the R&D laboratory planned to expand significantly in order to "preserve and extend [the company's] established markets" and "improve and extend the products and the processes."[68] Among the new research programs advocated by Moore were the development of new planar diodes and transistors and the "planarization" of Fairchild Semiconductor's entire existing transistor line. Another line of new R&D activity would be the miniaturization of electronic circuits—that is, microcircuitry. Further, Moore was interested in reorienting the laboratory toward basic research in order to strengthen the company's processing and design capabilities. In conjunction with this program of expansion in R&D and manufacturing, Robert Noyce sought to strengthen managerial control of the rapidly expanding firm. Experienced managers (among them Charles Sporck, who had worked in manufacturing at General Electric) were brought in to build a disciplined manufacturing organization.[69]

In March 1960, Fairchild Semiconductor announced its first planar transistor and diode products at the Institute of Radio Engineers show in New York. The announcements attracted considerable attention in the electronics industry, and the planar process was soon viewed as a major innovation that would reorient the technological direction for the semiconductor industry. In order to take part in the new planar and silicon technology, many semiconductor firms established crash programs. Texas Instruments and Motorola established competency in planar technology relatively rapidly and became significant competitors in planar transistors. Philco and Transitron, which had strong germanium product lines, were slow in bringing planar devices to the market, and were relegated to a secondary position in the industry in subsequent years. Planar technology combined with gold doping proved to be a lethal competitor for germanium transistors. Gold-doped planar transistors were much more reliable and had significantly better performance characteristics. They soon replaced high-speed germanium transistors in new military systems, especially digital computers. The planar process became the main process technology in the semiconductor industry and firmly established silicon as the main material for semiconductor electronics. Moreover, the planar process led directly to another transformative innovation: the planar integrated circuit.[70]

Miniaturization

In the early 1960s, the planar process gave Fairchild Semiconductor a significant competitive advantage in the contested arena of microcircuitry. Starting in the mid 1950s, research groups across the semiconductor industry became interested in the miniaturization of electronic circuits. The primary impetus for this flowering of microcircuitry projects was military demand. The U.S. military was interested in reducing the size and weight of electronics systems used in aircraft and missiles. The heavier the electronics systems were, the costlier and the more difficult it was to carry them in a plane or missile. The military also looked to microcircuitry as a way of improving the reliability of

Figure 1.7

Cover of *Electronic Daily*, 23 March 1960, with photo of Fairchild Semiconductor's booth at Institute of Radio Engineers show in New York. Left: Thomas Bay. Right: Jay Last. Note that the diagram of "the planar structure" does not include the silicon oxide layer. Fairchild Semiconductor's leaders sought to keep the use of the oxide layer a trade secret. Collection of Christophe Lécuyer.

electronics. Microcircuits could reduce the number of assembly steps and interconnections that were potential sources of failure.[71]

Directly supporting research on microcircuitry, the military services funded a large project at Texas Instruments in the "semiconductor integrated circuit" approach to microcircuitry, which was aimed at forming whole circuits in single blocks of semiconductor material. The military also supported other approaches to the miniaturization of electronic circuits, including hybrid and thin-film circuits. Hybrid circuits were assemblies of discrete transistors, diodes, resistors, and capacitors on a small ceramic plate. Thin-film circuits were made of evaporated films of material, forming resistors and capacitors, to which conventional transistors were added. The hybrid and thin-film approaches were pursued by the Diamond Ordnance Fuze Laboratory and many leading firms in the electronics industry, including RCA, Sylvania, Centralab, and the Bell Telephone Laboratories. Still other government-supported efforts toward microcircuits ranged from the prosaic to the exotic. Large programs to produce miniaturized packages for components were run through lead contractors such as RCA. Several laboratories explored cryogenic superconducting alloys and other materials for miniaturized devices.[72]

Several semiconductor corporations shared the common goal of producing a full circuit in a single piece of semiconductor crystal as a path to microcircuitry, but how to achieve this goal was far from obvious. Research groups approached the problem differently, but two main strategies can be distinguished. The first originated at Bell Labs. Researchers there advocated the pursuit of "functional devices"—blocks of semiconductor material that were chemically transformed so as to produce the function of an entire circuit. These functions would be achieved through the operation of the device as a whole, and without forming substructures for traditional circuit elements such as transistors, diodes, and resistors within the functional device. This far-reaching effort involved a reconceptualization of traditional electronic circuits. The other approach—pushed by Texas Instruments, by Sprague Electric, and ultimately by Fairchild Semiconductor—sought to fabricate electronic circuits in one piece of semiconductor material by creating structures in the material that performed the roles of traditional circuit components: transistors, diodes, resistors, capacitors and the like. In other words, the objective was to integrate an electronic circuit with transistors, diodes, resistors on one semiconductor chip.[73]

William Shockley, the former employer of Fairchild Semiconductor's founders, was a major proponent of the functional device approach. At Bell Labs, he had devised the PNPN diode (a switching device that performed an electronic function that would otherwise be accomplished by a circuit made of two transistors, a diode, and a resistor). In 1955, Shockley asked Ian Ross, a senior Bell Labs researcher, to start a new research group devoted to functional devices. Building on Shockley's PNPN diode work, Ross focused on designing and making a stepping transistor element (a single device that performed the function a counter circuit, without recreating all the components of a traditional counter circuit). To work on this project, Ross hired Arthur D'Asaro, a recent physics PhD from Cornell. Ross and D'Asaro first made a stepping element in germanium. When it became clear that the germanium device would not work very well, Ross left the project and D'Asaro focused on making a stepping element in silicon, using photolithography and oxide masking. The result was a device which performed an electronic function that would have required eight transistors, 26 diodes, and 27 resistors in a conventional electronic circuit. D'Asaro presented a paper on the stepping element at Wescon in the summer of 1959. Work on functional devices extended beyond Bell Labs. At the Shockley Semiconductor Laboratory, Shockley devoted a significant fraction of his senior staff, including some of Fairchild Semiconductor's founders, to the fabrication of PNPN diodes. This approach to electronic miniaturization was also adopted by Torkel Wallmark's group at RCA. Wallmark worked on a functional device that, like D'Asaro's, was based on the PNPN structure. This device performed the function of a shift register, a basic digital logic circuit.[74]

The research groups at other semiconductor firms that pursued semiconductor integrated circuits took a less far-reaching approach than the pursuit of functional devices. They aimed to create devices that provided circuit function by incorporating transistors, diodes, resistors, and capacitors in a piece of semiconductor crystal. Nevertheless, there were challenges with this more direct route to microcircuitry. One problem was how to isolate the different devices on the same piece of semiconductor crystal from one another. Electrical isolation was critical; otherwise current would flow from one device to the next, ruining their operation. Another question was how to interconnect the devices on the same piece of crystal. If the integrated components could not be electrically connected to one another properly, they would not form an integrated circuit. Integrated circuits would "raise the bar" for manufacturing technologies and process control significantly, as they would require much tighter tolerances than conventional transistor production.[75]

In the late 1950s, three firms were working on different schemes to realize this type of semiconductor integrated circuit. Among them was Texas Instruments, the largest manufacturer of silicon devices in the United States. In 1958, TI hired Jack Kilby, an engineer who had previously worked on a microcircuitry project in the hybrid and thin-film vein at Centralab. At TI, Kilby moved in the direction of forming a circuit in a piece of semiconductor crystal in his pursuit of circuit miniaturization. In September 1958, Kilby and several colleagues working at his direction made two circuits with all the basic circuit components—mesa transistors, resistors, and capacitors (the ability to form a mesa transistor implied the ability to make a diode)—formed in a single piece of germanium crystal. The first device performed the function of an analog circuit: a phase-shift oscillator. The second performed the function of a digital circuit: a flip-flop. Kilby solved the interconnection issue by joining the circuit elements together with gold wires that arced from spot to spot above the surface of the germanium. Kilby's solution to the isolation problem was to place the circuit elements far apart in the germanium sample, and even to cut a long trench through the crystal, the atmosphere filling the void providing "air isolation."[76]

These were the first working realizations of the concept of the semiconductor integrated circuit, and they were the subjects of considerable publicity by Texas Instruments, which put on a press conference to announce them to the public in early 1959. Kilby and Texas Instruments also filed a sweeping patent application for semiconductor integrated circuits on the basis of this work. In 1959, Texas Instruments was offering its flip-flop integrated circuit for sale to customers; later it obtained military and NASA contracts to develop other digital integrated circuits. However, TI quickly abandoned its original schemes for interconnection and isolation. New approaches emanating from Fairchild Semiconductor proved to be much more reliable, more manufacturable, and ultimately more successful. By incorporating these alternate approaches, TI remained a powerful entity in the nascent integrated circuit business.[77]

At the Sprague Electric Company in North Adams, Massachusetts, Kurt Lehovec, a solid-state physicist, considered the problem of isolation for integrated circuits in 1958. After listening to a talk on microcircuitry by Torkel Wallmark at a technical conference at RCA, Lehovec conceptualized an alternate approach to the use of wide spacing, complex geometries, or air isolation for the electrical isolation of components in semiconductor integrated circuits. He imagined using the primary structure employed in making semiconductor devices—the PN junction—to provide the sought-for isolation. From Lehovec's perspective, other approaches to isolation were complicated and expensive, whereas PN junctions were easy and cheap to make. By placing at least two PN junctions, properly biased, between the circuit elements of an integrated circuit, isolation could be achieved electrically. Lehovec's approach would come to be known alternatively as "PN junction isolation" or "electrical isolation." This was an important innovation that later became a central technology for manufacturing integrated circuits. However, Sprague Electric was not interested in Lehovec's innovation. In 1959 Lehovec filed a patent application he had prepared with the support of a patent lawyer, and a patent was issued in 1962. Because Sprague Electric made little use of the patent, and because Lehovec stopped working on integrated circuits, Lehovec's innovation did not receive wide attention.[78]

This flurry of activity around microcircuitry in the semiconductor industry in the late 1950s did not go unnoticed by Fairchild Semiconductor. The firm followed the work of Kilby and Texas Instruments through their connections to customers and the semiconductor research community. Indeed, several engineers and scientists at Fairchild Semiconductor had contemplated the possibility of putting an electronic circuit into a piece of silicon crystal. At Fair-child Semiconductor, it was Robert Noyce who creatively assembled a number of technologies and concepts into a comprehensive solution to the integrated circuit puzzle. In January 1959, Noyce was one of the few researchers at Fairchild Semiconductor who was intimately familiar with Jean Hoerni's ideas about the planar process and the planar transistor. Likely prompted by a discussion of the hybrid-circuit approach to microcircuitry by an engineer from American Bosch Arma who had visited Fairchild Semiconductor that month, Noyce conceived how the planar process could be used with PN junction isolation (which he arrived at independently from Lehovec) to create a semiconductor integrated circuit.[79]

In a patent notebook entry dated 23 January 1959, Noyce described how to interconnect the various devices on a single piece of silicon crystal by putting a conductive pattern of aluminum atop the insulating oxide layer covering the crystal. To solve the isolation problem, Noyce independently conceived Lehovec's approach of using several PN junctions between the circuit elements in the silicon crystal to electrically isolate them from one another. At the end of July 1959 and then six weeks later, Noyce filed patent applications covering these ideas for making a planar integrated circuit: two applications for PN junction isolation and another for aluminum interconnection atop the oxide layer. Initially, Noyce's applications on PN junction isolation were denied, but Fairchild Semiconductor's patent lawyers eventually succeeded in revising the applications, and the two isolation patents were issued in 1964. The claims of Noyce's isolation patents were relatively narrow, covering very specific instantiations of PN junction isolation. Their specificity may have been in reaction to the broader claims in the patent of Lehovec, who had filed his application only a few months earlier. The priority and the breadth of Lehovec's patent were later established through litigation between Texas Instruments and Sprague Electric over the patents of Kilby and Lehovec.[80]

The patent application that Noyce filed at the end of July 1959 covered the use of a metal interconnection layer atop the oxide layer, and was granted in 1961. This led to years of infringement litigation between Fairchild Semiconductor and Texas Instruments on the Noyce and Kilby integrated circuit patents. Fairchild Semiconductor won that fight, and Noyce's interconnection patent, along with Hoerni's planar patents, became the most prized possessions in Fairchild Semiconductor's patent portfolio.[81]

In parallel to this patenting work on the planar integrated circuit, Noyce asked Jay Last to initiate a crash microcircuitry project within Fairchild Semiconductor's R&D laboratory in the summer of 1959. This was largely a defensive response to Texas Instrument's lead on Fairchild Semiconductor in this field. The Wescon show was approaching, and Noyce wanted Fairchild Semiconductor to appear active in microcircuitry by debuting a device and having Last talk about it at the conference. Last's effort was less to create a viable product than to send a message to customers and competitors that Fairchild was active in microcircuits and at the forefront of semiconductor technology. Last rapidly made a hybrid circuit in a standard transistor package and presented the device to great fanfare at Wescon. Last's work led directly to the development of a line of hybrid circuits under the banner "Micrologic."[82]

A few months later, at the close of 1959, with support from Moore and Noyce, Last launched a major expansion of the Micrologic R&D program toward producing a semiconductor integrated circuit, like the one Kilby had made at Texas Instruments. Last would work toward creating an entire set of digital integrated circuits from which the logic of a digital computer could be constructed. While this same set of digital logic circuits would be pursued along hybrid-circuit lines, the Micrologic team would also follow Noyce's basic concept of the planar integrated circuit and would undertake the great challenge of reducing it to practice in an economically effective manner. For Last, placing the aluminum interconnection pattern on top of the oxide layer was a straightforward extension of the photolithographic approach to transistor production that the company had firmly in hand. The major challenge facing Last and his co-workers was isolation. It was clear to Last that the firm did not have the ability to practically undertake the multiple PN junction isolation scheme that Noyce had worked out. It required multiple, closely controlled diffusions that were beyond the firm's capacity.[83]

Last had to find another solution to the isolation problem. The first direction that Last devised was to place an insulating material between the circuit elements in the integrated circuit. He dubbed this approach "physical isolation." Insulating material, such as epoxy, would be deposited in deep trenches that passed from the back side of the silicon crystal all the way through to the covering oxide layer. Last fully anticipated the difficulties he would encounter with physical isolation. There was the challenge of aligning the trenches made from the back of the wafer with the circuit elements made by diffusion from the top surface. There would also be a search for an insulating material whose expansion and contraction behavior would be compatible with silicon. Last further realized that having the islands of silicon connected only by the oxide layer would make the devices more fragile.[84]

To tackle these problems, Last built up his Micrologic group. He recruited expert engineers who had worked at Texas Instruments, at the Diamond Ordnance Fuze Laboratory, and at other organizations. Among the recruits were James Nall (who had pioneered photolithography and hybrid circuits at the Fuze Laboratory with Jay Lathrop) and Lionel Kattner (who had previously manufactured germanium transistors at Texas Instruments). Last also collaborated closely with the device evaluation group in Fairchild's R&D laboratory, which was led by Robert Norman, on the Micrologic program. Last's group had expertise in devices and processes. Norman's group knew transistor circuits and digital circuit design. Norman and his group were instrumental in choosing the specific logic form for the Micrologic circuits. This was DCTL (direct-coupled transistor logic), a logic form using only transistors and resistors that was used in advanced, transistor-based digital computers for the military and the intelligence community in the late 1950s. From a production perspective, DCTL was attractive because it relied heavily on transistors, required few other circuit elements, and was thus easier to manufacture in silicon. Isy Haas, a member of Norman's group who was investigating the use of transistors in microcircuitry, began to work closely with Last's team on integrated circuit fabrication.[85]

Over a period of several months, Last's group developed the techniques required to make physically isolated integrated circuits. Under the direction of Last, who was skilled at coordinating the efforts of others, the Micrologic group devised new transistor

Figure 1.8
Photograph of physically isolated integrated circuit, from photo essay on microcircuitry in *Life*, 10 March 1961. Courtesy of Time & Life Pictures.

designs specially suited for a DCTL integrated circuit. They worked on improvements to the firm's diffusion and photolithography processes in order to meet the tight tolerances and small dimensions that were required. Using infrared techniques, they developed means for optically aligning the circuit elements on the front of the wafer with the epoxy-filled trenches on the back of the wafer. Another important focus of activity was the search for suitable materials to isolate the devices on the same die. In May 1960, Lionel Kattner succeeded in making a functional, physically isolated planar integrated circuit. But these first circuits were not reliable. They were brittle, and they broke easily. This led to a search for different insulating materials for the trenches. Kattner investigated many alternatives without finding a way of truly solving the problems. Nevertheless, the physically isolated planar integrated circuit established that the Micrologic group was moving in a productive direction, and that the planar integrated circuit was a viable approach. More immediately, the physically isolated planar integrated circuit had a substantial publicity benefit. One of these devices was given pride of place in a photo essay on microcircuits in *Life* magazine.

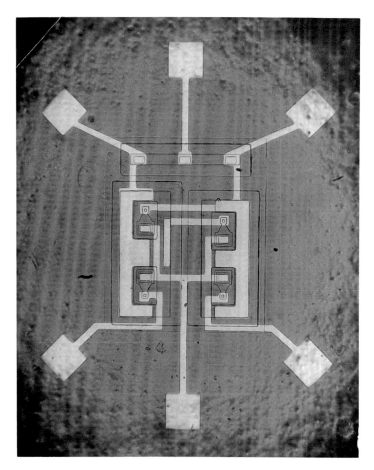

Figure 1.9
Photograph of the first planar diffusion isolated flip-flop circuit, September 1960. Courtesy of Lionel Kattner.

To Last and his colleagues, however, the physically isolated integrated circuit did not appear to be a product that could be easily manufactured in volume.[86] This realization led Kattner and Haas to revisit an idea that the Micrologic team had considered earlier: adapting Robert Noyce's isolation scheme to a more tractable form of PN junction isolation. This entailed leaving physical isolation completely behind. The electrically isolated planar integrated circuit that the Micrologic group considered would have a diffused well of doped material stretching from the front to the back of the wafer. This well would provide the necessary PN junctions to isolate the circuit elements. However, to form the well the engineers would have to diffuse from the front and from the back, the two diffusions meeting in the center of the wafer and thereby forming the complete well. Kattner and Haas worked to realize this new scheme. Using a new diffusion process for boron that had been developed within Fairchild Semiconductor's manufacturing organization, the pair diffused for 20 hours, creating the diffused wells. In the islands between the wells, the engineers used the planar process to form transistors and resistors. They then evaporated an aluminum film onto the oxide layer, patterning it with photolithography to interconnect the circuit elements. In September 1960, after several weeks of work, Kattner and Haas had an operational planar integrated circuit with electrical isolation. This electrically isolated planar integrated circuit was significantly more reliable and simpler to produce than the physically isolated version.[87]

Gordon Moore, head of R&D, selected the diffusion-based electrical isolation technology for use in building a family of planar integrated circuits for applications in computer logic. In March 1961, Moore and Robert Noyce convened a press conference to announce Fairchild Semiconductor's family of Micrologic planar integrated circuits. This was an important milestone. Fairchild Semiconductor was the first firm to announce a family of digital integrated circuits. It took six more months for Texas Instruments to do so. To design and fabricate their own family of integrated circuits, TI's engineers had to master the planar process. They also had to devise their own isolation scheme. This proved remarkably difficult. By early 1961, TI's management despaired of developing planar integrated circuits on their own and sought to gain access to Fairchild Semiconductor's technology by encouraging a group of Fairchild Semiconductor engineers, including Lionel Kattner, to start their own integrated circuit company. Not until the fall of 1961 did Texas Instruments announce its family of integrated circuits. Texas Instruments, which had originally held a significant lead in microcircuits, was now second in integrated circuits.[88]

Paradoxically, the development of the planar integrated circuit at Fairchild Semiconductor was disruptive for the firm. While many technical leaders in the organization recognized it as an important achievement, for large segments of the firm the planar integrated circuit initially appeared to be a distraction, a sideline. The rigors of meeting the rapidly increasing demand for the company's transistors and diodes were the utmost concerns for many in the marketing, sales, and production departments. For example, Tom Bay, the firm's sales manager, told Jay Last that the firm's R&D efforts would be better spent on serving and extending the transistor and diode businesses than on Micrologic. He also called for the cancellation of the integrated circuit effort. For many in the Micrologic program, their colleagues' preoccupation with existing product lines and occasional hostility to the microcircuitry effort seemed to indicate a misunderstanding of the great technological and commercial promise of integrated circuits.[89]

These differences of perspective on planar integrated circuits exacerbated instabilities in the organization stemming from the buyout of Fairchild Semiconductor by Fairchild Camera and Instrument just over a year earlier. As part of the buyout, Fairchild Semiconductor's founders received a substantial amount of Fairchild Camera and Instrument stock. Despite this windfall, the founders now were employees rather than owners, with unequal status relative to one another in the new organization. These changes caused stresses among the founders. And their windfall was a source of discontent for some outside the group of founders. Allison and some other top engineers felt that they too should have shared in the financial rewards.[90]

The promise of integrated circuits and the tensions arising from the buyout by Fairchild Camera and Instrument led the most important members of the Micrologic program to leave the firm to create spin-offs focused on integrated circuits. In January 1961, Jean Hoerni and Jay Last left to create Amelco Semiconductor as a division of Teledyne. Teledyne was a start-up designing military electronic systems in Southern California. Amelco produced advanced transistors and microcircuits for these systems. A few months later, David Allison, Lionel Kattner, and some other engineers in Fairchild Semiconductor's R&D laboratory established Signetics with financing from Lehman Brothers. Their new firm specialized in the design and production of integrated circuits. In late 1962, Robert Norman (the head of Micrologic design), along with one of Fairchild's top salesmen and some design and production engineers, left to form General Microelectronics, which, like Amelco and Signetics, concentrated on the new technology of planar integrated circuits.[91]

The development of the planar integrated circuit at Fairchild Semiconductor and the rapid pursuit of this technology by new start-ups marked a major milestone for the semiconductor industry, for computing, and for the digitalization of technology. The development of the first family of integrated circuits at Fairchild Semiconductor opened the era of silicon integrated circuits, which have come to pervade electronics. Over the last fifty years, integrated circuits have become far more complex. Whereas in 1961 an integrated circuit contained only a few components, in the late 2000s such a circuit might contain several billion components. With increasing capacities and decreasing costs, integrated circuits and digital technology have become increasingly essential to a wide range of industries and to the global economy. Used at first in computing and avionics, integrated circuits have become widely used in consumer electronics, in communications, in the automotive industry, in transportation, in health care, in financial markets, and in other major economic sectors. Integrated circuits were used by diverse industries to develop improved products and to develop entirely new sectors, including personal computers and Internet commerce. In the period 1957–1961, Fairchild Semiconductor set the developmental path on which silicon integrated circuits were used to invent the digital world.

2 Facsimiles and Interpretive Essays

Letter to Hayden Stone & Company

June 1957

Eugene and Rose Kleiner

Written by Eugene Kleiner with assistance from his wife Rose, this letter led to the formation of Fairchild Semiconductor.[1] Eugene Kleiner, born in Vienna in 1923, grew up in a well-to-do Jewish family. His father owned several shoe factories. When Germany annexed Austria in 1938, the family fled Vienna, moving first to Belgium and then to New York. In Belgium, Kleiner learned tool making, a trade he later practiced in the United States. During his stay in New York, he met his future wife, Rose Wassertheil, who had recently emigrated from Poland. Rose also came from an industrial family. Her father was a textile manufacturer. In New York, Rose studied sociology at Brooklyn College and later was employed as a social worker at the Quaker House.[2]

After serving in the U.S. Army during World War II, Eugene Kleiner obtained a bachelor's degree in mechanical engineering from the Polytechnic Institute of Brooklyn, with funding from the GI Bill. He later earned a master's degree in industrial engineering from New York University. Kleiner held engineering positions at the American Shoe Foundry Company, where he designed cigar-making machinery and gun loaders for the Navy. Later he worked at Western Electric, where he developed production tools for manufacturing telephone relays, the electrical switches used in the telephone system. At night, he taught machine tool operation at Brooklyn Polytechnic. In 1956, he and two Western Electric colleagues, Julius Blank and Dean Knapic, joined the Shockley Semiconductor Laboratory (henceforth referred to as Shockley Semiconductor), where they engineered crystal growers and other specialized equipment.[3]

The Kleiners' June 1957 letter was the outcome of months of turmoil at Shockley Semiconductor. William Shockley, the firm's founder, had antagonized his staff by staging public firings and demanding that his employees take lie-detector tests. Technological and strategic decisions made by Shockley were further sources of discontent. Shockley, who had initially focused his new firm on the making of diffused silicon tran-

Letter to Hayde Stone June 1957 (1)

This prospectus is to introduce a group of seven senior scientists and engineers who have been working together in the development of transistors and other semiconductor devices. Appendix I contains their biographical sketches. Because of seemingly insuperable problems with the present management this group wishes to find a corporation interested in getting into the advanced semiconductor device business. If such suitable backing can be obtained the present group can reasonably expect to take with them other senior people and an excellent supporting staff totaling about thirty people. Thus a backer has the opportunity to obtain at one time a well trained technical group by supplying enlightened administration and financial support.

This group of seven people, which represents a majority of the senior staff, is presently working at the Shockley Semiconductor Laboratory of Beckman Instruments, Il which is headed by Dr. William Shockley, who has recently received the Nobel Prize in Physics for his contribution to the invention of the transistor while working at the Bell Telephone Laboratories. The organization has been in operation for about a year and a half doing research and development in transistors. During this period much progress has been made in the field of silicon diffused devices. This has been accomplished at a cost of over a million dollars.

Our present dissatisfactions have arisen primarily from Shockley's confusing and demoralizing management. Although great scientific ability is indeed useful in attracting together such an ususually able group of technical people as we have, good administrative ability is necessary to use them effectively. Inadequacies in the leadership from this standpoint were brought as a last resort to the attention of Dr. A. O. Beckman. Some adjustments were made by him. However, they are insufficient to allow morale to rise to the point where we can rapidly accomplish success as a productive profit-making organization. Many people are seriously considering leaving the organization. A group feeling arose to the effect that rather than leave one by one, we would much prefer to stay together. We believe that we are much more valuable to an employer as a group.

We have an experienced and well-diversified group of men with background in the fields of physics, electronics, engineering, metallurgy, and chemistry. These men are not only outstanding in their own special field but have learned during the past year to work together effectively. We fully realize that it appears very paradoxical that the technical caliber of the group reflects the great attraction of Dr. Shockley for these people initially, yet the present pending breakup of the group reflects a later complete disallusionment with his leadership. Nevertheless, this is the situation as it stands. The horizontal ties in the group are strong and adequate technical leadership is present within it. It appears to have no person who has ambitions as a manager on the top level. As a result, it is the aim of the group to negotiate with a company which can supply good management. We believe that we could get a company into the semiconductor business within three months which would represent a considerable saving in cost and time.

Negotiations should be concluded as soon as possible in order to preserve the unity of the group. Details of the separation of the group from the present organization can be worked out later but it would be well to make this separation as quickly as possible after a commitment has been made.

We estimate that within three months after the organization has been started, barring unforseen delays in obtaining a suitable building, most of the important equipment can be in operating condition and the pilot production phase started. The pilot production and development phase will extend an additional six months during which time we expect to produce sample devices for prospective customers or for an internal market in the organisation with which we are associated. Mass production planning will then be initiated.

The initial products would be a line of silicon diffused transistors of usual design applicable to the production of both high frequency and high power devices. It should be pointed out that the complicated techniques necessary for producing these semiconductor devices have already been worked out in detail by

-3-

(3)

this group of people, and are not restricted by any obligation to the present organization. Also, it should be emphasised that we intend to carry on from the beginning a research program consistent with our manpower availability in order to attain and hold a superior position in the semiconductor field.

The final number of senior people who would leave the Shockley organization to form the nucleus of the new company would probably be about ten, the exact number depending on the timing of the negotiations and the conditions under which the new enterprise is set up. In addition to these senior personnel, we have an excellent supporting staff. While we have not approached them directly, we are confident on the basis of our past interaction with them that nearly all of them would choose to follow our group. In this specialised field this supporting staff has had to be trained at great cost of time and money. Because of this experienced staff, and also because of the group's own attachment to this lower San Francisco peninsula area, we would want to establish the operation here south of San Francisco.

It is estimated that the establishment of this new enterprise and its ~~maintenance operation during the first year~~ first year will require an expenditure in the neighborhood of $750,000. About one-third of this amount would be needed in the first three months in order to purchase initial equipment for the enterprise. Income from sales during the first year is not expected to reduce significantly the estimated capital outlay. This estimate allows for rental costs but does not include any expenditure for the construction of a new building. A more detailed listing of proposed first year expenditures is in Appendix II.

sistors, reoriented it toward the production of four-layer diodes, which were extremely difficult to make with any uniformity and whose market potential was more limited.[4]

The conflicts prompted some senior staff members to rebel against Shockley. The rebels included Gordon Moore, Jay Last, Eugene Kleiner, Jean Hoerni, Julius Blank, Victor Grinich, and Sheldon Roberts. They contacted Arnold Beckman of Beckman Instruments, Shockley's financial backer, and asked him to appoint a new, professional manager to whom they could report, with Shockley taking a more advisory role. After several meetings with the rebellious group, in which he considered new managerial arrangements at Shockley Semiconductor, Beckman decided to renew his support for Shockley. This decision put the seven young researchers in a difficult position. Having burned their bridges with Shockley, they felt that they had to leave. But they could not easily find similar jobs on the San Francisco Peninsula, where they enjoyed living. The electronics cluster on the Peninsula was still rather small, and no other firm was actively involved in the semiconductor business. The rebels also enjoyed working with one another and knew that they possessed a rare collective expertise in silicon devices and processes. This led Eugene and Rose Kleiner to write a letter to Hayden Stone & Company at the behest of the whole group. Hayden Stone was a small New York investment bank at which Eugene Kleiner's father had an account.[5]

The Kleiners' remarkably candid letter outlined the group members' difficulties with Shockley and their desire for collective employment. Seeking to attract a company that would employ the seven rebels as a group, the Kleiners emphasized the group members' technical credentials, their expertise in silicon technology, and their ability to work well together. These factors, the Kleiners argued, would allow the firm that hired the group to enter the silicon device business rapidly and at relatively low cost. It would also do so at little risk, since Shockley Semiconductor had no intellectual property rights on silicon device technology. The fundamental inventions in this area had been patented by the Bell Telephone Laboratories and could be easily licensed from them.

The letter also included the broad outline of a business plan. The Kleiners stated that the group would focus on the production of diffused silicon transistors and would operate an active research and development organization as a way to keep ahead of the competition. The letter suggested possible milestones for the new operation: setting up new facilities in three months, then six months of development and pilot production, then planning for large-scale production nine months after the firm's formation.

The letter was remarkably effective. Sent to a clerk in charge of the elder Kleiner's account, it was forwarded to Arthur Rock, a young analyst, and Alfred Coyle, one of the firm's partners. Rock and Coyle, who had previously been involved in the financing of semiconductor start-ups, were particularly receptive. The bankers saw potential in the group's silicon expertise and soon arranged for a meeting with them in San Francisco. Impressed, Rock and Coyle convinced the group—which now included Robert Noyce, another member of Shockley's senior staff—that, rather than look for collective employment, they should start their own company. This was a new and unfamiliar idea to these men, who had always envisioned working in the employ of existing corporations. Rock and Coyle also offered to raise the money for such a new firm. The researchers accepted the bankers' offer and decided to pursue their surprising suggestion. Together the researchers and the bankers reviewed the names of firms from the stock listings in the *Wall Street Journal*, circling any that they thought might be interested in having a semiconductor electronics operation. After contacting more than thirty companies from this list—including Litton Industries, North American Aviation, and Eitel-McCullough (a local manufacturer of vacuum tubes)—and encountering uniform disinterest, Rock and Coyle eventually found an investor: Fairchild Camera and Instrument, a military-oriented firm that made aerial cameras and other aviation-related equipment. It was interested in expanding into the semiconductor business. In September 1957, the group of eight signed a contract with Fairchild Camera and Instrument to form a new company: the Fairchild Semiconductor Corporation.[6]

Entries in Personal Notebook, Pages 21, 23, and 24

6, 11, and 18 November 1957

Jay Last

These notes from the first half of November 1957 reveal the initial orientations of the group of founders of Fairchild Semiconductor, as well as their awareness that speed would be essential to their start-up's survival in the intense competition among semiconductor firms. The notes were written by Jay Last in a personal notebook—a standard composition book—that Last carried with him to meetings and discussions.[7] In its pages Last recorded information about presentations that others made, decisions the group settled on, and items for him to follow up. There was no formal function for Last's note taking. Rather, it was a continuation of his practice of note taking during his quite recent graduate school days. The notes served to focus his attention during a meeting and acted as an aide-mémoire thereafter.[8]

Last, like his fellow founders, was a young man at this time—28 years old. Raised in Butler, Pennsylvania, he had earned an undergraduate degree at the University of Rochester, where he had specialized in physical optics. He had gone on to obtain a PhD in solid-state physics at the Massachusetts Institute of Technology. At MIT, he had used infrared spectrophotometers produced by Beckman Instruments in studying the structure of ferroelectric materials, and had formed a close association with Arnold Beckman and others affiliated with Beckman Instruments. Beckman Instruments offered Last a job in its instrumentation business. He turned it down, but did express an interest in finding an industrial research position in California.[9]

When Arnold Beckman established Shockley Semiconductor with William Shockley, in 1955, Beckman Instruments' management commended Last to Shockley as a possible hire. After a series of meetings on the East Coast, Last accepted a job offer from Shockley. He joined Shockley in Palo Alto in April 1956, immediately after completing his studies at MIT. At Shockley Semiconductor, Last worked closely with Shockley on theoretical studies of semiconductor physics and on experimental investigations of the electrical surface states that were negatively affecting the performance of four-layer diodes. After a year, however, Last's relationship with Shockley began to deteriorate. The same also happened with other members of the senior staff, leading to their departure and the establishment of Fairchild Semiconductor at the end of September 1957.[10]

After reaching their agreement with Fairchild Camera and Instrument, which secured them $1.38 million in financing over the next eighteen months with which to establish Fairchild Semiconductor and develop a diffused silicon transistor, the founders immediately resigned from Shockley Semiconductor. Their next order of business was to look for a suitable facility for their new firm. They considered a 40,000-square-foot building in nearby San Carlos that was about to be vacated by the electronics and instrumentation manufacturer Varian Associates. However, they judged that facility too large. Within just a week or so of their 1 October official beginning, the founders had found a much

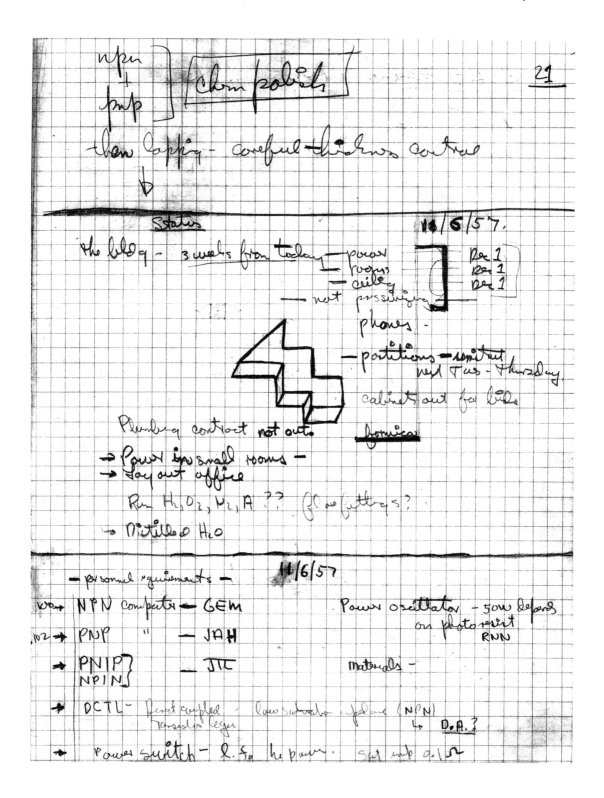

npn
+
pnp | Chem polish | 21

then lapping - careful thickness control

Status   10/6/57.

the bldg - 3 weeks from today — power   Dec 1
                                 — rooms   Dec 1
                                 — ceiling   Dec 1
                         — not pressurizing
                           phones -
                         — partitions — semi-trut
                                        next Tues - Thursday.
                         cabinets out for bids

Plumbing contract not out.   formica

→ Power in small rooms —
→ Lay out office
   Run H_2, O_2, N_2, A ?? (gas fittings?
→ Distilled H_2O

— personnel requirements —   11/6/57

vo→ NPN computer ← GEM   Power oscillator - 50w depends
                                        on photo resist
,02 → PNP   "   — JAH   RNN
→ PNIP}   — JT
   NPIN}   materials -
→ DCTL- direct coupled low saturation impedance (NPN)
          transistor logic   D.A. ?
→ Power switch - l. 5a hi power. Sat imp 0.1Ω

23

Staff meeting 11/11/57.   Host + Max.

hourly vs monthly   Green wax

[Requisitions — Project leader to $1000
           "   "   + Bob 5000
         > 5000 Policy committee

— Codex files ??

Tool list

Receiving and/or stockroom clerk.

procedures will be written up by Max

write up

— Patent Attorney —:

Staff Meeting 11/19/57

→ pow. transformers here: 2 weeks. to go   Finished by
→ ceiling: started today 2 weeks.   12/2/57
                                                  12/2/57

(this is only main power — no bench power)

→ plumbing, sewers etc } lind out
    gas, air

→ air handling — blowers, pressure: lind out.

→ small rooms: 12/15/57.

→ benches & lab: finished by Dec 1.
   cabinets: arrive this Thursday — also 6 Hoods.

  furnace benches: arrive today

→ phones: no estimate 2-3 weeks   DA6-6695 in 2 weeks
   + trunks

two estimates to J.B today

   1 up to 12/31/57
   2 up to 3/1/57

Hodgson called:
You Buy 12.6
Devito mgr.

Codex file: CSR

Patent agreement: nothing to steal (mining).

Patent attorney: Flair & Swain – wait on this.

When do we want to get into production:

Jan 6   Sawing   JB   ⇒ transfer to production date
         Orientation   CSR   Shawn
         Lapping (routine)   JT

         Crystal evaluation

Mar 3   photo etching   KNN
         raising diff N P N   SEM

Mar 17   evap & alloying   SEM

April 1 assembly N P N   R.B.

April 15 test & selection   UG

May 5   PNP Diffusion   JAH.

June 2   polish to thickness   JTC

June 15 P N I P   JTC

supervisors for production – low tech skills in general
∴ we write production specs.

Dec 1	Jan 6	Feb	∴ 13 more tech people by 2/1
offer	Sr. Eng. JAH.	2 tech	
1 Tech	2 tech	Sr. Eng. UG.	
middle			janitor new.
Hall			girl "
	6	3	

smaller building—14,400 square feet—at 844 East Charleston Road on the border of Palo Alto and Mountain View. The building, newly constructed, was little more than an empty shell, without utilities, a ceiling, or internal walls.[11]

Through October the founders met at their new address, discussing how to make the building suitable for developing and manufacturing silicon transistors. In a very direct way, their plans for transforming 844 East Charleston Road were an expression of their basic business and technological strategy. Their blueprints reflected their technological aims. An array of furnace benches was planned for developing diffusion and oxide masking processes. Small spaces for optical testing and photoresist use were planned for the pursuit of the new technique of photolithography. A dedicated space for evaporation equipment reflected the importance of developing new metallization techniques. More established processes for working with silicon material—crystal growing, lapping, and polishing—had specific places too. A device-development area, with tables, hoods, and sinks, was planned. For the time being, however, the founders had to restrict their time in their new building to daylight hours, for there was not even primary electrical service, and they had to use the rest room of a nearby gas station.[12]

On 6 November 1957, Jay Last met with his fellow founders twice. The first meeting concerned the new building and the efforts to get it ready by the beginning of December. (See notebook page 21.) Last's notes show that electrical service, telephone service, internal walls and partitions, and even a ceiling were three weeks away. Getting a plumbing contract out for the proper fittings to deliver the distilled water and the gases necessary for processing silicon devices was the order of the day. The founders' concerns about getting the building ready for work reflected an acute awareness of the importance of speed to their new business. Being among the first, if not the first, to bring diffused silicon devices to market would be their competitive advantage against larger firms (including Texas Instruments) that were already producing silicon transistors and were headed in the direction of diffusion.

In keeping with this sense of urgency, and despite the unfinished physical plant, the founders had a second discussion on 6 November 1957 in which they agreed on a set of silicon devices that they would explore as potential products. First on the list of possibilities was a diffused silicon mesa transistor in the NPN configuration. Last's notes capture this device as "NPN computer." (See notebook page 21.) This was shorthand for a transistor suitable for use in digital computers. The transistor's NPN configuration, the form of silicon transistor that the group had some experience pursuing at Shockley Semiconductor, was to be engineered by Gordon Moore. Jean Hoerni was given responsibility for developing a PNP version of the transistor for use in digital computers. However, forming good electrical contacts to the P-type regions was consistently difficult. Extra diffusion steps were necessary to heavily dope the P-type regions for making adequate contacts, and these steps added to the challenge of Hoerni's task. Setting the two founders at work to develop the rival configurations of the digital computing transistor (for only one of the two could be chosen as the first device to go into production) established an internal competition in the young firm, a competition that in the coming months would prove fruitful in generating both speed and innovations.[13]

The other product possibilities that the group discussed were more remote, but all were fundamentally connected to the manufacturing technology upon which the group was focused: diffusion in silicon using oxide masking and photolithography. Jay Last would explore transistor structures incorporating a layer of undoped or "intrinsic" silicon—"PNIP" and "NPIN." Bell Labs had recently originated the study of these structures for their potential as extremely fast-switching transistors that could also handle higher power. This combination of high frequency and higher power would make them ideal for use in digital computers. Whereas Bell Labs had used alloying methods to make these new structures, Fairchild Semiconductor's diffusion approach offered an attractive alternate route.[14] The newly hired engineer David Allison, with whom the group had worked at Shockley, would investigate a diffused silicon NPN transistor specifically designed for use in an emerging form of computer logic called direct-coupled transistor logic (DCTL). Robert Noyce would look at the possibility of making a power oscillator transistor within the context of his work on photolithography and photoresists.

In all the discussions, the founders' central strategy was consistent and clear. They would use their diffusion-based manufacturing technology to create a family of silicon transistors for use in digital computing. The basic approaches for this manufacturing technology had come to Fairchild Semiconductor's founders from Bell Labs though the conduit of William Shockley and his laboratory. For the founders, the batch processing at the core of the manufacturing technology was attractive both because of its potential for low-cost production and because of the flexibility it could afford. The emphasis on producing a suite of transistors and other devices for digital computing was more endogenous. Two of the eight founders had significant experience with digital computing. Robert Noyce had started his career at Philco, where he had worked on a high-speed germanium transistor that had been employed in early transistorized digital systems. Indeed, Philco actively promoted the DCTL logic form—an all-transistor logic that it had done much to create—for digital computers, and with it the firm's high-speed germanium transistors. Victor Grinich, the only founder with a formal education in electrical engineering, had worked on digital computers before joining Shockley. At the Stanford Research Institute, Grinich had designed transistor circuits for the ERMA digital computer project, a major effort to develop a specialized system for banking and check processing for the Bank of America. The experiences of Grinich and Noyce with the use of transistors in digital computing set the stage for Fairchild Semiconductor's focus, and perhaps also for its specific interest in the new, all-transistor DCTL logic form.[15]

On Monday, 11 November 1957, Jay Last recorded notes at the first "staff meeting" of the firm. (See notebook page 23.) Having assigned responsibilities for the product development projects, the group devised guidelines for the purchases of materials and equipment that would be required. Requisitions up to $1,000 were the prerogative of the project leader. Sums up to $5,000 could be used with the agreement of Robert Noyce and the project leader—one of the first indications of Noyce's rise as a "first among equals" in the fledgling firm. Noyce, owing to his tenure at Philco, was alone among the founders in having had a direct experience of transistor production. As a mark of both confidence and necessity, the group also discussed hiring a patent attorney. Not only would it be necessary to license basic transistor technology from Bell Labs and Western Electric, but also the group might need to protect inventions of its own.

Gauged by the extent of Jay Last's note taking, the next Monday staff meeting, which took place on 18 November 1958, was much more substantial. Eugene Kleiner and Julius Blank, the experienced production engineers who had worked closely together at Western Electric and at Shockley Semiconductor, continued their collaboration as founders of Fairchild Semiconductor. In particular, they took responsibility for readying the new facility and for constructing much of the required equipment, including crystal growers. The founders discussed in detail the estimated completion dates of various aspects of the building project. Though the benches for the diffusion furnaces were due to be delivered that day, electrical power and a completed ceiling were still estimated to be two weeks away. Bids were out for the plumbing and the air handling system, but they had no estimate for when phone service would be installed.[16]

Meeting in their unlit building, the men turned to estimates and plans for moving into production. Again, the importance of speed was implicit throughout the discussion. The group discussed a recent call from Richard Hodgson, a vice president of Fairchild Camera and Instrument who was the primary contact and supporter of the group within their East Coast backer. Hodgson reported that he had made an offer to Thomas Bay, a former sales executive with Fairchild Controls (a subsidiary of Fairchild Camera), to establish Fairchild Semiconductor's sales function starting in early December. The firm would begin pursuing sales before its facility even had sinks.

The group then moved on to address the question "When do we want to get into production [?]" (See notebook page 24.) Jay Last recorded the group's first attempt at a schedule for when the different components of their manufacturing technology would be solidly established and a list of who would assume primary responsibility for making them so. The techniques that the group believed would be ready first, in six or seven weeks, were those for making silicon wafers. Julius Blank was responsible for the sawing of silicon crystals into wafers. C. Sheldon Roberts would handle growing the crystals with the proper crystalline orientation. Last, drawing on his background in optics, would develop a routine lapping process for grinding the wafers flat.

The initial plan called for Robert Noyce to develop "photoetching" to a production-worthy stage by March 1958—three months hence—by which time Gordon Moore was to have settled on a stable process for the diffusion of the NPN transistor structure. By mid March, Moore was also to have worked out the processes for evaporating and alloying metal onto the transistors to form their electrical contacts. The goals for April called for the remainder of the steps for producing the NPN transistor to be in place. Robert Brown, a skilled technician working under Moore, was called upon to work out the steps for assembling the transistor—the attaching of leads and the placement within a protective package. Victor Grinich was responsible for developing the equipment and procedures for testing the devices during manufacture and selecting those transistors that met the product specifications.

Under this plan, the firm would possess the ability to manufacture the NPN transistor at the end of April 1958. This was the six-month lead time to first production that the group had originally articulated in Eugene Kleiner's letter to Hayden Stone & Company, and it was the primary expression of the group's emphasis on speed. The plan then called for the production processes necessary to widen the family of digital computing products to be readied in May and June. Jean Hoerni took the goal of solving the challenges of diffusion for the PNP transistor by May. Jay Last picked up two tasks for completion in June: developing a procedure for polishing the wafers to particular thicknesses, which would improve certain characteristics of the silicon devices, and developing a process for creating a PNIP transistor. The group was aware of the personnel implications of this rapid plan. They estimated that they would have to hire 13 people, ranging from senior engineers to technicians, to carry out this R&D program for establishing their manufacturing technology.

Entry in Patent Notebook

1 December 1957

Jean Hoerni

This entry in the patent notebook that Jean Hoerni kept at Fairchild Semiconductor is one of the most important documents in the history of semiconductor technology and the semiconductor industry.[17] It describes a revolutionary transistor structure (later to be called the *planar* structure) and the techniques for fabricating it. In the 1960s, Hoerni's planar process became the dominant approach to the manufacture of semiconductor electronics, including transistors and integrated circuits. It established a path of technological development that the semiconductor industry has pursued ever since.

Hoerni had been born into a banking family in Switzerland, and had obtained a bachelor's degree in mathematics and a doctorate in physics from the University of Geneva. He later received a second doctorate in physics from Cambridge University. In 1952 he had moved to the United States, where he had worked as a research associate under Linus Pauling in the chemistry division at the California Institute of Technology. At Caltech, Hoerni had continued his work in theoretical physics, specializing in electron diffraction. In the first half of the 1950s he had published a series of articles on the diffraction of electrons by molecules and crystals in *Physical Review*.[18]

Hoerni, who had been groomed for a career in academic science, reoriented his professional interests toward industry. He turned down an assistant professorship at Caltech that required a loyalty oath because of his opposition to that requirement. Knowing that his chances of finding an academic position in Europe were limited, he looked for a job in industrial research. After refusing the offer of a research position in radio science at the Bell Telephone Laboratories, he joined Shockley Semiconductor in 1956. At Shockley Semiconductor, Hoerni worked on an esoteric thermal semiconductor device, one of William Shockley's many ideas. Making use of his mathematical skills, Hoerni also calculated diffusion curves for dopants such as gallium, boron, and phosphorous in silicon. Diffusion curves—which plotted dopant concentration over junction depth given certain time and temperature conditions—helped researchers to calculate the diffusion rate and thereby adjust heating times and furnace temperatures to obtain the desired diffused junction. As Hoerni's relations with Shockley became increasingly tense, Shockley ordered him to fabricate four-layer diodes with Jay Last and C. Sheldon Roberts. This experience introduced Hoerni to experimental work and to the complexities of semiconductor device fabrication.[19]

Shortly after co-founding Fairchild Semiconductor, Hoerni recorded his ideas for a new transistor structure and techniques for producing it. That Hoerni carefully described these ideas in his patent notebook and had Robert Noyce witness his entry the very same day attests to the importance that Hoerni gave to his new ideas. Up to this time, all diffused silicon transistors were of the mesa form, with the emitter and base regions

December 1, 1957   Jean A. Hoerni

3

Method of protecting exposed p-n junctions at the surface of silicon transistors by oxide masking techniques.

The general idea underlying this invention is the building up of an oxide layer prior to diffusion of dopant atoms at those places on the surface of the transistor at which p-n junctions are expected to emerge from the body of the semiconductor. The oxide layer so obtained is an integrant part of the device and will protect the otherwise exposed junctions from ~~subsequent~~ contamination and possible electrical leakage due to subsequent handling, cleaning, canning of the device.

A second advantage resulting from the use of the technique to be described is the possibility of making contacts to the emitter, base and collector of a transistor on the same side of the wafer. In this way the contact to the collector on the back side of a thick wafer and its accompanying high series resistance may be avoided. The passive areas of the junctions can be kept at a ~~minimum~~ (compatible with areas required to attach a lead to the exposed part of the base of the transistor), irrespective of the overall size of the wafer.

The basic procedure to be used is as follows. A wafer (of usual dimensions) is cleaned and preoxidized. Using photoresist techniques or other masking techniques, the oxide is removed on a series of islands, of size comparable with the area desired for the emitter of the

4   transistor.   Jean A. Hoerni

Top view of
wafer

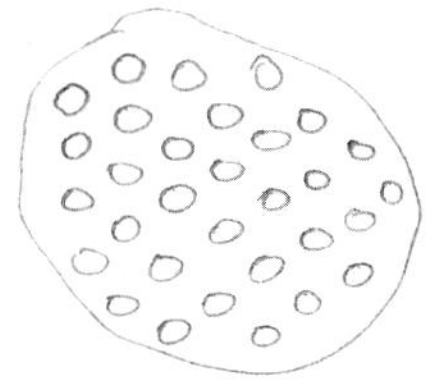

Fig. 1

Oxide layer removed within circles

The base and emitter regions are obtained by diffusion of impurities giving the desired conductivity type. The cross-section of across one of the unoxidized islands looks so after diffusion (for p type ~~bad~~ bulk material and a p-n-p transistor):

Fig. 2

It will be seen that in this way the parts of the silicon surface where the junctions emerge are masked at all ~~times~~ by the oxide layer. It is known that most impurities of interest (except Gallium) do not diffuse into the silicon wherever an ~~oxide~~ oxide layer is present. Contacts have to be made to the three regions, which requires that parts of the oxide layer be removed to permit these contacts. The structure shown on Fig. 2 is not suitable in that the width of the base exposed to the surface is only a few microns, and is too small to make a suitable contact. A design improving this ~~existing~~ situation is shown on Fig. 3:

Added oxide layer after diffusion of the base impurity
Original oxide layer

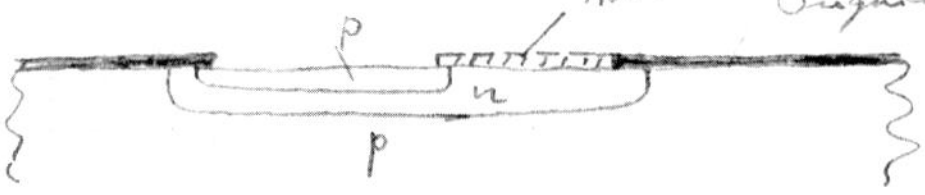

Read and understood Dec 1, 1957
R. N. Noyce

overlooking the collector region. Metal contacts were attached to the base and emitter layers on top of the transistor and to the collector layer on the bottom of the device. The transistor structure that Hoerni envisioned in his 1 December 1957 patent notebook entry was very different. The transistor included a layer of silicon oxide covering the top of the emitter and base regions—hence its flat or "planar" surface. All three metal contacts were made on the top surface of the device. More important, the layer of silicon oxide covered the transistor's PN junctions. This was a departure from the mesa structure, in which both the emitter-base junction and the base-collector junction were uncovered, exposed to the atmosphere.

In his patent notebook, Hoerni sketched the various steps for creating such a transistor structure. First, one would oxidize the surface of a silicon wafer by exposing it to steam, which would result in a silicon oxide layer covering the wafer. Then, using the photolithographic techniques under development at Fairchild Semiconductor, one would open up windows in the silicon oxide layer through which one would diffuse dopants, thereby forming the emitter and base regions of the transistor. In order to make the base region large enough for making metal contact with it on the top of device, Hoerni noted, one would have to regrow the oxide layer and use photolithography to open a new, smaller window for the emitter diffusion. The last steps included yet another regrowth of the oxide layer, and another round of photolithography to open up a new set of windows in it through which metal contacts would be made.

Hoerni's conception of the planar transistor and the planar process developed in the context of Fairchild Semiconductor's focus on oxide masking, a technique originally developed at the Bell Telephone Laboratories. In the spring of 1955, two Bell Labs researchers—Carl Frosch and Lincoln Derick—had observed that silicon wafers exposed to water vapor formed an oxide layer that protected the crystal surface from "pitting" and other damage during diffusion operations. The oxide layer prevented the wafer from eroding during lengthy and high-temperature diffusions. Frosch and Derick had also discovered that the oxide layer would prevent certain dopants, including boron and phosphorus, from diffusing into the crystal. Other impurities, such as gallium, could penetrate through the oxide layer and diffuse into the silicon wafer. This was an important finding, as the oxide layer could provide a selective mask against the diffusion of certain dopants, permitting their controlled introduction into silicon wafers. In June 1955, Frosch and Derick had circulated a memorandum on the properties of silicon oxide layers and on oxide masking techniques to their Bell Labs colleagues. One of the recipients had been William Shockley.[20]

Fairchild Semiconductor's founders had been introduced to the idea of oxide masking at Shockley Semiconductor—either through conversations with William Shockley himself or by reading the preprint of an article on oxide masking by Frosch and Derick that Shockley had circulated to his staff in December 1956. Shockley Semiconductor, as a Bell Labs licensee, received copies of articles in solid-state physics and engineering written by Bell Labs scientists that had been accepted for publication but had not yet been published. This particular preprint was an article by Frosch and Derick titled "Surface Protection and Masking during Diffusion in Silicon," soon to be published in the *Journal of the Electrochemical Society*. The paper presented many of the same results as Frosch and Derick's June 1955 memorandum. Shockley had sent the preprint to all members of his senior staff, Hoerni included. Understanding the significance of Frosch and Derick's findings immediately, they used oxide masking in making experimental diffused silicon mesa transistors at Shockley Semiconductor.[21]

In the 1 December 1957 entry in his patent notebook, Hoerni proposed going one step further than Frosch and Derick in the use of silicon oxide layers. He would use oxide layers to both create *and protect* the transistor junctions.[22] His idea was to use the oxide layer to create "nested diffusion" regions. Hoerni recognized that dopants diffused laterally as well as vertically in silicon crystals. When dopants were introduced into a silicon wafer through openings in the oxide layer, the dopants would diffuse under the silicon oxide mask and would form PN junctions that would be protected by the silicon oxide layer. This was important because PN junctions were the most sensitive parts of silicon transistors.[23]

Hoerni's second insight was to leave the oxide layer on top of the transistor after processing. This went against the conventional wisdom in the industry. It was widely accepted in the semiconductor community that the oxide layer that had served as a mask for diffusions was "dirty"—that is, full of contaminants that would have unwanted effects on the transistor's electrical characteristics. This idea of the "dirty oxide" seems to have originated at the Bell Telephone Laboratories in the second half of 1955. For example, in their patent application on oxide masking filed in December 1955, Frosch and Derick repeatedly discussed dipping the wafer in hydrofluoric acid in order to remove the oxide layer. The idea of the "dirty oxide" spread rapidly from the Bell Labs to the entire semiconductor community. That any oxide layer that had been exposed to diffusions should be removed and replaced by a "clean" re-grown oxide became a widely held belief.[24]

Hoerni immediately shared his idea of the planar structure and protected PN junctions with his Fairchild Semiconductor colleagues. Robert Noyce signed Hoerni's patent notebook entry on 1 December 1957. Moore recalls that he heard about the planar structure very early on, "not too far from the time [Hoerni] first put it in his notebook."[25] But Hoerni and his colleagues set these ideas aside for the moment as they focused on their plan to rapidly develop their manufacturing technology and, with it, a diffused silicon NPN or PNP mesa transistor. Most of the men concentrated on the design of an NPN transistor that could be used in digital computers. Hoerni, the theoretical physicist turned engineer, focused on using boron diffusion processes to create P-type regions of silicon in his pursuit of a PNP version of the mesa transistor. Hoerni's PNP transistor effort was a difficult project that took up most of his time until November 1958.[26]

An additional reason why Hoerni and the Fairchild Semiconductor group did not rapidly try out the planar structure and process is that it ran counter to the view and the approach that were conventional in the industry. "Our problems [at Fairchild Semiconductor]," Jay Last later noted, "were related to surface states under the oxide and the planar was probably going to compound [these problems] rather than cure them. It was just one of these things where you think, 'Well, it is probably not going to work anyhow, so why bother?' And it took until January of 1959 for Jean to decide to make one."[27] Not until then did Hoerni write a patent disclosure on the planar process and structure. He fabricated the first planar silicon transistor in March of that year.[28]

Entry in Personal Notebook, Pages 30–31

9 December 1957

Jay Last

At the close of 1957, the market for silicon semiconductor devices was both rapidly growing and overwhelmingly military. Texas Instruments had been supplying grown-junction silicon transistors for nearly three years, and Hughes Semiconductor had been producing silicon diodes for nearly as long. Predominant among the customers for these silicon devices were the manufacturers of electronic systems for military aviation and aerospace projects. The U.S. Air Force was dissatisfied with the reliability of the vacuum tubes and germanium devices in existing systems, and new programs for missile and airborne systems demanded even greater reliability. Silicon semiconductor devices, with their intrinsic tolerance for high temperatures, were looked to by the military as a path to the performance and reliability they sought.[29]

In December 1957, as Fairchild Semiconductor's founders continued to organize their firm, this larger context of the military market for silicon devices came into view. Jay Last's notes from the Fairchild Semiconductor staff meeting of 9 December 1957 (notebook page 30) record that the firm had "applied for security clearance for facility as Fairchild subcontractor." Fairchild Camera and Instrument, the backer of Fairchild Semiconductor, had a subsidiary company in Southern California, Fairchild Controls, that supplied electronic components to aerospace firms in that region, not uncommonly for classified programs. Manufacturers of components for military programs were often required to obtain security clearances for their facilities. Fairchild Semiconductor had a ready route to such security clearances through Fairchild Controls.[30]

H. E. Hale, an executive from Fairchild Controls, had visited Fairchild Semiconductor shortly before the 9 December 1957 staff meeting, and indeed Jay Last's notations about "security clearance" follow those about "Hales visit." Fairchild Semiconductor was operating under the aegis of Fairchild Controls, with Hale in the formal position of president of Fairchild Semiconductor. In practice, it was Richard Hodgson at Fairchild Camera and Instrument who was the main point of contact between Fairchild Semiconductor's founders and their corporate backer. Hale seems to have served as a conveniently positioned, seasoned executive who assisted Hodgson in his management and observation of the fledgling semiconductor operation.[31]

During his recent visit, Hale apparently had enjoined the Fairchild Semiconductor group to produce "accurate forecasts on budgets" and "sales." The remainder of Jay Last's notebook entry for the staff meeting on 9 December 1957 records the group's reaction to Hale's request. They focused on their plan for staffing and for purchasing of equipment and materials in order to get diffused silicon devices into production. In this planning discussion, the group forecast a growth in staff from 23 to 38 over the next

30   12/9/57

Staff meeting:

Hale visit: accurate forecast on budgets
                                                sales

Fairchild organization   Fairchild Controls } Components
                                                        Electronic
                                                        div
                                        ↓
                                wholly owned subsidiary
                                of Fairchild Camera

applied for security clearance for facility as Fairchild subcontractor

Mach net   → Harlan Lawler ← 220 +
Beauty clerk → Phil Peeters   ← 375 Keeping janitorial books - madison work

        Technicians Paul Hinchcliffe 1/2/58   400   Bus Ad
                    Swasky.   400   Criminology

By end of March:

3 girls   17 technical   Dibble dale
Phil   Tom Bay
Max   3 technicians } by Jan 1
Haley   Janitor

23 now   1 # Engineer → Jan
                    fast growing technician - Robert Jan 20
                    story   technician - Kleen story   "
                    autotest.   Sr Engineer - finish
                                  technician - Jan - Feb
                                  technician - finish Feb
                                  3 technician - March for people
                                        going to production

                                total 38

                                this is it except for will
                                production staff   budget.

31

⇒ make out a project budget; equipment
expend. material

(get predicted schedule from Bob)

written purchasing procedure.   PO costs vs $10-25
   no charge accounts PA Hardware, etc.

   Allan Chelsey — prospective Mgr.
   Ad in Tues or Wed for a Mgr.

~~Paint~~
Facilities
   Power: ON.
   Secondary power: owns day now
   Plumbing — almost done — leak in gas line
   Sewer   ≈   some more Cu tubing to go —
   Ceilings: almost done.
   Partitions: being painted now.
   Benches: start on Wednesday
   Wax floor this Tues perhaps
   Plows: all done
   Poly sinks: leg bind still 3 weeks to go

three months to establish the manufacturing process for diffused silicon transistors and to bring this process into production. They also elected to better organize their research, development, and engineering efforts by creating "project budgets," and to use purchasing orders rather than having "charge accounts" with the local hardware store and with other vendors. (See notebook page 31.)

Under the direction of Eugene Kleiner and Julius Blank, the new facility continued to be outfitted. The electrical power was on, the plumbing and ceilings were "almost done," the internal partitions were being painted, and the telephones were "all done." Julius Blank, the main engineer responsible for the facility, was a New York City native, the son of a luggage maker. Blank's studies at the City College of New York were interrupted by his service in the U.S. Army during World War II. After recovering from serious battle injuries, Blank was put to work repairing aircraft engines. After the war, he completed a degree in mechanical engineering at City College. After a stint with a manufacturer of industrial boilers in Ohio, he returned to the New York area as an engineer at Western Electric's plant in Kearney, New Jersey. There he worked on a variety of production problems connected to the high-volume manufacture of crossbar switching equipment for the telephone system. At Western Electric, Blank became acquainted with Eugene Kleiner and with Dean Knapic, another manufacturing engineer. (They shared a car pool.) When Knapic, who had made a name for himself by developing a new process for making relays at Western Electric, was hired by William Shockley to join Shockley Semiconductor, Knapic recruited Blank and Kleiner to Shockley's laboratory. Blank and Kleiner tackled a range of equipment and facilities needs at Shockley Semiconductor, continuing to handle these areas as founders of Fairchild Semiconductor.[32]

As Jay Last's personal notebook entry for 9 December 1957 reveals, the founders were looking outside their ranks for the professional management skills that would be required for building a silicon transistor business. Hodgson was assisting the founders on this front, talking to a variety of individuals who he thought might be interested and appropriate for the general manager position. With Hodgson's direct involvement, the search for a general manager was about to become national. In the middle of notebook page 31, Last wrote "Ad in Tues or Wed for a Mgr." An advertisement was placed in the *Wall Street Journal* for a vice president and general manager: "The man we are seeking must have wide administrative experience in semiconductor or electronic components field and broad industry relationships to help establish company as a strong competitor in the field. He will assume full responsibility for the management and expansion of this growing company." With this listing, Fairchild Semiconductor announced itself and its ambitions to a national audience, and attracted the interest of Ewart M. Baldwin, a high-level manager in charge of the manufacture of silicon diodes at Hughes Semiconductor.[33]

Entry in Personal Notebook, Pages 35–37

2 January 1958

Jay Last

On 2 January 1958, Fairchild Semiconductor's founders listened to Robert Noyce describe his meeting, two weeks earlier, with IBM engineers in Owego, New York. The three pages of detailed notes that Jay Last wrote during Noyce's account of the meeting showed how much importance the group placed on the event—Fairchild Semiconductor's first serious discussion with a potential customer.

Noyce, who had just turned 30 years old, had been raised in Iowa. The son of a minister, Noyce was known for his charisma, his competitiveness in diving, and his aptitude for science during his undergraduate years at Grinnell College. Introduced to semiconductors and transistors at Grinnell, Noyce went on to pursue a PhD in solid-state physics at MIT. In 1953 he completed a dissertation on experimental investigations of the electrical surface states of various materials. Passing on job offers from both Bell Labs and IBM, he accepted a position in the newly organized transistor department of the Philadelphia-based firm Philco. At Philco, he concentrated on a new form of high-speed germanium transistor, created using a novel manufacturing technique called electro-chemical jet etching. Noyce worked on the physics of this "surface barrier transistor," while his colleagues at Philco promoted their use in direct-coupled transistor logic.[34]

William Shockley, who had heard Noyce deliver a paper on Philco's high-speed transistor at a 1955 meeting of the Electrochemical Society and been impressed by the young researcher, recruited him to Shockley Semiconductor at the start of 1956. Noyce enjoyed a close working relationship with Shockley and a leadership position within the research staff at Shockley Semiconductor. As a result, he was initially reluctant to align himself with his dissatisfied co-workers. However, as conditions deteriorated at Shockley Semiconductor and discussions began with Arthur Rock and Bud Coyle of Hayden Stone & Company, Noyce agreed to join Fairchild Semiconductor's founders.[35]

Noyce's experiences at Philco with Air Force-sponsored programs on transistorized digital computers were important background in his traveling to Owego with Tom Bay, Fairchild Semiconductor's newly hired sales manager. Their meeting with the IBM engineers on 20 December 1957 was at the invitation of IBM's Military Products Division, which had been set up two years earlier to fulfill two IBM contracts that were central to the United States' capabilities for nuclear war fighting: IBM held the contract to create the data-processing centers for the networked SAGE air defense system and a contract to create a new on-board digital computing system for navigation and bombing in a new version of the B-52 long-range bomber. Additionally, by December 1957, groups in the U.S. defense establishment and at IBM Owego had started to work on a digital computer for a new strategic bomber to replace the B-52.[36]

Since 1954, the Air Force's Strategic Air Command had supported a secret project to design a supersonic long-range bomber to replace the B-52, with competing design

1/2/58   Report on IBM meeting   R.N.N.   35
                        Dec 20

3 general categories

    low power   150 mw at Room temp
→   core drivers   1W
    Servo drivers   ½-1 amp   10W out at 100°C. (Available from GE, TI)
                                            saturation resistance poor

<u>What they want for computers</u>

                    would like   can get. (n p n, selected)

collector R_{cs} <u>10 Ω.</u>   100 Ω
saturation

input h_{ib} 39 Ω   50 Ω.   1 ma
resistance

                    h_{fe} 70   80   20 ma.

grounded $f_{\alpha b}$ 20   30
base

                    C_{ob} 1.6 μμf.   20V.

collector V_{cb} 40V   > 25.   Used in a 28V
breakdown   system

power P 125 mV   1mw/°C.
dissipation

they need good matched pnp's to go along with those.
(can be can only be done with Double Diffusion - no matter
                                            techniques usable)

Reliability - GE pre-bakes at 200°C.
              Rover rather than glass seals.

Want to cut out all random catastrophic failures
put in a detergent filled bomb at 50 psi -
Shock tests
                                            Jeter Co.

Samples by end of first quarter - 20-50 or so.
Quantity requirements in a year.   20-60,000

36 they will go to Ge + air-conditioning if they can't get Si

Clamped RC coupled logic

haven't thought in terms of large signal parameters yet.

symmetric transistors to simplify the logic

Core Driver

DC β	150mo	60-100
f_α		>2 mc.
h_{ib}		30 Ω
IW @ 100°C.		(not realistic) ~250ma

should be specified

$I_c = 150$ ma

$V_b <$

$I_b <$

V_{ce}	60V	(this is high)
R_{cs}	2 Ω	(can get 100 Ω)
V_{eb}	2V	
rise time τ	.25 μsec.	

Hughes transistor may come close to this.

They will use 2000-3000 of these now (contracts out now).

10 computers at 100-200 each. will pay $100 each.

for first 500

- this will be used as a high freq power switch -

main thing - get the saturation resistance down! backside diffusion

this is a vacant area in transistors at the moment -

TI   903 ⎫
Ge   ⎪
Transistor ⎬ all getting into 5 mc area.
Hughes   ⎪
Motorola   ⎪
Raytheon   ⎭

② Edpro - Pioneer -   using to drive servo amplifiers
                      low freq (DC).
                      gain at 100°C (also gain at -50°C - need
                                      good lifetime for this)

Diffusion advantages: Disadvantages

make pnp   lifetime (low β)
high α   hard to make contacts.
oxide mask - interdigitate   (high saturation resistance)
put in intrinsic layers.
uniform large area.
low base resistance
easy to collector heat sink
(avoid encapsulation)
handle a large no. of elements at once

∴ push own pnp.
  interdigitation

smallest island 5×5 mils at the moment.
Completely surround the emitter.

should we head for the core driver now?

get top side structure on uph
try to jock B up.
Back side diffusion as soon as lapping is in good shape
Bob Noyce a masking
~~Buss~~ & cutoff no problem now —

teams at North American Aviation and Boeing. The new bomber's requirements called for it to fly at Mach 3, at high altitudes, carrying massive nuclear payloads, and to have an extremely long range. In December 1957, North American Aviation had won the design competition for the new aircraft, which would soon become known as the B-70 Valkyrie. IBM Owego had a subcontract to design the Valkyrie's on-board computer system, which would handle navigation, bombing, and missile guidance. The project engineers for the on-board computer were looking for diffused silicon transistors. Having heard of Fairchild Semiconductor through a news report, they contacted the firm about its transistor products. The IBM engineers invited Robert Noyce and Tom Bay to Owego in order to educate the pair about their requirements for the transistors in this computer system.[37]

As Jay Last recorded at the top of page 35 in his notebook, the transistors that IBM Owego required fell into "3 general categories." The first category, "low power," was IBM's largest transistor need for the Valkyrie computer, as measured by sheer number of parts. These were the transistors that would form the logic of the computer, and their distinctive requirement was very low power dissipation. The computer was not to produce much heat of its own, and it was not to consume much electricity. The second category of IBM transistor needs that Jay Last noted was "core drivers." The primary memory for the on-board computer, for storing programs and the like, was a magnetic drum. However, much faster magnetic core memory was used for handling data in a "random access memory." Fast transistors capable of handling significant current were needed as the "core drivers" for this random access memory—to read and write data to it and provide the information to the main computer. The third category of transistor needs for the IBM system was "servo drivers"—much higher power transistors used to control the aircraft's servomechanisms for automated piloting and targeting.[38]

Last recorded Noyce's recitation of the characteristics that IBM Owego "want[ed] for computers"—that is, for the numerous, low power dissipation logic transistors. In addition to charting the electrical characteristics that IBM desired against the characteristics that were currently available in silicon junction transistors, Last recorded the technological reason behind IBM engineers' interest in Fairchild Semiconductor. As Noyce reported to the group, "they need good matched PNP's to go along with these [NPN transistors]." Last quickly noted: "can only be done with double diffusion—no meltback techniques usable." The IBM Owego system designers wanted to build their computer logic from matched sets of PNP and NPN transistors. As Last noted on the top of page 36, such "symmetric transistors [were sought] to simplify the logic [design]." Solid-state diffusion was the only known way to produce the matched logic transistor pairs that IBM Owego wanted. The processes of grown and alloy junctions practiced by their much larger and better-established competitors, Texas Instruments and General Electric, simply could not provide such pairs.

Moving beyond the technical advantage of their diffusion approach for making the matched pairs of low power dissipation logic transistors, Noyce discussed IBM Owego's emphasis on *reliability*. The on-board computer for navigation and bombing would have extremely stringent requirements for reliability, and high reliability was required for all the components used in the system. The transistors would be no exception. To serve IBM, Fairchild Semiconductor would have to produce reliable transistors. IBM's emphasis on the reliability of electronic components was indicative of an increased awareness of and activism against unreliable electronic systems and components by the U.S. military. The military, and in particular the Air Force, was dissatisfied with the frequent failure of electronic systems, which recent reports had traced to reliability problems with the components used to create these systems. As a result, the military was demanding that its suppliers utilize more reliable components, emphasizing semiconductor devices over vacuum tubes, and propagating methods for measuring reliability.[39]

At the bottom of page 35, Last listed some of the information that Noyce had gleaned from IBM about what the other transistor producers did to enhance reliability, and the sort of reliability testing that IBM would require. General Electric, Last noted, "pre-bakes" their transistors at 200°C before sending them out, to ensure their high-temperature reliability. For the reliability of the packaging of the transistors, IBM engineers suggested a multi-metal alloy "Kovar" for sealing the packaging "rather than glass seals." Finally, Last recorded that IBM would "want to cut out all random catastrophic failures" through stringent testing of transistors. Such testing included high pressures, placing transistors in a "detergent filled bomb at 50 psi," and "shock tests." Even before they had set the exact specifications for their first transistor product, Fairchild Semiconductor's founders were absorbing the reliability requirements of potential customers in the military sector.

Most of page 36 of Last's notebook is filled with details about the second category of silicon transistors that IBM Owego needed for its project: the "core driver" transistors for the system's data memory. Most of the notations on page 36 describe various electrical characteristics that the IBM engineers needed for the core driver transistors. These characteristics describe a silicon transistor that was both relatively fast switching and capable of handling medium power loads. One important electrical property associated with the required medium-power capability was R_{cs}, the "saturation resistance" of the transistor. Sometimes also called "collector saturation resistance," this denoted the inherent electrical resistance of the transistor when fully turned on, allowing current to move through it. IBM Owego wanted a saturation resistance of 2 ohms. The lowest that was then available in silicon transistors was 100 ohms. Since, as Last recorded, a transistor from Hughes "may come close" to this low saturation resistance requirement, the "main thing" for Fairchild Semiconductor would be to "get the saturation resistance down!" Immediately after this imperative, Last wrote "backside diffusion." Here was another possible technical advantage of Fairchild Semiconductor's diffusion approach: diffusion from the bottom of the silicon wafer could be used to lower the saturation resistance to the required level.

Last's notes on Noyce's report concerning core driver transistors contain more than technical requirements and competitive information. They also contain a number of reasons why core driver transistors would be an attractive business opportunity for Fairchild Semiconductor. First, IBM had an immediate need for a substantial quantity of core driver transistors, and was willing to pay a high price: "they will use 2000–3000 of these now (contracts out now)" and "will pay $100 each for first 500." Moreover, since, as Last wrote, "this will also be used as a high freq power switch," the volume demand for the core driver transistor would be even larger at IBM. Critically, Noyce reported, such a fast-switching, medium-power silicon device "is a vacant area in transistors at the moment." An entire market for silicon transistors was thus open to Fairchild Semiconductor through the core driver opportunity at IBM.

Page 37 of Last's notebook records the ensuing discussion among Fairchild Semiconductor's founders about the competitive situation in this "vacant area in transistors," the advantages and disadvantages of the group's diffusion approach for both the logic transistor and core driver needs of IBM, and the direction in which the firm should head. At the top of the page is a list of semiconductor manufacturers that were pursuing the type of high-frequency transistors required by IBM for its core drivers and were moving to occupy the "vacant area in transistors" that Fairchild Semiconductor's founders had discerned. These were the leading transistor manufacturers of the day: Texas Instruments, General Electric, Hughes, Motorola, and Raytheon.

It was the relative advantages of Fairchild Semiconductor's diffusion approach for addressing IBM's transistor needs that would be the basis of the firm's chances in this competition. Among diffusion's perceived advantages was the ability to make silicon transistors in both the NPN and the PNP configuration with many of the desired electrical characteristics. Moreover, the diffusion and oxide masking approach was seen to confer a strictly economic advantage: the ability to manufacture transistors in a batch process, and hence at lower costs—in Last's words, the ability to "handle a large no. of elements at once." The disadvantages were low gain (due to poor carrier lifetimes in silicon), the difficulty of making metal contacts to diffused silicon transistors, and high saturation resistance.

At the bottom of the page, Last wrote "Back side diffusion as soon as lapping is in good shape." The point of that was to lower the saturation resistance. Fairchild Semiconductor's founders planned on using diffusion and oxide masking to create the NPN and PNP pairs of logic transistors as well as the low saturation resistance core driver transistor. The first meeting of the team in 1958 closed with an open question: "Should we head for the core driver now?" That question would be addressed in the weeks to come.

Entry in Personal Notebook, Pages 47–48

10 February 1958

Jay Last

Through regular staff meetings and informal discussion, Fairchild Semiconductor's founders and their co-workers engaged in a continued refinement of their technology, product, and business objectives in early 1958. Their main goal, however, remained unchanged: to develop a manufacturing process for diffused silicon transistors as soon as they could, and to introduce these devices to the market. Their specific tactics for accomplishing this goal began to take form in early February of 1958 with their selection of a first product, their submission of a first product quote, and the arrival of their newly hired vice president and general manager, Ewart Baldwin.

After Noyce and Bay's initial meeting with the IBM Owego engineers in December and the founders' discussion of IBM's needs in early January, the group quickly selected IBM Owego's core driver transistor as their first product. Achieving IBM's desired electrical specifications ("specs") was judged by the group to be within the grasp of the approach to manufacturing diffused silicon transistors that they were pursuing. On 8 February 1958, as Jay Last wrote on page 47 of his notes, Fairchild Semiconductor submitted a formal quote to IBM Owego for a sample supply of diffused silicon transistors meeting their core driver specs. The quote called for 100 of these sample transistors—in either the NPN or PNP configuration—to be delivered in six months' time (that is, in August of 1958) at the price of $150 each. The specifics of Fairchild Semiconductor's technology and product objectives were quickly forming, leaving open only the question of whether the first product would be of the NPN configuration or the PNP configuration.

Days before, Ewart ("Ed") Baldwin had joined Fairchild Semiconductor as its vice president and general manager, at nearly the same time that the IBM Owego quote went out. Baldwin had been an engineering manager for Hughes Semiconductor, and had accumulated experience in that firm's booming silicon diode business. He had responded to Fairchild Semiconductor's advertisement in the *Wall Street Journal*, and had impressed Richard Hodgson with his wide managerial experience and his familiarity with the emerging silicon semiconductor business. At the first staff meeting he attended (on Monday, 10 February 1958), Baldwin brought two important insights to the table.[40]

First, he suggested that Fairchild Semiconductor could "sell our rejects." In this, he was bringing into Fairchild Semiconductor a business practice that had been in use for several years among producers of transistors and diodes. The complexity and sensitivity of semiconductor manufacturing processes almost assured a variation in the critical electrical or other specifications of the devices produced. Devices falling outside of a particular product's specification range were rejected. Baldwin's suggestion was to look at "rejects" for one product not as waste but rather as parts fitting the specifications for *a different product*. In the specific case of Fairchild Semiconductor's first product, the

(47)

Staff meeting 2/10/58.   2/10/58

Baldwin here

Personnel requirements
Publicity blurb -

IBM Owego quote in 2/8/58

open for npn → pnp   6 mos. - $150 for 100

current gain question low temp β min 20 at -20

IBM will prob. need 2000-3000

Baldwin: Romo   sell our rejects β min down
           Hughes, etc}   is up

           Litton

           Sperry ??

                    Spec

BV$_{CEO}$ 40 V   P$_C$ 100°C   1W

BV$_{EBO}$ 2 V   T$_J$ 175°C

I$_{c max}$ 500 ma   I$_{CO}$(100°C) = 200μa max @ V$_{CO}$ = 30V

h$_{fe}$ I$_C$ 150ma   V$_C$ 10V   20

r$_{bb'}$ I$_c$ 50ma   V$_c$ 10V   40 Ω

f$_{hfb}$ I$_c$ 150ma   V$_c$ 10V   80 Mc

R$_{cs}$ I$_b$ = 10ma I$_c$ 150ma   10 Ω

C$_{ob}$ I$_c$ 10ma   V$_c$ = 10V   30 pf

EB → Electronic test gear for production needs emphasis

      Bernie Elminger → Electronic controls   3-4 technicians
                         automation, test instrumentation $13.5 + 10% bonus

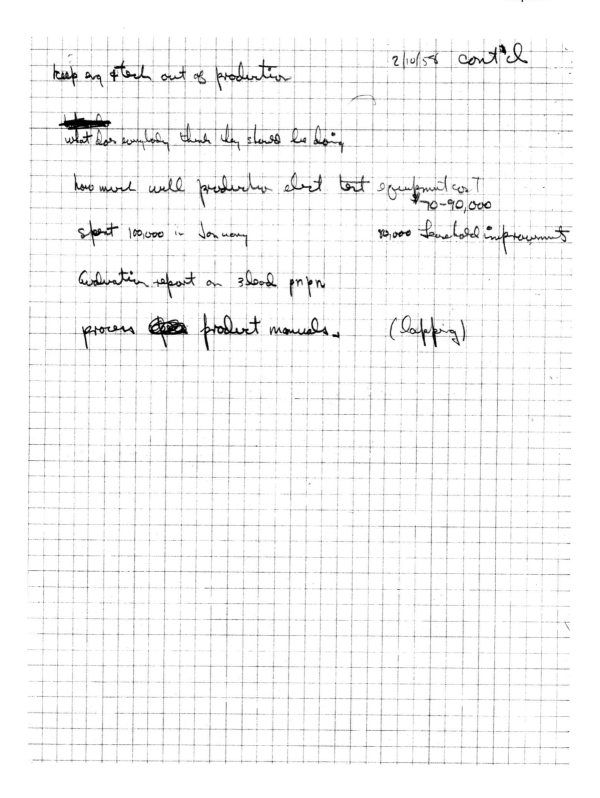

keep eng & tech out of production

~~_____~~ what does everybody think they should be doing

how much will production elect test equipment cost?
$70-90,000

spent 100,000 in January   80,000 leasehold improvements

evaluation report on 3,000 prpn

process ~~_____~~ product manuals.   (lapping)

2/10/58 cont'd

IBM Owego core driver transistor, Baldwin suggested that devices that did not meet IBM's stringent specifications could be sold to other manufacturers of electronics systems for missile, aerospace, and other military applications. Indeed, the firms Baldwin mentioned in February 1958 were the major firms engaged with aerospace computers: "Ramo" (meaning Ramo-Woolridge, a Hughes Aircraft spin-off and the leading contractor for the U.S. military's ICBM program), "Hughes" (meaning Hughes Aircraft and its associated aerospace, electronics, and semiconductor operations, constituting one of the largest suppliers of military systems), and "Litton" (meaning Litton Industries, which had established itself as an important supplier of military electronic systems for aerospace and communications applications). The relevant operations of all three firms were located in the Los Angeles area.[41]

Second, Baldwin reinforced the message that Noyce and Bay had received from IBM Owego concerning the importance of reliability. As the IBM engineers indicated, the reliability of components was a primary consideration for them in selecting components for building airborne computers for strategic nuclear bombers. It was reliability problems with germanium and grown-junction silicon transistors that had driven IBM toward Fairchild Semiconductor and its diffused silicon transistors. For Baldwin, the importance of reliability and the "sell our rejects" approach suggested that Fairchild Semiconductor should make a substantial effort in *electrical testing* as a manufacturing function. Exacting testing equipment and procedures would be required to determine which devices matched particular specifications, and how reliably they did so. For this effort, Baldwin proposed to hire Bernie Elminger, a testing expert, away from Hughes' semiconductor organization. Not only would Elminger require a substantial salary, but he would also require three or four technicians to work with him, and a capital investment of perhaps $90,000 in production electrical testing equipment. Baldwin later brought in Elminger and a group of other seasoned semiconductor-manufacturing engineers from Hughes. With Baldwin and the production engineers he recruited away from Hughes, Fairchild Semiconductor had acquired the skills in disciplined production that would be required to bring diffused silicon transistors to market, and to fulfill its quote to IBM Owego.[42]

Entry in Personal Notebook, Pages 50–52

17 February 1958

Jay Last

During the staff meeting of 17 February 1958 (the second meeting with Ewart Baldwin in his role as general manager), the Fairchild Semiconductor leaders constructed a detailed time line of requirements and responsibilities to get their new manufacturing technology in place and their first product shipped. Looking out farther, at six months *after* the hoped-for delivery of the first product samples to IBM, Baldwin discussed the type of organization that the firm would need to put in place for high-volume manufacturing. Noyce reviewed the R&D agenda for follow-on products that he believed could be developed quickly after completion of the first product.

The company had quoted IBM the delivery of 100 sample transistors by the first of August 1958, six months hence. Because of the great emphasis placed on reliability by IBM, and also by other military electronics firms and their Air Force customers, the firm would have to certify that the samples they delivered were indeed reliable: they would have to commit a number of good transistors to a "1000 hour life test." With the delicacy and novelty of the new manufacturing process, the group expected to have low yields initially. That is, they anticipated that the initial proportion of transistors that worked properly within the overall transistor production would be small. This anticipated low yield, along with the need to devote good transistors to reliability testing, meant that in order to fulfill the IBM quote the firm would have to get up to a "production rate 1,000 to 2,000 Xistors/wk [transistors per week] . . . about two months before August." Fulfilling their offer to IBM in August required getting into production in June.

In their meeting, then, the leaders looked to which functions would have to be readied by which date by the R&D organization for "pre-production manufacturing," that is, the earliest phase of manufacturing. "Mat. process" (materials processes), under the direction of C. Sheldon Roberts, was to be moved from R&D to pre-production by May. Under this rubric were the starting phases of the manufacturing technology, including growing high-purity silicon crystals, sawing them into wafers, and lapping and polishing of the wafers. Eugene Kleiner and Julius Blank were to "design and fabricate" the equipment required for "assembly," and do so by June. "Assembly" was shorthand for the manufacturing steps required to place the silicon transistor "dies" or chips into protective packages, which connected the chips to the leads and, in turn, to electrical circuits.

Also to be passed over from R&D to pre-production by June was the "Test" function, the responsibility of Victor Grinich. Grinich was the only electrical engineer among Fairchild Semiconductor's founders. His father, an immigrant from Croatia, had worked at a lumber mill. The V-12 College Program, which trained future Navy officers, had enabled Grinich to study electrical engineering at the University of Washington. He

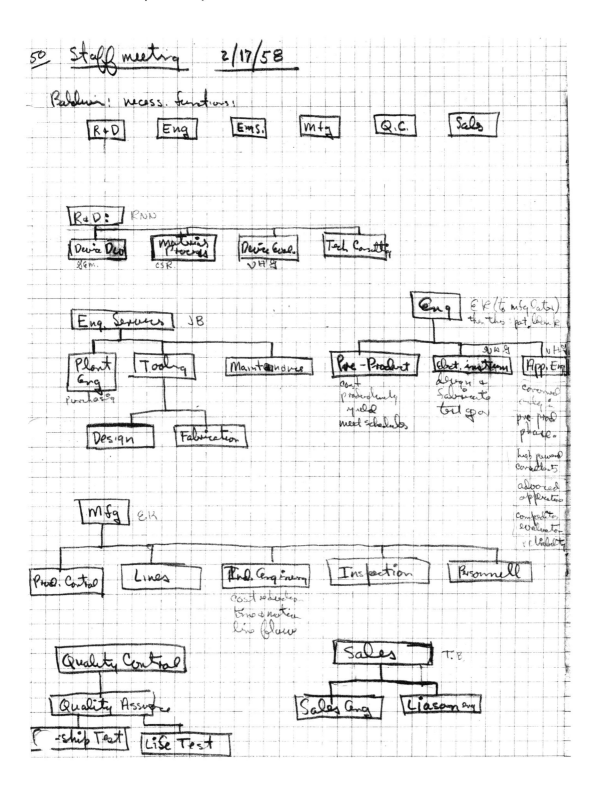

15'

the above will take place in 6 months or so after first product

IBM   100 samples   by Aug 1 - 58
we would have production rate of 1000 - 2000 Vistons/wk.
by this time   1000 hour life test
about two months before August.

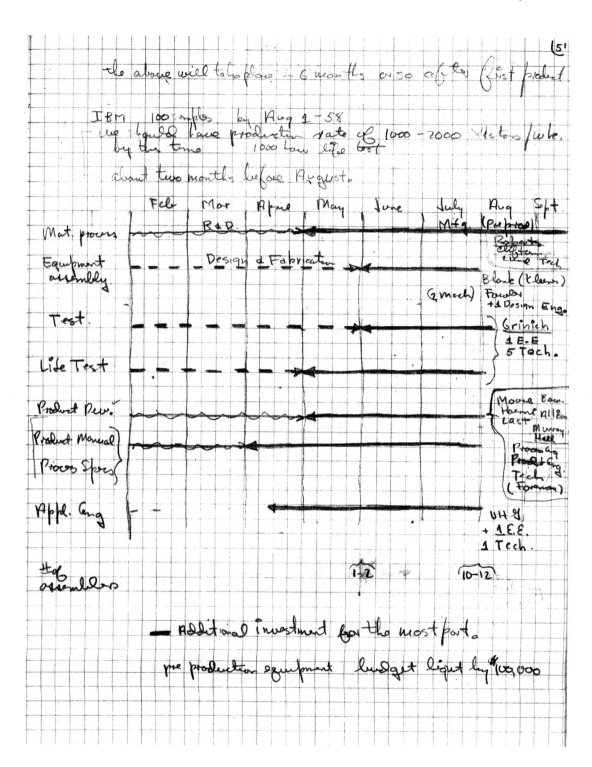

	Feb	Mar	April	May	June	July	Aug	Sept
Mat. process		R&D				Mfg	(Pre prod)	
Equipment assembly		Design & Fabrication					Blank (Kleen)	
Test					(2 mach)		Grinich	
Life Test								
Product Dev.							Moore	
Product Manual / Process Specs								
Appl. Eng							UH &	
# of assemblers					1-2		10-12	

— Additional investment for the most part.

pre production equipment   budget light by $100,000

5 ↩ <u>RNN</u>

Assume we have IBM Switch — what do we add?
(Same thing — smaller geometry — logic transistor
low power high speed)

add identical Xistor NPN instead of PNP (or v. versa)

Follow
this
line
} back side diffusion — accurate lapping

PNIP

Power Oscillator

PNP low R_cs
(NPN)

1 Amp PNPN

No
Major
Geomet.
changes

High Power Heat sinks   tens of watts

PNP }
NPN } power switch   simple geometry
PNPN 10⁺ amp   then interdigitation

•

speed time & effort on [interdigitation]   10W 100 mc.
                        [small geometry]

had then been recruited to join the electrical engineering department at Stanford University as a doctoral student. With funding from the Office of Naval Research, he had pursued advanced studies in circuit theory. After completing his doctorate in 1953, he had secured an engineering position at the nearby Stanford Research Institute (SRI). At SRI, he had designed transistor circuits for color television and for the ERMA computer, the first computer for banking applications. This experience with ERMA circuit designs had introduced Grinich to digital computing. It had also convinced him of the great potential of silicon transistors, which had just been introduced by Texas Instruments. After seeing an advertisement for a job at Shockley Semiconductor on the back cover of the *Proceedings of the IRE*, he had applied for the position. He had joined Shockley Semiconductor in June 1956.[43]

At Fairchild Semiconductor, Grinich was given charge (among other tasks) of developing all the instruments required to examine transistor performance and the tests to determine if the transistors functioned, and, if they did, to which electrical specifications. Very much connected to "Test," but due to be moved to pre-production earlier (by May, according to the developing schedule), was "Life Test." This function was also in the bailiwick of Grinich. It involved the electrical testing of good devices that had been in sustained operation for the required thousand-hour reliability trial. It was due earlier than "Test" in order that enough of the rare, good transistors could be devoted to the lengthy reliability testing.[44]

Developing the first product ("Product Dev"), and with it the manufacturing process, as well as writing up a "product manual" and the "process specs" for pre-production, were the joint responsibilities of Jean Hoerni, Jay Last, and Gordon Moore. Hoerni and Moore were engaged in parallel development efforts: Hoerni was developing a PNP version of the IBM core driver, while Moore was developing a NPN configuration. In April, the group noted that it would have to decide which of these two configurations was more nearly ready for production. Last was working on a variety of issues connected to photolithography, the new approach that the firm would use in connection with the oxide masking of diffusion.

The February plan called for "Appl. Eng." (applications engineering) to begin at about the same time that the first product moved into pre-production—that is, in April. Like "Test" and "Life Test," applications engineering would be under the direction of Vic Grinich. Applications engineering, as Baldwin explained to the group, involved the careful evaluation of competitor's products, in-depth reliability testing and analysis, and (more important) developing documentation on potential uses of the products.[45] In discussion of the plan, Baldwin determined that meeting their goal would require them to draw significant additional funds against the initial funding promised by Fairchild Camera and Instrument. He estimated that their previous pre-production budget estimates were $100,000 too low, and that the shortfall was attributable in no small part to an underestimation of the expenses for the equipment and procedures required for production and reliability testing.

Looking past the delivery of the first sample transistors to IBM, and at the coming six months (spanning into early 1959), Baldwin described the type of organization that the firm would have to build for high-volume manufacturing of the first transistor and subsequent products. (See notebook page 50.) In this, Baldwin was granting the firm the benefit of his experience at Hughes Semiconductor in the manufacture of silicon diodes for military markets. Baldwin's "necess. functions" were R&D, engineering, engineering services, manufacturing, quality control, and sales. Within these broad functions were activities that Moore, Last, and some of the other founders had not previously contemplated. Last's notebook captured some of the founders' initial thinking about where they might eventually find their places within the future organizational chart. What also became clear to the group was that they would need a significantly larger professional staff, with expertise that they themselves did not possess, and they would need to secure this staff quickly. Eventually, Baldwin would recruit many of the required professionals from the pool of his former colleagues at Hughes Semiconductor. The crux of Baldwin's approach and of his vision of the future organization was that the firm could expect its diffused silicon devices to be met with great demand, and that it would have to expand significantly in order to meet that demand. If it did not, then it would run the risk that one of its larger, established competitors would rapidly capture the market by rushing a diffused silicon transistor into production.[46]

At this same staff meeting, on 17 February 1958, Robert Noyce discussed future product development. Noyce laid the issue out simply: "Assume we have [the] IBM switch—what do we add?" (See notebook page 52.) The direction for an initial set of follow-on products appeared clear. If the same core driver transistor were made with "smaller geometry" (that is, smaller and with proportionally shrunken features), it would have electrical characteristics that would make it appropriate for a "logic transistor," used to make logic circuits in digital computers. It would be both "low power" and "high speed." IBM had expressed its need for large numbers of such silicon logic transistors for its airborne computer projects. Similarly clear was a continued effort to bring to production whichever core driver transistor configuration had come in second in the internal race between the parallel programs of Hoerni's PNP and Moore's NPN. IBM had indicated its desire for matched pairs of both logic and core driver transistors, identical in specifications but differing in their configuration.

Looking beyond these clear steps, Noyce discussed the product possibilities that could flow from continued R&D efforts on "back side diffusion" and "accurate lapping." Both of these processes were aimed at lowering the saturation resistance of the transistors, the electrical resistance a current encountered when passing through the transistor when it was fully on. Lowering the saturation resistance would give the capability of making improved logic and core driver-type switching transistors, and also, as Noyce pointed out, several different kinds of devices. All this could be accomplished without changing from the basic sizes or "geometry" of the first IBM core driver.

In this strategizing about the product paths that the firm could pursue, Noyce was hewing extremely close to the manufacturing technology he and his co-founders were developing for their first product. His ideas for the products that would follow the first core driver were the result of considering what could be done immediately, with no changes to the basic manufacturing processes, and also what could be done by extending the R&D efforts in which they were already engaged. There was no suggestion of developing new manufacturing approaches. Rather, the next products would be explorations of the available possibilities for what the manufacturing technology could provide. In this, the discussion reflected the founders' focus on exploiting the possibilities of the manufacturing technology that they were rapidly developing.

Entry in Personal Notebook, Pages 53–57

24 February 1958

Jay Last

From early in the formation of their group at Shockley Semiconductor, the founders of Fairchild Semiconductor acted consistently on the premise that there existed a demand for diffused silicon transistors in military applications. This assumption—that the greatest demand for diffused silicon transistors was to be found among the producers of military airborne computers and aerospace systems—was strongly reinforced for the group by Robert Noyce's February 1958 trip to the Los Angeles area. Los Angeles had long been a center of the aircraft industry, and that industry had successfully expanded its scope in the 1950s to include missile and space technologies. Three of the major producers of ground-based, airborne, and missile-based computer systems for the military were located in the area: Ramo-Woolridge, Hughes Aircraft, and Litton Industries. Fairchild Controls, which supplied components to this aerospace and electronics complex, was located in the region too. In mid February 1958, Robert Noyce visited these three potential customers as well as Fairchild Controls. He recounted his experience to the other Fairchild Semiconductor founders and Ewart Baldwin during their staff meeting of 24 February 1958.[47]

Ramo-Woolridge, the lead contractor for the Air Force's ICBM development program, Noyce reported, had "transistorized almost everything." (See notebook page 53.) That is, for both ground-based and onboard systems in the missile program they had moved away from vacuum tubes to transistors for considerations of size, weight, high-temperature performance, and reliability. However, Noyce learned, they were "down on T.I. because of reliability." Again, the Fairchild Semiconductor group heard, as they had from IBM Owego, that the prime dissatisfaction that their potential customers had with their most serious competitor was with the reliability of their silicon transistors. The Ramo-Woolridge story was repeated at Noyce's visits to the airborne computer and ground-based computer groups within Hughes Aircraft. The airborne-computer group at Hughes was using silicon transistors because of their advantages over germanium transistors ("low leakage"). While this group "need Si [silicon] now" because of the higher reliability of silicon transistors, the ground-based computer group was "not so rushed." The ground-computer group was concerned about the general reliability of transistors, and had tried using Texas Instruments' grown-junction silicon transistors. The ground-computer group "got stung on reliability and variability so they are shy on Si now." Ramo-Woolridge and Hughes underscored the lesson heard from IBM: the great demand for silicon transistors was in military airborne computers, and the competition with Texas Instruments and others would be won or lost on reliability. The feedback from Litton Industries, which was also working on airborne computers, was nearly identical to that from Ramo-Woolridge, Hughes, and IBM Owego. After listening to Noyce's report

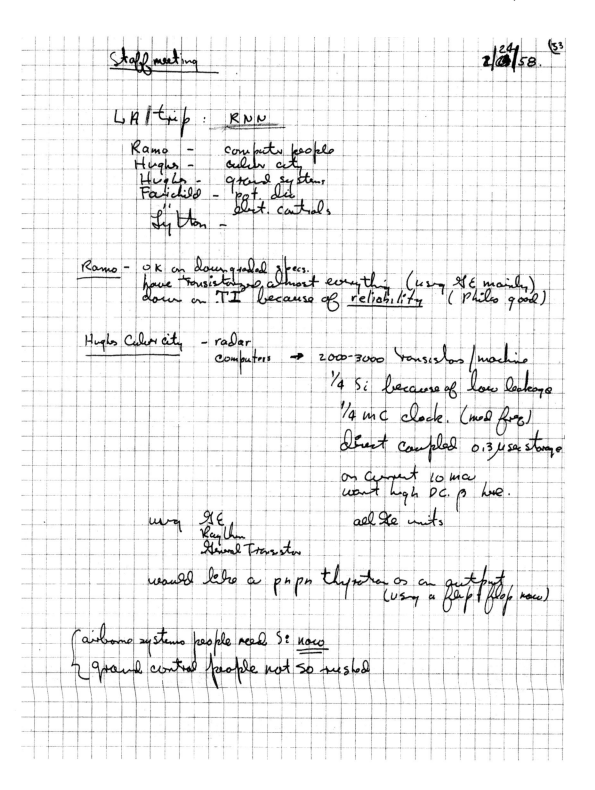

Staff meeting   2/24/58.   53

LA / trip :   RNN

Ramo –   computer people
Hughes – culver city
Hughes – ground systems
Fairchild – pot. dir
  "
Litton –   elect. controls

Ramo – OK on downgraded specs.
have transistors almost everything (using GE mainly)
down on TI because of reliability (Philco good)

Hughes Culver city – radar
              computers → 2000-3000 transistors /machine
                              ¼ Si because of low leakage
                              ¼ mc clock. (mod freq)
                              direct coupled 0.3 μ sec storage

                              on current 10 ma
                              want high DC β here.

      using GE   all GE units
            Raytheon
            General Transistor

      would like a pnpn thyristor as an output
                              (using a flip flop now)

⎰ airborne systems people need Si now
⎱ ground control people not so rushed

54 2/24 Cont'd

Hughs ground systems - dead audience

History - they went to TI silicon & got stung on reliability
& variability

so they are shy on Si now.

Fairchild Pot div. - they have shake table   60 g thru audio
96 hour test -
welding & metallizing

Lytton   pushing specs back up
using 900A & Si Transistor
↳ β change from TI design to production
½ mc clock circuits
higher V_{EB}
V_{CB} - 10 V -12 V at ~1 μA
base-emitter voltage ~ on - .7-.9 V.
10-20 mcs collector
3 Ω
higher β (~30)

applications: reading & writing magnetic storage
core driver   β≥20
pn pn thysistor to replace relays. 100 ma → 1 amp.

CB: ready market for our device with some slight increase
in specs.
we must get strong in reliability

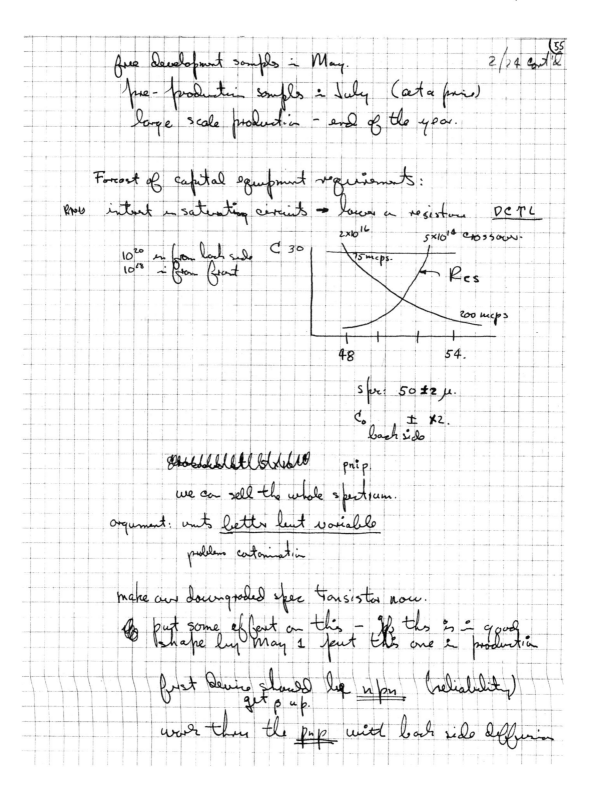

free development samples in May.

pre-production samples in July (act a price)

large scale production — end of the year.

Forecast of capital equipment requirements:

PNP₅   interest in saturating circuits → lower in resistance   DCTL

10^{20} in from back side
10^{18} in from front   C 30

2×10^{16} 5×10^{14} crossover.

75 mcps.

Res

200 mcps

48   54.

spec: $50 \pm 2 \mu$.

C_0 $\pm \times 2$.
back side

pnp.

we can sell the whole spectrum.

argument: units better lent variable

problems contamination

make our downgraded spec transistor now.

put some effort on this — If this is in good
shape by May 1 put this one in production

first device should be npn   (reliability)
get p up.

work then the pnp with back side diffusion

low R_α

pnip.

start with 20 Ω cm p type
50 Ω cm p type.

increase thickness 50 ± 2
100 ± 4

EB: Conclusions:

Target NPN IBM Owego with downgraded specs.

	FEB	MAR	APRIL	MAY	JUNE	JULY	AUG
Mach + equip (new)	3000	13,100	3,600 36,000	10,600	5600	4600	4200
Mach + equip (misc)	—	4000	3 000	—	—	—	—
Test equipment	5800	6100	5300	27,300	27,300	27,300	2,300
New estimate	Σ 8800	23,000	11,900	37,900			

ΣΣ = 80,000

Mach + equip (new) 72,650 asap
(no desks
no furniture ...) } 8,000

Life test equipment * } ≈ 10,000.
General life test

Σ = 92,000

Pre-product
(free samples)

Diff between old & new estimate = 12K.

Eng. Samples.
2000 / week.

Start production
buildup here.
to get to 20,000/week
200 - 300 K

welder
evaporator
slicer
metal grower.

already have.

racks
vibration
shock

[5]

<u>Income estimates for this year</u>

July 1000/week @ 25% yield

$\frac{1}{2}$ for life test

∴ 100 salable /week @ $30 - 150 ea

avg = $50

∴ income $5000 /week. July $ = 20,000

End of year 10,000 /week at a lower rate.

price down by 3×

yield up by 2×

Aug   15 K/week

increase 10K/month

5	July
15	Aug
25	Sept
35	Oct
45	Nov
55	Dec

~ 200K

then up exponentially

± a few months

2.5 - 3 million sales next year in this device

<u>if they are reliable</u>

(left margin, vertical): to get production done by day by end of year.

at the 24 February 1958 staff meeting, Baldwin was quick to summarize the lesson that Fairchild Semiconductor should take about the actual size and character of the existing market for diffused silicon transistors. Last recorded Baldwin's summation as follows: "[There is a] ready market for our device with some slight increase in specs. [We] must get strong in reliability." (See bottom of notebook page 54.)

The group discussed how these improvements to electrical characteristics and reliability could be addressed through their manufacturing processes, again returning to the use of back-side diffusion to lower the saturation resistance of their core driver transistor. At the time, Gordon Moore was spearheading the effort to develop the NPN version of the core driver transistor, and Jean Hoerni was working on the PNP version. Gordon Moore had been trained as a physical chemist. He had obtained a bachelor's degree in chemistry from the University of California at Berkeley and a doctorate in chemistry and physics from the California Institute of Technology. Moore had done research on the spectroscopy of gases at the Applied Physics Laboratory, a military laboratory managed by Johns Hopkins University, before joining Shockley Semiconductor in 1956 as the company's first chemist. After the formation of Fairchild Semiconductor, Moore had become the head of the device-development section in the R&D laboratory, where he was in charge of engineering the company's first product and coordinating the processes for fabricating it.[48] At the end of February 1958, Moore still had a few more weeks to make the final decision about which device configuration to deliver first to IBM Owego, but the technical discussion was trending toward Moore's own NPN version. Indeed, Last's notes indicate that reliability considerations were tipping the scales toward the NPN: "first device should be npn (reliability) . . . work thru the pnp with back side diffusion." (See notebook page 55.)

At the staff meeting of 24 February 1958, Baldwin revisited the estimates of the capital equipment expenditures that would be needed to bring the first core driver transistor to production. His new estimate, including the need for the "life test equipment" and "general life test" gear for reliability trials including "vibration" and "shock," had risen by almost 10 percent. (See notebook page 54.) More important, Baldwin was pointing to June—just before the first sample transistors would be delivered to IBM—as the month in which the firm would have to start a significant "production buildup" to "get to 20,000 [transistors]/week" "by end of the year." The capital cost for this buildup would be an additional "$200–300K," two to three times the capital investment they were contemplating to get the first device into pre-production. Baldwin's rising estimates would place significant strains on the initial funding to which Fairchild Camera and Instrument had agreed.

Baldwin believed that his plan for the rapid and costly expansion of the firm was justified by the sales income that such growth would engender. He forecast that the production of the core driver transistor could be steadily increased through the end of 1958, first meeting the 100 samples for IBM with production in July and then steadily expanding production to 55,000 transistors per month by December 1958. With this increase in production, Baldwin anticipated, as was typical for semiconductor devices, that the price would drop by "2×" while the yield would be "up by 2×." Even with this drop in price and increase in efficiency, he predicted further expansions of production volume to be "up exponentially" in 1959, leading to "2.5 to 3 million [dollars in] sales next year on this device," but adding the emphatic qualifier "if they are reliable." (See notebook page 57.)

Entry in Personal Notebook, Pages 63–65

10 March 1958

Jay Last

Fairchild Semiconductor reached an important milestone on 2 March 1958, when it received a purchase order from IBM Owego accepting Fairchild's quote to provide 100 core driver transistors at the price of $150 each. The firm had booked its first sale. With IBM's purchase order, Fairchild Semiconductor instantly gained a measure of credibility in the electronics industry. IBM, a notoriously selective and demanding customer, had chosen to buy devices from the start-up. Helping Fairchild Semiconductor to secure this order from IBM was, reportedly, a timely visit by Sherman Fairchild (the founder of Fairchild Camera and Instrument and its majority owner) and Richard Hodgson to IBM's president, Thomas Watson Jr. Managers at IBM Owego had concerns about Fairchild's production capabilities and financial soundness. To overcome these reservations, Sherman Fairchild—who was also IBM's largest individual shareholder and who chaired the executive committee of IBM's board of directors—met with Watson and asked him to buy silicon transistors from the new venture. Fairchild Semiconductor received its order from IBM shortly thereafter.[49]

In early March 1958, the IBM purchase order reinforced the opinion among the leaders of Fairchild Semiconductor that a substantial market for their first product existed among airborne-computer manufacturers. At a policy meeting on 10 March 1958, Thomas Bay laid out his picture of the market opportunity and what it could mean for the future of the firm. Bay, who had joined Fairchild Semiconductor in December 1957, was an experienced sales and marketing manager. A native of Chicago, Bay had come from a modest background. Like Victor Grinich, he had attended college with financing from the V-12 Navy College Program during World War II. He had obtained a bachelor's degree in electrical engineering at MIT. After teaching physics at the University of Vermont, he had accepted an engineering position in Chicago at Underwriters Laboratories, a product safety certification organization with extensive testing facilities. This experience had convinced the gregarious Bay that he did not want to work as an engineer.[50]

Bay had moved into sales at a Chicago firm that made electric motors and fans. In 1951, he had joined Fairchild Camera and Instrument's sales force. At first he had represented the firm's products in the East and the Midwest. Later he had worked as a sales manager at Fairchild Camera's potentiometer division, where he had become acquainted with analog computers used in military avionics. Convinced that digital computers would soon replace analog computers in the military market and that, as a result, the potentiometer division had little future, he had left Fairchild Camera in 1956 to join Industrial Nucleonics, a manufacturer of radioactivity measuring devices. When

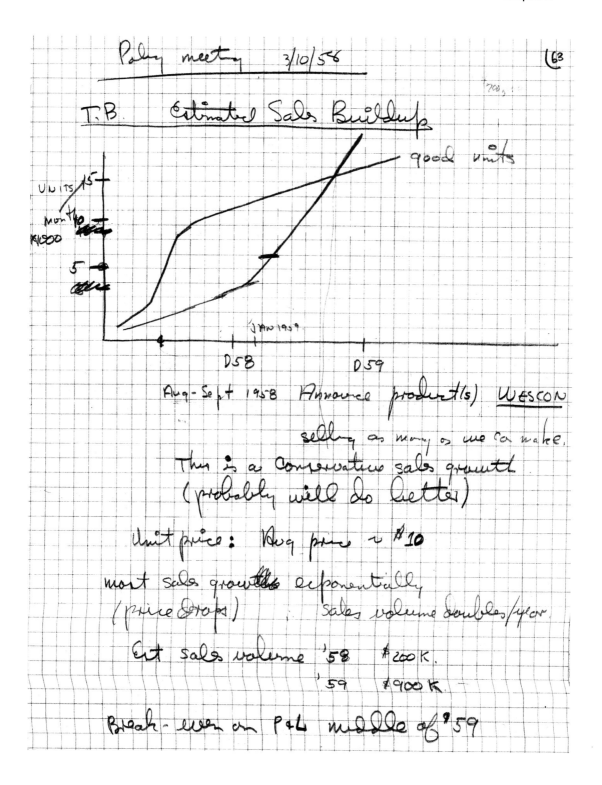

Policy meeting   3/10/58   ⌐63

T.B.   Estimated Sales Buildup

                                                        9000 units

Aug-Sept 1958   Announce product(s) WESCON

              selling as many as we can make.

     This is a conservative sales growth
     (probably will do better)

     Unit price: Avg price ~ $10

     most sales growth exponentially
     (price drops)   sales volume doubles/year

         Est sales volume '58 $200K.
                          '59 $900K

     Break-even on P+L middle of '59

1958   produce 23,600   good units

3600   we keep for test

2000   give away

18000   available for sale

have 3-4 months inventory on hand.

(to get increased equipment to allow for increased sales)

EB - we should be able to double this sales picture

MARKET: SRI late '56   predicted 1957 sales   3,000,000   Si transis.
                                            1958   8,000,000
                                            1959   19,000,000

TI exported 15,000,000 semiconductors 1957. out of total sale $65 M

∥ ~ 1,000,000 units

- Transitron - Coming up -

2-3% of business is conservative estimate

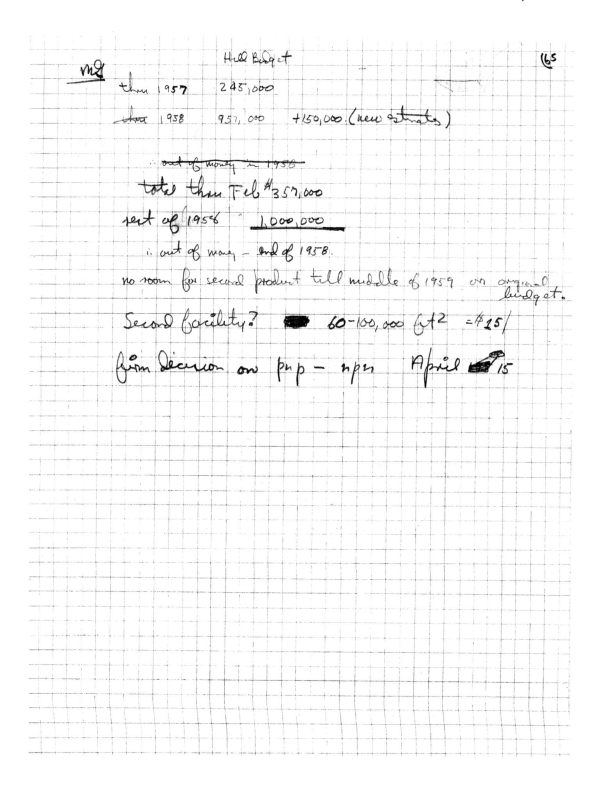

mg

Hill Budget

65

thru 1957   245,000

~~thru~~ 1958   957,000   +150,000 (new estimate)

~~out of money in 1958~~

total thru Feb #357,000

rest of 1958   1,000,000

∴ out of money — end of 1958.

no room for second product till middle of 1959 on original
budget.

Second facility?   ▬   60-100,000 ft² = #15/

firm decision on pvp — npn   April ▬ 15

Hodgson, the Fairchild Camera vice president mainly responsible for Fairchild Semiconductor, looked for a sales manager and a general manager for the new firm, he contacted Bay, asking him whether he would be interested in the positions. Bay, who liked the founders and understood the potential of silicon devices for digital computing, became the firm's sales and marketing manager.[51]

At the policy meeting on 10 March 1958, Bay presented an "Estimated Sales Buildup" to Baldwin and the founders in which he forecast that, with conservative estimates of yield improvement and sales growth, in one year's time the company would be selling as many of the core driver transistors as it could produce. (See notebook page 63.) The leftmost curve on the graph that Last recorded in his personal notebook represented Bay's projected growth in the number of "good devices" that the company could produce each month. The shape of this curve was the product of expanding production lines and also gains in manufacturing yield that could be expected from experience gained in high-volume production. The rightmost curve on the graph represented Bay's "conservative" sales projection, according to which the public announcement of the core driver transistor toward the end of 1958 at the Wescon electronics show would engender a steep and steady rise in sales volume.

While putting forward this conservative forecast, Bay believed it was quite possible that sales for the first Fairchild Semiconductor transistor would "probably do better," following an established pattern in electronic components: sales would "grow exponentially"—"sales volume doubles/year"—while "price drops." Even with more conservative expectations, Bay estimated that the sales volume would rise from $200,000 in 1958 to $900,000 in 1959, meaning that the firm would "break-even on P&L [profit and loss] middle of '59." However, Bay underscored that even this sales picture would require "increased equipment to allow for increased sales." (See notebook page 64.) In Bay's view, Fairchild Semiconductor would capture "2–3%" of the overall silicon "business." Responding to Bay's presentation, Baldwin felt that this general estimate was overly conservative, opining "We should be able to double this sales picture."

At the policy meeting of 10 March 1958, the leaders then moved on to confront some of the practical challenges that they would face in executing this plan for rapid expansion. The first challenge they discussed was financial. Given their original budget from Fairchild Camera and Instrument, they would be "out of money" at the "end of 1958" were they to follow this expansion plan, which called for expending a million dollars over the next nine months. As a result, there would be "no room for second product till middle of 1959 on original budget." Baldwin was pushing the idea that the firm needed a "second facility" of about "60–100,000 ft^2" for expanded manufacturing. At an estimated cost of $15 per square foot, this would require an additional investment of at least a million dollars.

Baldwin's expansion plans carried significant risk. If the founders could not develop the manufacturing process on schedule, or if the core driver transistor failed to meet the requirements of electrical performance and reliability demanded by the makers of military aerospace computers, the firm would find itself with no sales and out of money. Like many start-ups before and after, Fairchild Semiconductor was betting the firm on the success of its first product. The policy meeting closed with a reminder of just how far the group would have to travel in the coming months to deliver their first product: the schedule demanded that they make a "firm decision on PNP–NPN"—that is, on the configuration of the first transistor they would manufacture—by April 15.

Entry in Personal Notebook, Page 75

17 April 1958

Jay Last

The manufacturing process that Fairchild Semiconductor's founders and their colleagues had made great strides in developing by April 1958 was noteworthy in that it incorporated the approaches of diffusion, oxide masking, and photolithography. Notwithstanding these new approaches, the process had several characteristics in common with more established semiconductor device manufacturing and, indeed, electronic component production more generally. These common characteristics were complexity and sensitivity. As had been the case with the production of vacuum tubes, and as was then the case with the manufacturing of other semiconductor diodes and transistors, the process that Fairchild Semiconductor had developed for its first silicon transistor involved at least dozens and perhaps hundreds of actions. This complexity was matched by the sensitivity of the end results to the successful performance of these many actions consistently and in the correct order. The proportion of "good" devices emerging from the production line—the yield—was thus delicate and highly variable. Yields often dropped catastrophically and unexpectedly, and restoring them to their typical range required backtracking through the production sequence to try and determine which process step had gone awry.[52]

Because of this complexity and sensitivity, electronic component manufacturers had, for decades, written detailed manuals that contained exacting specifications of the many actions involved in the production sequence as well as information about the design and desired specifications of the product. These manuals, called "product manuals" or "process manuals," were used in the hand-off of a new manufacturing process or product from R&D or pre-production to manufacturing, and were often revised after the transfer with corrections and additions. Once in manufacturing, the manuals were used to guide the tasks of line workers. These manuals were a prime tool that the electronic components manufacturing sector used to establish and maintain stable, disciplined production.[53]

Ewart Baldwin and the semiconductor manufacturing engineers he had recruited from Hughes's components production organization were familiar with the industry practices surrounding process and product manuals. Indeed, Baldwin had discussed the need for process and product manuals at the very first staff meeting of Fairchild Semiconductor that he attended. By 17 April 1958, the need for such a manual was pressing. At a meeting called to discuss the state of technical developments, the founders of Fairchild Semiconductor and a select group of their colleagues were given crash assignments to develop the "product manuals" in the next two weeks, by the "first of May." In fact, a "rough draft" of the various manual sections was due at the next "Tech Meeting."

175

Tech Meeting   4/17/58.

   Product Manuals.

                                                          WED 10:15
                                                          New meeting date

   Xtals, orientation   - CSR.

   Saw & Lap   JTL   Lap to

   Basic Design   UH6
                               DA
                               JAH.

   Diffusion   JAH
                               DA.

   Photo Processing   RNN
   Masking   JTL.

   Evap, Alloying   ⎫   GEM.
   Dicing   ⎬   R. B.
   Baking   ⎪
   Mounting   ⎭
   Welding

   Test Procedure   UH9.
   & Characteristics

   FINISHED BY FIRST OF MAY

      WEDNESDAY AM — PRODUCT MANUAL ROUGH DRAFT

                                              3rd person.

The reason the manual was needed urgently was that the transfer of the manufacturing process from R&D to pre-production and manufacturing was to happen in May in order to keep to their schedule and plans, most immediately for the delivery of the 100 core driver transistors to IBM. The division of technical labor that the group adopted for creating the manual was unsurprising, reflecting the existing distribution of technological responsibility among the founders. The order of the manual sections would largely follow the flow of the manufacturing process itself. C. Sheldon Roberts had responsibility for the section on growing silicon crystals and determining the crystalline orientation of these silicon crystals. Roberts came from an old and established Vermont family. After commencing studies in metallurgical engineering at the Rensselaer Polytechnic Institute, he had been drafted into the military. He had attended radar school during World War II. After the war, he had completed his bachelor's degree at RPI, then had obtained a doctorate in metallurgy at MIT, where he had worked under the direction of Morris Cohen, a major figure in postwar metallurgy and materials science. For his dissertation, Roberts had studied metals used in the fabrication of gyroscopes. In the early 1950s, he had worked for the Dow Chemical Company and had done noted research on magnesium. But he had become increasingly interested in semiconductors. When William Shockley had asked Morris Cohen to recommend a very good metallurgist who might be persuaded to join Shockley's new firm, Cohen had put Shockley in touch with Roberts. Roberts had joined Shockley Semiconductor in 1956.[54]

Following Roberts' section on crystal growing in the process manual under development in April 1958 were the procedures for sawing the crystals into individual wafers and for lapping these wafers to give them flat surfaces. Both sawing and lapping were the responsibilities of Jay Last. The section on the "basic design" of the transistor fell to Jean Hoerni and Victor Grinich. In this work, Hoerni and Grinich collaborated with David Allison.

The son of American missionaries, David Allison had grown up in China. In 1938, he had moved to the United States, where he had completed high school. After two years in the Navy, he had enrolled at Columbia University, where he had received a bachelor's degree in physics. He had later worked at Federal Telegraph, an IT&T subsidiary, where he had engineered selenium rectifiers. In 1956, he had joined the junior staff of Shockley Semiconductor.[55]

While working at Shockley Semiconductor, Allison had obtained a master's degree in electrical engineering at Stanford University through its Honors Cooperative Program, which allowed engineers with jobs in industry to do graduate work at Stanford on a part-time basis. Allison had joined Fairchild Semiconductor quite soon after its establishment. Indeed, he had missed the opportunity to be a founder by forgoing a meeting at Gordon Moore's home to which he had been invited. It was at that meeting that the membership of the founding group had been finalized. At Fairchild Semiconductor, Allison had worked closely with Moore and had emerged as one of the firm's leading experts on diffusion.[56]

It also would fall to Hoerni and Allison to specify for the process manual the exacting diffusion techniques at the very core of the manufacturing technology. Last's list of responsibilities for sections of the manual has Robert Noyce assigned the section on the "photoprocessing" involved in oxide masking. Though Noyce had made photolithography the focus of his technical contributions to the firm, Jay Last increasingly took responsibility for this area, as Noyce was frequently called upon to make external sales calls and other visits. It was Last who, in the end, wrote the manual's section on "photoprocessing." The related process of "mesaing," which involved the use of metal masks, evaporated black wax, and acid etching, was the also responsibility of Last in terms of both actual development and manual writing.[57]

Gordon Moore and one of his technicians, Robert Brown, were called upon to write a significant portion of the manual, covering all the procedures for evaporating and alloying metals onto the transistor to form electrical contacts, "dicing" the individual transistors from the wafer, "baking" the transistor die at elevated temperatures to stabilize them, "mounting" the die onto the headers of the packages through which they would be connected to electrical circuits, and "welding" the tops of the packages onto the header, protectively sealing the mounted die within. Lastly, Victor Grinich would detail for the manual the electrical testing procedures that would be used throughout the production process to separate out defective devices, and to certify the electrical specifications of functioning transistors. In describing many hundreds of actions and factors in this manual, the founders and their colleagues were attempting to explicate in words the rich tacit knowledge they had developed over many months of working on the manufacturing technology.[58]

Internal Progress Report

1 May 1958

Gordon Moore

This internal progress report, written by Gordon Moore at the start of May 1958, discusses late-stage developments in the engineering of Fairchild Semiconductor's first product, the core driver transistor for IBM.[59] The formality of the report is indicative of more standardized practices of internal communication and coordination as the firm's staff grew in tandem with the variety of its interconnected activities. Moore discussed two important developments: the creation of a stable metallization process and the decision to bring the NPN transistor, rather than the PNP, into production first.

By April 1958, the R&D group had made significant progress with many of the manufacturing processes required to make the silicon mesa transistor. Diffusion, oxide masking, and photolithography were now under control. The main outstanding problem was the choice of metal with which to make the transistor contacts. For several months, Moore and the other founders had experimented with forming these contacts using various metals and alloys: silver, a silver-gallium alloy, a silver-phosphorous alloy, and the combination of a layer of aluminum with a layer of silver. None of these attempts had proved fruitful. The difficulties of forming electrical contacts to the mesa transistor were several. The ideal was to find metals that could form a mechanically strong, stable, low-resistance connection with intrinsic, P-type, and N-type silicon. Many metals simply formed a new and unwanted PN junction when placed into contact with the silicon. Indeed, "alloy-junction" transistors and diodes were made in just that fashion. Other metals simply formed poor or unreliable electrical contacts.[60]

These failures led Moore to explore other metals and approaches in April 1958. At Robert Noyce's suggestion, he experimented with aluminum for making both the emitter contact and the base contact of NPN transistor. This "all-aluminum" or "single-metal" approach had the advantage of diminishing the number of manufacturing steps and thereby reducing the potential for errors in the production process. Using aluminum for both emitter and base contacts was, however, a highly counterintuitive move. Aluminum, a P-type element, could reasonably be expected to make a good contact to a P-type material but also to create an unwanted PN junction when alloyed to an N-type region. To prevent the creation of a PN junction between the aluminum contact and the N-type material, Moore developed a new process in which an aluminum film was alloyed to the N-type material at 600°C. Moore also changed the diffusion process to heavily dope the N-type emitter layer as another way of avoiding the formation of an undesired PN junction. This successful all-aluminum process for forming the transistor contacts was a major innovation. Aluminum later became the metal of choice for making contacts to silicon devices throughout the semiconductor industry.[61]

The second important development that Moore discussed in his internal progress report was the decision to bring the NPN transistor, rather than its PNP counterpart,

FAIRCHILD SEMICONDUCTOR CORPORATION

Progress Report   May 1, 1958

By: G. E. Moore

Approximately ninety transistors were canned during the month, much below the prediction of 450 made in the previous report. Of these, some 62 were canned on the last two days, indicating, at least, that things were improving at the end.

The metallizing and alloying problems existing in the last few months were eliminated for the npn by switching to pure aluminum for the metal. No similar solution exists for the pnp structure. Primarily on this basis the final decision for our first product was made. It will be the npn. Device characteristics prove that the aluminum makes good contacts to both emitter and base regions of the npn. The emitter-to-base voltage required for the transistors to pass 150 ma is consistently between 0.9 and 1.0 volt.

An in-process check point has been instigated immediately after dicing. By examining each of the dice on the curve tracer at this time we can ssure that only good material goes on to be mounted. This test is economical until the percentage of good dice exceeds 90%, a goal for which we must strive. At the moment yields of 60% here are considered good. Principal reasons for rejects are:

1. Emitter-to-collector shorts that exist in the
bulk material after diffusion.

2. Emitter-to-base shorts caused usually by poor
registry of the photoresist masks or occasionally by specks
of unremoved metal. It might be pointed out that regions
of very bad registry are eliminated by inspection during mesaing. Only the boarderline cases get this far.

3. Premature breakdown of the emitter-collector characteristics of unknown origin, but quite certainly a bulk phenomenon.

We hope that rejects due to the second cause will soon
disappear with the new jigs in use. The first and third problems are not understood in principle, so more research is required. A sudden rash of trouble with regard to emitter collector shorts or premature breakdown could be disasterious
when the line is rolling. Other remaining problem areas are a
as follows:

1. Attachment of the dice to the headers. We are
now using pure tin as a solder on electrodlessly plated nickel
surfaces. Many of these contacts have failed mechanically,
while an even greater number have been of high resistance and/
or injecting. Work on a gold alloy as solder looks promising
as the eventual solution.

2. Surface phenomena in the canned devices. Surface breakdown seems to be fairly frequent and non-reversible. More trouble seems to exist in the sealed units, which have been baked and sealed in dry, inert atmosphere, than is found in room ambient. Empirical work here is now possible, since the supply of transistors is adequate.

3. Our final header is not yet being used.

All these problems mean that it is only slightly significant to start life tests at present, although they are to be started immediately, since slight significance is better than none -- certainly the results should yield minimum lifes for our final device.

On the positive side of the leger we have:

1. The clean-up to restore h_{FE} and I_{co} after mounting requires only a thorough rinse with D.I. water.

2. The gold bonds to the aluminum are sticking tightly, none having failed on the well alloyed surfaces; even under 20,000 g centrifugal force.

3. Welding is adequate. None of the 200 cans sealed for leak testing leaked at greater than 10^{-8} std cc/sec. None of the Kovar-type at $>5 \times 10^{-12}$ cc/ second with 99% of them having undetectable leaks to 4×10^{-13} cc/sec. Only about 30% of the compression headers showed observable leaks.

-3-

Prediction for May: We will can 1200 transistors, including at least 100 meeting all of the IBM specifications. Continuing to limit our production rate will be lack of a steady flow of dice ready to be mounted.

into pre-production. This was a decision that Moore himself had made in his role as head of device development.[62] By this time it was clear that the PNP was still very far from manufacturability. It faced two major problems. The gold solder used to attach the transistor die (or chip) to the header of its package created a N-type layer on the back of the transistor, transforming the PNP transistor into a four-layer PNPN structure, similar to a PNPN power switch. Additionally, Hoerni had not found suitable metals for making good contacts to the emitter and the base of the PNP. He devoted considerable effort to the use of silver for these contacts. However, the silver would "tarnish," or corrode, which would diminish its performance. And the contacts were not mechanically sound. It took six additional months for Hoerni to solve the PNP's back-side and metal-contact problems.[63] Despite these difficulties with the PNP, Hoerni did not take Moore's decision to choose the NPN transistor as the company's first product well. According to other founders, Hoerni was, in fact, furious. Hoerni's competitiveness spurred him to make a number of significant innovations in the coming months. One of these innovations was to put his planar ideas into practice; another was to use gold doping to make a faster-switching NPN transistor.[64]

Although the NPN mesa transistor was closer to production than the PNP, Moore and his group still faced significant challenges with it. Much of Moore's memorandum is devoted to these remaining problems. Some difficulties were related to assembly—the processes by which the silicon chip was attached to the package. Others had to do with photolithography. The masks were often misaligned, which required the development of tools that controlled the motion and location of the masks ("jigs"). In troubles from "surface breakdown," high electric fields at the edges and surface of a mesa transistor could cause the device to fail. Also troublesome were electric shorts between the emitter and base regions of the transistor caused by "specks of unremoved metal." As the Fairchild group would later discover, shorts caused by small particles would become a major reliability problem with both the NPN and PNP mesa transistors.[65]

Shortly after completing this progress report, Moore changed his position within the firm in order to follow the NPN transistor into production. He relinquished the leadership of the device-development section and became manager of engineering. Engineering, at the time, included pre-production engineering as well as applications engineering and electronic test instrumentation design. The main task of Moore's pre-production team was to work out the final problems with the NPN transistor and to continue to transform the techniques developed in the lab into carefully specified manufacturing processes that could later be transferred to high-volume manufacturing.[66]

Entry in Personal Notebook, Page 80

7 May 1958

Jay Last

While intently focused on delivering their first silicon transistor, the founders neverthe-less also kept abreast of the latest research that might have a bearing on their manu-facturing technology, or on semiconductor electronics more generally. They routinely attended a variety of scientific, engineering, and industry meetings. Members of the firm who attended a technical meeting would report back to the larger group about developments that struck them as particularly significant. One of the stops on this research circuit was the meeting of the Electrochemical Society, a leading venue for the presentation of research work on semiconductor materials. In early May 1958, Jack Clifton, a junior engineer at Fairchild Semiconductor, delivered an internal briefing on the most recent meeting of the Electrochemical Society that he had attended. Clifton, who had worked with Fairchild Semiconductor's founders at Shockley Semiconductor, had joined the new firm quite soon after its establishment. At Fairchild Semiconductor, Clifton worked closely with C. Sheldon Roberts on silicon-crystal growing.[67]

Clifton gave detailed descriptions of two presentations that he had seen at the Elec-trochemical Society meeting. One presentation covered a surface treatment of silicon devices developed at Hughes. The second presentation was by Martin M. "John" Atalla, a PhD engineer from Bell Labs who had been an active member of that organization's research effort on silicon oxide layers. This Bell Labs program had been initiated several years earlier, after Carl Frosch and Lincoln Derick had established that silicon oxide lay-ers could protect silicon surfaces during diffusion processes and could also be used for diffusion masking. At the 1958 Electrochemical Society meeting, Atalla had presented experimental results demonstrating that silicon oxide layers could also be used to *electri-cally stabilize* these same silicon surfaces. By that time, researchers at Bell Labs and other organizations had firmly established that variable electrical conditions occurred on the surfaces of semiconductor materials, and that these "surface states" could significantly alter the performance of semiconductor devices. Surface states were a major contributor to reliability problems in semiconductor devices. Atalla's was a major finding, insofar as the protection of the silicon surface and its electrical stabilization were critical for the reliability of silicon devices.[68]

Jack Clifton's report on Atalla's new finding may have acted as a spur to Jean Hoerni. Six months earlier, Hoerni had written down his conception of using silicon oxide lay-ers as diffusion masks and for surface protection in order to produce a new, "planar" transistor structure. Hoerni's conception broke significantly with earlier work on the use of silicon oxide layers, in that he proposed leaving in place oxide layers that had been exposed to diffusion processes as an integral part of his new transistor. At Bell Labs, where the most advanced research on the use of silicon oxide layers was taking place,

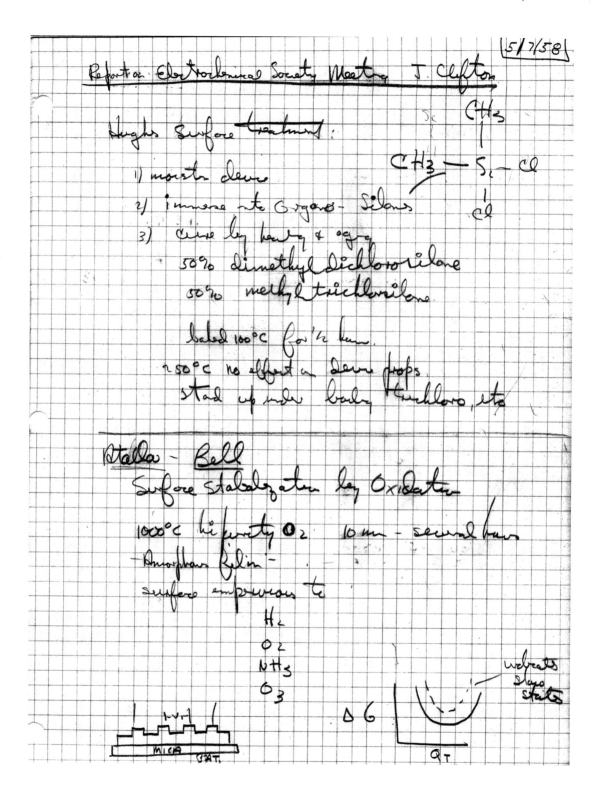

5/7/58

Report on Electrochemical Society Meeting   J. Clifton

Hughes Surface treatment:

1) moisten device

2) immerse into Organo-Silane

3) cure by heating & aging

50% dimethyl dichlorosilane
50% methyl trichlorosilane

baked 100°C for ½ hour

250°C no effect on device props
stand up under baking trichloro, etc.

Atalla - Bell
Surface Stabilization by Oxidation

1000°C hi purity O_2 10 mm - several hours
Amorphous film -
surface impervious to
H_2
O_2
NH_3
O_3

Δ G

Q_T

indicates slow states

MICA SPT.

such exposed layers were uniformly considered "dirty." That is, they were seen as possible sources of contaminants that would ruin the electrical characteristics of the device, and consequently they were removed near the end of processing. This had been the practice of Frosch and Derick earlier, and it was the practice in Atalla's latest work. The structures that Atalla had worked upon were formed by diffusion operations, but the exposed oxide layers had been stripped, and a new, "clean" oxide layer had been grown atop the rigorously cleaned silicon surface. For Hoerni, Atalla's work may very well have signaled that Bell Labs researchers were active in areas very close to his conception of the planar process. Moreover, Clifton's report may have reinforced Hoerni's interest in his planar process ideas, raising a question about whether the exposed, "dirty" oxide layers he thought of using would be able to provide the same very useful electrical stabilization that (as Atalla had shown) clean oxide layers could provide.

The second presentation that Clifton reported on to the technical group at Fairchild Semiconductor was also concerned with the protection and electrical stabilization of the surfaces of silicon devices. Researchers from Hughes Semiconductor detailed a new technique of forming a silicone polymer on the surface of silicon diodes. This polymer coating protected the surface of the diodes from contamination and from powerful etchants. It also enhanced the electrical characteristics of the diodes. The Hughes researchers' report mentioned coating a single diffused PNP transistor with the epoxy coating, with improved electrical amplification abilities as a result.[69] For Hoerni and the other members of Fairchild Semiconductor, the message from the Hughes presentation would have been that the major players in the semiconductor industry were actively developing a variety of strategies for surface protection and electrical stabilization of silicon devices. Together, the reports from Bell Labs and Hughes Semiconductor offered a measure of the intensity of the competition.

Entry in Personal Notebook, Pages 86–90

27 May 1958

Jay Last

As May 1958 came to a close, Fairchild Semiconductor had yet to deliver a single device to a customer. The founders were working feverishly to improve their manufacturing technology, to move the NPN mesa transistor through pre-production in order to deliver the first 100 units to IBM Owego at the start of August, and to develop the PNP mesa transistor to the point where it could be routinely produced. Yet the information that the group had gathered from potential customers—producers of airborne computers and military avionics systems—had convinced Ewart Baldwin that there was a very large market opportunity for these products. Baldwin, in turn, had successfully convinced the founders of Fairchild Semiconductor and the leaders of Fairchild Camera and Instrument that the semiconductor firm would have to expand quickly to capitalize on this opportunity. As Baldwin explained, the coming twelve months would have to witness significant advances and explosive growth on a number of fronts.

At a "policy meeting" in late May 1958, Baldwin laid out the essence of his expansionist argument to Fairchild Semiconductor's founders. It was the same plan he had convinced Fairchild Camera and Instrument's vice president, president, and chairman to support during recent visits. His plan, to seize the available market for diffused silicon mesa transistors, and to remain competitive with established firms, was to build a large manufacturing facility (capable of a weekly output of 100,000 devices) by the end of 1959. With manufacturing at such a scale, Baldwin convinced his colleagues that yields could be improved, prices could be competitively reduced, and revenues could be steadily expanded. The economics of rising yields and falling prices that came with the high-volume manufacturing of semiconductor devices were familiar to Baldwin from his experience in the silicon diode business at Hughes Semiconductor. With similar high-volume manufacturing of the NPN and PNP mesa transistors, Baldwin was convinced, yields would increase from 20–25 percent to 65–70 percent. These increasing yields and the rise in the number of units sold would make it practicable to lower the price of a the mesa transistor from $150 per transistor (the price of such a transistor sold to IBM in August 1958) to $15 or even as little as $7.50 in the second half of 1959. In fact, Baldwin's estimates of $3.5 million to $4.9 million in total revenues by the end of 1959 implied that Fairchild Semiconductor would pass the break-even point for operations at the end of 1959, and would earn enough to repay Fairchild Camera and Instrument's expanded investments for the large new manufacturing plant by the spring of 1960.[70]

As the crux of his plan, Baldwin emphasized the need to immediately build a new facility about five times larger than the current one, and to have it ready for occupancy by April 1959. Again, he drew on his experiences with high-volume manufacturing at Hughes Semiconductor for his estimates of facilities and staffing. The new

POLICY MEETING — 5/27/58

rpt on visits of Hodgson Carter, Fairchild.

we have to get lrg mfg. facility in operation at end of 1959 beginning of 1960.

We have to get up to 100,000 units a week by end of 1959.

Three product buildup

Units / week.

n p n   4000-6000- week
p n p   ~2000 /week
p n p n — pilot line

New plant ready for occupancy April 1. in order to meet growth rate

End of 1959 —

n p n   30,000/week ⎤
p n p   30,000   ⎥ total ~100,000
p n p n.   30,000   ⎦

these are manufacturing numbers —

Yield will go from 20% → 70% by end of year n p n
                   25% → 65% by end of year p n p.
                   25%

this will give us 60,000 devices salable /week by end
of 1959.

Cumulative number of units produced:

<u>end of 1959</u>   500,000   npn   <u>good units</u>

                   350,000   pnp

                   200,000   pnpn.

Use rule of thumb — 3-4 months inventory on hand.
∴ Sales lag by this time interval

<u>Cumulative sales in $</u>

Assumptions   npn   avg price $20 this year 1958

                          $10-12 first half of 1959

                          $15 - 7.50 second " of 1959.

                          $5   1960.

          pnp   some price

          pnpn $20 first half of 1959

                         $10-12 Second " "   "

                         $5-6   1960.

If these prices hold, we should have accumulated
            <u>high figures</u>   <u>low figures</u>
      2.8 million dollars.   2.
      1.4   .9
       .8   .7
      ─────   ─────
      5.0   3.5 million
      4.9 million   by end of 1959.

96/ Based on 200 transistors/assembler/week on a balanced line,
Min of 80 ft² / assembler.

Assembler buildup   40 end of 1958

450 end of 1959.   (2 shifts
max 250
at one time)

∴ we need 250 × 80 = 20,000 ft² for assembly
and test.

for supporting facilities we need ~ 30,000 ft².

Pre - prod.
A E
E I
S E   Sustaining engineering
E Srg Services
Sales
Admin

Eng   12 - 15,000 ft²

Eng ser 10-12   ft²

Sales   2,000

Admin   3,000 ft²

Misc   5,000   5,000 ft²   Sales
admin
stores, etc.

Cafeteria, large 5,000

Total : 55 - 57,000 square feet bldg needed.

189

Assemblers $290/month   180% overhead

monthly costs   130,000   end of 1959.
                  130,000   overhead
                  200,000   remaining payroll.

                  450,000   total operating expenses
                1,250,000   monthly sales

Operating break-even late 1959
total expense break even spring of 1960.

Fairchild's total investment log. at max point
    $3,500,000   exclusive of buying building
    This would add $1,250,000

    this does not include any sales money
    this does not include material either

How many professional people
        applications engineers   7-10   administration 7-8
        instrumentation   4-5   technicians   ____
        sustaining eng.   7-8   Design   6-B.
        pre-production   10   shop   8-10
        sales   10 in field
        quality control   4-5
        manufacturing   7-8

90

∴ 100-150 professional people

this gives a total of 600-650 people by end of 1959.

50 R&D people. half professional

Location — Carter — go where cheapest — Arizona
max of 100,000 ft² per bldg   union problems.

stay away from area of aircraft industries

Fairchild likes small towns

July 1   Sites available

Redwood city north — nothing available

10 acres to
get
100,000 ft²

East Bay — Oakland out for Carwoming

Bohannon — $1/ft² lease only they build bldg

Stanford $25,000 acre.   get financing

across street $30,000 acre   lease only

near Bayshore 5 feet of fill— $50,000 acre
                                      total.

South   Mt. view cheap but noisy

Sunnyvale — Keefer road $9-12,000 acre.

San Jose — too far away

Los Gatos — no utilities but cheap.

Saratoga

55,000–57,000-square-foot building would house 450 new "assemblers," each of whom would take 200 transistors per week through assembly and testing. It also would house expanded "professional" staff for sales, quality control, manufacturing, administration, design, pre-production, sustaining engineering, applications engineering, and other functions. The expanded professional staff would number from 100 to 150. Research and development would remain in the original building for the time being, the staff increasing to 50 ("half professional"). "This gives," Last wrote, "a total of 600–650 people by the end of 1959." Thus, the firm sought both to hire a large number of people and to create a suitable building for them to produce 100,000 transistors per week.

The selection of the site for the new production plant was critical economically and also in terms of labor relations. Baldwin estimated "10 acres to get 100,000 ft^2" as the ratio of lot to facility size, so the price of land would be a significant factor in the economics of the new plant. Additionally, John Carter, president of Fairchild Camera and Instrument, had offered Fairchild Semiconductor his personal advice about choosing a site and size so as to avoid the prospect of a unionized workforce. He suggested going where labor and land "were cheapest—Arizona." The suggestion was plausible, for Motorola's semiconductor manufacturing operations were based there. Carter noted that "Fairchild [Camera and Instrument] likes small towns," but that each building should be less than 100,000 square feet in size to avoid "union problems," and that the firm should "stay away from areas of aircraft industries," which commonly had strong union presences.[71]

It appears, however, that Fairchild Semiconductor's founders never considered a site outside the Bay Area for the new plant. In his notebook, Last recorded Julius Blank's report on land availability and costs in possible locations from San Jose to Oakland. Both the East Bay and San Jose were eliminated, in Blank's estimation, because they were "too far away," or inconvenient to reach from the original Charleston Road facility, which the founders clearly intended to keep. The immediate environs were expensive, whereas prices were much lower to the north and to the south. No suitable plots were available to the north in Redwood City, but to the south Blank found "Mt. View cheap but noisy." Also farther to the south, Blank found Sunnyvale and Los Gatos to be inexpensive alternatives. The founders were narrowing their list of possible sites to the communities to their immediate south on the San Francisco peninsula—the region that would become known as Silicon Valley.[72]

Entry in Personal Notebook, Page 95

30 June 1958

Jay Last

In 1958 the ambitions of Fairchild Semiconductor were very much dependent on per-suasion. Ewart Baldwin had to convince the top executives and board members of Fairchild Camera and Instrument—Sherman Fairchild, John Carter, and Richard Hodg-son—to approve Fairchild Semiconductor's plans and provide the required funding. At the regular weekly "policy meeting" at Fairchild Semiconductor on 30 June 1958, Baldwin reported on the prospects for their plans after his meeting with John Carter and Richard Hodgson. As Jay Last recorded in his notebook, Baldwin had won their approval, but with a price. The price was increased pressure for the start-up: Fairchild Camera and Instrument demanded commitments to specific results by the end of 1958. For Fairchild Semiconductor, meeting these commitments was a critical measurement for its backers at FCI. If the commitments were not met, the viability of the overall plan would be called into question, and the continued financial support of FCI for the plan might be revoked.[73]

As Baldwin recounted, Fairchild Camera and Instrument had accepted Fairchild Semiconductor's forecast of expenditures through the end of 1958, assenting to the additional $204,000 that the group advised that they would need for equipment and materials. Fairchild Camera and Instrument had also "agreed in principle" to the "new facility," but had emphasized that the start "date [was] not decided." As an alternative, the FCI board approved the renting of a few thousand additional feet of factory space in 1958, and an increase in the number of employees to 128. The clear implication was that FCI wanted to see these commitments met before moving forward with the new plant and the expansion more generally. The new commitments that Baldwin had made to the FCI board were for specific levels of sales and revenue to be reached by the end of 1958 (six months hence). Income of $500,000–$700,000 was to be generated from the sales of 15,000–20,000 mesa transistors. Presumably, if these commitments were met, a start date for the new plant would be approved by FCI, which would give practical sanc-tion to the overall expansion planned for 1959.

Evidently, the founders of Fairchild Semiconductor took these sales and income commitments to be significant challenges. For Jay Last, the concern he recorded in his notebook was less that the commitments could not be met than that meeting the com-mitments might set an unrealistic expectation or might front-load too many of the sales. "Will this pressure," Last wondered, "make us look bad in 1959?" Until Fairchild Semi-conductor was on a firm and profitable footing, its fate would hang on the perceptions of the FCI leadership.

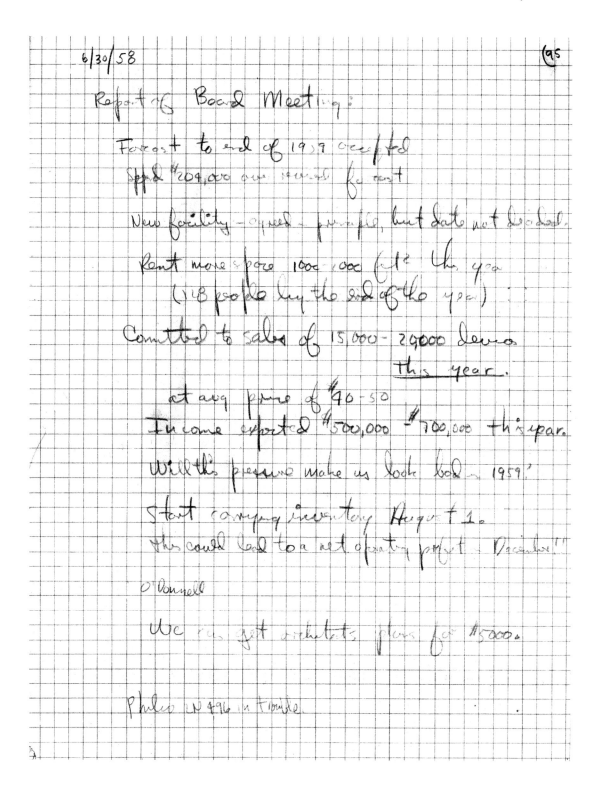

6/30/58   (95

Report of Board Meeting:

Forecast to end of 1959 accepted
$spend 204,000 over second forecast

New facility — agreed — principle, but date not decided.

Rent more space 1000 × 1000 (late this year
(128 people by the end of the year)

Committed to sales of 15,000 – 29,000 devices
this year.

at avg price of $40 – 50

Income expected $500,000 – 700,000 this year.

Will this pressure make us look bad — 1959?

Start carrying inventory August 1.
this could lead to a net operating profit — December !!

O'Donnell

We can get architects plans for $5000.

Philco LN 496 in trouble.

Entry in Personal Notebook, Pages 97–98

5 August 1958

Jay Last

After Fairchild Semiconductor shipped the 100 NPN mesa transistors to IBM Owego in time to meet the 1 August delivery deadline, on Monday, 5 August 1958, many of the founders gathered for an "R&D Meeting" to review their "active" programs and to decide on new activities. Most of the active efforts had been ongoing for some time and were directly connected to the manufacturing processes developed for the mesa transistors. "Resistance Grower" (notebook page 97) was shorthand for an effort to develop a new, inexpensive, and robust form of silicon crystal grower.

Typically, silicon crystal growers incorporated radio-frequency (RF) heating sources for generating the steady high temperatures that were required. Though these RF heating sources had the advantage of not contaminating the silicon with any unwanted materials, they were expensive and required large power supplies. Resistance heating used coils that were advanced cousins of the heating elements found in ovens or toasters. These coils were possible sources of contamination for crystal growing. But resistance growers were far less expensive to create and operate. C. Sheldon Roberts and Julius Blank were involved in an effort to design and build resistance-heated crystal growers at this time. Their eventual success allowed Fairchild Semiconductor to rapidly expand its silicon production capability, the resistance growers giving the firm cost advantages.[74]

Even more closely connected to the then-current manufacturing process were the continued effort to improve the function and reliability of the NPN mesa transistor and the ongoing program to tackle the difficulties associated with fabricating the PNP mesa transistor. A persistent effort to turn the complexities of bonding the PNP mesa to its package into a virtue by making a PNPN power switch also reflected the grounding of Fairchild Semiconductor's R&D program in manufacturing technology. The notation "Backside" in the list of active R&D programs (notebook page 97) referred to the months of work aimed at lowering the saturation resistance of the mesa transistors. The lower the electrical resistance of the mesa transistor in its saturated or fully conducting state, the better its performance in low-power logic applications and in medium-power applications such as core drivers. The main contributor to this resistance was the mesa transistor's thick collector region. To lower the resistance of this "back side," the R&D group was pursuing at least three approaches: diffusion, alloying, and etching. Diffusion and alloying would change the resistivity through chemical changes. Etching would simply thin the layer, resulting in reduced resistance.[75]

The group had also initiated some R&D work beyond that required for making silicon mesa transistors. "Intermetallics," second on the list of active R&D projects (notebook page 97), stood for activities that C. Sheldon Roberts had initiated on producing crystals of compound semiconductor materials. By mixing elements from groups 3 and 5 of the

97

R&D Meeting   8/5/58

Action

1. Resistance Grown   Lifetime
2. Intermetallics   IR Transmission
                                      Imperfection
3.   NPN   50% DA Ellison
4.   PNP
5.   PNPN
6.   Backside { Diffusion
                  Alloying
                  Etching }

Start:

1. μwave diode   Pit alloy (100)
2. Small Geometry ← pull away.

Antimony furnace being set up for high doping

130   NaOH etch.

                                    p^{23} gradient
                                    μμf.
                                    area 10^{-5} 10^{-4} cm^2
90μ
                                    [Pearson - Acta Met.
                                      selective etch

98

Put Pillory
Straight mesa.
Uhlir method.

March 1

good logic unit — small geometry

CSR — InSb, — Zoning

(Ga As)   "

① Add dopant InSb crystals

② the work on GaAs single flag by horizontal
growing — a graphite boat
closed system — controlled As
partial pressure — a separate
reservoir
reaction between Cu + As

→ Phillips Res Reports

periodic table, one could produce a material exhibiting semiconducting properties. Roberts was investigating indium antimonide and gallium arsenide, in particular the use of Bell Labs' zone heating techniques to purify and crystallize these "intermetallics." (See notebook page 98.) Indium antimonide and gallium arsenide had been subjects of ongoing work in the semiconductor industry, for high-speed transistors and diodes could be formed from them. Such high-speed (even microwave-frequency) devices were of great interest to the military for computing, aerospace, and communications applications.

The active programs on "lifetime" and "IR Transmission" were much less of a departure from Fairchild Semiconductor's silicon manufacturing technology. Controlling the "minority carrier lifetime" in silicon transistors was a perennial concern as this electrical property was central to both the amplification potential and the switching speeds of mesa transistors. One way lifetime was addressed in this period was by looking at the addition to the transistor of materials that either "gettered" (that is, drew out) contaminants that reduced lifetime or directly boosted it. In the coming months, Jean Hoerni would initiate a novel investigation of gold doping that would result in a new process that would be adopted widely. "IR transmission" was a technique for using infrared radiation to image the layers and regions of the silicon wafer and the transistor structures. Through examination of the passage of infrared radiation through these features, "imperfections" could be identified.[76]

The two new R&D activities that the group decided to "start" were device-development projects. First on the list was a project on a microwave diode, a high-frequency device desired by the military for a host of applications. Second was an effort on a "small geometry" transistor for computer logic, a potential product that the group had discussed for months. Apparently, after delivery of the first NPN mesa transistors to IBM it was time to move the logic transistor into the active product pipeline along with the PNP mesa transistor and the PNPN power switch. This logic transistor would require significantly better control of the transistors' dimensions and hence would require improvements in photolithographic techniques.

In all, the R&D review of early August 1958 was very much concerned with maintaining the existing directions in strategy and in specific projects. The strategy was to stick close to issues immediately at hand—rendering the next devices into manufacturable products, looking at what could be done readily with the existing silicon technology—and extending out with a limited number of further-reaching efforts. In maintaining direction on specific projects, the founders kept their eyes on fixed on semiconductor devices that addressed the military market in digital computing and aerospace applications.

Print Advertisement by Fairchild Semiconductor Corporation

10 August 1958

Starting in August 1958, Fairchild Semiconductor advertised its first products—the 2N696 and the 2N697—in the trade press.[77] Produced under the general direction of Thomas Bay, the head of sales and marketing, this print advertisement had two purposes: to position the 2N696 and 2N697 as general-purpose transistors that could be used in a wide range of military applications and to promote Fairchild Semiconductor Corporation to the electronics systems industry.

The advertisement emphasized the fact that the 2N696 and the 2N697 met the requirements for two types of applications. Their switching speeds made them useful in digital circuits and, more generally, in computing. At the same time, they had low saturation resistance. In other words, the inherent electrical resistance of the transistors, when fully turned on, allowed higher currents to move through them. As a result, the 2N696 and 2N697 could be used for such higher-power applications as core memory drivers, or when low power dissipation was at a premium (as it was in many aerospace and avionics systems). The ad also prominently mentioned that Fairchild Semiconductor's transistors operated at high temperatures. This was very important, since the military was increasingly requiring suppliers to produce electronics systems and components that worked reliably at high temperatures.

The advertisement also promoted Fairchild Semiconductor, presenting a very specific image of the firm. It introduced a new and unknown firm, by emphasizing expertise in diffusion, research prowess, and manufacturing capability. Potential buyers needed additional persuasion to buy products from a start-up. The more Fairchild Semiconductor could do to reassure these buyers about its abilities to survive and to deliver, the more likely it was that they would place orders. This problem was particularly acute for Fairchild Semiconductor because procurement officers of large military contractors, who were the primary buyers, highly valued supplier dependability and viewed small, untried firms such as Fairchild Semiconductor with suspicion. In the face of such anticipated skepticism, Bay's advertisement presented the firm as a "research-production team" that was "uniquely experienced" and possessed a "singleness of purpose."[78]

This advertisement was particularly effective. Published for the first time on 10 August, it generated 1,000 customer inquiries in less than three weeks. The 2N696 and 2N697 attracted significant attention because, as the founders of Fairchild Semiconductor had foreseen in January 1958, they filled "a vacant area in transistors." (See facsimile of 2 January 1958 entry in Last's personal notebook.) Texas Instruments' silicon transistors, produced by grown-junction techniques or by a combination of grown-junction and diffusion, operated at significantly lower frequencies. At the same time, germanium

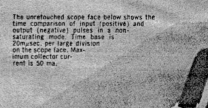

transistors had high frequency but failed at high temperatures, requiring expensive and bulky air-conditioning equipment if they were to be used in military systems. As a result of this competitive landscape, sales of Fairchild Semiconductor's transistors increased rapidly. In August and September 1958, the company sold $65,000 worth of transistors. Total sales reached $440,000 in the fall of 1958. Almost all of these sales were to military laboratories and military system contractors.[79]

Entry in Personal Notebook, Pages 99–101

25 August 1958

Jay Last

Two weeks after the debut of Fairchild Semiconductor's NPN mesa transistor in the press and at a major trade show, the corporation's founders gathered with sales manager Tom Bay and general manager Ewart Baldwin for a "policy–info meeting" at their building on Charleston Road. Walt English—a board member of Fairchild Semiconductor, and one of a number of executives and accountants from FCI who regularly visited the "California group" to take the measure of their activities—joined them. By chance, by design, or through a combination of the two, the reports that English heard were nothing less than thrilling.

Robert Noyce and Tom Bay had traveled to Wescon in early August to introduce the NPN mesa transistor. Wescon was the major show sponsored by the Western Electronics Manufacturers' Association, a trade group established during World War II to represent the interests of electronics firms located in the western United States. Wescon included a large exhibition as well as talks and presentations. Noyce's jubilant report of his experience at Wescon was the fulfillment of Fairchild Semiconductor's strategies and hopes. Last's notes of Noyce's recounting began with "big interest at booth—from competitors as well" and went on to conclude "we scooped the industry." In less than ten months, the founders had gone from meeting in Last's apartment to delivering a novel silicon transistor created using a new batch-manufacturing technology—a product that met the requirements of one of the most stringent customers in military digital computing.

Not only had Fairchild Semiconductor scooped the industry; it did not appear to Noyce that there was any pressing danger of real competition. "Nobody ready to put something like this on market," Last's recording of Noyce continues. "2N560 Bell closest competitor—No prospect of anybody getting in our way in the immediate future." Western Electric had just announced its 2N560 transistor, a diffused silicon NPN mesa transistor that was similar in many respects to the Fairchild Semiconductor product. However, Western Electric's process for making the 2N560 was very different: for example, it did not employ photolithography, different dopants were used in the diffusion processes, and both aluminum and silver were used for forming contacts. These differences added complexity to the process. Further, Bell Laboratories and Western Electric were legally limited in what they could do with the 2N560. An anti-trust consent decree with the U.S. government had been the basis for Bell Labs' and Western Electric's granting numerous and affordable patent licenses for their basic transistor technology and for their active technical support of their licensees. This same consent decree precluded Western Electric from manufacturing transistors for anything other than the telephone system's internal uses, with possible exceptions for military work. Thus, although

99

8/25/58   Poling - info meeting —
           (Calif group + Walt English)

RNN - Woscon Show —
      big interest at booth from competitors as well.
      we scooped the industry - nobody ready to put
      something like this on market. 2N560 Bell closest
      competitor - No prospect of anybody getting - one way
      in the immediate future.

transistor

EK - Personnel situation
     Hughes - PSI in bad shape morale-wise

          Metz coming up from PSI.

          Instrumentation still a problem

          O'Keefe coming - Philco oriented

          Ashmad — Application engineer
             best response from NY Times - Electronic News.

Bay   Sales picture

          Response extremely gratifying at show

          Electronic Equipment Ad — 407 responses
          ad went out 8/10   + 30 letters & telegrams

          within first 10 days.

          Requests for quotes for sample quote

          order for 500 IBM - Poughkeepsie

          Bobb — 200-500 Sperry   order this week
                  200-500 Arma
                  200   GE - Utica   Σ = 1000-2000
                 (...?) Burroughs

Gem Product Selection

up above 1000 ferral seals/week for the first time

furnaces in operation   70 wafers/day

10 ferral seals/wafer = 700/day.

∴ several hundred a day   1500 this week.

big lead will occur on testing

yield jumped to 37%

Bay (cont'd)

total # of inquiries ~ 1000 all told.

Bevin - IBM avego -   will order at least 2000-3000 today

open orders now - 550

shipped   ~   250-275

expected orders   5000-6000

"we can sell the 5000 units we expect to make this year without any trouble"

unit price will probably hold up to 40-50 up thru ~~December~~

101

Booked to date   262   #36,000.

On order   540   #28,000

Julie Blak — cost estimate on new bldg — 15 ft² with primary distribution, air conditioning

15
16
15,000
4 $,000
$
$

Timing scale on bldg — 9 months from initiation Shaved a month or so.

the 2N560 was a close technological competitor, it could do little harm to Fairchild Semiconductor's market prospects.[80]

These market prospects were the subject of Tom Bay's lengthy report at the 25 August 1958 "policy–info meeting" concerning the response that the sales organization had witnessed to the Fairchild Semiconductor transistor. "Response extremely gratifying at show" is how Last began his notes on Bay's "sales picture." According to Bay, this interest at Wescon was matched by the reaction to the print advertisement that had run in *Electronic Equipment* on 10 August: "407 responses + 30 letters and telegrams."

Bay then ran through a long list of "requests for quotes." Digital computer and military systems houses—IBM Poughkeepsie, Sperry, American Bosch Arma, GE Utica, Burroughs—requested quotes for lots of samples ranging from 200 to 500 devices. IBM Owego was expected to re-order another 2,000–3,000 transistors the very day of the meeting. In sum, Bay expected orders of 5,000–6,000 transistors. Fairchild Semiconductor already had shipped 250-275 devices and had orders in hand for 550. Bay expected the price of a transistor to average $40-$50 for several months. Last quoted Bay's conclusion: "We can sell the 15,000 units we expect to make this year without any trouble." Fittingly, Gordon Moore reported on "production" in his new role as head of the engineering organization. The information he provided was encouraging, giving credence to the expectation that the firm could fulfill the many orders that were coming in. Manufacturing had passed a production volume milestone, "up above 1,000 final seals/week for the first time." That is, 1,000 transistors had made it to the step of being sealed in their packaging and moving on to final testing during the week. With manufacturing yields up sharply from the twenties to 37 percent, Moore predicted that the manufacturing organization would be sealing "several hundred a day, 1,500 this week." Even though a "big bind will occur on testing," Moore warned, his production rate would meet Bay's expectation for the supply of transistors that would be available to ship.

Eugene Kleiner and Julius Blank also reported to the group, covering two important aspects of Fairchild Semiconductor's plan for rapid expansion: personnel and facilities. Kleiner discussed the need for a large number of technical hires. The firm was benefiting from the fact that "Hughes [and] PSI [Pacific Semiconductors] [were] in bad shape morale wise," which made it easier to recruit experts from these Southern California semiconductor firms. Print advertising for recruiting was also bearing fruit. Kleiner reported that the "best response [was] from NY Times—Electronic News." Blank continued to lead the effort to find a site for the firm's new manufacturing plant, to design the facility, and to get time and cost estimates for the project. Again, Blank's report was positive. Cost estimates remained at the expected level of $15 per square foot, and the construction "timescale" was "9 months from initiation—shaved a month or so."

Entry in Personal Notebook, Pages 106–108

15 September 1958

Jay Last

Through the 1950s, the semiconductor industry's practice surrounding intellectual property—patents and trade secrets—was a mixture of pooling and trading. That basic transistor technology as well as fundamental manufacturing processes had been generated and patented by Bell Labs and Western Electric was certainly central in this. As a result of AT&T's anti-trust consent decree, and bolstered by a desire among Bell System scientists and engineers to see their efforts widely and quickly employed, the basic intellectual property necessary for entering the semiconductor industry was available in the form of low-cost licenses from Bell Labs and Western Electric. This relatively easy trading of intellectual property, and the concentration of the semiconductor industry on a fairly closely clustered array of manufacturing approaches and device designs, meant that intellectual property generated by the industry was often overlapping, and also that most firms needed intellectual property held by others. As a result, firms sought to establish a strong pool of patents that could be traded with other firms in cross-licensing agreements.[81]

Not infrequently, cross-licensing involved a relatively small payment from one firm to another, reflecting a perceived disparity in the value of the patent pools or in the bargaining positions of the firms. Nevertheless, the prevailing practice was one of trading, of exchange, with each firm seeking to secure freedom to operate rather than actively attempting to shut a competitor out. A more assertive form of patenting practice began to emerge in the later 1950s at Texas Instruments. TI began submitting a far larger number of patent applications amassing more and more patents, and asking for much higher payments for access to them. Patents, at TI, were becoming a valuable source of revenue in their own right and also a way of straining the financial resources of competitors.[82]

In contrast with this practice of patent trading and licensing deals, semiconductor firms simultaneously worked intently to develop trade secrets and keep them just that. Such trade secrets, often centered on specific materials and their use in the manufacturing process or on particular techniques for using equipment, were in many ways more valuable than patents. They were often very difficult for competitors to uncover.[83]

By 15 September 1958, the time had come for Fairchild Semiconductor to contend with patents. The R&D group had discussed the need to tackle patenting and patent licensing earlier in the year, but had deferred much of the related activity to this point, when the NPN mesa transistor was in production. After reviewing the nature of patents and patent applications, the founders discussed their selection of John Ralls from a local firm of patent lawyers, Lippincott and Smith, as Fairchild Semiconductor's patent attorney. They then engaged in a brainstorming session on "patentable ideas." (See notebook page 106.) The session elicited many new ideas from across the group—new forms of

106   9/15/58   R&D Meeting

Patents
Description of invention - what is new, what advantages
Description of applications

Patentable Ideas:
Single metal contact. (?)   BTL used this at putty knife factory
we used this at putty knife factory
claim on another patent.

automatic   [Selective plating,
indexing   [pullaway techniques etc.   CSR

[John Rolls - Lippencott & Smith   - proposed patent attorney]

[A method of machining by use of a gaseous etch.
        Boron pits

[Diode with oxide overlap.   (IAH)
[collector only under emitter

[Thick base PNPN   voltage drop to switch by
                          conductivity modulation

[Shorted base - emitter PNPN - non-surface switching
        2 terminal

[Turn off pnpn with a pulse JH?

107

Ni plating for n-type diffusion, leading Ga diodes

watch on μwave diodes - file as soon as possible]

Status reports:

JAH - 10 Ω cm - new injecting contact
various soldering techniques
bond directly to Si triode

VHS p-p-n - evaluate switching times
p-n-p - switching times comp to npn, lower storage time
small gap n-p-n $R_b C_i$ 1000-1500

CSR pull away investigations
multi-metal - immiscible liquids
preferentable plating (chem plating)
silicone + iron

crystals - can grow 110 112 flats
resistivity control - good shape

get out good In Sb -
then Ga As - (L.D.)

JC - Resistance grower - no reproducibility, yet
lifetime - good slope

PTC int - dopants in collector junction
solute elements in solder junction
phys characteristics - switching, lifetime, softness.
low continuous is wetting of surface while dia.

106

DA — dep function problems — β too high for [illegible] — [illegible] problem

if base width is narrowed [illegible] is not good enough

phos diffusion 1100 → 1200 to get a reasonable [illegible] time

this cuts β fortunately as well

softness coming in again recently.

1 hour of oxidation — 1 hour of [illegible] diffusion gives thick enough oxide layer

1 μ loss slotted (4 fingers) this will be continued —

_____

Write progress reports on the first — have this meeting on 10th – 15th.

— get a line foreman — set up services

four-layer PNPN devices, gaseous etching, and selective plating for "automatic index-ing," among others.

Of particular note were two ideas that made it to Last's list from the discussion: "single metal contact" and "diode with oxide overlap." The use of aluminum to form the transistor contacts was a major advantage for Fairchild Semiconductor, greatly simplifying its manufacturing process. A patent for this practice would be a valuable trading item, but there was some concern about the viability of patent application for this practice. Next to "single metal contact" Last wrote "BTL using" (referring to Bell Telephone Laboratories). Below "BTL using" he wrote "we used this at putty knife factory." "Putty knife factory," an allusion to the humorist H. Allen Smith's recent book *Life in the Putty Knife Factory*, was Last's joking name for Shockley Semiconductor. The following year, Gordon Moore and Robert Noyce would nevertheless file a successful patent application on "single metal contact," which proved a valued addition to the firm's storehouse of intellectual property. The second idea of note was Jean Hoerni's mention of forming a "diode with oxide overlap." Hoerni's interest in his concept of using silicon oxide layers to protect the junctions of devices at their surface, which he had recorded in his patent notebook in December 1957, had not waned. With his diode suggestion, Hoerni was proposing to patent the concept of the planar process using the simpler structure of a diffused silicon diode as the illustrative case, rather than the planar transistor structure. The planar process remained consistently at the forefront of Hoerni's mind in the context of patenting.[84]

From "patentable ideas," the men turned to more immediate tasks, offering "status reports" on their current activities. (See notebook page 107.) Because Last's notebook was an aide-mémoire, few of the entries concern his own activities. However, at this meeting Last surely must have updated the group on his work to develop the microwave diode to which the firm was looking as a new product. Hoerni discussed his ongoing difficulties with the development of the PNP mesa transistor, particularly his attempts to find a suitable way to mount the transistor to the package header. Phil Flint, a newer member of the organization, was working for Hoerni, devoting his time to detailed studies of the mounting materials and procedures. Vic Grinich reported on his electrical studies of the PNPN, PNP, and "small geometry" NPN devices. C. Sheldon Roberts told the group that he had routine crystal growing using the radio frequency heaters in "good shape," and that he was looking into producing "intermetallic" compound semiconductor crystals and was exploring various plating techniques. Roberts' co-worker Jack Clifton was using the new resistance-heated crystal grower that Kleiner and Blank had assembled. There was "no reproducibility yet" (that is, the properties of the crystals varied widely from run to run), but "lifetime—good shape," indicating that the contamination that had been expected to come from the resistance heating coils was not, in reality, an issue. Lastly, David Allison updated the group on his project to develop the "small geometry" NPN transistor for computer logic applications. He was finding it necessary to adjust many of the processes to generate the desired electrical characteristics when working with the smaller dimensions.

In both the discussion of patentable ideas and the ongoing efforts, a greater organization of and an expanded scope for the R&D lab were in evidence. The time horizon of R&D projects was lengthening, they were beginning to explore more speculative ideas, and they were starting to engage in more fundamental studies to address ongoing problems with their product development efforts. Administratively, the R&D staff would now need to "write progress reports on the first" of the month, with the monthly R&D meeting occurring on the "10th to 15th." The circulation of written reports would begin to replace face-to-face interaction as the primary medium of communication and coordination.

Patent Disclosure

14 January 1959

Jean Hoerni

This document is less important for its content (its language replicates Hoerni's 1 December 1957 patent notebook entry in its entirety) than for what it implies about the development of the planar process at Fairchild Semiconductor.[85] On 14 January 1959, Jean Hoerni asked Mary Lou Weiss, a secretary, to type a patent disclosure reproducing notes on the planar process and on the planar transistor structure that he had jotted down in his patent notebook more than a year earlier. The patent disclosure was destined for John Ralls, Fairchild Semiconductor's patent attorney. Ralls, a partner at Lippincott & Ralls, a patent law firm in San Francisco, handled all of Fairchild Semiconductor's patent applications. What is significant about this document is that, after a year of sporadic attention to his planar ideas, Hoerni quite actively returned to them in January 1959. He was now convinced that his planar ideas were sufficiently important to warrant a patent disclosure. In the U.S. patent system, priority was given to whomever could prove that they were the first to "invent," rather than simply to whomever first filed an application. As a result, researchers produced formal patent disclosures to document the conception of an innovation at an early stage, while the patent application was being prepared.

Two factors appear to have rekindled Hoerni's interest in the planar process and planar transistor. One was a series of experiments in which Fairchild Semiconductor researchers (probably Hoerni and a technician named Paul Hinchcliffe) created a *partial* planar transistor: they left the oxide layer on top of the emitter-base junction (but not the base-collector junction) after performing their diffusion processing steps to form the emitter, base, and collector regions. It is likely that Hoerni and Hinchcliffe conducted these experiments in late 1958 or during the first two weeks of January 1959. They found that these partial planar transistors had higher gain (amplification) and were more electrically stable than conventional mesa transistors. These results, which were readily shared with the founders, attracted a great deal of interest at Fairchild Semiconductor. Moore recalled having been "very interested in them." It is likely that these results encouraged Hoerni to write the patent disclosure on the planar process and to move directly to fabricate fully planar transistors in which *both* junctions were covered by a layer of silicon oxide.[86]

The second factor that probably encouraged Hoerni to prepare his patent disclosure and to make a fully planar device was his alarm at reliability problems that Fairchild Semiconductor faced with its first products, the 2N696 and 2N697, in the fall of 1958. By this time the firm had shipped significant numbers of these devices to customers. To the founders' dismay, the firm's reliability engineers (and, presumably, its customers) had discovered that the electrical characteristics of many mesa transistors deteriorated

PATENT DISCLOSURE

Ref: Pgs. 3 and 4 of Fairchild Notebook No. 3; December 1, 1957
Jean A. Hoerni

Method of Protecting Exposed p-n Junctions at the Surface of Silicon Transistors by Oxide Masking Techniques

The general idea underlying this invention is the building up of an oxide layer prior to diffusion of dopant atoms at these places on the surface of the transistor at which p-n junctions are expected to emerge from the body of the semiconductor. The oxide layer so obtained is an integrant part of the device and will protect the otherwise exposed junctions from contamination and possible electrical leakage due to subsequent handling, cleaning, canning of the device.

A second advantage resulting from the use of the technique to be described is the possibility of making contacts to the emitter, base, and collector of a transistor on the same side of the wafer. In this way, the contact to the collector on the back side of a thick wafer and its accompanying high series resistance may be avoided. The passive areas of the junctions can be kept at a minimum (compatible with areas required to attach a lead to the exposed part of the base of the transistor), irrespective of the overall size of the wafer.

The basic procedure to be used is as follows: a wafer (of usual dimensions) is cleaned and pre-oxidized. Using photoresist technique, or other masking techniques, the oxide is removed on a series of islands, of size comparable with the area desired for the emitter of the transistor.

Top view of wafer.	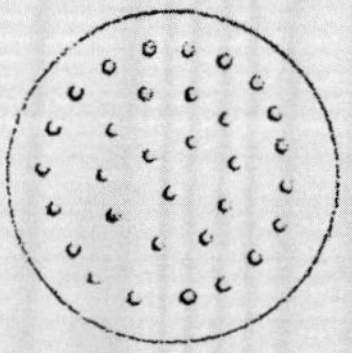	Oxide layer removed within circles.

Figure 1.

The base and emitter regions are obtained by diffusion of impurities giving the desired conductivity type. The cross-section across one of the un-oxidized islands looks so after diffusion (for p type bulk material and a p-n-p transistor):

Patent Disclosure, Jean A. Hoerni   Page 2
Method of Protecting Exposed p-n Junctions at the Surface of Silicon
   Transistors by Oxide Masking Techniques

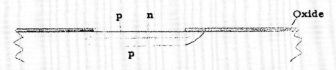

Figure 2.

It will be seen that in this way the parts of the silicon surface
where the junctions emerge are masked at all times by the oxider layer.
It is known that most impurities of interest (except Gallium) do not diffuse
into the silicon wherever an oxide layer is present. Contacts have to be
made to the three regions, which requires that parts of the oxide layer be
removed to permit these contacts. The structure shown on Figure 2 is not
suitable in that the width of the base exposed to the surface is only a few
microns, and is too small to make a suitable contact. A design improving
this situation is shown on Figure 3:

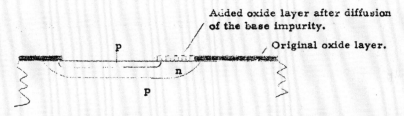

Figure 3.

JAH:mlw
1/14/59

over time. Even more worrisome, some of the devices failed catastrophically—that is, they unexpectedly ceased to operate.[87] This led Fairchild Semiconductor's leaders to launch a crash program to find the causes of the failures. Significant scientific resources were devoted to this. However it was Robert Robson, the foreman in charge of diffusion and photomasking, who discovered the failure mechanism. Robson found that the strong electric fields at the exposed transistor junctions, especially the base-collector junction, attracted specks of dust and metal—loose in the interior of the transistor package—that would ruin the transistors' electrical characteristics or would "short out" their junctions. This finding led Fairchild Semiconductor's engineers to look for the sources of the particles (nicknamed "unidentified flying objects"). It turned out that, among other sources, they came from the welding of the transistor package.[88]

Great efforts were made to clean up the welding process and reduce the number of particles in the transistor packages. But these efforts were only partially successful. The engineers did not eliminate the particles entirely. The production group developed new testing procedures in which they would tap the transistor packages with a pencil in order to identify the transistors that were most prone to failure (later, pencils were replaced with automated testers). In spite of these *ad hoc* testing procedures and the general clean-up of the manufacturing and assembly process, the failure rate of Fairchild's transistors remained unacceptably high for some of the firm's most demanding customers. For example, Autonetics specified that the transistors used in the navigational computer of the Minuteman missile have a far lower failure rate. To meet the requirements of these military suppliers, it was imperative to find other ways to improve the reliability of diffused silicon transistors. This challenge led Hoerni to revisit his planar idea and to make transistors in which both the emitter-base junction and the base-collector junction were protected by a layer of silicon oxide. Indeed, when Autonetics got wind of the development of the planar transistor, they indicated their eagerness to purchase some for evaluation. The new device was one of their only options for such stringent levels of reliability.[89]

In late January 1959, Hoerni began working toward the full realization of his planar idea. At first he sought to make a PNP planar transistor, the configuration he had used in his notebook entry and in the patent disclosure. He had already worked intently for months to develop the PNP version of the mesa transistor. The difficulties he encountered with trying to make the PNP planar transistor led him to rapidly switch to attempting a NPN version. In the first week of March 1959, Hoerni obtained functional NPN planar transistors and discovered that they had extraordinary characteristics. They were immune to the reliability problems of Fairchild Semiconductor's mesa transistors, and their electrical characteristics were much better. These findings generated considerable excitement at Fairchild Semiconductor. On the basis of Hoerni's disclosure, John Ralls filed a broad patent application covering both the planar process and the planar transistor in May 1959. Presumably in response to Patent Office actions, Ralls split the application into two in May 1960. The patent on the steps required to make a planar transistor, the planar process, was granted in March 1962, and the patent for the planar transistor structure issued in November of the same year.[90]

Raytheon and Hughes Aircraft soon challenged the planar patents. Raytheon, a large military electronics firm based in Massachusetts, sued Fairchild Semiconductor, claiming that the planar patents infringed on a Bell Labs patent by Jules Andrus. Andrus' patent covered the particular oxide masking techniques used in the fabrication some years earlier of a stepping transistor element by L. Arthur D'Asaro, another Bell Labs researcher. Andrus' patented approach had commonalities with Hoerni's scheme, including the use of photolithography and oxide masking techniques to diffuse dopants into the silicon crystal, but the patent indicated that the oxide layer had be taken off after each diffusion. Raytheon soon abandoned its case against Fairchild Semiconductor and took a license on the planar patents. More important, Hughes Aircraft filed an interference claim with the Patent Office on the basis of prior work by Hans Dill and other researchers in its semiconductor division. The Hughes lawyers argued that all the claims in Hoerni's planar patents had been anticipated by Dill and his colleagues.[91]

Roger Borovoy, who had succeeded Ralls as Fairchild Semiconductor's patent lawyer, chose to settle the lawsuit with Hughes out of court. According to him, Hughes Aircraft did not have much of case and would have lost the interference lawsuit in court. But the lawsuit would have significantly delayed the licensing of the planar process. The two parties agreed that one claim among the seventeen claims in Hoerni's planar patents belonged to Hughes—namely the idea of creating a plane surface with a nonconductive coating, possibly a silicone polymer in Hughes' case, on top of the silicon crystal. Hughes dropped the interference suit and assigned its claim back to Fairchild. In exchange, Hughes received a small share of the royalties on the planar patents. Because of the great importance of Hoerni's patents to the subsequent development of semiconductor technology, they became the basis of a highly lucrative licensing program. Along with Robert Noyce's integrated circuit patent, they brought Fairchild Camera and Instrument, Fairchild Semiconductor's parent company, more than $100 million in royalties between the mid 1960s and the late 1970s.[92]

Patent Disclosure

20 January 1959

Jean Hoerni

This patent disclosure by Jean Hoerni, dated January 20, 1959, documents his invention of what became known as "gold doping."[93] This invention furthered Fairchild Semiconductor's technical leadership in silicon transistors and, along with the planar process, did much to establish silicon as the dominant material used in semiconductor electronics. Gold doping considerably increased the switching speed of NPN silicon transistors, making them competitive with germanium transistors for computing applications. The patent disclosure on gold doping more formally reproduces an entry that Hoerni wrote in his patent notebook on the same day. On previous pages of the patent notebook—dated 5 November 1958, 3 December 1958, and 1 January 1959—Hoerni described his experiments on the effects of gold and iron doping on the electrical characteristics of transistors that led him to conclude that gold diffusion could considerably improve the performance of NPN transistors.[94]

In the fall of 1958, Fairchild Semiconductor's engineers began to encounter a significant degradation in the switching speeds of their NPN transistors. It was taking longer and longer for the transistors to switch. According to Hoerni, IBM contacted the group complaining that "the transistors didn't turn off."[95] IBM employed Fairchild's NPN transistors to drive memory cores. If the transistors did not turn off, the memory function of the computer was severely compromised. The slowdown in switching was an unintended consequence of changes that engineers had made to Fairchild Semiconductor's manufacturing processes. They had developed a new processing step in which they plated the back of the wafer with nickel and doped it with phosphorus. This was a "gettering" technique to draw out and nullify impurities in the bulk silicon of the transistor. The step was too effective, however. The "gettering" process continued for some time, even after the transistors had been shipped to customers, eliminating more and more impurities from the bulk silicon. There were so few impurities remaining that the minority carrier lifetime—an important property in transistor behavior—was so long that switching time was increased considerably. In other words, the transistors would take longer and longer to turn off.[96]

Hoerni discovered a remedy in the scientific literature. He found an article by a group at Bell Labs that discussed the use of gold doping for the fabrication of high-speed silicon diodes. Gold acted as a catalyst, speeding up the recombination of majority and minority carriers and thus decreasing minority carrier lifetimes. Inspired by this article, Hoerni thought of using gold doping to reduce minority carrier lifetimes and increase the switching speeds of NPN transistors. This was a highly unorthodox idea, however. Gold was widely viewed in the semiconductor community as an impurity that should be removed from transistors at all costs. At Bell Labs, gold was referred to as "deathnium"

PATENT DISCLOSURE

Ref: Pgs. 12,13,14 and 15 of
Fairchild Notebook No.3
January 20, 1959
Jean A. Hoerni

Selective Control of Electron and Hole Lifetimes in Semiconductor Devices

Several characteristics of semiconductor devices are strongly
dependent on the recombination rate, or lifetime, of electrons and holes
in excess of carrier equilibrium densities. So far, technological progress
has moved in the direction of ever increasing lifetime values. Present
obtainable lifetimes are indeed high enough that it is now possible and
feasable to reduce them in a controlled manner to a level consistent with
best device behavior. Considering the particular case of a transistor,
it is found, however, that the lifetime requirements are not the same in
the different regions of the transistor. In particular, high lifetime
values are desirable in the base material (since they yield high current
gains), whereas low lifetime values are desirable in the collector material
(in order to reduce storage effects when turning off a transistor used in
switching applications). In double diffused transistors, it is found that,
contrary to these requirements, the lifetime is lower in the diffused base
than it is in the collector (made of undiffused semiconductor).

The purpose of this disclosure is to describe a way in which the
lifetimes can be selectively controlled over semiconductor regions of
different polarities (p or n). In the particular case of the double
diffused transistor mentioned above, this procedure makes possible a
reduction in collector lifetime (leading to faster switching response)
without sacrifice in lease lifetime (or current gain).

The procedure to be described makes use of the properties of specific
impurities to affect the recombination rate of electrons and holes to a
different extent. In the steady state (or, in the general case, when trapping
effects can be neglected), electron and hole recombination rates, or electron
and hole lifetimes, are always necessarily the same in a given semiconductor
region. Electron and hole lifetimes defined in the text refer to lifetimes
τ_{no} and τ_{po} prevailing in strongly p-type material, or strongly n-type
material respectively. It can be shown that the electron and hole lifetimes,
τ_{no} and τ_{po} respectively, are related to the capture cross-section of the
impurities in question by

$$\tau_{no} = \frac{1}{v_n N \sigma_{no}} \quad , \quad \tau_{po} = \frac{1}{v_p N \sigma_{po}} \tag{1}$$

where v_n and v_p are the carrier thermal velocities, N is the density of
impurity centers, and σ_{no} and σ_{po} are the captive cross-sections in strongly
p-type and n-type material. On the basis of formula (1) selective lifetime

Patent Disclosure   - 2 -   Jean A. Hoerni
Selective Control of Electron and Hole Lifetimes in Semiconductor Devices

control may be achieved by doping the transistor with impurities for which
the difference between σ_{no} and σ_{po} is large. In our particular application of a npn transistor, the condition for reducing the storage time
without affecting the current gain is therefore $\sigma_{po} \gg \sigma_{no}$.
In the case of a pnp transistor the equivalent condition is $\sigma_{no} \gg \sigma_{po}$.

In silicon or germanium, impurities suitable for lifetime control
are those which cause deep energy levels close to the middle of the energy
gap between the valence and the conduction band. To mention a few, gold, iron,
nickel, copper, zinc, silver, manganese, platinum, have been found to have this
property. Contrary to the usual dopants of the third and fifth column of the
periodic table, the deep level impurities diffuse at a fast rate, so that it
is quite feasable to dope a transistor structure uniformly with them over a
time period in which further diffusion of the already present p and n regions
is negligible. Capture cross-sections of the deep level impurities are generally unknown, or only known at doping levels of little interest in device
fabrication. The available evidence, however, indicates that they are
large in some cases and likely to fulfill the inequalities quoted above.

The following give the particular application of gold doping in double
diffused silicon npn transistors. Subsequent to the usual diffusion of the
base and emitter dopants, gold is plated or evaporated on the collector side,
and diffused into the transistor over a time period and at a temperature
compatible with optimum concentration and uniform final doping. Representative
values are 30 minutes and 980 C. Under these conditions, the author has found
that the current gain, or h_{FE} values are hardly affected, whereas the storage
time after turn off of the transistor is reduced by a factor of 5 to 10. The
differential effect of gold on σ_{no} and σ_{po} is observed in an even more
striking way if pnp transistors of equivalent design are doped with gold under
the same conditions. Here the current gain values depend on hole lifetime and
drop to less than one hundredth of their original values. Clearly in the pnp
case, another impurity of effect opposite to gold remains to be found.

Read and Understood_____
                                R. N. Noyce
                                January 20, 1959

because of its effect on gain (amplification), an important characteristic of a transistor. In fact, Bell Labs researchers had developed nickel "gettering" as a way to remove gold particles from the bulk of the silicon crystal in order to improve transistor amplification.[97]

Hoerni reasoned that he could use carefully controlled gold doping to reduce the minority carrier lifetime in the collector region of the transistor and, at the same time, maintain longer lifetimes in the base region of the transistor. By doing so, he reasoned, he would improve the transistor's switching speed with short lifetimes in the collector *and* maintain the longer lifetimes in the base associated with high gain. In November and December 1958, Hoerni experimented with different gold diffusion techniques, varying the duration and temperature of the diffusions and searching for a way to dope the collector with gold without affecting the minority carrier lifetime in the base. After weeks of constant experimentation, he settled on a process in which he plated gold to the back of the transistor and then quickly diffused the gold into the collector region, heating the wafer to 980°C for 30 minutes. Gold doping had a striking effect on the switching speeds of NPN transistors, increasing them by roughly an order of magnitude without a deterioration in gain.[98]

Hoerni disclosed his invention to Robert Noyce on 20 January 1959, and later to Fairchild Semiconductor's founding group as a whole. Members of the group recall being surprised by Hoerni's results, which went against all accepted knowledge in the semiconductor community. But they also immediately understood the significance of Hoerni's invention, which increased the switching speeds of silicon transistors greatly. The group also quickly discovered that gold, like nickel, could act as a getter, drawing out impurities from the bulk of the silicon crystal. Fairchild Semiconductor soon protected Hoerni's invention, filing a patent application on gold doping. More important, Fairchild Semiconductor's manufacturing engineers rapidly integrated a gold diffusion step into their NPN production process. This step permitted the fabrication of fast-switching mesa transistors for digital circuits, such as the 2N1253 and the 2N706.[99] These gold-doped silicon transistors competed directly with high-speed germanium transistors in the computer market. Indeed, together with the planar process, gold doping enabled silicon transistors to emerge as the main semiconductor devices and ultimately to displace their germanium counterparts. Gold doping remained an important manufacturing process at Fairchild Semiconductor well into the late 1960s, when it was replaced by other ways of speeding up bipolar integrated circuits.[100]

Entry in Patent Notebook

23 January 1959

Robert Noyce

This entry in Noyce's notebook presents his solution to a problem of great interest and potential importance in solid-state electronics: how to design and fabricate a miniaturized, complete electronic circuit in a single piece of semiconductor material.[101] Noyce's solution—the planar integrated circuit—would soon animate a program at Fairchild Semiconductor. The success of this program to realize Noyce's concept would, in turn, establish the silicon planar integrated circuit as the main line of technological development in electronics. By January 1959, when Noyce penned this entry, researchers across the semiconductor community had devoted several years to various approaches to microcircuitry: making new forms of highly reliable and miniaturized electronic circuits containing both passive components (resistors and capacitors) and active components (diodes and transistors). This microcircuitry challenge was well known in the semiconductor industry by the later 1950s. As early as 1952, Geoffrey Dummer, a reliability engineer at the Royal Radar Establishment in England, had discussed the possibility of realizing electronic functions in a "solid block" of semiconductor material. In 1953, Harwick Johnson of RCA filed a patent application for the formation of a complete oscillator circuit in a single piece of germanium, and in 1957 a patent was issued.[102]

By the late 1950s, the approach to microcircuitry advocated by Dummer and Johnson—that of semiconductor integrated circuits, the forming of complete circuits in single samples of semiconductor material—was being pursued by several research groups, including the team at Texas Instruments led by Jack Kilby, a group centered on Torkel Wallmark at the RCA Laboratories, and a team directed by Edward Keonjian, the chief engineer at the American Bosch Arma Corporation. In fact, Keonjian and Kilby were formally collaborating on a project to design and build semiconductor integrated circuits in 1958 and 1959.[103]

Semiconductor integrated circuits were but one distinct approach among a variety of approaches to microcircuitry in the late 1950s. The main impetus for all these efforts was the push by the U.S. military and intelligence agencies to miniaturize electronic circuits. Circuit miniaturization was viewed as critical to reducing the size and weight of aerospace systems. Microcircuitry was also seen as a way to substantially increase the reliability of military electronics. In the mid 1950s, the various branches of the U.S. military and the National Security Agency began to support large programs aimed at microcircuitry across the range of approaches.[104]

Thin-film circuitry was one such approach. It had some commonalities with techniques for manufacturing printed circuit boards. Deposited films of various materials on an insulating substrate were used to form resistors, capacitors, and other passive components. The research frontier in this approach was on methods for making

70

This type of logic element can be carried much
further by multiple connections for deflection
electrodes, and multiple contacts on both
front and back surfaces. It would appear
that the resulting output voltages are suitable
for direct coupling, so many of these elements
are possible on one wafer.

January 23 '59

Methods of isolating multiple devices:
In many applications now it would be desirable
to make multiple devices on a single piece
of silicon in order to be able to make interconnections between devices as part of the manufacturing
process, and thus reduce size, weight, etc, as well
as cost per active element. Several considerations
enter here: First, the blocks of devices which
make up one unit should be large enough
that the number of external leads is
substantially reduced, realizing an economic
advantage in fabrication costs. Secondly, either

71

the number of elements must be small.
or the yield very high in order that
overall yield is high enough to be economic.
Some steps may be taken here in transistor
and logical design in order to make simple
high yield elements. Still some compromise
must undoubtedly be made. Third, the
method of making interconnections, should
fall naturally into the pattern of making
the elements. Fourth, Some method of surface
protection must be utilized.

　　　The following seems to meet most of these
requirements: Suppose we want to make
a diode matrix for a full adder.

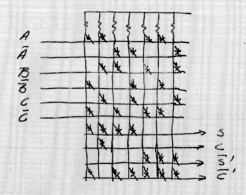

72

We start with, say high resistivity n-type or ʋ material. Then after oxidizing, a p-type impurity is diffused through holes in the oxide, diffusing all the way through the wafer

oxide

Then, after removing oxide on the top, an n-type impurity is diffused in:

metal connections are made, through the holes
in the oxide, to interconnect the diodes as desired
~~by evaporating metal~~
for a particular circuit.

Resistors might be made by either making two connections to one diffused island, or by coating the outside with resistive material, and making connections to it.

The important features of the above are
1. Isolating multiple units by including at least 1 p-n junction between them. more common will be the case where 2 junctions are included between the elements, and that one is always reverse-biased, regardless

73

of the polarity of the voltage between the elements.

2. Use of the SiO_2 layer as an insulator to isolate contact strips from the underlying ✓ Silicon.

3. Protection of junctions at the surface with an oxide layer.

The above is applicable to transistors as well as diodes.

A generalized logic element might be the following:

Logic Amplifiers.

Input →

Diode Matrix for Logical fcn

Output Lines.

DC Power + Bias.

Direct coupled transistor adder: Richards p 169

$$S = A \bar{B} \bar{C}$$
$$+ \bar{A} B C$$
$$+ \bar{A} \bar{B} C$$
$$+ A B C$$

$$C = A B \bar{C}$$
$$+ A \bar{B} C$$
$$+ \bar{A} B C$$
$$+ A B C$$

B —

A —

74

Full adder using Beam switching device:

One Beam device

1 Pulls Beam
0 Pushes "

no carry for ABC

This looks OK

condition ABC
looks bad

Equivalent from PNPN's   (could be npn's) (avalanche)

high-performance active components such as diodes and transistors from the same thin films. The thin-film approach was closely related to another research vein in micro-circuitry: hybrid circuits. In this approach, discrete active components—diodes and transistors—were inserted into arrays of passive components that were often formed by thin-film and printed-circuit-board techniques. These hybrid circuits would be placed within a single device package. The hybrid-circuit approach was pioneered by Jay Lathrop and James Nall (using photolithography) at the government's Diamond Ordnance Fuze Laboratory. Bell Labs' leaders also pushed an active program in hybrid circuits. While eschewing the semiconductor integrated-circuit approach, Bell Labs researchers were also active in functional devices. In this vein, researchers looked to create complete circuit functions in a new material structure, but without replicating traditional circuit components in the new structure. This was far-reaching research that nevertheless resulted in actual devices, including an array of PNPN structures and the stepping transistor element on which Ian Ross and L. Arthur D'Asaro collaborated and which D'Asaro succeeded in fabricating.[105]

Other strategies for microcircuitry ranged from novel materials to packaging. For example, at the close of the 1950s the Air Force funded a major program in molecular electronics at Westinghouse. The Westinghouse researchers' vision of molecular electronics had much in common with the Bell Labs researchers' conception of functional devices, but with perhaps a greater emphasis on the engineering of fundamentally new materials and the use of electron beams as a processing technique. In the end, the Westinghouse program increasingly focused on a novel way of producing silicon for making traditional devices such as transistors. Through its "Project Lightning," the National Security Agency funded a program at IBM and Arthur D. Little to make digital circuits from cryogenically cooled superconducting components. These circuits, the purpose of which was to greatly increase the speed of digital computers for cryptanalysis and cryptology, were highly miniaturized in order to fit inside vacuum flasks of liquid gases. The NSA also funded efforts at RCA and elsewhere in high-speed devices formed from compound semiconductors. Better known was RCA's lead role in the "Micromodule" program of the U.S. Army Signal Corps, a major program to standardize a miniaturized, modular packaging for circuit elements from which circuits of varying configuration could be formed for military electronic systems.[106] In view of the prominence of microcircuitry within the semiconductor community in the late 1950s, it is not surprising that several engineers at Fairchild Semiconductor (including Noyce) considered the integration problem.[107]

An event that may have animated Noyce's interest in microcircuitry was a visit to Fairchild Semiconductor by Edward Keonjian on 20 January 1959, three days before Noyce wrote this entry in his patent notebook. Keonjian was a senior engineer at the American Bosch Arma Corporation, a manufacturer of military avionics based in New York. At American Bosch Arma, he directed the design of a miniaturized guidance computer for the Atlas missile. The Atlas—the first American ICBM—was developed in a "crash program" by the military and its contractors in the second half of the 1950s. A major focus of Keonjian's Atlas computer project was the development of miniature circuits, especially hybrid circuits, for the central processing unit. Keonjian had designed miniaturized hybrid circuits for the project, but American Bosch Arma lacked the know-how to fabricate the required silicon transistors. Keonjian was looking to collaborate with a firm that had such silicon manufacturing capability. During his visit to Fairchild Semiconductor, Keonjian talked with the founders about "microminiaturized circuits," especially a full adder that he was developing for his airborne digital computer. A full adder is a logic circuit that performs addition operations. Keonjian discussed the possibility of working with Fairchild Semiconductor on the production of these hybrid circuits.[108]

Recent discussions with Jean Hoerni about the planar process were also critical for Noyce's formulation of his answer to the microcircuitry question. Noyce had long been aware of Hoerni's planar ideas. He had witnessed Hoerni's original patent notebook entry on his planar ideas in December 1957 and had heard about Hoerni's planar diode idea. Noyce also knew about the partial-planar transistor and its improved amplifying characteristics. In mid January 1959, Hoerni had even asked Noyce and Last to make photomasks for him to use in fabricating a PNP planar transistor. Of Fairchild Semiconductor's founders, Noyce was the one with the greatest knowledge of Hoerni's planar ideas.[109]

Hoerni's planar process gave Noyce a powerful tool with which to solve the microcircuitry problem. Indeed, the semiconductor integrated circuit that Noyce described in his patent notebook was a planar integrated circuit. The powerful tool provided by the planar approach was the layer of silicon oxide, which could be used as an insulator between the silicon crystal and a metal layer. This metal layer could interconnect various circuit components formed by oxide masking and diffusion in the same piece of silicon crystal. To electrically isolate these circuit components from one another, Noyce thought of using multiple PN junctions. These junctions would prevent current from flowing between the various components within the same silicon chip. Another insight that Noyce recorded in his 23 January 1959 patent notebook entry was that one could make resistors through diffusion techniques or by coating the oxide with a resistive material.

Because of his use of Hoerni's planar process, the integrated circuit that Noyce proposed in his patent notebook was significantly different from those invented by Jack Kilby and Kurt Lehovec in late 1958 and early 1959. At Texas Instruments, starting in the summer of 1958, Kilby had used mesa-transistor techniques to make integrated circuits. In addition to forming transistors, he had fabricated resistors and capacitors in a piece of germanium crystal. To isolate the various components electrically, Kilby had etched away portions of the germanium crystal. These air-filled gaps would provide the required insulation. In contrast, Lehovec of Sprague Electric had conceived of a semiconductor integrated circuit made using both grown-junction and alloying processes. The first step in Lehovec's process was introducing impurities into the semiconductor crystal as it was grown in a crucible. This resulted in a crystal bar with multiple PN junctions. Transistors were then fabricated by alloying techniques on one of the sides of the crystal bar. PN junctions provided isolation regions between the transistors. In his 23 January 1959 patent notebook entry, Noyce independently reinvented two of Kilby and Lehovec's ideas: making diverse circuit components in a single piece of semiconductor material and isolating components by creating multiple PN junctions.[110]

But Noyce went further than Kilby and Lehovec. He devised a novel method to interconnect the various circuit components that were formed in the piece of semiconductor material. In the patents and the early practice of both Kilby and Lehovec, these components were interconnected in a highly traditional way: through metal wires that arced above the surfaces of the semiconductor piece, spanning the locations to be connected.[111] Noyce, in contrast, proposed interconnecting the components in the same semiconductor piece by depositing metal lines—wires of a sort—on top of the insulating silicon oxide layer. Noyce's process for forming this interconnection layer was essentially identical to the process for forming the contacts to planar transistors in Hoerni's planar process. The surface of Noyce's integrated circuit was also protected by the silicon oxide layer. As Hoerni discovered in March 1959 when he succeeded in building the first planar transistors, surface protection by the oxide layer greatly improved the electrical characteristics of transistors and made them much more reliable.

To illustrate his idea of the planar integrated circuit, Noyce described a full adder— the very circuit that Keonjian had discussed with Fairchild Semiconductor's founders a few days earlier. Noyce's adder, however, was an all-silicon device, in contrast with Keonjian's hybrid circuit. Noyce described an adder that was an array of planar diodes in a single piece of silicon interconnected by metal contacts deposited on the silicon oxide layer. Diode arrays were a well-known form of computer logic, first conceived at the Bell Telephone Laboratories in the late 1930s and the early 1940s. Diode arrays had been used in some of the first digital computers built by Bell Labs, including the Tradic (an airborne computer for bombing and aircraft navigation). Noyce may have had direct contact with Bell Labs' computer program while he was with Philco in the mid 1950s, when Bell Labs had begun to employ Philco's "surface barrier" germanium transistors in a successor computer to the Tradic. As Noyce realized, the main advantage of diode-array logic was its simplicity. Unlike transistors, diodes were relatively easy to manufacture and could be produced with high yields. This was important because the higher the yield of each component in the circuit, the more likely it was that the circuit as a whole could be produced in an economic fashion. In essence, then, Noyce's choice of a diode array for his full adder was an argument for the manufacturability of his planar integrated circuit solution to the microcircuitry problem.[112]

Noyce went on in his entry to note that logic circuits could be made from arrays of transistors and other active components.[113] In the last page and a half of the entry, he drew diagrams of full-adder circuits made of transistors, beam switching devices (a recent conception of Noyce's), and PNPN switches (also known as thyristors). Interestingly,

Noyce's transistor circuit was a direct-coupled transistor logic circuit, a logic configuration originally developed at Philco. In the late 1950s, DCTL logic was used in several cutting edge computers. Sperry had used DCTL in military systems, Bell Labs adopted it for military airborne computers, and Philco had used it in what may have been the first fully transistorized computer: a desk-sized system, called Solo, that Philco developed for the National Security Agency. DCTL was the primary focus of Fairchild Semiconductor in digital logic during its earliest years, both because of its prominence in military and government computing and because of Noyce's and Grinich's previous experiences with the logic form. In fact, David Allison was looking to design a silicon transistor especially suited to DCTL circuits as early as November 1957.[114]

This notebook entry was the first step in Noyce's work on the planar integrated circuit. In subsequent months, he significantly refined and expanded upon the ideas he had jotted down in January 1959. Noyce's continued work probably was stimulated by developments unfolding at Fairchild Semiconductor and at its major competitor, Texas Instruments. In early March 1959, Hoerni demonstrated that the planar process led to significant improvements in transistor performance and reliability. This demonstration confirmed Noyce's idea that a surface-protected semiconductor integrated circuit was the way to go for microcircuitry. It was also in March 1959 that Texas Instruments organized a press conference to announce Jack Kilby's semiconductor integrated circuit—dubbed the "solid circuit"—at the Institute of Radio Engineers conference in New York. Unlike the logic arrays formed of single types of devices that Noyce had considered in January, Kilby's solid circuit was an oscillator made from a mesa transistor and several resistors and capacitors. It is likely that Kilby's solid circuit led Noyce to recast his ideas about planar integrated circuits as transistor-based rather than diode-based and to think more carefully about isolation and about forming passive components in the silicon substrate. In subsequent months, Noyce conceived different ways of making resistors and capacitors in the silicon chip. He also proposed various structures for planar devices, including one in which a transistor was made by triple diffusion. Using triple diffusion to form the transistor solved the problem of isolating the transistor from the other elements in the circuit, and it was a significant new invention. The planar transistors Hoerni had fabricated required two diffusions. Hoerni would diffuse the emitter and the base in the collector. Noyce proposed instead to diffuse the emitter, the base, and the collector in the substrate. The junction at the bottom of the collector would be reverse-biased. As Noyce noted in one of his patent applications of 1959, this bottom junction "served the important function of isolating the collector of the transistor from the grounded, underlying P-type region."[115]

At the end of July 1959, John Ralls, Fairchild Semiconductor's outside patent attorney, submitted a patent application that incorporated many of Noyce's earlier ideas for the planar integrated circuit and his new thoughts on passive components and on isolation. The application emphasized Noyce's novel method for interconnecting several devices on the same chip. A patent was issued in April 1961, but the Patent Office had disallowed one of the eleven original claims in Noyce's application, arguing that the claim on the method for forming the planar integrated circuit could not be combined with the ten claims that focused on the structure of the circuit, and in particular the interconnection scheme.[116] With the issuance of Noyce's device and lead structure patent, Texas Instruments filed an interference suit in May 1962. Texas Instruments claimed that Noyce's patent interfered with a pending patent application, filed by Kilby in January 1962, that was a continuation of an earlier patent application that Kilby had filed in February 1959. After the Board of Patent Interferences decided to split the claims of the Noyce patent between Fairchild Semiconductor and Texas Instruments, both firms filed appeals, each seeking complete rights to all Noyce's claims. After lengthy legal proceedings, these cross-appeals were settled by the U.S. Court of Customs and Patent Appeals. In essence, the Court again split the claims, Fairchild Semiconductor winning those connected to the planar interconnection scheme and Texas Instruments gaining those connected to the formation of all the basic circuit elements in a single piece of semiconductor material.[117]

Noyce and his lawyers filed the device and lead structure patent application at the end of July 1959. Several weeks later, on 11 September, Noyce and the same lawyers filed two additional patent applications. These two applications, both originally titled "Semiconductor Circuit Complex," further embodied Noyce's developing ideas about the planar integrated circuit approach, and in particular his ideas for using PN junctions to isolate the circuit components from one another in the chip.[118] Remarkably, these two patent applications by Noyce, which resulted in two patents issuing in 1964, appear to have eluded the notice of historians and chroniclers of the integrated circuit.[119] The historical neglect of Noyce's two isolation patents may be due to their eclipse by the high-profile litigation between Texas Instruments and Sprague Electric that ran concurrently with the battle between TI and Fairchild Semiconductor over the Noyce device and lead structure patent.

Texas Instruments filed suit over an alleged interference between the patent issued in 1962 to Kurt Lehovec of Sprague Electric and a pending patent application by Kilby, filed in 1962, continuing a patent application from May 1959. Lehovec's patent, originally filed in April 1959, contained broad claims on the use of multiple PN junctions to achieve isolation in a semiconductor integrated circuit—the idea that Noyce had conceived independently in January 1959. TI claimed that Kilby's patent applications of February and May 1959 anticipated Lehovec's claims. Litigation between TI and Sprague Electric dragged on into 1966 before the Board of Patent Interferences ruled in Lehovec's favor.[120] Lehovec's victory in the priority battle over PN junction isolation appears to have obscured the fact that Noyce did in fact have two patents issued on isolation schemes for planar integrated circuits—patents originating from his early ideas of January 1959 and with obviously close connections to and overlaps with Lehovec's work and patent.

Noyce's two patent applications of 11 September 1959 were centered on isolation schemes for planar integrated circuits, one application focusing more on structure and the other more on method. Both of Noyce's September applications were titled "Semi-conductor Circuit Complexes." In the application that resulted in U.S. patent 3,117,260 ("Semiconductor Circuit Complexes"), Noyce described the formation of a sort of inte-grated circuit blank—a silicon chip with large squares of doped silicon surrounded by a grid of silicon doped by the opposite dopant type. This grid would be formed by diffus-ing from both the top and the bottom of the wafer to form a well spanning the width of the chip. Each large square would be isolated from the adjacent squares by the PN junctions formed on the sides of the grid of material separating the squares. Within each square then, one could form various circuit elements—transistors, diodes, capacitors, resistors—using the planar process. These circuit elements could be interconnected by metal lines laid atop an oxide layer covering the chip. On the basis of this conception, Noyce's application originally contained broad claims to planar integrated circuit struc-tures employing PN junction isolation. Noyce's method-focused isolation application, which eventually resulted in U.S. patent 3,150,299 ("Semiconductor Circuit Complex Having Isolation Means"), covered the same basic system as his other patent applica-tion, but with greater detail on a variety of alternatives for including layers of intrinsic, undoped silicon within the PN junction isolation regions. On the basis of the descrip-tion of how these alternative PN junction isolation structures could be formed, Noyce made nineteen claims broadly covering methods for making PN junction isolation struc-tures in planar integrated circuits.[121]

Over the next several years, in successive revisions in light of criticisms and denials from the Patent Office, the claims of Noyce's interconnection applications were whit-tled down, reduced in number and scope, and largely restricted to structure rather than method. The reduction in the scope of Noyce's claims was due in part to the fact that both the Patent Office and Fairchild Semiconductor's patent lawyers were aware of the Lehovec patent. Nevertheless, in 1964, when Noyce's two isolation patents were issued, Fairchild Semiconductor controlled a significant portfolio of patents on planar inte-grated circuits, in addition to Hoerni's patents on the planar process. This was important, as the relative strengths and overlapping nature of Fairchild Semiconductor's and Texas Instruments' portfolios of patents on the integrated circuit led to a détente between the firms in 1966. In that year, the firms made a deal to cross-license their integrated-circuit patents to each other but to require other firms to make separate licensing deals with them. The royalties on these basic integrated circuit patents brought the two firms very substantial licensing revenues over the life of the patents.[122]

Entry in Personal Notebook, Pages 139–141

18 March 1959

Jay Last

March 1959 was an eventful month for Fairchild Semiconductor. At the start of the month, vice president and general manager Ewart Baldwin had left abruptly, having been with the firm only a year. Baldwin took other Fairchild Semiconductor employees with him, particularly those he had recruited from Hughes. He left to establish the semiconductor operations of Rheem Manufacturing in order to produce diffused silicon mesa transistors. His departure from Fairchild Semiconductor was, thus, a direct competitive move. Fairchild Semiconductor had proved that there was a market for diffused silicon mesa transistors. Baldwin believed he could establish an organization at Rheem that could outcompete Fairchild Semiconductor in the manufacture of these devices and win a major position in this growing market. Fairchild Semiconductor brought legal actions against Rheem Semiconductor and against Baldwin. The suit against Rheem alleged theft of trade secrets (a copy of Fairchild Semiconductors process manual was discovered at Rheem); the suit against Baldwin accused him of breaching a confidentiality agreement. In what would become a typical pattern in Silicon Valley, these lawsuits were settled out of court.[123]

Unfortunately for Baldwin and his efforts at Rheem, his departure occurred just before Jean Hoerni's demonstration of a fully planar NPN transistor in early March 1959. The greatly improved electrical characteristics and reliability of the planar transistor, as well as its basic compatibility with the manufacturing technology that Fairchild Semiconductor had developed to create mesa transistors, quickly convinced the firm's founders that Hoerni's planar process and planar transistor constituted a major innovation. Jay Last's entries in his personal notebook from an "R&D Planning Meeting" held on 18 March reflect this rapid appreciation of the importance of the planar approach. Baldwin and Rheem were thus aiming in the direction from which Fairchild Semiconductor was quickly moving away.[124]

Last's entries from the 18 March planning meeting indicate that the discussion began with a review of the existing deadlines that the R&D group would have to meet in order to keep the firm's product introduction on schedule. For example, R&D was due to transfer the PNPN switch to the pre-production organization at the start of July, when the organization would be located in the new manufacturing plant. This would allow the firm to fulfill its delivery "commitments" for 1,500 devices by the end of the year. The bulk of the meeting, however, was a discussion of a major re-orientation of the R&D laboratory's activities in reaction to the results that Hoerni had recently demonstrated with his planar NPN transistor.

"New programs" was the heading Last used in his notes for this discussion at the meeting. (See notebook page 140.) The focus of these new programs was summarized as "SURFACES." The improved reliability and electrical characteristics of the planar

3/18/59   139

R&D planning meeting

PRE PROD   PRODUCTION

1140   MARIS   (OCT 1)

4500   JULY 1 (NEW BLDG)

pnpn   5500   JULY 1 (NEW BLDG)

1040 (338 replacement) SEPT - OCT

8000   OCT 15 (when 1140 goes out)

10 at 1A

Commitments

5500 — 1000 in Sept. (Aeronutronics)   low voltage.
       500 by Dec. (Sperry)

140

New programs: 3/18/59

<u>SURFACES</u>

| OUTMODE THE MESA — OXIDE MASKING —
| HIGH VOLTAGE
| LEADS

<u>Shockley:</u>
- Thin base layers —
- Alloying thin layers —
- Oscillations under emitter — impurity interactions
  GaAs.

<u>Sah:</u>

Boron - high + low doping
oxide masking —
problem of scaling shots
metals as getters + lifetime controllers
new phenomena devices - Read diode.

<u>Moll:</u>

surface protection + stabilization   (low melting point)
get leads out —   glasses
    surface problems in general — effect of ions
    surface cleanliness — producing + maintaining
    high temp contacts —
long range - oxide + sulphide glasses - ionic conductivity

Jay

power device
1090-338
1040-
small gom pulp.
micro-min program

parametric amplifier diode —   various forms

IBM
large areas - high power.

time schedule - personnel schedule
objectives

3/18/59

transistor that Hoerni had created were the results of his new approach to using silicon oxide layers on the surface of the silicon wafer. Here, "SURFACES" denoted the oxide layer, the silicon wafer surface, the aluminum contacts, the metal leads, and the interfaces between them. Under the banner of "SURFACES," the first item on Last's list of new goals was "OUTMODE THE MESA—OXIDE MASKING." This was an effort to develop Hoerni's fledgling planar approach into a robust manufacturing process, yielding planar transistors that would, in many ways, render the mesa transistor obsolete. The second new activity was "HIGH VOLTAGE," a deeper look at how surface phenomena were connected to high-voltage characteristics in Fairchild Semiconductor's devices. The third item on Last's list, "LEADS," placed an ongoing issue that the R&D organization struggled with in the new context of more basic studies of surfaces and their interfaces: difficulties encountered in forming good attachment of leads to the contacts on devices as part of the assembly process.[125]

The remainder of Last's notes captured comments from the leaders of groups within Fair-child Semiconductor's R&D organization on the efforts they would pursue. C. Sheldon Roberts and his colleagues would continue to work on semiconductor crystals, but their research on "alloying thin layers" was directly in keeping with the new emphasis on surfaces. Jean Hoerni's research program was largely unchanged, since it already embodied a central concern with surfaces. "Oxide masking" meant Hoerni's continued development of the planar process and the planar transistor. Hoerni's longstanding interest in boron diffusion would continue, as would his development of gold doping: "metals as getters + lifetime controllers." G. Worden Waring, a PhD from MIT, led a chemistry group in the R&D laboratory that was almost entirely devoted to surfaces and their effects.

The R&D organization was thus moving toward fundamental studies of surfaces in response to Hoerni's demonstration of the planar NPN transistor. This marked an important new direction for the R&D organization, and for the firm as a whole. This was the opening of the company's reorientation to planar technology. Another technological reorientation discussed at this meeting was the beginning of an active program in microcircuitry that would eventually lead to the making of planar integrated circuits. In one of the rare instances in which Jay Last recorded notes of his own contributions to the meeting discussions, he noted the list of device development efforts that would be carried out under his direction. All but one of the efforts were for devices that had been mentioned in earlier meetings, including "small geometry" transistors and microwave diodes. The new effort, characterized as "micro-min pro-gram," microminiaturization program, was circled, indicating extra attention or interest.[126] (See notebook page 141.)

By this time, the founders of Fairchild Semiconductor probably were familiar with the efforts in microcircuitry at Texas Instruments and at the American Bosch Arma Corporation. Through contact with Edward Keonjian, the founders had learned of American Bosch Arma's efforts in hybrid circuits for ICBM computers. Indeed, Keonjian had raised the possibility of partnering with Fairchild Semiconductor on the hybrid circuits. It may have been through Keonjian, who had also formed a collaboration with Jack Kilby on miniaturized circuits, that the founders had learned that Kilby planned to announce Texas Instruments' microcircuit at the IRE meeting in New York City in less than a week after the 18 March meeting. Whatever proximate cause, the Fairchild Semiconductor R&D group decided to enter the microcircuitry race with a new, explicit project under the direction of Jay Last.

The move to planar technology and miniaturized electronic circuits was a major shift for the founders of Fairchild Semiconductor. In the fall of 1957, they had oriented their firm toward the manufacture of silicon mesa transistors. In the next year and a half, they developed a manufacturing technology and designed several mesa transistor products with the goal of establishing the company as a major producer of mesa transistors. But by March 1959, the founders found themselves in a very different place than they had originally anticipated. Now focusing on making mesa transistors obsolete, they sought to develop a new kind of silicon transistor, the planar transistor. They were also aiming at fabrication of microcircuits.

"New Products Steal the Show"

Leadwire, volume 1, number 3

September 1959

In July 1959, Fairchild Semiconductor's leaders created a newsletter, titled *Leadwire*, to share company news with their rapidly expanding workforce. The third issue of this employee newsletter, dated September 1959, publicized the introduction of new Fairchild Semiconductor products at the Western Electronics Show and Convention (Wescon).[127] It was at Wescon that, a year earlier, the company had announced its first transistor, the 2N696. The devices the company introduced at the 1959 Wescon were a fast-switching logic transistor, a hybrid circuit (a flip-flop, a basic building block of digital logic), and tunnel diodes.

The fast-switching transistor, the 2N706, was a NPN mesa transistor. To obtain greater switching speeds than the original 2N696 mesa transistor, David Allison and other engineers at Fairchild Semiconductor had pursued better control of the photolithography process. Having done so, the team significantly scaled down the dimensions of the firm's first NPN mesa transistor, creating the long-planned "small geometry" version of the core driver transistor for use in logic applications. The resulting transistor, the 2N706, was one-fourth the size of the original 2N696.[128] In a second version of the 2N706, Allison and his group also incorporated gold doping, the process developed by Jean Hoerni in late 1958 and early 1959. Gold doping produced short minority carrier lifetimes, resulting in even greater switching speeds. With both smaller dimensions and gold doping, the 2N706 was considerably faster than the firm's first transistor. More important, it was faster than germanium transistors. This increase in switching speed opened up a large market for the new transistor in the logic circuits of military computers.[129]

At Wescon, Fairchild Semiconductor also announced a set of experimental devices: a hybrid circuit and several tunnel diodes. In 1958, Leo Esaki, a Japanese physicist working at Sony, had invented the tunnel diode. The tunnel diode, based on quantum-mechanical effects at a PN junction, could operate at higher frequencies than existing junction diodes. It generated great excitement in the semiconductor industry and was widely viewed as a promising device for computer and microwave circuitry. Most semiconductor firms, Fairchild Semiconductor included, invested in tunnel diode research. For example, General Electric's engineers developed germanium and silicon tunnel diodes. These devices were announced with great fanfare by GE in July 1959. Competing with General Electric, Fairchild Semiconductor announced its silicon tunnel diodes at the August 1959 Wescon.[130]

A year earlier, in August 1958 (the month after Esaki's public announcement of the tunnel diode), Jay Last, Fairchild Semiconductor's head of device research, had initiated work on high-speed diodes (tunnel diodes and parametric amplifier diodes) and on the processes for making them. He first fabricated diodes with mesa techniques and then

Aug 1959

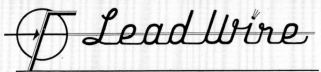

VOLUME I   MOUNTAIN VIEW – PALO ALTO , SEPTEMBER 1959 , NUMBER 3

NEW PRODUCTS STEAL THE SHOW

In addition to unveiling our new 2N706 logic transistor at the recent Western Electronics Show and Convention at the Cow Palace, FSC made the headlines on two other fronts.

Fairchild's entry into the field of microcircuitry was the subject of the lead article in "Electronic News," the industry newspaper of Wednesday, August 19. The article described early laboratory models of our "packaged circuit" module, this one a 20mc flip flop circuit containing four active elements and mounted in a TO-9 transistor case.

Locally dubbed the "hexistor" because of the six leads protruding from the case, the flip - flop circuit module was prominently displayed in the FSC booth at Wescon. Developed principally by Jay T. Last, the new device occupies the middle ground between conventional component design and the widely publicized "molecular engineering"concept.

Gordon E. Moore, head of R & D, noted that the major advantage of our design is that it allows the use of conventional mounting and wiring techniques while still effecting considerable savings in size and weight. Plans are to expand the packaged circuit concept to include gating and adding circuits, thus opening completely new areas in computer design.

Another front on which Fairchild was active was in the display of introductory models of our new "Esaki diode." Our units were developed by C. T. Sah on principles first reported in 1958 by Japanese scientist Leo Esaki. The new diode has several unique properties: verv little effect of temperature on its operation, frequency capability of 2000 mc, and ability to act as a very low noise amplifier.

These units will make it possible to use inexpensive solid state components in the front end of a TV tuner or FM set.

Introduction of the 2N706 logic transistor continues to be the big news, however, as it is the enthusiastic reception of this device which prompted the forecast that we will have 2000 employees by 1960, occupying 120,000 square feet of plant space.

```
┌─────────────────────────────┐
│   NUMBER OF EMPLOYEES        │
│           631                │
└─────────────────────────────┘
```

used Hoerni's planar process to make them. Another Fairchild Semiconductor researcher active in the tunnel diode area was C. T. Sah. Sah had received a PhD in electrical engineering from Stanford and worked with Fairchild Semiconductor's founders at Shockley Semiconductor. At Fairchild Semiconductor, he worked in the physics section of the R&D lab under Hoerni's supervision.[131]

The other experimental device debuted by Fairchild Semiconductor at Wescon was a hybrid circuit. Called a "packaged circuit module" in the *Leadwire* article, this device constituted Fairchild Semiconductor's response to the announcement by its chief competitor, Texas Instruments, that it had made a "solid circuit" (a semiconductor integrated circuit) in March 1959. By the summer of 1959, TI was actively marketing integrated circuits. Fairchild Semiconductor's leaders felt that they needed to demonstrate that they too were working at the cutting edge of semiconductor technology. In a meeting with Last in late July or early August 1959, Robert Noyce, then the firm's general manager, said: "TI was making noises about integrated circuits, and Fairchild should show the flag in some way at Wescon in late August to show that Fairchild was also working in this area."[132]

In subsequent weeks, Last constructed a hybrid-circuit flip-flop—a circuit that used its two stable states to hold one bit of digital information (a 0 or 1). The flip-flop was one of the simplest digital circuits. Last mounted four transistors on a ceramic plate and formed resistors by drawing graphite lines on this plate with a pencil. These components were interconnected with fine wires. Last then put the ceramic plate into a typical transistor package. This combination of discrete devices and integrated packaging was part of the hybrid circuit approach to microcircuitry. In August 1959, as Noyce had hoped, Last's hybrid circuit received significant attention at Wescon and was the subject of a lead article in *Electronic News*, a trade publication widely read in the electronics industry. Fairchild Semiconductor was now in the microcircuitry business.[133]

The hybrid-circuit project and the tunnel-diode project had very different outcomes. Within a year, Sah abandoned his research on tunnel diodes to concentrate on more promising devices, including field-effect transistors. Tunnel diodes had turned out to be very difficult to use in electronic circuits. But Last's hybrid-circuit project blossomed into a substantial research program. In late 1959, Last and his group engineered more hybrid circuits of the type that he had shown at Wescon. More important, Last's "Micrologic" section, using the planar technology Jean Hoerni had developed, experimented with ways of making integrated circuits in a single piece of silicon crystal. They succeeded in making the first functional planar integrated circuit—also a flip-flop—in May 1960.

Internal Memorandum

5 November 1959

Gordon Moore

Written by Gordon Moore in November 1959, this memorandum details the R&D laboratory's plan for 1960.[134] By the time he wrote this memorandum, Moore had directed the laboratory for about five months. He had succeeded Robert Noyce as head of R&D in May 1959, after Noyce became Fairchild Semiconductor's general manager. After the departure of Ewart Baldwin, Richard Hodgson (vice president of Fairchild Camera) and the founders of Fairchild Semiconductor decided not to seek outside management again. Instead, they opted for a stratification of the founders, with Noyce taking overall leadership responsibility for the firm and Moore taking the technological reins. Hodgson also became more involved in the management of the company. Between May and November 1959, with this new management organization, the firm had made significant strides. It had filed a series of patent applications covering two fundamental innovations: the planar process and the planar integrated circuit. It had introduced new transistor products to the market such as the 2N706, the fast-switching mesa transistor for logic applications. It also had grown significantly. The number of employees had increased from 344 in May 1959 to 855 in November 1959. By the fall of 1959, Fairchild Semiconductor had emerged as a significant player in the semiconductor industry.

Building on these accomplishments, the firm's leaders were intent on solidifying its position in the business of advanced silicon transistors. But they also wanted the firm to diversify into new products and new markets, and do so through internal research and development. Moore's memorandum on the R&D program for 1960 reflected these priorities. Addressed to Richard Hodgson, it advocated both a significant expansion and a reorientation of the firm's R&D activities. The R&D laboratory, which until then had focused on transistors and related fabrication processes, now was to be tasked with the development of new products—diodes, microcircuits, and "memory elements" (components used in computer memory)—for the firm's main customers: companies building digital computers for aerospace (predominantly military) applications.

Perhaps most important, Moore proposed to reorient the laboratory toward basic research. His goal was to move beyond the trial-and-error engineering that had characterized much of the lab's activities to that time, and to build a research program investigating the fundamentals of silicon technology. In this, Moore followed an important trend in industrial research in the United States after World War II. In this period, private corporations made much greater investments in basic research than they had done previously. The general expectation in U.S. industry was that basic research would lead to technological breakthroughs.[135] For Moore, a basic research program on silicon technology had several desirable uses beyond product breakthroughs. He saw basic research as a way to attract talented scientists and to tackle the complex and often intractable

J. Hoerni

R. Hodgson

cc: R. N. Noyce

Semiconductor Corporation
Corporate
Summary of Projected R&D Program
    for 1960
By: GEM -- 11/5/59

The projected activities of the R&D Department are designed to fulfill four
major responsibilities:

1. Supply a flow of new products to production.

2. Keep abreast of and investigate new areas for potential products to
    preserve and extend our established markets.

3. Perform research to understand processes and phenomena associated
    with both existing and new products in order to improve and extend
    the products and processes.

4. Establish and maintain the technical reputation of the company outside
    of the company.

Up until recently a majority of the effort has been expended on the first
of these areas. It is now important that the activities be broadened to
assure our continued technical leadership in transistors and related fields.

SPECIFIC PRODUCT DEVELOPMENT PROGRAM

I. Transistors

    Considerable work aimed specifically at the development of new transistor
    types is still required. The devices under consideration are as follows:

    a. Those necessary to fill out a family of double-diffused, silicon
        transistors including:

        1. Protected versions of our present PNP and small geometry units.

        2. A small geometry PNP.

        3. The group of NPN high frequency high power transistors (about 20
            watts) of which the X6000 is the first.

        4. A transistor optimized for r.f. applications.

        In addition we would like to extend the size of units in this family
        to both larger than the X6000 and smaller than the FT-1140. These
        last extensions will be started during 1960, although development
        will extend into 1961.

    b. A pair of devices, probably electrically similar to our 4000 series
        and 1140 series, whose construction and specifications are optimized

R. Hodgson

Page 2

Summary of Projected R&D Program
for 1960
By: GEM -- 11/5/59

- -

with respect to eventual manufacturing costs. This pair of devices
should allow us to establish a large commercial market.

II. Diodes

A family of switching and general purpose diodes, probably about four
by the end of 1960, that will cover the large market applications for the
near future, must be developed.

NEW PRODUCT ORIENTED AREAS

I. Microcircuitry

We are convinced that microcircuitry is an important trend. Our transistor
techniques are applicable to the production of microcircuits. Because
the most difficult problems in microcircuitry have evolved around the
active elements, i.e. transistors, the transistor manufacturers are in
the best position to develop this concept. We propose to expand considerably in this area, both with respect to direct work on microcircuits
and the advancement of the underlying technology. An important facet of
such an effort is close interaction between those people making the circuits
and those familiar with their applications so that the best compromises
regarding specific circuits can be obtained. This implies a very strong
evaluation and application effort in conjunction with the device effort.

Our approach is to develop a new set of components, the first group of
which will be for the computer market. These new components will perform
complete circuit functions. They might include flip-flops, gates, adders,
shift-registers, digital delay lines and the like. Eventually, sets of
these components will be able to replace over 90% of all the circuitry
in high speed digital computers. A most important point concerning our
approach that has not been recognized by others is that it appears that
the manufacturing cost for complete circuits will be less eventually than
it is for the conventional components necessary to duplicate the circuit
functions.

II. New Materials

While it seems that it will be some time before the newer semiconductor
materials are a factor in the transistor market, the potentialities of
higher temperature and higher frequency operation cannot be overlooked.
For some other devices, such as parametric diodes and tunnel diodes, these
materials may be useful in the near future. We must stay abreast of
developments with these materials. Our program here is to evaluate samples

R. Hodgson   Summary of Projected R&D Program for 1960
Page 3   By: GEM -- 11/5/59
-- --

of the best material we can obtain or prepare and to acquire the
technology to handle these materials. When the material and the
technology are ready we will attempt some device development.

III. Microwave Devices and Special Diodes

The extension of solid state devices into the microwave frequency range
is an important goal, which we plan to pursue. As yet, the most promising approaches are the tunnel diode and parametric-diode. At least one
other diode structure has been suggested as a microwave oscillator. We
wish to extend the work in this area of microwave devices, especially
with respect to the tunnel diode, potentially a formidable competitor
to the transistor.

IV. Memory Elements

Present computer memories are relatively slow and bulky. They also
represent a computer component that we do not yet produce. We propose
to expand into this area. How far we go in this direction depends upon
how successful we are in attracting the right person. It is possible that
this problem could lead to work in ferromagnetic materials, thin films,
superconductors, or semiconductors, all of which have been suggested for
memory elements in the past.

SUPPORTING RESEARCH AND TECHNOLOGY DEVELOPMENT

Many important technical problems remain even with respect to the processing
on our standard transistor types. These include both problems for which we
have an empirical cure of the witchcraft variety and those with which we
just live at present. These problems effect yeild, limit electrical performance and control reliability of our transistors and diodes. In addition,
the devices we are producing now are near the limit of the capabilities of our
present processing. It is necessary that we undertake the basic research and
technology development required to understand our present limitations and
advance the state of the art to remain in our position of leadership. Some
of the work done in this area will result in important scientific contributions and can be published without endangering our proprietary position.
This is very important in attracting and retaining scientific personnel.
Some of the areas in which we plan work are listed below. This list will
certainly change as new information unfolds.

I. Interactions of Imperfections in Semiconductors

Evidence exists that some important yield problems are closely tied to
the interactions of impurities and other imperfections. These same
effects limit the performance of semiconductor devices to well below any
basic limitation that exists according to present theory. While the

R. Hodgson   Summary of Projected R&D Program
                                                  for 1960
Page 4   By: GEM -- 11/5/59
-- --

scientific content alone makes study in this area extremely interesting,
its obvious practical importance makes it imperative that we understand
the mechanisms. Techniques required for these investigations will
include low temperature measurements and radioactive tracer studies
as well as the conventional electrical and optical observations.

II. Surface and Interface Studies

No semiconductor laboratory seems complete without its surface studies.
The historical role of surfaces on yield and reliability of semiconductor
devices certainly justify this extensive effort. Our approach can be
somewhat different than have been those of other companies, since we
feel that the problem is basically solved by our protected structures.
This type structure now allows us to study the silicon -- silicon
oxide interface in some detail. Early experiments have shown unexpected
electrical effects at this interface. Control of these effects is
important in our protected structures. The understanding of these
interfaces may result in new device ideas as well as shed some light
on the role of oxygen in silicon.

III. Semiconductor Films and Epitaxial Growth of Small Crystals

The possibility of replacing single crystal wafers with evaporated or
chemically deposited films of semiconductor material offers potentially
considerable advantages in fabrication ease and certain device properties.
At present such ideas are a long way from realization. Considerable work
must be done before one can hope to realize the potential advantages.
We propose to study such films and to develop technology to handle and
use them. As an example of a potential advantage of this method is the
possibility of doping during deposition by decomposition from the gas
phase. This would allow one to tailor impurity concentration profiles
to a degree presently unobtainable.

IV. Silicon

There are still problems and strange phenomena in silicon that it would
be in our best interest to understand. Also, the study of other ways
of growing crystals and the growth of crystals with special properties
is necessary.

V. Thin Film Metallurgy

An important part of our processing involves the alloying of thin metal
films to silicon. This has been done on an empirical basis that does
not assure that the final process is optimum. In order to improve this

R. Hodgson   Summary of Projected R&D Program for 1960
Page 5   GEM -- 11/5/59

----

area, we need to do more basic work in these systems where the usual
metal-semiconductor results are modified by the important effects of surface energy and trace impurities.

VI.   Diffusion

Our present devices are about up to the limit of our diffusion technology. There are several areas into which the technology can be
extended. We plan to improve the control of concentrations and to
explore such possibilities as out-diffusion (diffusion of impurities out
of rather than into the silicon), and the diffusion of impurities other
than the standard onces. We hope to obtain such practical results as
a method of controlling storage time in PNP transistors.

One of our advantages up until now has been our ability to shift emphasis
as the need and/or opportunity arose. We will try to preserve this to a
considerable extent, but will maintain the continuity of some long range
efforts. Beyond doubt, the above list will be extended several times before
the end of 1960 and some of the projects suggested above will die in their
infancy.

                                                   Gordon E. Moore

GEM:hb

bcc: J. Hoerni
      J. Last
      C. S. Roberts
      W. Waring

problems that the firm encountered in *manufacturing*. Fundamental studies could lead to both new products and a greater mastery of existing production technology.[136]

To strengthen Fairchild Semiconductor's position in the silicon transistors business, Moore called for the development of a large family of planar transistors. By November 1959, Fairchild's pre-production engineers had made significant strides in bringing the planar version of the 2N696, Fairchild's first NPN mesa transistor, to the manufacturing stage. This transistor would be introduced at the Institute of Radio Engineers convention in New York in March 1960. Moore was interested in converting all the firm's products to planar versions. He also advocated the development of new planar transistors for a variety of radio-frequency (r.f.), power, and digital applications. This strategy—building an entire family of products—was common in the semiconductor industry, and indeed in the entire electronics industry, at the time. The goal was to market all the components that a customer would need for a particular product or system.[137]

In another departure from earlier strategies, Moore proposed to develop two new planar transistors aimed at *commercial* applications. So far, the firm had focused exclusively on the military market. As Moore was aware, expanding into the commercial market would require substantial cuts in manufacturing costs. Commercial customers were much more price-conscious and price-constrained than military contractors. In other words, silicon transistors would have to be offered at prices approaching those of germanium transistors, the transistors then used in commercial equipment. To reduce manufacturing costs, Moore proposed to "optimize" the construction of planar transistors.[138]

Building on the expertise the firm had acquired in transistors, Moore advocated the design of two new categories of products—planar diodes and microcircuits —for 1960. In the summer and fall of 1959, Hoerni revived the planar diode idea he had mentioned at a staff meeting nearly a year earlier. Hoerni had learned that the mesa silicon diodes then on the market suffered from the same reliability problems as Fairchild Semiconductor's first mesa transistors. Dust and other small particles attracted to the exposed junction could cause the device to fail. This created a potential market for planar diodes among reliability-conscious military contractors. Intent on exploiting this business opportunity, Hoerni designed planar diodes. In collaboration with Frank Grady, the firm's operations manager, he pushed the firm to go into the diode business and to build a new plant dedicated to diode manufacturing. Hoerni's advocacy was successful. Fairchild Semiconductor introduced planar diodes to the market in March 1960 at the same time it announced its first planar transistor.[139]

Another research thrust advocated by Moore was in the area of microcircuitry. In his memorandum, Moore developed the argument that it would be economically feasible to make planar integrated circuits, and that this was "a most important point that had not been recognized by others." (See page 2 of memorandum.) Perhaps the most prominent of these "others" was Bell Labs, where the top leaders espoused the view that semiconductor integrated circuits would be extremely difficult if not impossible to produce economically. Each component on the integrated circuit would individually have a low manufacturing yield, and as a result the yield for the whole circuit would be very close to zero. This view was advocated by Jack Morton, the vice president in charge of the semiconductor program at Bell Labs, and it led him to set aside promising work in the direction of silicon integrated circuits and to focus the Labs' resources on the development of hybrid circuits.[140]

In contrast, the stance of Moore and his colleagues at Fairchild Semiconductor was that it was not the yield of each individual component in the integrated circuit that was meaningful, but rather the yield of the integrated circuit as a whole. What was important was for the individual components to perform well enough for the overall integrated circuit to meet its desired specifications, not whether or not each of the individual components met some set of specifications. Moreover, drawing on their close scrutiny of the yield of transistors in manufacturing, Moore and his colleagues were learning that defects were not evenly and randomly distributed across wafers during manufacturing. That is, defects were clustered, and thus there were regions of high yields and lower yields on a single wafer. By extension, this implied that the Fairchild Semiconductor's researchers might expect to observe the same high-yield regions in making planar integrated circuits. These perspectives overturned the prevailing economic argument against semiconductor integrated circuits. Moore and his colleagues held that, as engineers gained more experience in the production of integrated circuits, the manufacturing cost for an integrated circuit would be less than the cost for an equivalent circuit built from assemblies of discrete components. This realization gave significant impetus to the "microcircuitry" program at Fairchild Semiconductor.[141]

By November 1959, Jay Last (with input from Victor Grinich and from Robert Norman, a systems engineer who had joined Fairchild Semiconductor from Sperry in August) had defined the broad outlines of this microcircuitry program. Fairchild Semiconductor would focus on making planar integrated circuits and would design a whole family of circuits that could be used in digital computers for aerospace applications. Much of this work would be collaborative. It would require close interaction between circuit engineers (Norman and his group) and device and process experts (Last and his team). Moore called for the investment of significant resources to make digital integrated circuits a reality.[142]

In addition to these product-oriented programs, Moore promoted a shift to basic research in order to strengthen the firm's processing and design capabilities. In particular, he called for research projects aimed at gaining a better understanding of manufacturing processes, especially the planar process. For example, he advocated studying the interface between the silicon oxide layer and the silicon crystal, which he presciently viewed as critical both for improving the manufacturing process and for developing new devices based on surface effects. Another area of research identified in Moore's memorandum was crystal growing, especially the forming of very thin crystal layers by epitaxy. Epitaxy is a process whereby a layer of silicon crystal is deposited onto a silicon wafer, matching the crystal structure of the underlying wafer. This was another approach to forming layers of P-type, N-type, and intrinsic silicon that could be used in device production. In 1961 and 1962, epitaxy emerged as a critical process for the manufacture of silicon transistors and planar integrated circuits.[143] Moore's memorandum also called for "basic" research on diffusion, aluminum films, and imperfections in silicon crystals, all of which were essential to the fabrication of advanced products and were known to affect manufacturing yields.

Hodgson and Noyce supported the research program outlined by Moore. Financial resources did not figure in their decision. The substantial profits generated by the firm's family of mesa transistors financed the laboratory's expansion in 1960. With this expansion, results came rapidly throughout the year. The laboratory's device-development section designed a family of planar transistors and diodes. Last and his group fabricated the first planar integrated circuits and started the development of an entire family of digital integrated circuits. Hoerni and the physics section initiated new studies on epitaxy and field-effect transistors. But the development of a commercial transistor (referred to internally as the "cheapie") failed. When it became clear that the cheapie would not appreciably lower the cost of planar transistors, Moore wound the project down in late 1960.[144]

Beyond these immediate outcomes, Moore consistently used the underlying strategy of his 1959 memorandum to guide Fairchild Semiconductor's research and development in the first half of the 1960s. A much greater emphasis was given to basic research. For example, Andrew Grove, Edward Snow, and Bruce Deal conducted fundamental studies on the interface between silicon and silicon oxide. They discovered that sodium and certain other elements severely degraded the electrical characteristics of transistors, particularly a very new form of transistor known as the MOS field-effect transistor. The work of Grove, Snow, and Deal was an important step in the development of MOS transistors and integrated circuits, which would come to dominate semiconductor electronics in the 1970s.

By 1968, when Gordon Moore left Fairchild Semiconductor to co-found the Intel Corporation, the Fairchild Semiconductor laboratory was the most productive and innovative R&D operation in the semiconductor industry. It had also become a large organization in its own right, with more than 600 scientists and technicians.[145]

Leadwire, **Volume 1, Number 5**

November 1959

The November 1959 issue of Fairchild Semiconductor's employee newsletter contained two articles that covered transformational changes at the company in the past several months. The first of these changes was a new round of major physical and business expansions, with related changes and additions to the management of the firm; the second was the purchase of Fairchild Semiconductor by Fairchild Camera and Instrument at the end of September 1959 in an exchange of stock valued at $3 million.[146] These developments were profoundly changing the nature of Fairchild Semiconductor, and they were to have lasting consequences for Fairchild Semiconductor's future and for the future of the silicon semiconductor industry more generally.[147]

The headlines on the front page of the November *Leadwire* announced a substantial "expansion program" well underway at the firm during the fall of 1959: "FSC TO BUILD MILLION DOLLAR DIODE PLANT" and "$75[0],000 Addition For Mountain View." ("$75,000" was a typographical error.) North of San Francisco, in San Rafael, a million-dollar plant for the mass production of diodes was planned to be completed by June 1960. In January, diode production was to begin in a smaller rented facility in San Rafael while the new plant was under construction. South of San Francisco, in Mountain View, Fairchild Semiconductor's transistor plant, constructed the year before at a cost of $1 million, was to undergo a major expansion at the end of 1959. As one of the articles pointed out, the expansion would "double the space we now have." In addition to this combined $1.75 million capital investment in manufacturing plants, plans to create a new R&D facility in Mountain View were already underway. (In 1962, a large new R&D facility was opened, but located in the Stanford Industrial Park in Palo Alto.[148]) These capital investments represented a third round of financing by Fairchild Camera and Instrument. The first round had been Fairchild Camera and Instrument's initial investment of $1.38 million in funding to start Fairchild Semiconductor and bring the mesa transistor to production. The second round had come in 1958, when $1 million had been invested to build the transistor manufacturing plant in Mountain View.[149]

The diode plant represented an expansion of Fairchild Semiconductor's business in silicon devices to include the mass production of silicon diodes. The diodes that Fairchild Semiconductor planned to produce at the San Rafael plant were planar diodes with gold doping—high-speed switches for digital computers. Fairchild Semiconductor's leaders looked at the planar diode business as one defined by low-cost, extremely high-volume production. This emphasis on mass production was evident in the details that *Leadwire* provided on the individuals who had come to fill the "key positions" in the diode operation. Robert E. Freund, who would act as assistant division manager and head of engineering for the diode operation, was poached from Hughes' silicon diode manufacturing organization, where he had been an engineering manager. Irving Michaelson, who

Vol. I, No. 5   Fairchild Semiconductor Corp., Mountain View, Calif.   November 1959

FSC TO BUILD MILLION DOLLAR DIODE PLANT

Bob Freund Will Manage Marin Facility

Our million-dollar diode plant in Marin County will be another first for Fairchild. When the 50,000-square-foot installation is completed in June 1960, we will be the only major industry in the area.

The exact location of the 10-acre site is two miles north of San Rafael on the east side of Highway 101 just inside the north city limits.

The plant will be built facing the frontage road just off the freeway. In case you're

BOB FREUND

driving up that way, the property is approximately across from the Terra Linda housing development. The building will be built to our own specifications and every detail has been planned to make the plant an ideal facility for semi-conductor production.

Until the new plant is finished, diode manufacturing will be housed in temporary leased quarters in San Rafael. There a 5,000-square-foot facility is being readied for operation by January 1, 1960.

Now a pilot line is in the process of being established in the Research and Development Laboratory, where three basic diodes are under development by the R & D group.

Choose High Level Staff

Frank Grady will manage the diode division. His assistant division manager and head of engineering will be Robert E. Freund, formerly manager of Diode and Rectifier Engineering at the Semiconductor Division of Hughes Aircraft Company, Newport Beach, California. Bob began work with Fairchild two weeks ago. He's a 1954 University of Pittsburgh graduate with a B.S. in physics. After receiving his degree, he was awarded a graduate assistantship at Pitt and also was chosen to be a research fellow with the Mellon Institute. In 1958 he went to Hughes Semiconductor, where he was appointed chief device engineer. Bob and his wife, Dolores, will live in San Francisco.

The entire management staff for the diode plant has not been completed but

so far the following people have been chosen to fill key positions:

Don Rogers, who's been our western regional sales manager, operating out of the Los Angeles office, will serve as diode sales manager; chief accountant will be Stan Vieth. Stan comes to us from Hughes Aircraft Company in Los Angeles. Bud Seyoer will leave his production supervisor job at Mountain View to become production manager. Irving Michaelson, manager of tooling, just joined us. He's been tooling manager for CBS-Hytron Division. Before that he occupied a similar position at Texas Instruments in Dallas. Niel Dorwood, a recent West Point graduate, will be production supervisor.

$75,000 Addition For Mountain View

Our plant here in Mountain View won't be left out of this expansion program. Fairchild will spend $750,000 on an addition to be started in December that will double the space we now have. The two construction programs will run concurrently.

By the time the Mountain View addition is complete, our plant plus utility and parking areas will have practically used up our 10-acre plot of ground. This means we will have to purchase more land in Mountain View when we get ready to build further additions. This time is not far off as it is planned to build entirely new separate facilities for R & D at Mountain View, so that the less-than-ideal Palo Alto location can be abandoned.

WHAT FCI STOCK PURCHASE MEANS

The recent purchase of Fairchild Semiconductor Corporation by Fairchild Camera and Instrument Company, still a frequent coffee-break topic, has raised points that should be clarified.

There was a time when businesses were built on the maxim, "Let this year's earnings pay for next year's expansion." Today this is unheard of. When FSC was formed, its founders had only their brains and experience to go on. They needed a few million dollars to make hardware immediately out of ideas which, if left dormant, would surely be picked up by others. Here the fabled backyard workshop approach was out of the question. To get off the ground spectacularly at the first attempt, a solid financial backing was necessary.

This backing did not come with no strings attached. Usually, when a large corporation finances the organization of (Continued on Page 2)

NUMBER OF EMPLOYEES
855

Bob Noyce talks to press at conference held by FCI recently at Waldorf Astoria in New York to release information on merger of FCI and FSC. Left is Richard Hodgson, executive vice president of FCI.

JIM NALL WINS HIGHEST PRIZE

Jim Nall, R & D Lab, is one of five who share in a $25,000 Department of Defense award for work in circuitry micro - miniaturiza-tion.

JIM NALL

Secretary of the Army Wilber M. Brucker presented this highest official award to Jim and his four colleagues in a Pentagon cere-mony recently.

Working as a science team at the Army's Diamond Ordnance Fuse Laboratories (DOFL), Washington, D.C., in 1957, the group developed a new process to fabricate printed micro-circuits. By using photog-raphy and lithography in combination with other techniques, they constructed sub-assemblies so small and compact that an electronic system can be made with 1,000 components per cubic inch compared to the 30 to 50 possible using conventional components.

This decrease in size and weight is of vital concern to space scientists, because it takes, for example, 12,000 lbs. of effi-cient Vanguard-type launching equip-ment to deliver a one-pound payload to Mars.

These tiny circuits also will be used to bring non-military products like wrist-watch radios and briefcase size electron-ic brains one step closer to a counter display at the corner department store.

FSC-FCI MERGER

(Continued from Page 1)

a new entity, the newcomer is either operated as a division of the parent com-pany with the parent having absolute control over its every move, or as a wholly owned subsidiary where the fledgling is responsible only in a loose sort of way to its benefactor. FSC be-came at the outset an affiliate of FCI, meaning that we had our own officers and policies and were connected to Syosset, Long Island, mainly by purse-strings.

Since FCI did not own us at the out-set, obviously they had to have some compensation for the risk they were taking in underwriting the organization of our Company. They put up funds and took in return an option to purchase us at any time within eight years after they "loaned" us the money to get started. If we had flopped, the "loan" would prob-ably have been written off as a bad debt. If, however, we boomed, they had the option to buy back FSC from its found-

Jim's printed micro-circuit process is very much like the photolithographic technique used in making offset (or litho-graph) printing plates. A pattern of cir-cuitry and components is created on a ceramic wafer by a photographic proc-ess. Then the process is completed by exposing the image to a special light to develop it. A series of these wafers can be stacked together to form a complete circuit sub-assembly. Because of extreme miniaturization, the work must be done under microscopes.

This is the third round of applause for the group's breakthrough in miniaturiza-tion. In January of 1958 Diamond Ord-nance Fuse Laboratories awarded them a Certificate of Achievement. In turn, DOFL was presented with the first an-nual Miniaturization Award (sponsored by Miniature Precision Bearings, Inc.).

Jim's colleagues in the DOFL team were T. A. Prugh, Silver Spring, Md.; Mrs. Edith M. Olson, Washington, D.C.; Norman J. Doctor, Wheaton, Md.; and Dr. Jay W. Lathrop, Dallas, Texas.

Joins DOFL in 1956

He joined our research staff in August of this year. Majoring in chemical engi-neering at the University of Kansas City, Jim's schooling was interrupted by a World War II tour of duty in the South Pacific with the Navy Medical Corps. He received his B.S. degree at George Wash-ington University in Washington, D.C., then joined the staff of the Electron Tube Laboratory at the National Bureau of Standards. In 1956 he transferred to the DOFL when it was separated from the Bureau. Jim, his wife, Lexie, and their two children live on Torwood Lane in Los Altos.

ers at any time at a previously agreed-upon price.

Trade for FCI Stock

Before the purchase, ownership of FSC was vested in a number of parties, including all of the original founders. The 1,065 outstanding shares of FSC stock had an indeterminate value since none had ever been traded on the open market. After the pooling of interests, the owners received shares of FCI stock instead of money. Thus the founders traded 100 percent ownership of an un-traded company for about 1/25th of the total outstanding common stock of FCI.

Gene Spencer, our administration manager, came to FSC in July from Lockheed's Missile and Space Division in Palo Alto, where he was Manager of Administrative Planning for their Research Department. Gene and his wife, Kath-ryn, are active in Los Altos PTA and Cub Scout-ing. This comes as no surprise when you know they have three sons, Mike, 10; Pat, 8; and Jeff, 5. Gene graduated from the University of California in 1949 with a B.A. degree in eco-nomics. His MBA degree in industrial manage-ment came from the University of Southern California.

PLAY HOST TO IRE GROUP

FSC played host on October 27 to nearly 100 computer engineers who held their monthly meeting at our plant. They were members of the Seventh Regional IRE Professional Group on Electronic Computers.

At 7:30 p.m. they saw the FSC color movie in the employee lunchroom, which was converted to a little theatre-lecture hall. A Cook's tour of the manufacturing facility came next. Guides Mary Allen, Wanda Chamberlain, Mary Eksa, Alma Ferguson, Carolyn Himsworth, Marilyn Jacobs, Betty McFadden, Flora Stone and Jan Wilson took the engineers through the production lines while swing shift assemblers were working so that the visitors could see actual transistor manufacture in progress.

At 8:30 Jay Last gave a short talk on his "hexistor," locally dubbed because of the six leads protruding from its case. The talk concerned microminiaturiza-tion as applied to computer electronics in general, as well as to the hexistor. After the talk, which was enthusias-tically received, the Party Givers served refreshments to the guests.

"LEADWIRE"

NEWS STAFF

Publisher .... Dick Lewis
Editor .... Rosemarie Daley Hensel
Sports Editor .... Doreen Hembrow
Make-Up .... Alex Karuzin
Reporters and Columnists: Mike Julian, *R & D Reporter*; Mary Sickinger, *Foreign Correspondent*

would develop manufacturing equipment for Fairchild Semiconductor's diode production, came from a similar position at the CBS-Hytron Division of CBS, a major manufacturer of miniaturized vacuum tubes. Fairchild Semiconductor had selected management for its diode operation that would bring into it established skills and approaches for mass manufacturing from existing diode producers and from the vacuum tube industry.[150]

The emphasis on driving down the costs of diode manufacturing marked another early move of Fairchild Semiconductor toward commercial markets in addition to the military market. If the costs of silicon diodes could be lowered, the devices might prove attractive to the producers of commercial computer systems, which at the time were prodigious consumers of diodes for logic circuits. This early tilt toward commercial markets fit the strategy laid out in Gordon Moore's comprehensive R&D report from this same month. In the report, Moore called for the development of two new transistors "whose construction and specification are optimized with respect to eventual manufacturing costs. This pair of devices should allow us to establish a large commercial market."[151]

While diode expansion brought in new staff familiar with mass manufacturing from the worlds of diodes and vacuum tubes, it also provided new openings into which established managers could be moved in order to make way for outside manufacturing experts to be brought into the firm to discipline transistor manufacturing. For example, Frank Grady, who had previously overseen transistor manufacturing, became the general manager of the diode division, and Charles Sporck was hired away from General Electric to apply that firm's famed manufacturing disciplines, skills, and structures to Fairchild Semiconductor's expanding transistor production.

The third headline on the front page of *Leadwire* was "WHAT FCI STOCK PURCHASE MEANS." At the end of September 1959, Fairchild Camera and Instrument made the decision to exercise its option to buy Fairchild Semiconductor in an exchange of stock. In the deal that established Fairchild Semiconductor, Fairchild Camera and Instrument agreed to lend the new company $1.38 million in exchange for an option to purchase it at a set price. Within two years, Fairchild Camera and Instrument would pay $3 million to buy Fairchild Semiconductor. From four to seven years out, the price would increase to $5 million. In the end, Fairchild Camera and Instrument waited just two years to exercise its option. Each of the eight founders had each purchased 100 shares in the firm when it was established, for $5 each. With the Fairchild Camera and Instrument purchase, these 100 shares were exchanged for roughly $250,000 worth of Fairchild Camera and Instrument stock. This was a substantial windfall—$250,000 was about 15 times Jay Last's then-current annual salary, and was enough to purchase four houses at the median home value in California for 1960. The other beneficiaries were Hayden Stone & Company (which had arranged Fairchild Camera's financing) and two Fairchild Semiconductor employees: Frank Grady (then head of transistor manufacturing) and Thomas Bay (the sales manager). When Richard Hodgson and the founders had recruited Ewart Baldwin as general manager in early 1958, they had offered him the option of buying 100 shares of Fairchild Semiconductor stock. Baldwin, however, never bought the stock.

After Baldwin defected to form Rheem Semiconductor, Bay and Grady were given the opportunity of buying into the company.[152]

For Fairchild Camera and Instrument (FCI), the close of 1959 was an extremely opportune moment to exercise its option on the promising new firm and also to pour additional funds into its continued expansion: Fairchild Camera's market capitalization had skyrocketed, making its acquisition of Fairchild Semiconductor by an exchange of stock very attractive financially. When FCI's top management had made their initial deal with Fairchild Semiconductor's founders, FCI's stock was trading in the 20s on the American Stock Exchange. In 1958, the value of the stock had roughly doubled, routinely trading in the 50s. In the summer of 1959, the value of the stock climbed wildly, quadrupling from its value the previous year to trade in the 200s in August 1959. While the stock slid in September and October to the mid 100s, it rebounded to the low 200s in November.[153]

The remarkable increase in the value of Fairchild Camera stock can be explained by the firm's expansion into a variety of electronics businesses and its successful entry into semiconductors through its financing of Fairchild Semiconductor. In the second half of the 1950s, Fairchild Camera became a mini-conglomerate. It acquired a series of electronics companies, many of them concerned with digital technologies. Another reason for the run-up in the value of Fairchild Camera stock was Wall Street's increasing infatuation with electronics in the late 1950s. Analysts and investors viewed electronics as a "growth industry" with significant potential for capital gains. A speculative movement into electronics and other "high technology" stocks ensued. (The term "high technology" emerged at that time to denote firms active in military-oriented technologies and businesses.) Fairchild Camera was a beneficiary of this speculative movement in "high technology" securities. But it was not the only one. Many electronics firms located on the San Francisco Peninsula, among them Hewlett-Packard and Varian Associates, saw the value of their stock climb in the late 1950s.[154]

FCI's purchase of Fairchild Semiconductor was a major topic of conversation at the latter firm in the fall of 1959: Why did it happen? What did it mean? Who else should share in the financial windfall? *Leadwire* addressed some of these questions, but its coverage could not put this "coffee-break topic" to rest. The purchase generated a great store of entrepreneurial energy within Fairchild Semiconductor, which would have great consequence for the expansion of the semiconductor industry in Silicon Valley. For the founders, the purchase meant that they were able to make decisions about their careers and futures with few personal financial constraints. This financial independence, along with their conversion from owners to employees, created an inherent instability in their relations with Fairchild Semiconductor and Fairchild Camera and Instrument. In addition, David Allison and some other members of the staff felt slighted that they had not shared in the financial windfall. Others simply took inspiration from the founders' success, and contemplated doing the same thing for themselves.[155]

This buildup of entrepreneurial energy at Fairchild Semiconductor, generated by the FCI purchase, was a major factor in the waves of departures and spin-offs from the firm in the early 1960s. At the start of 1961, Jean Hoerni and Jay Last left to found Amelco, Teledyne's division specializing in silicon integrated circuits. Sheldon Roberts and Eugene Kleiner soon joined them at Amelco. That same year, a significant fraction of Fairchild's integrated circuit organization joined with Allison to form Signetics, another producer of silicon integrated circuits. At the end of 1962, another group of engineers, led by Bob Norman, left Fairchild to found yet another manufacturer of integrated circuits, General Micro-electronics.

The second page of the November 1959 *Leadwire* contained an article on James Nall, a chemist in Fairchild Semiconductor's R&D lab who had won an award from the U.S. military for his work on microcircuitry. Nall's experience provides a telling illustration of the entrepreneurial ferment that followed the purchase of Fairchild Semiconductor by Fairchild Camera and Instrument. Nall had developed the photolithographic approach to semiconductor fabrication while working closely with Jay Lathrop at the Diamond Ordinance Fuze Laboratory in 1957–58. In August 1959, Nall brought his photolithography expertise to Fairchild Semiconductor's integrated circuit effort. He stayed at Fairchild Semiconductor only until 1962, when he left to form his own integrated circuit company, Molectro.[156]

Within about two years, then, the centripetal forces created by the perceived promise of planar integrated circuits and the entrepreneurial energies produced by the Fairchild Camera acquisition caused Fairchild Semiconductor to lose many of its technological leaders to spin-offs. These Fairchild losses were Silicon Valley's gain, as these spin-offs further established the region as a center for semiconductor electronics.[157]

Device Drawing

22 December 1959

Lionel Kattner

Lionel Kattner designed the pattern of metal interconnections for the first planar integrated circuit, a "flip-flop," in December 1959.[158] Flip-flops were circuits that could operate in one of two states, providing a basic building block for digital computer logic.

Kattner had worked at Fairchild Semiconductor for about five months. The son of a pastor who ministered to German communities in Oklahoma and South Texas, Kattner had received a bachelor's degree in chemistry from Southern Methodist University. He had worked as a chemical engineer at the Hanford Works, the nuclear complex in Washington State, where he had helped design a chemical process for the separation of plutonium. Enlisting in the military at the end of the Korean War, he had become an officer and handled nuclear components for the Navy. In 1958, he had joined Texas Instruments, where he became a product engineer on a manufacturing line for germanium mesa transistors. Unsatisfied with Texas Instruments' "brute force" approach to semiconductor engineering, he had accepted a position in the R&D laboratory of Fairchild Semiconductor in July 1959. In the next several months, he learned about silicon technology and photomasking before joining Jay Last's "microcircuit" research group.[159]

In September 1959, Robert Noyce asked Jay Last to establish a new research group focusing on microcircuits. Among the technologists Last recruited to the group were Kattner, Isy Haas (a circuit engineer who had previously worked in the device evaluation section), and James Nall (a new hire who had pioneered photolithography techniques at the Diamond Ordnance Fuze Laboratory). The group worked closely with Robert Norman, a circuit and systems engineer who headed Fairchild's device evaluation organization. Last's and Norman's main goal was to fabricate planar integrated circuits.[160] These circuits would be made of planar devices interconnected by a layer of aluminum deposited on top of a protective and insulating layer of silicon oxide covering the devices in the silicon crystal.

Members of this group—which soon became known by the marketing term for Fairchild's planar integrated circuits and hybrid circuits, "Micrologic"—designed a family of hybrid circuits and a family of planar integrated circuits for digital computers in aerospace (primarily military) systems. Digital circuits could be made using a variety of logic forms, distinguished by the types of components used to form the circuits and how these components were connected. Fairchild Semiconductor's family of planar integrated circuits was designed for the direct-coupled transistor logic (DCTL) form. DCTL was a well-known circuit configuration at the time. It had been pioneered at Philco. It had been used in a number of advanced digital computers sponsored by the military. It had an advantage of simplicity, requiring only transistors and resistors. Creating silicon transistors particularly suited to DCTL circuits had been among the earliest of Fairchild's

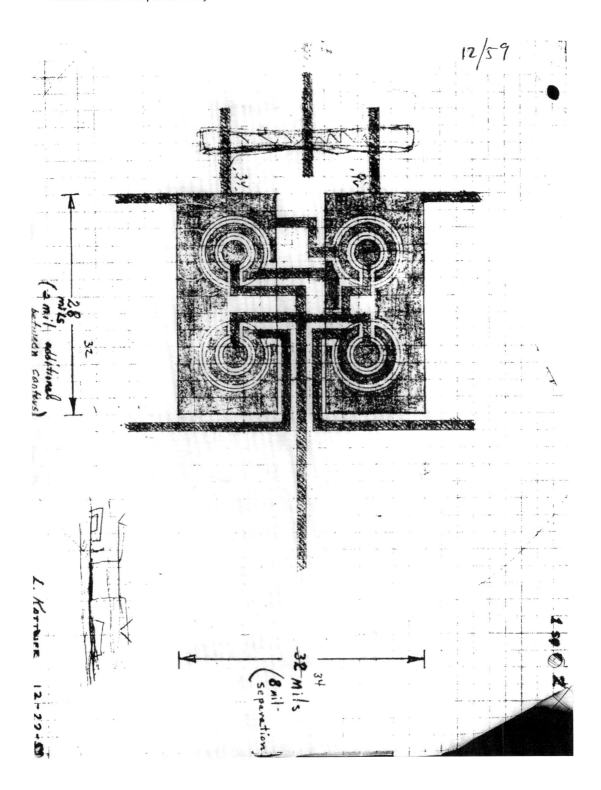

R&D goals. Indeed, given Fairchild's expertise in transistor fabrication, Last and Norman expected that DCTL integrated circuits would be less difficult for them to manufacture than circuits of other logic forms. Moreover, many of Fairchild Semiconductor's customers for transistors, the makers of aerospace computer systems, would be familiar with DCTL.[161]

Fabrication challenges were uppermost in Last's and his group's concerns. The family of digital circuits could be designed relatively easily. The major question was how to fabricate them. A particularly difficult issue was determining how to electrically isolate the different transistors in the same silicon chip from one another. Several possible means appeared to be impractical. In his patent application on the device-and-lead structure (interconnections) for the planar integrated circuit of July 1959, Robert Noyce had proposed using transistors formed with three diffusions (collector, base, and emitter), which would make the transistors electrically isolated from one another. Unfortunately, Fairchild Semiconductor's engineers did not have the capability of making triple-diffused transistors. Diffusing the base and emitter regions into a diffused collector ruined the collector's electrical characteristics.[162] Additionally, Noyce had suggested using diffusions from both the back and the front of wafers to form insulating wells or trenches in his patent applications of September 1959 on isolation schemes for planar integrated circuits. The prospect of diffusing boron completely through the wafer was a daunting one for the Micrologic team, as such long diffusions would be very difficult to control and would cause significant damage to the wafer.[163] This approach seemed impractical. At that time, boron diffusions lasting 15 minutes were a challenge. Diffusing boron for 20 hours—the duration that would be required for making the isolation regions—was out of the question.[164]

These considerations led Last to conceive another isolation scheme in the fall of 1959. He thought of creating isolation regions by physically inserting an insulating material between the transistors in the same circuit. As depicted in the rough sketch at bottom left of Kattner's interconnect pattern, the circuit would be made of planar transistors (depicted sideways in the sketch). A deep trench, reaching up to the silicon oxide layer on top of the silicon wafer, would separate the transistors. This trench would then be filled with an insulating material such as epoxy. Thereby, all transistors on the chip would be isolated from each other. An aluminum pattern on top of the silicon oxide layer would interconnect the transistors on the chip, creating an electronic circuit.[165]

Last decided that his team should first pursue this "physical isolation" approach because he judged it the most immediately promising route and thought that it would prove that it was in fact possible to make a functioning planar integrated circuit. The vehicle for this effort, Last decided, would be a DCTL flip-flop—a simple circuit requiring only four transistors and a resistor. (Last's first hybrid circuit also had been a flip-flop.) Norman did the circuit engineering for the flip-flop while Last and his group worked on the processing. An important task in the processing efforts was to design the aluminum interconnection pattern that would link the transistors and the resistor electrically. The group went through several iterations of this interconnection design. On 2 December 1959, Kattner devised and drew the final version. This drawing was used to make the masks for the actual fabrication of the aluminum pattern on the flip-flop circuit.[166]

Noticeable in Kattner's drawing are the four transistors (the circular shapes) and the resistor (the rectangular shape at the top of the interconnect pattern). Two pairs of transistors can be distinguished. These transistor pairs were separated by a moat-like structure corresponding to the epoxy-filled grooves on the back of the wafer.[167] Another moat-like structure separated the transistor pairs from the resistor. The dark lines and regions represented the aluminum layer forming the transistor contacts and interconnecting the five components on the chip. The aluminum film covered much of the chip's surface. Kattner expected the film to crack in some areas, and he reasoned that additional aluminum coverage would help mitigate the effects of these cracks. Kattner's expectation of cracking was due to the fact that the aluminum pattern would cover a chip made of different materials (epoxy, silicon, silicon oxide), bringing in mechanical instabilities. The chip would create stress and strain in the aluminum film.[168]

Kattner's drawing also recorded changes in the flip-flop's interconnect pattern. At first, Kattner worked with the idea of having a pattern interconnecting the four transistors that would be 32 mils by 28 mils. (A mil is a thousandth of an inch.) His goal was to make the transistors as small as possible so that they would occupy the smallest possible area on the chip. Kattner later realized that the separation between the two transistors in a pair was not wide enough. The phosphorus and boron diffusions used to make the base and emitter regions of the transistors would spread out laterally, and as a result the two transistors would overlap each other. This led Kattner to expand the separations between the transistors, which in turn translated in larger overall dimensions for the flip-flop's interconnect pattern. The final dimensions were 34 mils by 32 mils.[169]

Designing the interconnect pattern was the first of many steps required to make a physically isolated flip-flop circuit. Indeed, the fabrication of such a planar integrated circuit stretched Fairchild Semiconductor's manufacturing technology to the limit. Making the flip-flop would require significantly better control of the lateral and vertical dimensions of the transistors and would necessitate notable improvements in diffusion. Making a physically isolated flip-flop also created materials problems and processing problems that the firm had never faced before. For example, the group had to find insulating materials with the same coefficient of expansion as silicon in order to fill the grooves isolating the different transistors. Without such a material, the silicon oxide layer and the aluminum film on top of the chip would fatally crack with changes in temperature. Another important problem was aligning the trenches formed in the back of the wafer with the transistors diffused from the top. Precise alignment was essential to the fabrication of a functional flip-flop.[170]

Entry in Patent Notebook

23 February 1960

Jay Last

Jay Last, Lionel Kattner, and other members of the Micrologic group were well on their way to fabricating a physically isolated planar integrated circuit by February 1960.[171] The idea of the physically isolated integrated circuit that Last had proposed in the fall of 1959 was now sufficiently promising that he wrote a two-page entry covering it in his patent notebook (a separate volume from his personal notebook) on 23 February 1960. His goal in doing so was to secure the physically isolated circuit idea as Fairchild Semiconductor's intellectual property. Texas Instruments, Fairchild Semiconductor's chief competitor, was particularly aggressive in filing for and enforcing patents. It was also clear that Texas Instruments was intent on establishing a strong patent position in integrated circuits. As a result, it was imperative for Fairchild Semiconductor to file patent applications on integrated circuits as well. The firm had to build its own patent portfolio in order to defend itself against Texas Instruments. Fairchild Semiconductor's leaders were less concerned about being precluded from pursuing the integrated circuit business by patent interference lawsuits (this was impossible in the intellectual property regime of the late 1950s and the early 1960s) than about avoiding having to pay large licensing fees to Texas Instruments. A solid patent portfolio of its own would give Fairchild Semiconductor a strong bargaining position in negotiations with Texas Instruments. Similar reasoning was at work in Fairchild Semiconductor's filing of the patent applications on gold doping, the planar process, and the planar integrated circuit in the spring and summer of 1959.[172]

In his patent notebook, Last summarized his ideas for physically isolated integrated circuits (referred to here as "micrologic elements"). He proposed to isolate the various devices in the same chip by etching grooves between them and by filling these grooves with an insulating material such as epoxy. In his entry, Last described the process by which physically isolated integrated circuits could be produced. He proposed etching a groove on the back of the silicon wafer and having this groove reach up to the silicon oxide layer on top of the silicon wafer. The groove would then be filled with epoxy. This scheme created isolated islands of silicon crystal where transistors and other devices could then be fabricated. Evaporating an aluminum pattern on top of the silicon oxide layer would then interconnect these devices. Using this notebook entry, John Ralls, Fairchild Semiconductor's patent lawyer, filed two patent applications on August 15, 1960: "Solid-State Circuitry Having Discrete Regions of Semiconductor Material Isolated by an Insulating Material" and "Method of Making Solid-State Circuitry." Patents were issued in 1964 and 1967 respectively.[173]

58   2/23/60

<u>Physical isolation of micrologic elements</u>

The problem exists in our micrologic elements of separating
electrically collectors of various transistors making up the circuit.
This can be done ~~ellll~~ by diffusing in an insulating layer or the
like (see patent application of Noyce) or by physically separating
the devices. For physical isolation, the oxide on the surface
can be used to keep the structure mechanically intact, and to
allow leads, deposited before etching, to remain
continuous ~~llllll~~ after the devices are physically
separated. This eliminates the problem of having to
make an electrical connection across the moat.
The desired structure (not to scale)

thermally grown oxide

shown for case where 2 bases are connected   evap Alum.   thermally grown oxide

epoxy filled

59

the set of processing operations to accomplish this (the transistor and leads are omitted for simplicity - only the oxide layer is shown.

black wax protector
oxide
Si

Area to be removed.

Paint with wax or use thermally grown oxide in the proper pattern.

black wax
oxide
Si
wax or thermally grown oxide

now etch with an etch + etching procedure that gives

a high ratio of $\dfrac{Si \ etching \ rate}{SiO_2 \ etching \ rate}$ (preferably ∞)

Etch out the dotted area.

Pot with epoxy. - Remove black wax - coat with epoxy on top surface for mech. strength + stability. the desired structure is thus obtained.

similar material

EPOXY
SiO2
Si
Si
EPOXY

JHart
2/23/60

Entry in Patent Notebook

26 May 1960

Lionel Kattner

In March 1960, Lionel Kattner began to focus on the fabrication of physically isolated integrated circuits.[174] At the end of May, after a few unsuccessful attempts, he fabricated the first functional planar integrated circuit: the flip-flop for which he had designed the interconnection pattern. This entry in Kattner's patent notebook (titled "FF-105," after the experimental run number) records the steps Kattner followed in making the flip-flop circuits.[175] The complexity of the process is striking. There were 44 steps. Most of the steps were chemical in nature and involved the use of a wide variety of substances: epoxy, waxes, photoresists, solvents (including acetone and trichloroethylene), and etchants (including hydrofluoric acid, nitric acid, and various mixtures of these acids). Ammonium fluoride was used to decompose the silicon oxide layer. Toxic boron and phosphorus-based gases were used in diffusion.[176]

Two sequences within the fabrication steps can be distinguished in Kattner's notes. In the first part of the process (described in the first two pages of his notebook entry), Kattner employed Fairchild Semiconductor's techniques for making planar NPN transistors. These included a succession of oxidation, photomasking, etching, and diffusion steps. Kattner even employed gold doping, the technique Jean Hoerni had developed to increase the switching speed of NPN transistors. Kattner then evaporated aluminum on top of the wafer. Using the pattern he had drawn by hand in December 1959, Kattner selectively etched out the aluminum film to form the flip-flop's interconnection pattern on top of the chip.

In the second part of the process (described on the third page of the notebook entry), Kattner employed novel techniques that had been developed by other engineers in the Micrologic group for the sole purpose of fabricating physically isolated integrated circuits. For example, he used etching techniques perfected by the group to create grooves in the silicon crystal without damaging the silicon oxide. (The etchant was a mixture of nitric and hydrofluoric acid originally developed at Bell Labs.) The precise alignment of the transistors processed on top of the silicon chip with the grooves on the back of the chip was critical. To align the transistors with the grooves, Kattner employed a complex optical apparatus conceived by Jay Last and engineered by Jim Nall. Exploiting the fact that silicon is transparent to infrared light, this equipment enabled them to "look" through the wafer and line up the aluminum interconnect pattern with the isolating grooves on the back of the wafer.[177]

Indicative of the delicacy and complexity of Kattner's process was its yield, the percentage of good circuits coming out of the fabrication process. Kattner had started with 27 wafers, each containing 70 potential circuits. He obtained only one functional

<u>FF-105</u>   <u>5-26-60</u>

Started 27 N Type .4-.5 Ω cm wafers
which were previously etched to ~ 130μ thick
These wafers were then cleaned and oxidized
for 1 hr @ 1160°C using wet O_2 (Flowrater
SA 18008, flow rate of 19, water bath with
variac @ 20v

Ten wafers were coated with KPR & spun
& dried @ 100°C for 2 min.   (30 sec @ 3200 RPM)
Wafers then exposed using FF-1 mask (base
diffusion) with carbon arc lamp for 10 sec.
Wafers then developed in Hot TCE vapors
for 30 sec followed by bake for 25 min
@ 150°C
Wafers then etched in ammonium fluoride
etch (~ 10 min) until oxide removed.
Wafers then placed in acetone & KPR
striped with cotton swab.
Wafers then subjected to boron pre-dep
in furn 36 U @ 1034°C (see procedure)
Resultant $V/I = 14$ Ω
Wafers then diffused with boron in (7U)
$V/I = 31$, $x_j = 19-20$ fringes
(See Boron diff procedure) $1° = .273$ fringes

Wafers then processed in photoresist using mask # FF 2 (Emitter collector oxide removal) Wafers given phosphorus predep for 45 min @ 1010°C using dry N_2 in Flowrater #SA18202 with flow of 1. Resultant V/I of .81 Ω (desired I = .9 Ω)

Wafers were then etched in HF on backside only followed by gold evap of ~.1 mil thick. Wafers then diffused @ 1000°C for 18 min. Backside of wafers were etched using aP-8 to remove excess gold & chemically polish surface to wafer thickness of 70-80 μ.

Wafers then subjected to Emitter diffusion – oxidation step. 15 min @ 1000°C with dry O_2 Flowrater #SA18202, flow of 5. Followed by bubbling O_2 in hot H_2O for 3 hrs and 15 min.

Wafers then given photoresist step oxide removal FF-3 mask (backside oxide masked)

Wafers then evaporated with Aluminum 50 mg with wafer temp @ ~300°C followed by 50mg al with wafer cold

Wafers then applied with KPR & exposed with mask # FF-4 & metal removed in NaOH. KPR not stripped.

Wafers then alloyed for 4 min @ 582°C (KPR-oops)

Wafers then KPR'd on backs only. Using infra red source & detector mask #FF-5 lined up with aluminum pattern on front side, then exposed & oxide etched.

Wafers then mounted face down in glycol phthalate wax on slide. A jet of CP-6 etch alternately ~ 5 sec intervals was used to etch thru silicon leaving islands masked by oxide.

Wafers then lined up with teflon mold and cavities filled with furane epoxy Type 3 & cured 1 hrs @ 40°C followed by 3 hrs @ 80°C & then glycol phthalate, heated to flow point and mold with epoxial units removed. Units removed from mold & given additional cure of 150°C for 1 hr.

These units then mounted in 8 pin TO-18 headers using gold epoxy to connect swap flip flop pattern to pins. All epoxy then cured for 3 hr @ 150°C.

out of 10 units one was good however due to T_5 (gold lifetime control inadequate) operational freq was limited to .5 mc. Other units had open interconnections due to faulty casting of epoxy.

flip-flop, and it displayed poor electrical characteristics because of an ineffective gold doping step. Although this yield was abysmal, the making of a flip-flop circuit with physical isolation techniques was an important milestone in Fairchild Semiconductor's Micrologic program. It proved that it was indeed possible to make planar integrated circuits. In the next year, Last's research group capitalized on this finding and developed more practical ways of making integrated circuits.

Entries in Patent Notebook

7 August, 31 August, and 13 September 1960

Isy Haas

These entries in Isy Haas' patent notebook from September 1960 document the development of the first *electrically* isolated planar integrated circuit, the manufacturable form of such devices that would be the focus of development from this point forward.[178]

A native of Turkey, Haas had graduated from Robert College, an English-speaking school in Istanbul. He had then obtained a master's degree in engineering at Princeton University in 1957. After working as a circuit engineer at Univac, a producer of mainframe digital computers, he had joined Fairchild Semiconductor in July 1958. At Fairchild Semiconductor, he had worked in the device evaluation section of the R&D organization, under Victor Grinich, before joining Jay Last's Micrologic group in August 1959. In Last's group, Haas worked closely with Lionel Kattner. Haas designed DCTL circuits and engineered planar NPN transistors suitable for this DCTL circuitry. He also tested the physically isolated flip-flops that were fabricated by Kattner. To his consternation, Haas discovered that these flip-flops had significant reliability problems. The devices failed when they were subjected to temperature cycling tests, in which they experienced very low and very high temperatures (these tests were required for military products). The flip-flops' insulating material would expand and contract at these extreme temperatures. As a consequence, the layer of silicon oxide would crack, and that would result in broken interconnects. This reliability problem made it very difficult to bring the physically isolated integrated circuits into production.[179]

The poor reliability of physically isolated integrated circuits led Haas to contemplate other ways of isolating the components in a planar integrated circuit. Two such schemes had been proposed at Fairchild Semiconductor in the second half of 1959. In his patent application on interconnections for planar integrated circuits, Noyce described a circuit made of triple-diffused transistors. These triple-diffused transistors were isolated from one another by the junctions that these transistors formed with the surrounding P-type wafer. Noyce also proposed an alternative diffusion approach in his two patent applications on isolations for planar integrated circuits. In this alternate approach, wells or trenches formed by diffusing from both the top and the back of the wafer would provide isolation.[180]

Haas was aware that Noyce's idea of the triple diffused integrated circuit was not then technically feasible. Engineers in the R&D laboratory did not know how to control the collector characteristics of triple diffused transistors. However, Haas thought the idea of diffusing isolating wells through the wafer had real potential. (According to Kattner, the idea of reviving this diffused isolation scheme emerged in conversations he had with Haas.) Haas made calculations showing that it was possible to diffuse boron from both sides of the wafer in order to create a P-type well that would isolate NPN transistors

August 31, 1960   127

Electrical isolation

An effort is being made to obtain electrical isolation without actually having triple diffused transistor. The method used is probably not entirely original as the author recalls hearing of a similar approach. The present suggestion is to diffuse far enough boron in n type material uniformly from the back and around a specified geometry through the front thus having a device completely surrounded by reverse biased junction at all times. We also have the advantage of only having to

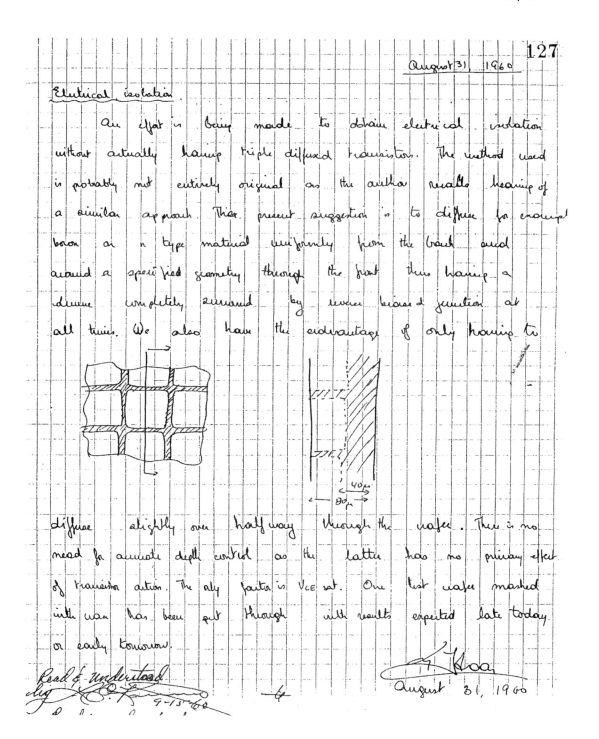

diffuse slightly over half way through the wafer. There is no need for accurate depth control as the latter has no primary effect of transistor action. The only factor is V_{CE} sat. One test wafer masked with wax has been put through with results expected late today or early tomorrow.

Read & Understood

9-13-60

August 31, 1960

20   August 7, 1960

Preliminary Results on Electrical Isolation.

Two test runs, one at 6 hrs & the other at 18 hrs
were made on 3 Ω-cm material. The first gave a
diffusion depth of 100 fringes (27μ) and the second a diffusion
depth of 180 fringes (49μ) The latter was repeated with the
right pattern (5th mask as FF) and will now be put through
the FF mill to make devices) Junction hardness was tested
and was found to have reputable leakage and breakdowns
greater that 40v at 10μa.

Read & Understood by   Read & understood
                      9-15-60   by Samuel D M Fox
                                   September 15, 1960   August 7, 1960

Preliminary results on diffused flip-flop.   September 13, 1960
        A few flip-flop wafers (run 139) were made from 3 Ω-cm
material. A couple of wafers were tested on the 3 point probe
with . L. Kattner and we have shown that :
        1) We have good transistor action (β ~ 20)
        2)   "   "   electrical isolation. Sharp breakdowns.
After metalizing, we had all around shorts (almost) and
it was decided that this is very probably due to the
insufficient oxide thickness grown on the base and emitter
surfaces. This run   consisted of   unglazed . 80μ

wafer.

The problems we have observed were:

1) The V_{CE} sats. were possibly high in some of the transistors but we can't be sure that this (0.8v) is not due to the improper contact.

2) The isolation current might not have been as low as it really should be for a f.f. to be proud of, but still this cannot be blamed on poor diode characteristics.

3) We definitely have poor contact problems because measurements on base input characteristics are completely inconsistent.

Conclusion:

I'll wager anything that we can make good electrically isolated flip-flops "if we can make good transistors to go on them"

Read & Understood by
9-15-60

September 13, 1960

Read & understood by C.
Samuel M. Fok September 15, 1960

from each other. Last supported him in this interest.[181] Haas and Kattner knew of recent advances in diffusion techniques made by the pre-production group in Fairchild Semi-conductor's plant in Mountain View and thought that these techniques made diffused isolation regions possible. The pre-production group had developed a boron diffusion process, using a new compound: methyl borate. This process was much more controllable than the processes based on boron oxide and boron trichloride that had been used previously at Fairchild Semiconductor.

The methyl borate process had the added advantage of not damaging the surface of the wafer as rapidly as earlier processes. This was extremely important, because the formation of isolation regions would require very long diffusions—on the order of 20 hours. In contrast, the conventional boron processes allowed only 15 minute diffusions. Longer diffusion times severely eroded the surface of the silicon wafer. In early August 1960, Haas and Kattner began experimenting with long methyl borate diffusions. According to Kattner, they did this on their own time at night or on weekends, while they devoted their workdays to addressing the reliability problems of physically isolated flip-flops.[182]

The entries in Haas' patent notebook document the various steps that he and Kattner took to make integrated circuits with diffused isolation, which they referred to as "electrically isolated" (in contrast to "physically isolated") devices. The 7 August entry discusses experiments that the two men designed to test the idea of using the methyl borate process to make isolation regions. They diffused boron from only one side of the wafer for 6 hours; then, in another experiment, they diffused it for 18 hours. In the second experiment, they obtained a P-type well that was 49 microns deep. This was a very promising result, as it proved that it was possible to diffuse both sides of a very thin wafer and have the diffused region meet in the middle. (The thinnest wafer the group could make at that time was 75 microns thick.) Haas and Kattner repeated the 18-hour experiment, this time creating a P-type isolating well with photomasking techniques. (For this they needed a fifth mask; the other four masks would be used to create the planar transistors.) They found that the P-type wells made with the methyl borate technique had good isolating properties. This entry was witnessed a week later by Kattner and by Samuel Fok, an engineer who worked on photolithographic techniques in Last's Micrologic group.

By 31 August, the electrically isolated integrated circuit appeared promising enough for Haas to document it in detail in his patent notebook. Haas' entry included two drawings: a view of the top of the wafer and a cross-section of the same wafer. These drawings showed the wells isolating semiconductor islands. NPN transistors and resistors would be formed in these islands.[183] (See notebook page 127.) Overall, Haas' structure looked very similar to the physically isolated integrated circuit, the main difference being that the isolation region was made of diffused silicon rather than an insulating material such as epoxy. Haas also recorded that in collaboration with Kattner he had recently processed P-type wells both from the top and the back of the wafer.

Haas' 13 September entry reported the results obtained on another batch of wafers. (See notebook page 128.) With this batch, Haas and Kattner had processed entire DCTL flip-flops. They had achieved good isolation regions and made functional transistors. But the circuits were marred by electrical shorts, which they attributed to insufficiently thick silicon oxide layers. These mixed results led Haas to write: "I will wager anything that we can make good electrically isolated flip-flops 'if we can make good transistors to go on them.'" Within two weeks, Haas and Kattner processed another batch of wafers and succeeded in creating functioning, electrically isolated flip-flops. Last, elated, devoted greater resources to the effort on electrically isolated integrated circuits. In the next few months, Kattner and Haas continually improved their processes for making these DCTL flip-flops. The Micrologic group also started to design an entire family of such DCTL digital circuits, starting with gates and moving to half-shift registers, half-adders, buffers, and counter adapters. These were all the digital circuits required for the central processing unit of a computer.[184]

Note on Micrologic Elements

22 September 1960

Robert Norman

At the request of Fairchild Semiconductor's sales organization, Robert Norman wrote this internal brief to provide the sales representatives with answers to questions that they felt they would have to answer in order to sell planar integrated circuits to actual customers.[185] Norman was the head of the device development section in the R&D department. A graduate of Oklahoma Agricultural and Mechanical College, Norman was a circuit and systems engineer. He had worked at Sperry Gyroscope, where he helped design small digital computers for submarines and the Sergeant and Polaris missiles. Norman, who had joined Fairchild Semiconductor in August 1959, soon became an important player in the Micrologic program. With his experience with logic circuits at Sperry, he helped convince Jay Last and Victor Grinich to choose DCTL as the logic form for the firm's first integrated circuits. Norman's suggestion found a receptive audience, since the firm had pursued an interest in designing a transistor specifically for DCTL since early 1958. Norman directed the design of Fairchild's family of DCTL integrated circuits and oversaw the testing of prototypes.[186]

Norman also aggressively promoted Fairchild Semiconductor's integrated circuit program to the electronics industry and the semiconductor research community. In the winter, spring, and summer of 1960, he gave talks on Fairchild Semiconductor's Micrologic devices at Wescon, at the IRE show in New York, at the Solid State Circuits Conference, and at a military conference on guidance and control systems. In these presentations, Norman consistently implied that the program was more advanced than it actually was. For example, at the IRE show in March 1960, Norman discussed the entire family of DCTL integrated circuits even though the Micrologic group had not yet fabricated the first physically isolated flip-flop. In this and other presentations, Norman usefully employed a deliberate ambiguity that Fairchild's managers had created by referring to both their hybrid circuits and their anticipated planar integrated circuits as "Micrologic elements." The talks that Norman presented at a number of venues in 1960 were intended to show that, like Texas Instruments, Fairchild Semiconductor was active in microcircuitry, that it was making significant progress, and that microcircuitry was an important new direction in electronics. Norman also wanted to alert systems engineers to the potential of integrated circuits for military computers. Perhaps most important, Norman understood that promotion was a fundamental component of innovation: one had to generate significant interest in a new technology for it to reach fruition.[187]

Norman's brief on Micrologic elements represented an additional step in his promotion of planar integrated circuits. He structured the brief around questions that would be of particular interest to systems engineers: What circuit functions will Fairchild Semiconductor provide? When will these circuits be on the market? How can they be used?

FAIRCHILD SEMICONDUCTOR CORPORATION

R & D DEPARTMENT

DEVICE EVALUATION SECTION

1. How does Fairchild propose customers accomplish testing of solid modules?

Micrologic elements are digital functional blocks and will have clearly defined specifications. These will establish by test that they do function and that they are compatible with other micrologic elements. A fairly simple test setup can be used for incoming inspection as well as customer reliability evaluation of all micrologic elements.

2. What in Fairchild's estimation are the problems purchasing people will encounter when selecting vendors?

The problems purchasing people will encounter are some of those encountered in dealing with any completely new type of part. Decisions in the next one to two years will be largely affected by engineering evaluations of the competitive parts. Some weight can be given to the past performance of the vendor in technological areas similar to those involved in making the micro-miniature modules. There is no point certainly for the next one to two years in expecting any sort of compatability among the products of different vendors. There may be in addition a wide variation in the reliability and usefulness of the products.

3. What circuit functions are presently available and what can be expected within a year?

No micrologic elements are presently available. Within a year the full family of elements will be available. This family includes:

1. Flip-flop
2. Half-shift Register
3. Half Adder
4. Buffer
5. Gate
6. Counter Adapter

These elements will be available in both the TO-5 and TO-18 size

- 2 -

packages. Output coupler elements capable of accepting micrologic
inputs and driving loads of the order of 100 V, 1 amp. are anticipated. It is not now known whether these will be available within
a year. No parts other than the above will normally be required in
a computer logic section.

4. How does this concept fit in with existing circuitry?

Micrologic elements can be fairly easily used to implement existing computer logical designs. These elements, thus, can be used
to build a logic section which can be readily adapted to be compatible with other portions of the system. In this case, the
whole logic section would be replaced. It would generally not be
feasible to replace circuits on an individual basis with micrologic elements.

5. Can it be integrated in part; or must it be designed system-wide?

As implied in the answer to question four above, it is generally
not economical to inter-mix micrologic elements with standard
circuitry. Micrologic is most economically used when the elements
are assembled as integral sub-units or units.

6. What are the overall characteristics regarding input and output, and are
they flexible enough to be tailored at buyer's specifications?

As implied in the answer to question one, the input and output characteristics of micrologic elements are designed to assure the compatability of the elements. The input characteristics are specified in
terms of equivalent micrologic loads. The output characteristics
are specified as micrologic load driving capability. Numerical test
methods are designed to assure this capability. Since these are
binary functional blocks, which either function compatibly or do not,
tailoring of specifications is not applicable.

7. Any comments on grown circuitry, wafer depositions and micro-circuitry?

Micrologic elements are fabricated by diffusing planar transistors
and resistors on a continuum of silicon and depositing interconnections on top. These elements are fabricated using the same batch
processing techniques used in the manufacture of transistors. For
this reason the cost and reliability figures on these elements are

- 3 -

expected to be very similar to those of planar transistors. The
TO-5 size package is basically a standard transistor package and
allows a lead configuration which is suitable for printed circuit
interconnection of these elements. The TO-18 size package which
will also be available will require more sophisticated interconnection techniques such as welded wire assembly.

How can they be tested? What should firms consider when they purchase integrated circuits? Norman promised a full family of digital integrated circuits within a year. He also stated that these circuits (referred to in the text as "micrologic elements," "solid modules," or "micro-miniature modules") would be standard, off-the-shelf components. In other words, the integrated circuits would not be tailored to the requirements of specific customers. The Micrologic circuits would be compatible with one another and would include all the circuits needed to make the central processing unit of a digital computer.

Prominent in Norman's brief was his discussion of the testing of integrated circuits. Testing was a central function within military systems firms. All semiconductor devices purchased by military contractors underwent rigorous "inspection" and testing before being assembled into systems. The issue of testing was particularly prominent for integrated circuits because they were entirely new types of components. Further, they required a shift from established methods for individual component testing to the testing of whole circuits. In his write-up, Norman argued that the testing of integrated circuits would not be as difficult as one might think, and that the circuits could be tested with a fairly simple set-up. Testing, however, would remain an important issue for integrated circuits in subsequent years. Indeed, the challenge of devising tests for integrated circuits proved to be one of the main obstacles to their widespread adoption in the electronics industry.[188]

In his brief, Norman discussed a broad range of factors that systems firms needed to take into account when making purchasing decisions for integrated circuits. Evaluating circuits for speed and reliability would be critical. Systems firms would also need to take into consideration the prior performance of semiconductor suppliers in order to ascertain their ability to meet their delivery commitments. (Semiconductor firms were notorious for being late in their shipments.) Norman argued, further, that other semiconductor companies would introduce different proprietary families of integrated circuits to the market, and that these families would not be compatible with one another. In other words, a systems firm would not be able to build a single system with integrated circuits bought from different vendors. On both of these points, Norman was prescient. Late delivery and product-family "lock in" would become major problems for the customers of integrated circuits in the 1960s and thereafter.[189]

Lecture Notes

30 September 1960

Jay Last

In late September 1960, Jay Last jotted down notes for a talk that he was to give to his colleagues in Fairchild Semiconductor's R&D laboratory.[190] (Last made his presentation on 30 September.) By this time, the Micrologic program had come under direct criticism from some *within* the company. Thomas Bay, the head of sales and marketing, was particularly vocal. At a management meeting in mid September, Bay castigated Last for the company's large investments of effort, attention, and money in integrated circuits. Bay went on to declare that the Micrologic program should be shut down. After this outburst, concern grew in the Micrologic group about the firm's commitment to its effort, and to integrated circuitry more broadly. It was in this context that Last presented his talk on the program to the R&D laboratory. His goal was to address three foundational questions about the firm's push into integrated circuits: "What we are doing—Why we are doing it—Why should we at Fairchild do it?"[191]

Last pointed out that the miniaturization of electronic circuits was the focus of intense activity in the electronics industry. He noted that at least thirty corporations had research groups working on various kinds of miniaturization projects, and he cited three of them: RCA, Sylvania, and Varo. RCA's engineers worked on micromodules, a packaging scheme for microcircuitry. Micromodules were made of stacks of small ceramic plates, with electronic components affixed to the plates. These stacks were then encapsulated in plastic. The U.S. Army Signal Corps invested significant resources in this technology and gave $15.4 million in R&D contracts to RCA to develop it in the late 1950s. Sylvania also had a Signal Corps contract for a packaging approach to microcircuitry. Researchers there were developing a miniature "pancake" version of traditional transistor packages. Varo Inc., a military-oriented electronics firm based in Texas, focused on another microcircuitry approach. In 1957, it received a contract from the Office of Naval Research to make thin-film circuits. Thin-film circuits were circuits in which transistors and passive components were formed from layers of films, deposited on a substrate by evaporation or sputtering.[192]

The main impetus for this flowering of microcircuitry projects was military demand. The military was keenly interested in reducing the size and weight of the electronics systems used in aircraft and missiles. Size and weight of electronics systems were at a premium because of how they affected overall system design. For example, designers of ICBMs sought to decrease the weight and size of avionics equipment in order to reduce the thrust required of the missiles' engines. Another important force behind miniaturization was a parallel push, again by the military, to improve the reliability of electronics systems. In the mid 1950s, the reliability of these systems was very limited. Avionic electronic systems failed on the average every 70 hours, creating significant maintenance

MICROLOGIC PROGRAM   TALK TO LAB 9/30/60   9/30/60

What we are doing — why we are doing it. —why should we at Fairchild do it

Trend toward miniturization for its own sake   own power
                                                   weight
                                                   military airborne sys)

Other reasons come in   lower cost
                         higher reliability   }   — 3×10^{10} cm/sec   100mc operation
                         better performance 10^{-8} sec
                                                                               300 cm

———————————————————————————

Programs underway   RCA   micromodule program.   — supplying xistors

                       VITRO   supply active devices

                       SYLVANIA. — hermetic sealed active devices

                       about 30 companies doing 1 thy or another now.

———————————————————————————

FAIRCHILD STARTED on this road as well.

        header metallized — put in all sorts of components

        multiple bonds

Look at xistor Mfg process shows the way to go:

        1140 xistor
        o o o o o o o o
        o o o o . o o o o
        o o o o o o o o

        1" across   10 mils

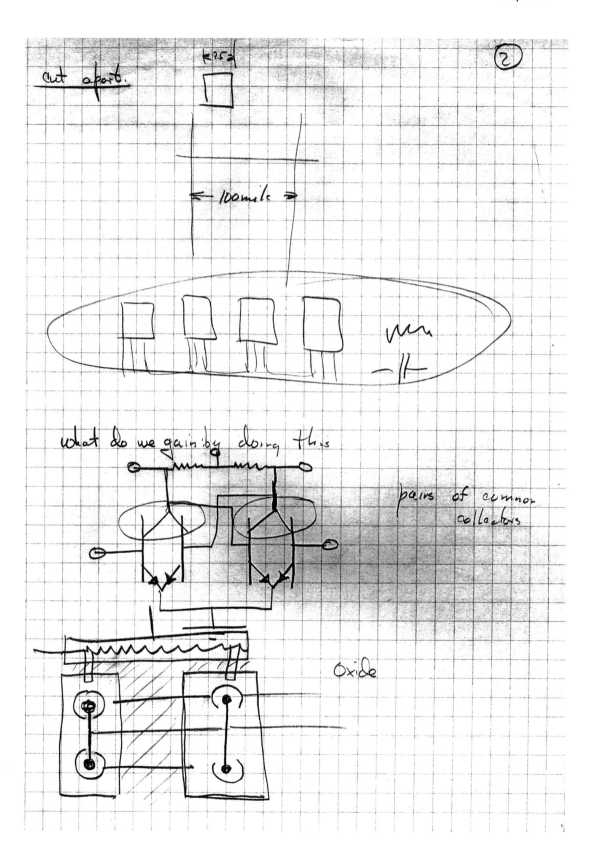

Cut apart.

←25→

←100mils→

what do we gain by doing this

pairs of common collectors

Oxide

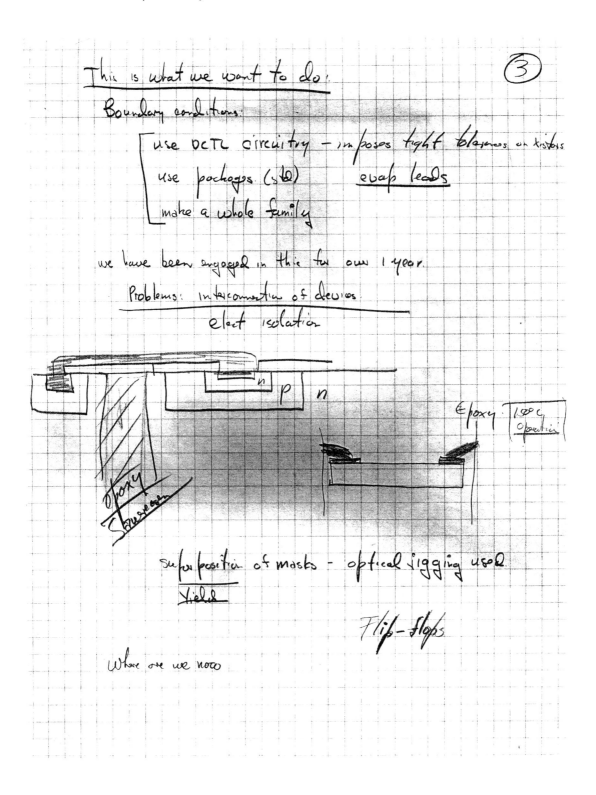

This is what we want to do.

Boundary conditions:

- use DCTL circuitry — imposes tight tolerances on tistors
- use packages (std)   evap leads
- make a whole family

we have been engaged in this for over 1 year.

Problems: interconnection of devices

elect isolation

Superposition of masks — optical jigging used.

Yield

Flip-flops

Where are we now

problems. This led the military to push for greater reliability. Creating miniaturized cir-cuits was one of the ways in which greater reliability could be achieved, as miniaturized circuits would avoid problems related to the assembly of components on printed circuit boards. These assembly problems were one of the main causes in failure of electronics systems.[193]

In the second part of his talk, Last reviewed the course of Fairchild Semiconductor's Micrologic program since its inception in the summer of 1959. The program started with the development of hybrid circuits, which Last referred to as "headers, metalized, all sorts of components." (See first page of lecture notes.) These hybrid circuits were made of transistors and passive components attached to a ceramic plate and interconnected through wires or patterned, thick films of metal. An example of these hybrid circuits was the flip-flop circuit Last had made for the Wescon in August 1959. The main defect of this approach, Last underscored, was related to the "multiple bonds" required to attach the many diverse components to the ceramic plate. Thus, the hybrid circuit approach did not avoid the reliability problems associated with assembly that plagued electronic systems with a large number of discrete components.

In moving on from the hybrid circuit approach to planar integrated circuits, Last observed, a "look at xistor mfg [transistor manufacturing] process shows the way to go"—that is, toward the batch-production approach of Fairchild's silicon manufactur-ing technology, including the planar process. Last's sketches at the bottom of his first page of notes and the top of his second page give some indication of the argument he made about the planar transistor manufacturing process showing the way for Fairchild to pursue microcircuitry. The first sketch shows planar transistors arrayed on a wafer, along with a diagram of a planar transistor. The second sketch shows that when the tran-sistors were divided from the wafer into dice, increased spacing had to be used between the transistors on the wafer to allow for the dicing operation. Further, the second sketch shows the additional increase in the size of a multi-transistor circuit when these diced, individual transistors were put into packages and then interconnected into a circuit. In this diagrammatic argument, Last indicated that the planar integrated circuit approach would lead to smaller and cheaper circuits than either the hybrid circuit approach or the discrete component circuit approach. With the planar integrated circuit, components could be placed closer together in the wafer, and there would be less wasted space associ-ated with "cutting apart" the circuits from the wafer. The final drawing Last made was of the first planar integrated circuit, the flip-flop, showing the circuit's diagram and a top-down view of the chip, with a resistor, two transistor pairs, and isolation regions.

In the third page of his notes, Last discussed the overall goal of the Fairchild program: the design and manufacture of a family of DCTL planar integrated circuits—circuits made from components produced on the same chip, interconnected by "evap[orated] leads," and placed in standard packages. In short, the goal was to provide the basic DCTL building blocks for the logic systems of digital computers. Last also talked about the problems that the group had encountered in fabricating these circuits. He focused on the challenge of electrically isolating the circuit components from one another, and on what was then the most highly developed approach within the program to meeting that challenge: physical isolation with an insulating material such as epoxy or sauereisen (a porcelain-based material). Last drew a cutaway view of a physically isolated circuit showing two transistors whose collectors were isolated by a deep well filled with an insulating material. Last also discussed the difficult issue of aligning the transistors on the top of the wafer with the grooves on the back of the wafer where the inert material would be deposited, mentioning the optical system using infrared light that the group had developed. Last concluded his talk notes with the phrase "where we are now," presumably meaning that he intended to discuss the current state of the Micrologic program. It is not certain if Last mentioned the very recent work by Haas and Kattner on isolation by diffusion ("electrical isolation"), which was to become the dominant approach for the Micrologic program in coming months.

Company Profile

Solid State Journal, **Volume 1, Number 2, September-October 1960**

Fairchild Semiconductor did not sell its products directly to final consumers. It sold components to the engineering and manufacturing organizations of systems producers that, in turn, delivered their system products to the end user. At this remove from the final consumer, the need for Fairchild Semiconductor to actively shape external perceptions and the reputation of the firm may not, at first blush, have appeared obvious. However, such shaping of perception and reputation was of great importance to Fairchild. To win sales, it was important for the firm to project an image that would increase the confidence of engineers, scientists, and managers at systems producers in Fairchild Semiconductor as a dependable manufacturer of desirable electronic components.

In the fall of 1960, an opportunity to project such an image for Fairchild Semiconductor came in the form of a new entrant to the electronics industry trade press, the *Solid State Journal.* Horizon House launched the *Solid State Journal* in 1960 to cover the burgeoning semiconductor industry, patterning it on the *Microwave Journal,* a respected trade publication for the microwave tube and system industry. Like its predecessor, the *Solid State Journal* offered industry insiders a selection of industry news, company profiles, and semi-technical articles. In the second issue, dated September-October 1960, Fairchild Semiconductor was featured in the "company profile."[194]

In the profile, representatives of Fairchild Semiconductor—likely Robert Noyce and Tom Bay, the only two Fairchild Semiconductor employees directly quoted in the piece—emphasized certain aspects of the firm, relegating other aspects to the background. The result was a glowing portrait, bordering on the openly celebratory, that glossed over the fact that Fairchild Semiconductor continued to face fierce competition and significant challenges in the second half of 1960.

The article opened with a brief review of the origins and the rapid growth of the firm during its three-year history. The language of this review projected an image that was consistent with the language and themes surrounding the presidential campaign of John F. Kennedy, which was underway at the time. The founders of Fairchild Semiconductor were presented as successful, superiorly competent, and forward-looking. The piece emphasized the youth, "brains," and ambition of the founders, and by extension, of the firm. It cast Fairchild Semiconductor's origins as a "reverse Horatio Alger story." In contrast with the sort of firm that was built slowly from the initial work of a "struggling idealist" in a "garage," Fairchild Semiconductor was characterized as an example of a group of whiz kids—the best and brightest—securing major backing to get big fast, building the most modern facilities, hiring the "best men" for all functions, and concentrating on the most forward-looking technology and products. The photographs selected for the profile reinforced this image. The photo of the founders projects youth

COMPANY PROFILE

FAIRCHILD SEMICONDUCTOR CORPORATION
Mountain View • California

Fairchild's main offices and transistor manufacturing plant in Mountain View, Cal. This 68,000 sq. ft. building will be expanded to more than 130,000 sq. ft. beginning later this year.

When some future historian sets out to write the history of the solid state electronics industry there will be more than passing mention of the "Fairchild Formula and Philosophy."

The formula will be the reverse-Horatio Alger concept that surrounded the founding of Fairchild Semiconductor Corporation of Mountain View, California, just 36 months ago this September — and the philosophy will be that of the founders who were able to attract so many of the nation's top minds and talents in such a short time.

Fairchild's original semiconductor device was the double-diffused silicon transistor — now commonly called the silicon mesa transistor — which the Fairchild people jumped into at a time when several firms had a lengthy head start on development programs. Fairchild developed the unit and put it into production a full year before any other manufacturer came out with a similar device.

But to go back to the beginning . . .

Recap

The dilemma faced by eight young California scientists in the fall of 1957 might have overwhelmed men of lesser vision and faith. It merely spurred these eight to greater ambition.

Engaged in advanced electronic work, the firm with which they were working offered them little promise for the future. Their obvious choice, as one member later expressed it was, "to leave singly and evaporate; or to stay and make something of the existing organization." Ultimately they chose a less obvious solution, to set up their own shop.

In industry lore, the classic Horatio Alger tradition provides that the struggling idealist, having attracted others to starve with him, establishes his embryo business in a garage. This course for a variety of reasons was impractical according to Dr. Robert Noyce, now vice president and general manager. In the group were six PhD's: 32-year old Noyce, with a Doctorate in physical electronics and solid state physics; Gordon Moore, 31, who has a PhD in chemistry and physics, and is now Director of Research and Development; Victor Grinich, 35, Associate Director of R and D, with a PhD in E.E.; Jay Last, who, at 30, was the youngest of the founders and is now head of the micrologic element development section; C. Sheldon Roberts, 33, who received his Doctorate in the field of metallurgical engineering; and Swiss-born Jean Hoerni, a 35-year-old with the rather unique distinction of possessing two PhD's in physics (one from the University of Geneva, and the other from Cambridge). Two other members of the original group were Eugene Kleiner, now Manager of Manufacturing Engineering; and Julius Blank, Engineering Services Manager.

Rather than struggle in someone's garage, they decided to seek out a New York investment banking firm for help. Kleiner initiated contact with Hayden, Stone and Company to explore the possibilities of financial backing. Hayden, Stone drafted a list of companies that might entertain a proposal — among them Long Island's Fairchild Camera and Instrument Corporation. At about that time, John Carter, 37, had become president of Fairchild.

"The company had studied the possibility of entering the semiconductor field a year earlier," Dr. Noyce explained, "but had not found a competent group. Consequently, they were primed and eager to go along if our ideas seemed practical."

Arrangements were made to exchange visits, Richard Hodgson, Fairchild executive vice president, first visiting the West Coast. By the time Kleiner was ready to visit Fairchild's New York plant, the group finally had attracted the one person they wanted most — Dr. Noyce.

(While he was fully aware of their activities, he had been reluctant to abandon his efforts to strengthen the organization with which they were associated, and only did so when the prospects of that company appeared to take a downward turn).

The Eastern meeting resulted in a firm deal. The new company, Dr. Noyce pointed out, "borrowed a name and capital." They first located at Palo Alto, best known as the home of Stanford University, 35 miles from down-town San Francisco. What they gave Fairchild, in addition to scientific knowledge, was the right to merge their company with the parent organization at the former's option. In October of 1959, Carter of Fairchild did just that.

"I think that one remarkable thing at the time our company was formed," Dr. Noyce related, "was that we essentially had no person with specific prior experience in managing or administering this type of operation. It always has been my opinion that brains are more important than experience."

Option Taken

When Carter picked up the option, the original eight, plus Hayden, Stone and two others who joined later, received 19,900 shares of Fairchild Camera Stock, with a market value of over $3,000,000. On this day, Fairchild's original group had grown to 750 (and to more than 1100 today).

The new Fairchild Semiconductor Corporation started work in about 14,000 square feet of leased space at 844 Charleston Road in Palo Alto. (The same plant today, since expanded to 24,000 square feet, has about 110 employees as the firm's Research and Development laboratories). In late 1958, Fairchild opened its present head-

quarters and transistor plant in nearby Mountain View which now has about 740 employees in the 68,000 square-foot building.

In the fall of 1959, Fairchild created the Diode Division across the Golden Gate Bridge from San Francisco in San Rafael; today it has about 165 employees producing diodes in 8,500 square feet of leased area. Under construction is a modern 50,000 square foot diode plant at 4300 Redwood Highway, San Rafael. The Reliability Evaluation Division in Mountain View and the Instrumentation Division in Palo Alto add another 15,000 square feet of space and about 100 more employees.

The diode plant at San Rafael now under construction is located in one of the most picturesque and charming areas of California's postcard coastline. It has practically no industry, and thus represents a dramatic example of the new philosophy of business which recognizes that in highly specialized fields, stress must be placed on location and environment in order to attract scientists, research specialists and production personnel.

Rapid Growth

In summation, from a handful of employees (including the eight founders) and 14,000 square feet of leased space in the winter of 1957, Fairchild Semiconductor has grown in three years to five plants (116,000-square feet) with more than 1100 employees.

This high rate of expansion — many times faster than industry growth during the same period — is generally accounted for by two key factors: the high degree of technical competence of the founders, and the forward-looking attitude of the parent corporation. Resisting the temptation to try to turn the newest arm of the corporate

Left to right: In Fairchild Semiconductor waiting room — Dr. Gordon Moore, Dr. Sheldon Roberts, Eugene Kleiner, Dr. Noyce, Dr. Grinich, Julius Blank, Dr. Jean Hoerni and Dr. Jay Last.

A technician is shown measuring furnace temperatures in the diffusion area. In the diffusion process the silicon wafer is heated to just below its melting point, and an impurity — in the form of a gas — is diffused into the wafer.

complex into a money-maker overnight, Fairchild Camera executives took the opposite tack by pouring huge sums of money into the budding division. The result was that the California contingent had sufficient backing to permit all of the things they wanted to do, including the hiring of some of the best men available in the important areas of engineering, manufacturing and sales; and the full development of a product, without the common pressure to release a new item before it's ready. This philosophy of concentrating on tomorrow's profits instead of today's, though not new, (it's always accepted in principle, but all too seldom practiced), paid off handsomely for Fairchild. Although figures for the semiconductor branch are not published separately, a spokesman indicated that they began adding to the corporate coffers after only 15 months, and are now solidly in the black. In terms of sales, the volume has grown from a few thousand in 1958 to over $7 million in 1959, with a level of $30 million indicated in 1960.

One management man recommended by Fairchild Camera who proved to be of key importance was Tom Bay, now Semiconductor's marketing manager, in charge of sales. He has been instrumental in putting Fairchild Semiconductor into sales orbit. The company's first order — for 100 transistors at $150.00 each — was recorded shortly after his arrival in December of 1957. The company got a second from the same customer, IBM, for both the same dollar and price six months later. Even then it hadn't made any public announcement of its product, this coming at the WESCON convention in August of 1958. The product was the first silicon mesa transistor.

Dr. Noyce and his R and D group under Dr. Moore list the company's major achievements to date as: the NPN and the PNP double diffused silicon transistor line, the development of the "planar structure" for diodes and transistors, the ultra-fast silicon diode line and the program of "micrologic elements."

New Products

In the immediate future, perhaps some time late this year, Fairchild will introduce a new product line — "micrologic elements." Essentially, this approach to the microminiaturization program is a complete set of "build-

ing blocks" that will handle all the arithmetic or logic functions of a basic computer.

The firm announced the first step in its "building block" program at the 1959 WESCON with the display of the first 20 mc flip-flop circuit package. At the time, Dr. Noyce said this Fairchild approach represented the "middle ground" between present circuit packaging and the advent of microscopic computer sub-systems.

Assembled, the elements can perform all the logic of a digital computer. In short, the micrologic elements represent all the components of a computer, except the input, output circuits and the memory system.

In choosing a name for the development, Fairchild places the emphasis on the logical functions to be performed rather than treating the elements as circuits built of individual components. For this reason, the term "micrologic" is preferred to the more common terms "micro-circuitry" or "micro-electronics" for describing this development in the technology of high density packaging of digital logic functions.

Ultimately, Fairchild believes it can manufacture the micrologic elements at less cost than the semiconductor devices required to perform the same function in conventional circuitry. Bay believes the new line of elements will have a number of distinct advantages including cost and the fact that the elements can be used "today, with today's manufacturing facilities."

Fairchild worked out the concept on the basis that the typical transistor with the can removed has abundant space to package rather complex transistor circuits on the same header. Most of the micrologic elements contain the equivalent of several transistors, diodes and resistors and will fit easily into a JEDEC TO-5 outline with eight leads. The same elements are being proposed in a JEDEC TO-18 outline.

Even though the Fairchild concept brings these computer elements into a greatly reduced space, further reductions are still possible under current techniques. How-

Testing of electrical characteristics of individual transistor dice (each smaller than a pinhead) must be done under a microscope. This is one of many testing procedures along the transistor production line.

Shown above is a transistor assembly line. Here the assemblers perform under microscopes the exacting operations required to attach individual transistor die (smaller than a pin head) to the header, a gold plated circular platform on which the transistor die is mounted, attach gold leadwires from the transistor die to the posts, and weld the hair-fine wires.

ever, until the reductions are possible in other portions of a computer — especially the memory system — progress will be slower. There is not too much point for a "pea-sized" logic element and a "barrel-sized" memory system, is the way the Fairchild developers put it.

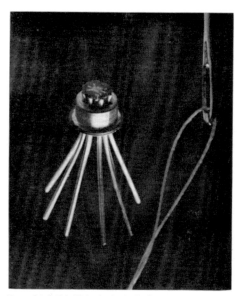

Pictured is a Fairchild micrologic flip-flop circuit. This prototype unit represents the first in a full line of micrologic elements to be produced by the company. These elements will handle all of the arithmetic and logic functions in a basic computer.

For the more distant future, Fairchild has a variety of products in the development stage to broaden the product base.

Objectives

The executives at Fairchild define their objectives in simple terms: "To develop semiconductor products for sale at a profit."

Dr. Noyce added, "We are not in business to sell development as such. Our philosophy has the advantage of production flexibility which permits us to shift away from less promising areas and invest our technical talent where it will do the most good." Fairchild believes that new product research programs should be supported out of company funds.

Regarding the development of future projects, he added, "Industrial research may look into the future as far as it can look back on a successful history. The longer the history of success, the more money will be available for far reaching programs. Therefore, in our early history our research was focused on this problem at hand: organization for production.

"Since having a brief but successful history behind us, we can now tackle longer range projects. We have broadened our base to include fundamental work on new material, and exploratory work on new techniques and operating principles. Our research effort now includes double the personnel and space the entire company utilized two years ago."

Regarding production mechanization, Fairchild believes that before a company concerns itself with automation, it should first spend money on whatever product engineering is necessary to affect yield improvement. In this way a manufacturer changes or eliminates certain production processes before he designs mechanization to perform these processes. The practice has been one of the factors which has contributed to Fairchild's prodigious success.

and confidence, and the other photos show advanced production taking place in a new, modern facility.

The company profile trumpeted Fairchild Semiconductor's success by two criteria: rapid growth and technological achievement. It detailed how the company had grown in three years to encompass five plants, with a combined size of 116,000 square feet, housing 1,100 employees. It noted that the firm had $7 million in sales during 1959 and anticipated $30 million by the close of 1960. Technological achievement was defined by a list of product accomplishments provided to the journal by Robert Noyce and Gordon Moore: mesa transistors, planar diodes and transistors, gold-doped planar diodes, and "micrologic elements." These achievements were all real, yet they did not constitute a complete account of Fairchild Semiconductor's true situation.

There were 1,100 employees by September-October 1960, but in March 1960 there had been 1,400. The reduction in staff was due to increased competition from other firms, especially Texas Instruments, in the mesa transistor business, and to the internally generated competition between mesa and planar transistors for Fairchild Semiconductor sales. Moreover, the U.S. military had begun to scale back some of its procurements. Though the *Solid State Journal* printed Fairchild Semiconductor's figure of $30 million for projected sales in 1960, the actual figure came in at $21 million—a sizable increase over 1959's total, to be sure, but lower than the projection by nearly one-third.[195]

The profile's extended discussion of the Micrologic program also served to mask the real challenges that Fairchild Semiconductor faced for technological leadership. The basic message of the profile was that the firm's Micrologic products constituted a complete set of "building blocks" for creating computer logic—building blocks that would soon be competitive with traditional discrete component approaches on *cost*. In this, the profile conflated the two microcircuitry approaches that were active under the Micrologic banner toward the end of 1960. The hybrid circuit approach launched by Jay Last at the end of 1959—in which multiple individual transistors and resistors were interconnected to form a circuit within a single package—had expanded to include a number of computer logic "building blocks." These same building blocks were the objective of a parallel effort to create planar integrated circuits. However, the planar integrated circuit efforts were in many respects behind the hybrid circuit program. Physically isolated planar integrated circuits had been created, and were produced in limited number within the R&D lab. However, the physically isolated circuits were plagued by reliability problems. The first of the electrically isolated integrated circuits had just been fabricated in September of 1960. It was far from manufacturable when the profile was published. The conflation between the hybrid circuit approach and the planar integrated circuit approach—in this and in other public presentations—gave the impression that Fairchild Semiconductor's technology and products were farther along than they actually were. In this, Fairchild Semiconductor was one of many firms in the semiconductor industry that exaggerated how close products were to actual delivery. In fact, Fairchild Semiconductor had started out quite a bit behind Texas Instruments, its main rival in the development of semiconductor integrated circuits at this time. Fairchild Semiconductor's Micrologic program was feverishly attempting to get out in front of Texas Instruments in microcircuitry with its planar integrated circuit approach.

While avoiding these issues of competition and challenge, the *Solid State Journal* article contained several revealing insights into Fairchild Semiconductor's manufacturing focus and strategy. A quotation from Robert Noyce nicely described the firm's focus on developing a manufacturing technology for diffused silicon transistors and the expanding scope of its research program: "Industrial research may look into the future as far as it can look back on a successful history. The longer the history of success, the more money will be available for far reaching programs. Therefore, in our early history our research was focused on the problem at hand: organization for production." Noyce also described a major difference in manufacturing technology approach between Fairchild Semiconductor and three of its major competitors: Texas Instruments, Motorola, and Philco. By late 1960 these competitors were far into major efforts in the "automation" and "mechanization" of transistor production. These automation efforts were aimed at lowering the production costs of transistors. Though automation could accomplish this goal, Noyce pointed out, automation and mechanization also locked a firm into particular manufacturing processes. Fairchild Semiconductor, Noyce explained, had adopted a more flexible approach, focusing on "whatever product engineering is necessary to affect [*sic*] yield improvement." He continued: "In this way a manufacturer changes or eliminates certain production processes before he designs mechanization to perform these processes." Fairchild Semiconductor sacrificed the benefits of automation for the freedom to rapidly change and adapt its manufacturing processes, as in the case of the planar process. "This practice," the *Solid State Journal* profile concluded, "has been one of the factors which have contributed to Fairchild's prodigious success."

Internal Progress Report

1 October 1960

Jay Last

In this internal progress report, Jay Last provided a formal review of the integrated circuit program.[196] Like other monthly reports from the R&D laboratory in the early 1960s, this report on the Micrologic section contained an overview, written by the section head, of the work accomplished during the previous month, along with detailed discussions on the work of the section's researchers. The first four pages of the progress report are reproduced here. The rest of the report is of lesser historical significance.

In this report, Last reviewed the status of the three approaches to microcircuitry that the Micrologic section pursued in September 1960: hybrid circuits ("Phase I"), physically isolated integrated circuits ("Phase II"), and diffusion or electrically isolated integrated circuits ("Phase III"). After Last fabricated a hybrid circuit flip-flop in August 1959, work on hybrid circuits continued. By late September 1960, engineers in the Micrologic group had designed a set of digital hybrid circuits, which the firm eventually marketed as "special products." The special products group at Fairchild had its own production facility in which workers assembled hybrid circuits and "matched transistor pairs." Transistor pairs were hybrid circuits composed of NPN and PNP transistors. Invented by Jean Hoerni, the pairs sold extremely well in switching applications. With the transistor pairs and the hybrid circuits designed by the Micrologic section, the special products group had sales of about $2 million in 1961.[197]

Most of Last's October 1960 report, however, was devoted to physically and electrically isolated planar integrated circuits. In September 1960, physically isolated integrated circuits had received most of the Micrologic group's attention. Considerable efforts were devoted to improving the manufacturing process and to solving reliability problems with these devices. Physically isolated circuits were made of islands of silicon crystal surrounded by epoxy resin and covered by a layer of silicon oxide. Temperature changes expanded or contracted the epoxy and the silicon to different extents, leading to cracks in the silicon oxide layer and also the aluminum interconnecting the components on the chip. In August and September, Lionel Kattner experimented with new insulating materials to replace the epoxy resin. He examined a variety of organic and inorganic materials before finding two materials that possessed expansion and contraction behavior close to that of silicon crystals: sauereisen and another type of epoxy. Sauereisen was a porcelain-based material manufactured by Sauereisen, Inc., a Pennsylvania-based firm. Kattner also explored the possibility of employing Pyroceram, a ceramic glass produced by Corning Glass. Kattner found that Pyroceram-based integrated circuits had poor reliability characteristics, but that the ones filled with sauereisen and the new epoxy resin withstood better the standard reliability tests required of military components.[198]

The most important news conveyed by the report was the successful fabrication of electrically isolated planar integrated circuits (flip-flops). The diffusion approach to

F.S.C. - CONFIDENTIAL

FAIRCHILD SEMICONDUCTOR CORPORATION

RESEARCH AND DEVELOPMENT DEPARTMENT

PROGRESS REPORT - MICROLOGIC SECTION   October 1, 1960

MICROLOGIC ELEMENTS PHASE I   (J. Nall)

Micrologic elements are under construction in the TO-5 configuration for electrical
and mechanical evaluation. Twelve counters and 12 half adders have been completed
and will be delivered within the week. These elements are fabricated using the
basic techniques as described in previous reports.

Physical Isolation Phase II

Flip-flops using the DCTL dumbbell pattern with diffused resistors have been
fabricated and large numbers are being evaluated at the present time. All the
elements which have been sent to evaluation will be evaluated for electrical and
mechanical characteristics. Several materials for insulation and mechanical
support of the elements have proven to be usable. (Reported by S. Fok and
L. Kattner.)

Investigation into a more suitable material and process of interconnection to
the TO-18 and TO-5 package are being considered. (Silver paint vs. gold epoxy,
etc.) A new set of masks for the flip-flop are being made and new elements will
be made soon.

Electrical Isolation Phase III

Electrical isolation studies are underway with considerable interest and there
are indications of feasibility by a few operative elements. More effort will be
placed on this phase of the program.

DCTL Transistor

The DCTL transistor studies have been given the highest priority in order to
finalize on a true DCTL flip-flop. Masks have been made and devices have been
constructed using a so called keyhole pattern and a fan keyhole pattern. These
patterns were designed to give the desired electrical characteristics utilizing
spreading resistance to meet our R_b (> 100 ohms) requirement. A considerable
number of these devices have been made and the evaluation indicates that the

Progress Report - Micrologic Section

Page 2   October 1, 1960
- -

DCTL Transistor (cont.)   (J. Nall)

keyhole or fan structure will satisfy our DCTL requirements. However, the
fan geometry appears to be the more desirable pattern. More DCTL transistors
will be fabricated to insure reproducibility of the device.

Topographical Control and Optical Jigging

There will be a two week delay in receiving the automatic numerical control
system. The fabrication of the servo system and mechanical portion has been
completed. The usual readout section is being assembled by our Instrumentation
group.

Studies are continuing on the lateral shift of patterns with final results expected
within the month.

Several optical jigging units are in various stages of fabrication. A total of
3 new optical jigging setups will be available for general use within the month.

The production of masks has increased during the past month, both from the diode
plant and the transistor plant. Improvement in the quality is expected when we
can control the dust fallout.

PHASE II ELEMENTS   (L. Kattner)

Effort this month was centered on evaluation of our best encapsulating systems in
addition to supplying Device Evaluation Section with a suitable number of devices
for initial evaluation. To date we have both an inorganic system and an organic
system which have withstood environmental testing other than 1000 hour life test.
All data to date indicate that both systems can be thermally cycled and shocked
up to 200°C without catastrophic results. In addition, a number of devices were
subjected to mechanical tests to determine failure point but no failures occurred
with available test equipment short of smashing the devices with a hammer. The
microthene mounting system as reported last month has failed to show any promise
after two successful tries. The Chemistry Section is assisting in the determination
of a suitable solvent.

Progress Report - Micrologic Section
Page 3   October 1, 1960
- -

Phase II Elements (cont.)   (L. Kattner)

Phyroceram was tried in the new approach to physical isolation in fusing glass
into the isolation region. This has not been successful thus far. Different
glass systems will be tried as soon as more time is available.

Presently several hundred operating DCTL devices are being fabricated using both
the inorganic (Sauereisen) and the organic (Isochem epoxy) systems. These
devices will be subjected to additional testing including 1000-2000 hr life
test information.

Phase III

Rather marked success has been obtained in the development of electrically
isolated DCTL flip-flops. In cooperation with and at the suggestion of I. Haas
two "quickie" runs were made with good results in both cases. Since 3 ohm-cm
material was used for bulk resistivity, device characteristics are not optimum,
however, they do operate. Currently several runs are in process using 0.5 ohm-cm
material which should improve the operating characteristics. Collector capacitance
is increased in this system compared to Phase I and II elements. It is anticipated that it can be held to approximately 10 times or less.

DCTL TRANSISTOR   (I. Haas)

The DCTL transistors with the latest base masks are being evaluated. To date,
we have tested the transistors with the keyhole and the modified keyhole (fan).
The first runs made out of 0.3 Ω cm starting material proved to be satisfactory
for fan-out. Their speed, however, (average propagation delay time) was
appreciably large 45 nsec, 23 nsec at room temperature. The former corresponds
to transistors having beta's of 400 or more and the latter of around 200.
These high beta's were mainly due to very early Early Effects, (punchthrough
0.5 - 6 volts). The room temperature fan-outs (20) can therefore be due to
unusually (and uncontrollable) high beta's. Before the DCTL transistors can be
optimized, we must get transistors having beta's around 50-100 that don't punchthrough below 10 volts minimum. The saturated switching speed is expected to
improve if beta is decreased.

Progress Report - Micrologic Section

Page 4   October 1, 1960
- -

DCTL Transistor (cont.)   (I. Haas)

Nothing conclusive can be said in comparing the keyhole versus the modified keyhole (fan). The two runs which have been compared were too different in DC characteristics to be conclusive. The remaining problem is the overlapping diodes. The one run with the fan-shaped base had the higher betas, yet did not show noticeable deterioration of this effect. The reason for this has been discussed in a meeting. One run using lower starting resistivity (0.1Ω cm) showed an appreciable effect of the overlapping effect as was to be expected. The way to go is therefore most probably to higher (around 0.5Ω cm) starting material resistivity.

The ratio of the base imput impedance in saturation to that out of saturation cannot be determined to use this as a tool in evaluating the transistors. The impedance of the emitter base breakdown seems to be only partially affecting this measurement which leads one to believe that we have a spreading resistance effect at the edge of the emitter.

Electrical Isolation

A method was suggested to obtain electrical isolation and prototypes were made with the close cooperation of L. Kattner. The process is not yet under satisfactory control. We have made about 8 units that prove the feasibility of the concept. However, only two of these had no apparent defects. One of these was given to R. Norman's group. In general, these units were slow (no life-time control). V_{CE}'s were high due to high starting material resistivity and there was a large spread among the DC parameters.

LONG DIFFUSIONS   (J. Campbell)

Since joining Fairchild on September 1, activity has been confined mainly to the learning of present technology. A limited study has been started on the possibilities of obtaining high resistivity material after long diffusions. This is of interest for electrically isolating active regions of micrologic circuits. The chief complication at this time appears to be the necessity of the Au diffusion for lifetime control of the finished device.

component isolation in integrated circuits began as a side project for the Micrologic group. Kattner and Isy Haas worked on these circuits on their own time in evenings and weekends. After several weeks of dedicated effort, Haas and Kattner completed and tested the first functional diffused or "electrically isolated" integrated circuits on 27–29 September. This was an important breakthrough. Electrically isolated integrated circuits offered a promising alternative to physically isolated integrated circuits. They were made of a single slice of silicon crystal, and as a result they would be more reliable than physically isolated integrated circuits. Moreover, their fabrication was far more compatible with Fairchild Semiconductor's diffusion-based manufacturing processes.[199]

Last believed that the electrically isolated circuits had great promise. "Electrical isolation studies are underway with considerable interest," he wrote, "and there are indications of feasibility by a few operative elements. More efforts will be placed on this phase of the program." In the next few months, Last partially reoriented his group toward the making of electrically isolated circuits. The Micrologic group pursued both physically isolated and electrically isolated circuits, but the latter were ascendant.

In late December 1960, Gordon Moore, as head of the research and development department, made the decision to concentrate on electrically isolated circuits and to fabricate a whole family of digital circuits based on this technology. Kattner made most of the circuits in this family in early 1961. By March 1961, the work had sufficiently progressed for Fairchild Semiconductor to announce its family of DCTL planar integrated circuits at the IRE show in New York. This family of integrated circuits was an important milestone in the history of semiconductor technology. These were the first planar integrated circuits to be commercialized, establishing the main line of development in semiconductor electronics to the present.[200]

Internal Memorandum

1 December 1961

Robert Graham

In this memorandum, Robert Graham, the marketing manager for Micrologic and special products (that is, planar integrated circuits and hybrid circuits) at Fairchild Semiconductor, discussed the state of the Micrologic program in late 1961.[201] Graham addressed his memo to Fairchild's sales force and circulated it to Gordon Moore, Robert Norman, Philip Ferguson (the head of the device development section in the R&D laboratory), Robert Schultz (the applications engineering manager), and Graham's own supervisor, Thomas Bay.

By this time, the men who had pioneered planar integrated circuits—Jay Last, Lionel Kattner, and Isy Haas—had all left Fairchild Semiconductor to start new semiconductor firms. In January 1961, Last and Jean Hoerni established Amelco Semiconductor as a division of Teledyne, a military electronics firm based in Southern California. Last and Hoerni were soon joined at Amelco by Haas. Last's and Hoerni's new company concentrated on integrated circuits and field-effect transistors, but also developed a substantial business in application-specific hybrid circuits for military systems. A few months after Last and Hoerni left Fairchild, Kattner founded Signetics in collaboration with three other Fairchild Semiconductor researchers: David Allison, David James, and Mark Weissenstern. Signetics' business plan was to produce custom integrated circuits—that is, circuits of the customer's specification rather than standard functions such as a flip-flop. This was a business opportunity that Fairchild Semiconductor had not yet addressed.[202]

Graham's memorandum discussed recent developments at Fairchild Semiconductor: sales of integrated circuits, the transfer of the family of integrated circuits to production, and the firm's recent move into "custom circuits." "We are at a point now where we can discuss Micrologic as a true product," Graham wrote in his memorandum. He estimated that Fairchild's sales of integrated circuits would reach half a million dollars by the end of December 1961. These sales were to military laboratories and systems firms that bought Fairchild Semiconductor's integrated circuits in small quantities for evaluation purposes. To support increasing sales of integrated circuits, Graham enlarged his group by hiring a circuit engineer who focused on marketing. His job was to help potential customers design Fairchild Semiconductor's Micrologic circuits into their products. Graham's other direct report worked on special products (hybrid circuits), which had significantly greater sales than integrated circuits.[203]

Another development that Graham noted in his memorandum was the transfer of Fairchild Semiconductor's family of electrically isolated planar integrated circuits from the R&D department to the manufacturing plant. As Graham noted in his memo, this had been a delicate undertaking involving close collaboration between R&D engineers and manufacturing engineers. Transitioning products from the laboratory to the plant

RD 2/20/62

12/1/61

FAIRCHILD SEMICONDUCTOR
A Division of Fairchild Camera and Instrument
Inter-Department Correspondence

TO: All Field Sales   CC: T. Bay   DATE: December 1, 1961
                                     R. Schultz
                                     R. Norman
                                     M. Siegel
SUBJECT: Micrologic Status Report   P. Ferguson   FROM: R. F. Graham
                                     G. Moore   Special Products &
                                                            Micrologic

----

We are at a point now where we can discuss micrologic as a true product. Our shipments by the end of December will be in the $500,000.00 region and the current
backlog is about 5K units, almost all of which is shipable in December. This
means that in January we will have 6K to 10K units ready for sale! From that
point on it will be a matter of demand.

The liaison which has been maintained between R and D, Production and Marketing
has payed off very well in that with our most complex product we have been able
to go through the transition to a production item without selling ourselves into
a deep hole. We are currently turning out all but the "H" at Mountain View. The
first "C" and "B" elements will be shipped this month and by January will be in
good supply. The "H" element will be moving sometime after mid December. Our
latest element, "R" (full shift), will be coming out in the latter part of January
or the first part of February. This element will cut the number of cans in the
shift registors by a factor of 2.

Pete Schink is now aboard and will be handling the micrologic effort in the same
areas, Ben Anixter is handling Special Products. Pete is very competent on
digital and analogue circuitry and should be able to handle most of those sticky
customer problems.

One hundred thousand dollars worth of mask making equipment has been purchased and
is being installed here in Mountain View for making custom circuits and for
modifying current product slightly. This will leave the R & D unit free for new
products and will improve turn around time for special circuits greatly. In line
with the idea of special circuits Don Farina is coming right along with the
Fairchild "Kit" devices. This will be a set of nine functions all isolated from
one another on a .150" chip and arranged so that many logic functions of diodes,
resistors and transistors can be built up quickly on one piece of silicon by
making only one additional mask (Metalization).

The Kit layout is as follows:

1	2	3
4	5	6
7	8	9

1. Tapped Resistor
   100Ω to 6KΩ
2. Resistor
   2.5KΩ to 20KΩ
3. 5ea Common Cathode
   Diodes
4. 3ea Common Anode
   Diodes
5. 2N708 Type
6. 2N708 Type
7. 2N709 Type
8. 2N1253 Type
9. Resistor
   5KΩ to 20KΩ

was notoriously difficult in the semiconductor industry. The transition involved scaling up laboratory techniques. Compounding this challenge was the fact that the instruments used in the laboratory were often different from factory equipment. It was often necessary to send the R&D engineers who had developed the new products to the factory. Graham also noted that, in addition to the original circuits developed by Haas and Kattner, the R&D laboratory was about to transfer a new integrated circuit, a full shift register, to the factory in Mountain View. This shift register represented one more step toward miniaturization, as this single chip performed a function that had required two chips in Haas and Kattner's original circuit family.

Graham detailed Fairchild Semiconductor's recent expansion into customizable circuits. It is likely that this expansion came partly in response to the formation of Signetics and its building of a custom circuit business. Fairchild Semiconductor's management viewed the Signetics group as a significant threat that had to be challenged at every turn. One way of besting Signetics was to compete with it in the custom circuit arena. In his memorandum, Graham noted that the factory in Mountain View (rather than the R&D laboratory) would be in charge of custom circuit design and fabrication, and that it had made a substantial investment in photolithographic equipment for that reason. The plant would also make customizable circuits (referred to as "kit" devices in the memorandum). As Graham indicated in his drawing, the "kit" was a silicon chip divided into nine isolated regions. Each region would contain Fairchild's most advanced transistors, diodes, and resistors. Fairchild's engineers would then design a special aluminum pattern interconnecting the various components on the chip in order to produce the specific electronic circuit that each customer desired.[204]

As Graham soon discovered, the demand for integrated circuits, especially custom circuits, turned out to be very limited in the early 1960s. Few of the small orders received in 1961 were followed by production contracts. Of the initial orders, only two led to significant sales: one from the AC Spark Plug Division of General Motors and one from the Instrumentation Laboratory at MIT. The Instrumentation Laboratory used the gate in Fairchild Semiconductor's Micrologic circuit family to build the guidance computer for the Apollo spacecraft. AC Spark Plug employed the firm's circuits to make a flight-control computer. Fairchild Semiconductor's sales of integrated circuits grew slowly from $500,000 in 1961 to $1.1 million the next year. Sales amounted to about $1.1 million in the first half of 1963.[205]

Adoption of Fairchild Semiconductor's integrated circuits was gradual for a variety of reasons. The integrated circuits did not perform as well as equivalent circuits made of discrete transistors and resistors. They were also much more expensive than circuits composed of discrete components. Only customers with very large budgets and unyielding miniaturization and reliability requirements chose Fairchild Semiconductor's circuits.

Moreover Fairchild's planar integrated circuits were in competition with hybrid circuits, which possessed many of the performance advantages of circuits formed by discrete devices—especially their ability to perform to highly exacting specifications. These precise specifications were extremely important for linear circuits, which were of great interest to the producers of military electronic systems. Hybrid circuits were, therefore, a major business for Fairchild and for Amelco and other spin-offs through the early 1960s, competing with the product lines of planar integrated circuits advanced by these very same firms. The seriousness of this competition between hybrid circuits and planar integrated circuits was evident in a "keynote panel discussion" among leading figures in the semiconductor research community at the 1965 International Solid State Circuits Conference. A panel on "Hybrid Versus Monolithic Circuits" organized by James Goldey of Bell Labs included many of the leading figures in microcircuitry: Ed Davis of IBM, Ed Sack of Westinghouse, Jack Kilby of Texas Instruments, Jay Last of Amelco, and Gordon Moore of Fairchild Semiconductor. As late as 1965, the competition between hybrid circuits and planar integrated circuits was still active.[206]

Sales of planar integrated circuits increased gradually relative to sales of Fairchild's earlier transistor products. This was attributable to skepticism toward integrated circuits among the relevant technical communities. The skeptics emphasized doubts about yields, testing, performance, and reliability with planar integrated circuits. Proponents and producers of integrated circuits addressed these doubts through a variety of panels, presentations, and publications in the first half of the 1960s.[207]

Another factor in the relatively slow adoption of Fairchild's circuits was the fact that the Micrologic group had not fully taken the needs of customers into account when it had chosen its logic configuration for its planar integrated circuits. It had chosen DCTL which relatively few system designers knew about outside of advanced military computing. And few engineers knew how to test these circuits.[208] In contrast, the Signetics group pursued a more widely used form of digital circuitry—diode-transistor logic (DTL)—and was initially more successful than Fairchild in the marketplace.[209]

There was another, deeper reason for the slow adoption of Fairchild Semiconductor's in-tegrated circuits in the military market. Circuit engineers of military system firms saw integrated circuits as a threat to their livelihood and opposed their use in the design of new systems. Only when the military began to force its contractors to use miniaturized circuits in new weapon systems, starting in the summer of 1963, did Fairchild Semiconductor's sales of integrated circuits increase significantly, growing to $2.6 million in the second half of 1963 and $6.2 million in 1964.[210]

Indeed, the mid 1960s marked something of a turning point for planar integrated circuits. With the incorporation of epitaxial techniques into silicon manufacturing technology, the production of planar integrated circuits became much easier and more robust. More important, as manufacturing groups gained more and more experience with the production of integrated circuits, microcircuits became much cheaper than equivalent circuits made of discrete components. These technological and economic factors, along with the military's edict, led to a significant increase in the use of planar integrated circuits in military and commercial systems by 1966. That year, sales of planar integrated circuits approached $120 million, half of those sales captured by semiconductor firms in what would be soon called Silicon Valley.[211]

Conclusion

Between 1957 and 1961, Fairchild Semiconductor's founders and engineers responded to the challenges posed by a set of interconnected "logics" in pursuit of their initial goal of producing diffused silicon devices for the military computing market. The first of these logics was silicon logic, encompassing the properties and characteristics of silicon, silicon oxide, other materials, and the equipment and processes used to handle and transform these materials. Silicon logic often resisted the intentions of the Fairchild Semiconductor researchers, presenting them with great uncertainties and novel roadblocks. At other times, silicon logic provided the researchers with new avenues to pursue, recasting their goals and intentions. Such was the case with the two most fundamental innovations at Fairchild Semiconductor in the period 1957–1961: the planar process and the planar integrated circuit. Both of these innovations rested on the particular properties of the oxide layers that form on the surface of silicon crystal.[1]

Yet these innovations also were fundamentally shaped by the other formative logics: user logic and competitive logic. The user logic of the makers of military digital computers—their technological requirements and their emphases on reliability and miniaturization—were critical in shaping the goals of the Fairchild Semiconductor researchers. These military requirements for reliability and miniaturization led to the planar process and the planar integrated circuit. So too the competitive logic of the other firms in the semiconductor industry led to the concentration on manufacturing capability, speed of action, and flexibility at Fairchild Semiconductor, all of which created a local context in which the planar process, the planar integrated circuit, and other innovations could be developed and moved into production rapidly. Responding to these three logics, Fairchild Semiconductor achieved a position of technical and business leadership in the semiconductor industry between 1957 and 1961. It made a transition from a small start-up to a large, profitable enterprise offering a broad set of devices for military digital computing, including the most promising form of microchip.

Fairchild Semiconductor's innovation of the planar process and the planar integrated circuit put the firm at the forefront of semiconductor technology. It remained the main center for semiconductor innovation for much of the 1960s. It also maintained its advantage in manufacturing processes. In turn, Fairchild Semiconductor's processing capabilities enabled its engineers to develop and manufacture successful products, including very fast computer transistors and commercial transistors used in television circuits, that other firms were not able to make. Fairchild Semiconductor also produced high-speed digital integrated circuits for computing (first using only the DCTL logic form, but later using the DTL and TTL configurations too), and it developed "analog" or "linear" integrated circuits such as operational amplifiers.[2]

Another area of technological innovation pioneered by researchers in Fairchild Semiconductor's R&D organization was MOS (metal oxide semiconductor) integrated circuits. These circuits were based on a new type of transistor, the MOS field-effect transistor, that differed significantly from Fairchild's previous junction transistors and integrated circuits but was nevertheless amenable to fabrication using the planar process. In particular, Fairchild engineers developed CMOS (complementary MOS), a variant of MOS technology with certain performance advantages. MOS (and later CMOS), representing both a manufacturing technology and an integrated circuit form, came to dominate digital electronics starting in the 1970s. In conjunction with these product and process innovations, Fairchild Semiconductor's R&D laboratory emerged as the main center for basic research on device structures and materials in the semiconductor industry. Among the most significant work done at Fairchild Semiconductor were studies of the interface between the silicon crystal and silicon oxide that identified the main causes of instabilities at this interface, thereby making MOS and CMOS technology viable.[3]

Fairchild Semiconductor's managers also led the way for the semiconductor industry in opening up commercial markets for silicon technology. At first, the firm had grown by actively serving military markets for silicon transistors. In this, Fairchild's founders were in lock step with their competitors: silicon electronics meant military electronics. Nevertheless, Robert Noyce and Gordon Moore took initial steps toward commercial markets as early as 1959. Moore initiated research projects that aimed at developing transistors for commercial markets. Around the same time, mass production specialists from General Electric and CBS-Hytron were recruited to reorganize Fairchild Semiconductor's manufacturing operations for high-volume production. Higher volumes and lower manufacturing costs would be essential for commercial products. Charles Sporck (who had worked as the manager of a capacitor manufacturing line at General Electric, where he had produced millions of components) joined Fairchild Semiconductor's manufacturing organization in 1959 and became the director of its Mountain View plant the next year.

In 1962 and 1963, Fairchild Semiconductor's leaders intensified the firm's movement toward commercial markets and users, even as it continued to address the requirements of their core customers in the military market. To meet the volume and price requirements of commercial customers, Sporck relentlessly pushed for increases in production volumes and a concomitant decline in manufacturing costs. He also played a significant role, with Robert Noyce, in moving the assembly of transistors and integrated circuits to Hong Kong and South Korea as a way of lowering labor costs. System firms serving commercial markets were much more price-conscious than military contractors. Commercial producers also needed transistors and integrated circuits in greater quantities. The decision of Fairchild's leaders to pursue larger commercial markets was predicated on the position it had attained and the capacities it had developed by addressing military markets. Through these efforts, Fairchild broke open these commercial markets for silicon discrete devices and integrated circuits during the 1960s. In following decades, commercial markets would eclipse military markets for silicon integrated circuits.[4]

One important component of Fairchild Semiconductor's success in opening commercial markets for silicon electronics was an extensive effort in applications engineering. From the firm's very beginnings, its leaders had emphasized the writing of applications notes that detailed the characteristics of the firm's devices and the ways these devices could be used in military systems. Fairchild Semiconductor's managers greatly expanded these applications activities, and in the early and mid 1960s they re-oriented them toward commercial users. The firm's applications engineers produced notes explaining to potential customers how to use Fairchild devices in order to improve their existing products or develop entirely new products. These applications engineers also developed prototypes of toys, television sets, and automotive components that incorporated the company's silicon diodes, transistors, and integrated circuits. The engineers showed these prototypes to potential customers as demonstrations of what could be done with silicon electronics. Fairchild Semiconductor's sustained applications engineering program and declining manufacturing costs enabled the firm to build up a significant commercial business in the consumer electronics industry and among manufacturers of commercial computers.[5]

Other manufacturers of silicon components in the semiconductor industry rapidly adopted Fairchild Semiconductor's manufacturing and device technologies, following the firm into commercial markets. By 1962, both Texas Instruments and Motorola had mastered planar transistors and integrated circuits and brought products to the market that competed directly with Fairchild Semiconductor's. For example, in 1962 Motorola introduced a line of planar transistors that captured a significant fraction of the market for silicon transistors in the computer industry. A few years later, Texas Instruments marketed a family of silicon planar integrated circuits of the TTL logic form that were widely used in military and commercial applications.[6]

Beyond its re-shaping of established semiconductor firms through intense competition, Fairchild Semiconductor was also the source of an increasing number of start-ups and spin-offs. Entrepreneurs established these new firms in order to exploit technologies—particularly integrated circuit technologies—originally developed at Fairchild Semiconductor. They also adopted Fairchild's methods for opening up new markets for integrated circuits. The spin-off integrated circuit firms populated Silicon Valley, arriving in two waves. Men from Fairchild's Micrologic program who had pioneered planar integrated circuits established the companies of the first wave of spin-offs. In 1961, Jay Last and Jean Hoerni established Amelco Semiconductor, the semiconductor division of Teledyne, a newly formed military electronics firm based in Southern California. Arthur

Rock, the analyst from Hayden Stone & Company who had been instrumental in the establishment of Fairchild Semiconductor, was involved in the financing of Teledyne, and also in Last and Hoerni's formation of its Amelco semiconductor division. Soon after Last and Hoerni departed Fairchild, so too did David Allison, Lionel Kattner, and several other Fairchild Semiconductor engineers; they then established Signetics, the first firm solely focused on integrated circuits. Two other integrated-circuit spin-offs that had origins in the Micrologic group at Fairchild were Molectro and General Microelectronics (GME).[7]

In the mid and late 1960s, a second wave of spin-offs emerged out of Fairchild Semiconductor and from the first wave of its spin-offs. In the main, these firms commercialized MOS integrated circuit technologies developed at the older firms, creating markets for them in computer memories, digital watches, and calculators using many of the business practices pioneered at Fairchild Semiconductor. For example, Intel Corporation, formed by Noyce and Moore in 1968, initially concentrated on making MOS integrated circuits for computer memory. The firms of this second wave of spin-offs, like those of the previous wave, exhibited many of the same dynamics as Fairchild Semiconductor in its start-up phase: they initially exploited technologies developed elsewhere, they emphasized speed and focus to establish themselves in a fiercely competitive environment, they pursued growth through innovation, and they underwent very rapid expansion (often followed by a period of consolidation). In addition, many start-ups experienced the same entrepreneurial pattern that Fairchild had experienced: their founders left after three years in order to start new companies.[8]

An important factor in the formation of these integrated circuit firms, especially the second wave of start-ups, was the emergence of the venture capital business in Silicon Valley. To a large degree, this business grew out Fairchild Semiconductor. In 1961, Arthur Rock's experiences with financing Fairchild Semiconductor and Teledyne and the contacts he had developed in the electronics industry on the San Francisco Peninsula persuaded him to start a venture capital partnership in San Francisco, in collaboration with Thomas Davis (who had previously invested in the microwave tube business in Northern California). Among Davis and Rock's investors were several of Fairchild Semiconductor's founders, including Jay Last, Jean Hoerni, Eugene Kleiner, and Sheldon Roberts. Davis and Rock, in turn, invested in start-ups in the Bay Area and in Southern California and generated fantastic financial returns. These results convinced local technology entrepreneurs to move into the venture capital business too. Among them was Eugene Kleiner, who in 1972 established Kleiner Perkins, a major venture capital partnership. The venture capitalists invested in new semiconductor spin-offs from Fairchild, Amelco, and GME. For example, Rock financed both Intel and Intersil (a firm, started by Jean Hoerni, that made MOS integrated circuits for digital watches). Most of the thirty-odd firms that entered the semiconductor industry in Silicon Valley in the late 1960s and the early 1970s obtained some of their financing from these venture capital partnerships.[9]

It was this group of firms—Intel and the other start-ups established in Silicon Valley in the late 1960s and the early 1970s—that, along with Motorola and Texas Instruments, digitalized the human-built world. The critical technology that they developed was MOS integrated circuits, the variant of the planar integrated circuits originally developed at Fairchild Semiconductor. Critical among these MOS integrated circuits for the process of digitalization were microprocessors and microcontrollers ("computers on a chip"), which made possible digital control of existing electromechanical technologies and the development of entirely new, digital products such as the personal computer. From the 1970s through the 1990s, Fairchild's successor firms, Texas Instruments, Motorola, along with semiconductor firms in Asia and Europe, created enormous markets for microprocessors, microcontrollers, and other types of MOS circuits in a wide variety of industries. They opened up these markets in two ways: by dramatically reducing the price of electronic functions through greater integration and by investing significant resources in helping customers integrate digital processing techniques into their products and systems.[10]

Using MOS microprocessors and microcontrollers to control automotive engines, machine tools, or scientific instruments required considerable engineering expertise, and such expertise resided largely in researchers and engineers within semiconductor companies. Indeed, engineers at Intel, the firm that developed the first microprocessors, devised design aids—"development systems" that were in essence small computers—to help their customers design microprocessors into their own products. For several years, Intel had greater revenue from these design aids than it had from microprocessors. The applications engineering group at Intel also designed prototype scientific calculators and video games to demonstrate what could be done with the firm's first microprocessors. Judging these efforts critical for the adoption of new microprocessors and microcontrollers, semiconductor firms continued to invest heavily in applications engineering well into the 1990s. Such was the challenge of digitalizing industrial and commercial products.[11]

A critical aspect in the development of MOS integrated circuits such as microprocessors and microcontrollers—an aspect that has allowed for the extraordinary suffusion of digital circuits through a wide range of industries—has been *scaling*. Since the late 1960s, Intel, Texas Instruments, Motorola, and other semiconductor firms have systematically invested in the development of silicon manufacturing technology in order to reduce or "scale down" the size of transistors, the basic components of integrated circuits, and to produce more and more complex circuits containing more and more transistors—a phenomenon often referred to as Moore's Law.[12]

The scaling of integrated circuits though continual investment in developing silicon manufacturing technology has resulted in an exponential increase in the functionality of integrated circuits and an exponential decrease in the cost per electronic function. Because of the batch nature of silicon manufacturing technology, scaling has allowed digital electronics to become ever cheaper and more powerful. The steady drop in the cost of electronic functions opened increasingly large markets for integrated circuits and digital processing techniques, resulting in continued digitalization of industries and technologies.[13]

Major advances in silicon manufacturing technology were required for researchers and engineers to maintain the path of scaling. Among these advances was the adoption of polycrystalline silicon for forming the gates of MOS transistors. (Gates control the flow of electrons from the source to the drain of MOS transistors.) Pioneered at Bell Labs and at Fairchild Semiconductor, and brought to production at Intel, silicon gate MOS technology enabled the fabrication of chips much denser than could be made with other techniques. Indeed, it was the silicon gate MOS transistor that engineers and researchers persistently scaled down from the early 1970s to the late 2000s. This great reduction in the size of MOS transistors required a long series of innovations in manufacturing processes, including improvements in photolithography and the adaptation of ion implantation (a technique originally developed in nuclear physics) to semiconductor manufacturing. Ion implantation allowed much greater control over the introduction of dopants into silicon crystals than the diffusion technology initially used at Fairchild Semiconductor. As a result, it permitted the fabrication of much smaller and much faster MOS transistors.[14]

As semiconductor firms became more adept at producing ever-smaller MOS transistors, they encountered the challenge of designing more and more complex chips containing ever-greater numbers of transistors. In the 1960s, chip engineers designed integrated circuits mainly by hand, with paper and pencils. Using opaque films and tapes, technicians translated these drawn designs into physical layouts for forming and interconnecting all the components in a chip. The layouts were then used to produce photolithographic masks. This manual approach to circuit design and layout was practical for chips with hundreds or even thousands of transistors. It became increasingly uneconomical for integrated circuits containing tens or hundreds of thousands of components.[15]

To address the challenge of designing chips with enormous numbers of transistors, starting in the late 1960s and the early 1970s, semiconductor firms pioneered the development of computer-aided methodologies and tools for the layout and the design of integrated circuits. Research groups at universities also developed software tools for integrated circuit simulation. Out of these developments emerged the electronic design automation (EDA) industry. New firms, including Mentor Graphics (1981), Daisy Systems (1981), SDA Systems (1983), and Synopsys (1987), spun off from university laboratories and semiconductor companies. They produced several generations of computer-aided design programs and systems, each addressing a greater level of chip integration. These tools allowed semiconductor firms to take full advantage of scaling and to design ever more powerful MOS microprocessors, microcontrollers, and other types of microchips.[16]

The digitalization of existing industries and technologies, and the creation of new digital technologies using integrated circuits (especially microprocessors), represented enormous technological and commercial opportunities that Silicon Valley entrepreneurs and venture capitalists rapidly exploited. These individuals were uniquely positioned to understand and capitalize on the opportunities opened up by the new chips. Many had worked for Fairchild Semiconductor or for other semiconductor firms and thus were intimately aware of what could be done with microprocessors. A case in point is Donald Valentine, a former sales and marketing executive at Fairchild Semiconductor who entered the venture capital business in the early 1970s. On the basis of his knowledge of the microprocessor, Valentine and his venture capital partnership, Sequoia Capital, invested in Apple Computer and in other start-ups making microprocessor-based systems. Valentine also invested in Atari, which made video games. Another leading venture capitalist with roots in semiconductor technology was John Doerr, who had marketed microprocessors at Intel. In 1980, Doerr joined Kleiner Perkins, the venture capital partnership founded by Fairchild Semiconductor co-founder Eugene Kleiner. For much of the 1980s, Doerr and his colleagues at Kleiner Perkins financed new microprocessor-dependent ventures, among them Compaq, Sun Microsystems, Lotus, and America Online.[17]

Massive venture capital investments supported the formation of new microprocessor-based industries. These industries appeared in two waves, from the 1970s through the 1990s. In the second half of the 1970s, the commercial production of personal computers took hold in Silicon Valley at start-ups such as Apple, Cromemco, and Osborne. These firms built their microcomputers around the early microprocessors coming out of Intel, Zilog, MOS Technology, and Motorola. Funded by Silicon Valley's venture-capital community, and employing experienced managers from Intel and Fairchild Semiconductor, Apple Computer rapidly emerged as the region's dominant maker of personal computers. It introduced a series of innovative systems, including the Macintosh (1984). In turn, Apple's rapid expansion fueled the growth of the software and disk-drive industries in Silicon Valley.[18]

A second wave of microprocessor-based firms emerged later, focused on workstations and computer networks. In the early and mid 1980s, research groups at Xerox's Palo Alto Research Center (PARC) developed new computer workstations and networking technologies, drawing on earlier exploratory efforts at the Stanford Research Institute and at university laboratories. Engineers at Stanford University and at the University of California at Berkeley did innovative research in computer architecture and networking with funding from the Defense Advanced Research Projects Agency, an agency of the Department of Defense. John Hennessy at Stanford and David Patterson at Berkeley engineered RISC (Reduced Instruction Set Computer) microprocessors. Jim Clark developed the "Geometry Engine," an integrated circuit for processing three-dimensional computer graphics. Efforts at Stanford to build a complex computer network led to the design of a powerful workstation, the Stanford University Network (SUN) computer, in the early 1980s. William Yeager, a Stanford engineer, developed one of the first packet-switching routers for the Stanford network. These new technologies (and others, including a version of the Unix operating system developed at Berkeley) were commercialized by Cisco Systems, Sun Microsystems, Silicon Graphics, MIPS Computer Systems, and other start-ups. In the 1980s and the first half of the 1990s, these firms established themselves as suppliers of networking routers and advanced workstations.[19]

The continued development of silicon manufacturing technology supported an explosive growth in personal computing, computer networking, and software from the 1980s to the present. Through the appropriation of these technologies and the utilization of more powerful and cheaper microchips, engineers in previously existing industries have digitalized their technologies, often to transformative effect. Consumer electronics may have been the first sector to be affected by MOS microprocessors as a variety of firms, especially in Japan, employed them to produce calculators. More important, the use of microcontrollers became pervasive. Designers employed microcontrollers to improve product performance in many industries. In the automotive industry, for example, engineers increasingly used microcontrollers to increase engine efficiency, reduce emissions, and control safety features.

In many other cases, digitalization did more than augment older electromechanical and other technologies, products, and systems. It replaced a variety of existing technologies and practices with software and digital hardware. Perhaps most prominent in these radical transformations is the digitalization of communications, the convergence of communications and computing. With this convergence, forged through the replacement of analog with digital approaches in telecommunications, and with the proliferation of microcomputers and computer networks, the Internet developed rapidly. The Internet and the wireless voice and data communication systems tied to it—resting atop digital silicon integrated circuits—were major forces in large-scale technological, economic, and cultural change in the 1990s and the 2000s.[20]

By the 2000s, the silicon technologies and business activities that were developed in the late 1950s to provide new components for military digital computers had moved remarkably far beyond their original contexts of silicon, user, and competitive logics. The semiconductor industry, fueled by venture funding, had used these silicon technologies and these business activities to create exponentially more powerful and cheaper digital electronics. With them, other firms and industrial sectors acted in concert with producers of digital electronics to digitalize existing technologies and to create new, fully digital technologies. In this, they helped to transform the human-built environment into a digital world.

Appendix: Semiconductor Technology in the Late 1950s and the Early 1960s

The historical documents that form the core of this book are traces of an intensive technological effort. The explication and interpretation of these documents, therefore, contains many technical terms and concepts. While the interpretive essays have been written to make them accessible to the reader, those without some prior exposure to silicon semiconductor technology may find portions of the interpretive essays to be challenging. It is for these readers, and for those desiring a quick general review, that this appendix is addressed. It presents a general introduction to the technical terms and concepts in the silicon semiconductor technology of the 1950s and the early 1960s. It employs terms and concepts that were used in the 1950s and the 1960s. Most of these terms and concepts are still in favor in the semiconductor community at the time of this writing. Indeed, it is the central project of this book to elucidate how Fairchild Semiconductor came to establish the main line of technological development in silicon electronics and digitalization in the period 1957–1961.

Through the late 1950s, the basic building blocks of electronic systems—computers, radios, radar sets, etc.—were electronic components, discrete parts each having a distinctive electrical behavior. Circuits, performing an electrical function, were constructed by the interconnection of a set of components. Electronic systems were formed from interconnected circuits.[1]

Diodes and Transistors

There was an enormous variety of electronic components by the mid 1950s. Within this variety, a basic taxonomy of components can be described. At the most general level was the division of components into the classes of *active* and *passive*. Active components were those few capable of power gain—amplifying the strength of an electrical signal. Passive components were the much more numerous parts that were not capable of this action. In the mid 1950s, the dominant form of active component was the vacuum tube. Thousands of different vacuum tube designs provided a wide range of electrical behaviors, from simple amplification to the generation, broadcast, and reception of radio and microwave signals. Vacuum tubes were complex and delicate assemblies of metal electrodes, filaments, and grids arrayed inside evacuated glass bulbs. They produced prodigious amounts of heat, and they failed often. At the time, the most common passive components were resistors, capacitors, and diodes. Resistors, providing electrical resistance in a circuit, were frequently formed by small carbon rods or wound lengths of metal wire. Capacitors, storing electrical charge, were known by the materials used to form them: paper, mica, ceramic, tantalum, electrolytic, etc. Diodes, acting like one-way valves in the flow of current in a circuit, often took the form of a simplified vacuum tube.[2]

In the late 1940s, vacuum tubes began to face a rival form of both passive and active electronic components: solid-state or semiconductor electronics. During World War II, vacuum tubes were used in unprecedented numbers, especially for communications. Tubes provided amplification for long-distance telephone signals, for long-range microwave transmission and receiving, and for both long- and short-distance radio communication and broadcasting. In a related military technology, radar employed a range of tubes for the tracking of ships and aircraft. The U.S. government also funded the construction of early digital computers, employing thousands of vacuum tubes as switches and amplifiers. In both the radar effort and the digital computer effort, semiconductor "crystal" diodes were developed and employed. The success of these crystal diodes led to a substantial effort in solid-state electronics at the Bell Telephone Laboratories and elsewhere. In 1948, Bell Labs publicly announced the creation of a solid-state active component, the transistor, that offered power gain and could provide the switching and amplification functions previously available only with vacuum tubes.[3]

The first transistor—called the point-contact transistor—had much in common with solid-state crystal diodes: they were both formed by affixing the sharp point of a metal contact wire (or wires) to the surface of a solid piece of semiconductor crystal. In this, these first semiconductor components were far smaller and simpler than vacuum tubes, and had the potential to be cheaper, better performing, and more reliable. In many respects, for these semiconductor components, the piece of crystal was the device. Semiconductors are chemical elements that are neither poor nor excellent conductors of electrical current. The most commonly used semiconductors for electronic components are germanium and silicon. Semiconductors, like most elements, possess a crystal structure in solid form (the solid state). Most often, this structure is polycrystalline—a jumble of regions of geometrically regular single crystal, the boundaries between them, and a variety of defects and dislocations in the crystal structures. Under certain conditions, a substantial piece of semiconductor may form one unified single crystal, with a regular geometry in the placement of the semiconductor atoms throughout. When a semiconductor crystal is contaminated or "doped" with certain other chemical elements, the ability of the material to conduct an electrical current may be altered in a controlled fashion. Doped semiconductor material may be either N-type or P-type (as explained below), N or P denoting the character of the doping and of the resulting electrical properties. Both the crystal structure and the chemical composition of a piece of semiconductor material are important factors in determining its electrical properties, such as conductivity.[4]

In the crystal diode, also known as a point-contact diode, the sharp metal wire that impinges on the surface of the crystal forms a "junction." The back of the crystal is attached to a metal plate, which does not form a junction but rather provides simple low-resistance electrical contact to the device called the "base contact." The operation of the point-contact diode centers on the junction formed by the wire to the surface. The following explication assumes the case of an N-type semiconductor crystal. When a voltage is applied between the point contact and the base contact, through the semiconductor crystal in one direction (from the plus to minus sides of the power source, e.g., a battery), the junction formed by the wire point and the crystal exhibits a low electrical resistance, allowing a current to flow easily through the bulk of the crystal to the base of the diode. This arrangement of the voltage is called *forward bias*. When the voltage is applied in the other direction, from the minus side to the plus side of the power source, the junction between the point and the crystal exhibits a high electrical resistance, preventing the passage of current through the diode. This arrangement of the voltage is called *reverse bias*. For P-type semiconductor material, the directions of the voltages to provide forward and reverse bias would be the opposite configurations. The primary function of a diode is to control the passage of current through it like a one-way valve or switch. The point-contact diode accomplishes this through the bias applied to the point contact.[5]

In a point-contact transistor, two junction-forming points touch the surface of the semiconductor crystal, with a very small distance separating them. One of these point contacts is termed the *emitter*, the other the *collector*. Again, metal contact is made to the back of the semiconductor crystal without forming a junction, providing a low-resistance *base* contact. The following explication assumes the case of an N-type semiconductor crystal. The emitter contact is forward biased by a voltage in the plus to minus direction; the collector contact is reverse biased by another voltage in the minus to plus direction. Thus, the emitter junction has low resistance and the collector junction has high resistance. If the emitter and the collector are placed closely enough to one another, the crystal provides an interaction between current flowing through the

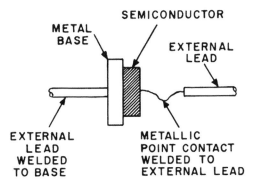

Figure A.1
Point-contact diode. U.S. Army.

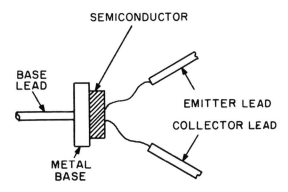

SEMICONDUCTOR

BASE
LEAD

EMITTER LEAD

COLLECTOR LEAD

METAL
BASE

Figure A.2
Point-contact transistor. U.S. Army.

emitter and current flowing through the collector. A small input current in the emitter produces an increase in the output current in the collector. Owing to the contribution of the semiconductor crystal, the increase in output is larger than the input. The transistor thereby produces power gain, and can be used not only as a switch but also to provide amplification.[6]

The manner in which the semiconductor crystal provides power gain in the transistor will be more fully explored in the following description of an alternate form of transistor: the *junction transistor*, developed in the early 1950s, which soon eclipsed the point-contact transistor as the dominant form of transistor. Junction transistors—also known as *bipolar transistors*—would later be largely replaced by MOS field-effect transistors, used in integrated circuits from the later 1960s to the present day. The junction transistor was the main vehicle through which semiconductor components and integrated circuits were firmly established in the 1950s and the 1960s. Initially, semiconductor component manufacturers used the element germanium to form junction transistors. In the later 1950s, firms began to employ the element silicon for making junction transistors, and silicon replaced germanium almost entirely in the 1960s. The following section focuses specifically on silicon junction transistors for these historical reasons, and also because the manufacture of silicon junction transistors was one of the central efforts by Fairchild Semiconductor in the late 1950s.[7]

Silicon Junction Transistors

Silicon, one of the most abundant chemical elements on Earth's surface, is a relatively poor conductor of electrical current—a semiconductor. Silicon has a high melting point and readily forms silicon oxides in reaction with oxygen, much as iron readily forms iron oxides (rust). By adding atoms of very particular chemical elements (dopants) to a silicon crystal, the ability of the crystal to conduct electrical currents can be increased in a controllable fashion. In a crystal of undoped or "intrinsic" silicon, the electrons of the silicon atoms form strong bonds with the surrounding silicon atoms, leaving few free electrons available for conducting an electrical current—hence the high resistivity or poor conductivity of intrinsic silicon. When atoms of the chemical elements from Group 15 of the periodic table—the nitrogen group, formerly known as Group V—are added to the silicon crystal, their electrons form bonds with the surrounding silicon atoms in such a way that one electron remains free to travel through the crystal and carry an electrical current. These dopant elements are known as *donors* for granting these free electrons to the crystal, with the resulting material known as *N-type* for these negatively charged current carriers. Examples of donor dopants are phosphorus, arsenic, and antimony.[8]

Elements of Group 13 of the periodic table—the boron group, formerly known as Group III—are also employed as dopants for silicon crystals, and are known as *acceptor* dopants. Examples of acceptors include boron, gallium, and indium. When an acceptor atom forms bonds with the surrounding silicon atoms in the crystal, it lacks the number of electrons required to make the same number of bonds as would a silicon atom. The acceptor atom can be thought of as needing to borrow an electron from another atom in the crystal to complete its bonds with the neighboring silicon atoms in the crystal. By accepting such an electron, the dopant atom creates a deficit (a "hole") in the structure. Like a free electron, this "hole" is able to move about the crystal, and it acts as a positively charged current carrier. Semiconductor material doped with acceptors is known as *P-type* for these positively charged current carriers.[9]

In N-type and P-type material, both electrons and holes are present. In N-type material, the excess electrons are the majority carriers of current and the holes are minority carriers. In P-type material, the situation is reversed, with excess holes as the majority carriers and electrons as the minority carriers. The new form of transistor that rapidly replaced the point-contact transistor and was the primary type of transistor well into the 1960s—the junction transistor—was based on the behavior of the boundaries or junctions between regions of P-type and N-type semiconductor material, known as "PN junctions." Using reverse and forward bias, a single PN junction could be made to form a diode. With two PN junctions and the use of reverse and forward bias, a transistor could be made.[10]

In the area surrounding the junction between P-type material and N-type material, a "depletion region" forms—a region depleted of both mobile electrons and mobile holes. In the course of their regular motion throughout the crystal, holes from the P-type region and electrons from the N-type region will migrate across the junction, canceling one another. What remains in this region of cancellation are positively charged donor atoms and negatively charged acceptor atoms, creating an electrical field. The electrical field of the depletion region serves as a barrier to the movement of both electrons and holes across it. When a voltage is applied to a PN junction in the minus-to-plus direction, the mobile holes in the P-type region are attracted to the negative terminal of the power supply, and the mobile electrons of the N-type region are attracted to the positive

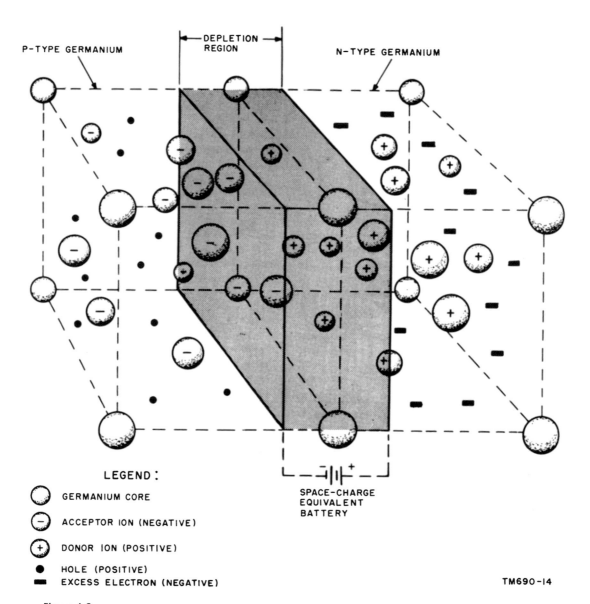

Figure A.3
Idealized representation of a PN junction in a sample of germanium, showing donor and acceptor dopant atoms, majority and minority carriers, and the depletion region. U.S. Army.

terminal. This serves to widen the depletion region, creating an even greater barrier to the flow of current. This high-resistivity junction is reverse biased. When the voltage is applied to the PN junction with the opposite polarity, in the plus-to-minus direction, the mobile electrons and holes are repelled into the depletion region, causing it to narrow and lowering the barrier to the flow of current. This low-resistivity junction is forward biased. In this way, the forward or reverse biasing of a single PN junction produces a diode—a one-way valve or switch for current.[11]

A junction transistor is formed of three distinct areas of doped semiconductor material and the two PN junctions existing between these three doped areas. For purposes of explanation, the case of an NPN transistor (a sandwich-like structure of N-type, P-type, and N-type silicon) will be used. The alternate form of junction transistor, the PNP transistor, operates in the same fashion, but with the polarities and the majority and minority carriers reversed. A junction transistor has three areas: an "emitter," a "base," and a "collector." In an NPN transistor, the emitter and collector are N-type regions separated by a P-type base. Thus there are two PN junctions in the device: an emitter-base junction and a collector-base junction. Three metal contacts are made to the structure to form the transistor: one to the emitter, one to the base, and one to the collector. These contacts, unlike the contacts of the point-contact diode and the point-contact transistor, do not form junctions. Called ohmic contacts, they exhibit a stable, low resistance. Through these contacts, the junction transistor is connected to a surrounding circuit and to power sources.[12]

In normal operation, an NPN transistor has its emitter-base junction in forward bias and its collector-base junction in reverse bias. This causes the depletion region of the emitter-base junction to narrow, allowing electrons to flow into the base from the emitter. The base region is particularly thin in the junction transistor, so that many electrons injected into the base from the emitter avoid combining with holes present in the base. The injected electrons that avoid the holes in the base are then attracted into the N-type collector region. The electrons are attracted to the positively charged donor atoms in

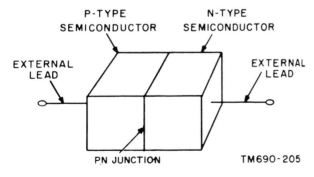

Figure A.4
PN junction diode. U.S. Army.

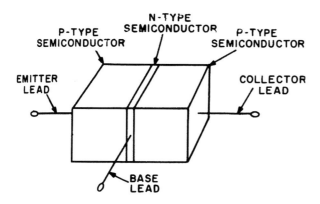

A. PNP JUNCTION TRANSISTOR

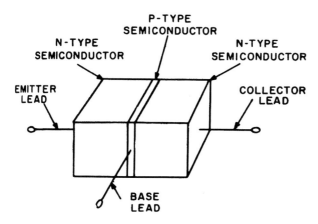

B. NPN JUNCTION TRANSISTOR

Figure A.5
PNP and NPN junction transistors. U.S. Army.

the widened depletion region around the reverse-biased collector-base junction and
also to the positive terminal of the collector-base power supply providing the reverse
bias. The injected electrons that reach the collector region cause the collector current
to flow. Because the current from the low-resistance emitter-base junction increases the
current across the high-resistance collector-base junction, the junction transistor provides power gain or amplification. With the control of reverse and forward biasing, the
junction transistor can also function as a switch, allowing and shutting off the flow of
current from emitter to collector.[13]

When junction transistors are employed for a switching function, one of their characteristic properties is their *frequency*—the rate at which they can turn on and off, allowing

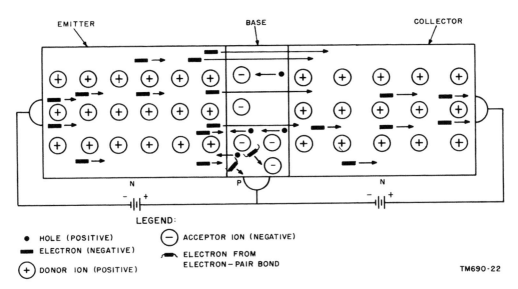

Figure A.6
Simplified representation of the behavior of an NPN junction transistor in the "on" state. U.S. Army.

or preventing the flow of current from the emitter to the collector. Because the flow of current in the junction transistor is governed by the movement of both electrons and holes throughout it, the speed of these movements leads to a junction transistor to have a particular *rise time* to turn on and a particular *fall time* to turn off. Together, the rise time and the fall time put an upper limit on the switching frequency of the transistor.[14]

All junction transistors are formed by doping regions of semiconductor crystal to create two PN junctions. Different processes for doping the crystal defined the basic approaches to manufacturing junction transistors. Two such approaches had achieved relative prominence by the mid 1950s: *grown junctions* and *alloy junctions*. In grown-junction technology, acceptor and donor dopants were successively added to a molten mass of silicon from which a long, cylindrical, single crystal of silicon was being carefully grown. By successively adding acceptor and donor dopants to the silicon melt, the grown crystal would possess successive layers of P-type and N-type silicon and multiple PN junctions.

The production apparatus for creating such single crystals of silicon was known as a *crystal grower* or *crystal puller*. The crystal grower could also produce single crystals of intrinsic, undoped silicon. A single crystal with grown junctions would then be sawed into small bars containing the three doped regions—either PNP or NPN—and the two PN junctions between them. Ohmic metal contacts were then made to these emitter, base, and collector regions, and the grown-junction transistor was complete.

The production of alloy-junction transistors began with a small piece of doped semiconductor crystal, either P-type or N-type. Depending on the type, a particular metal was chosen for alloying to both the top and the back of the crystal, either an acceptor or a donor metal. Heat was used to alloy the dopant metal to the two sides of the crystal, and after cooling the recrystallized regions containing the dopant metal formed the emitter and collector regions of the transistor. The unaffected bulk of the starting silicon crystal formed the base of the transistor. The alloyed metals provided ready contacts for the emitter and collector regions. With an ohmic contact made to the base region, the alloy-junction transistor was fully formed.[15]

A third approach to doping semiconductor crystals was being developed on an experimental basis in the mid 1950s: *diffusion*. In the "diffused junction" approach, layers of P-type and N-type material were formed in a piece of semiconductor crystal by exposing the crystal, at elevated temperatures within a furnace, to atmospheres containing vapors of acceptor or donor dopants. Dopant atoms diffused out of the vapor and into the semiconductor crystal, forming P-type or N-type layers in the crystal. In this way, an emitter and a base layer were formed in the starting crystal, the unaffected portion of which formed the collector layer. Such a junction transistor relied on two diffusions to create the emitter and the base, and hence is called a *double-diffused junction transistor*. Fairchild Semiconductor was established to develop a manufacturing process embodying this diffusion approach, initially for the production of a double-diffused silicon junction transistor. The next section of this appendix reviews the manufacturing process that Fairchild Semiconductor developed for the production of these transistors, also known as *silicon mesa transistors*. It considers the case of the NPN diffused silicon mesa transistor for the sake of simplicity, and for the reason that this was the form of transistor first produced by Fairchild Semiconductor.[16]

Silicon Mesa Transistors

The fabrication of NPN diffused silicon mesa transistors at Fairchild Semiconductor began with the production of single crystals of silicon. These long, cylindrical crystals had a diameter of approximately ¾ inch, and were produced using a crystal grower. A donor dopant added to the silicon melt yielded a crystal rod of uniform N-type silicon. A flat edge was then ground onto the crystal rod along its length, and the rod then sawed across its width to form many thin *wafers*. The earlier grinding operation thus provided each of the many silicon wafers with a flat edge that could be used for orienting and aligning the wafer during the processing steps that would follow. The wafers were then lapped—a form of grinding—in order to smooth the surfaces of the wafer, and given a final cleaning. Often this cleaning was a quick dip of the wafer into a strong chemical etchant—commonly a mix of nitric and hydrofluoric acids, which would dissolve the outermost layers of the wafer—followed by a water rinse. At this stage, a supply of multiple smooth, shiny, silver-gray wafers of N-type silicon would be at hand.[17]

The next stage of processing was the formation of the diffused layers in the silicon wafer. The diffusion process used high-temperature furnaces to drive dopant atoms from the atmosphere inside the furnace into the crystal of the silicon wafer. The temperature, the concentration of dopant in the furnace atmosphere, and the time of exposure

Figure A.7
Silicon wafers arrayed in a silica "boat" for placement in a diffusion furnace. Courtesy of McGraw-Hill.

together acted to control the depth or thickness of the diffused layers and the extent of their doping. The diffusion operation gave the ability to control the vertical dimensions of the junction transistor structure, by controlling the thicknesses of the diffused layers.[18]

The high temperatures and chemical reactions involved in a diffusion operation could cause damage (called *pitting*) to the surface of the wafer. Pitting would ruin the ability to form transistors. Researchers discovered that it was very easy to form a layer of silicon dioxide on the surfaces of these wafers, and that these silicon oxide layers could protect the surface of the silicon wafer from such damage during diffusion. Furthermore, some dopants were unable to pass through a silicon oxide layer to reach the underlying silicon wafer in a diffusion operation, whereas other dopants were able to diffuse through the oxide layer into the silicon wafer. For those dopants that were trapped by the oxide layer during diffusion, this opened the possibility for *oxide masking*—the use of a pattern of oxide on the surface of a wafer to control where dopants could diffuse into the wafer and where they could not. Thus, the oxide masking of diffusion provided the means to control the lateral dimensions of the junction transistor structure.[19]

With the vertical dimensions of the transistor structure controlled by the diffusion conditions, and the lateral dimensions defined by oxide masking, the diffusion approach provided the ability to carefully construct junction transistor structures. To employ oxide masking, however, required a technique for creating patterns in the oxide layer atop silicon wafers. The oxide layers could be formed with relative ease by placing wafers in a furnace and exposing them to a flow of oxygen or water vapor. The question of patterning the oxide layer for oxide masking was, then, the question of how to remove the oxide layer from specific regions of the wafer. The approach adopted by Fairchild Semiconductor for the patterning of these oxide layers was *photolithography*. The following account is of the photolithographic approach used at Fairchild Semiconductor during the period covered by this documentary history.

The photolithographic process began with what was essentially a black-and-white drawing of the pattern to be formed on the oxide layer. The drawing was a positive image: white where you wanted the oxide to stay, black where you wanted the oxide to be removed. Photographic techniques were used to reduce this pattern drawing many times over until it reached the scale of thousandths of an inch and matched exactly the dimensions of the pattern that was wanted on the oxide layer. Other photographic techniques were used to create a *mask*, often a glass slide about an inch square, which contained many repeated iterations of the pattern. The mask was placed in a metal frame so that it could be placed in a mechanical jig for alignment with the other masks required to make the transistor. The metal frame also protected the mask for the process of *contact printing* that was to follow.[20]

In contact printing, the oxide-covered silicon wafers were coated with a *photoresist*—a photosensitive coating. Exposure to ultraviolet and blue light caused a chemical reaction in the photoresist, with the exposed regions forming a polymer. Once polymerized, the exposed photoresist regions could withstand exposure to hydrofluoric acid, an *etchant* that can dissolve silicon oxide layers.

Contact printing proceeded by placing a photoresist-coated wafer against the mask, and then shining the light from an arc lamp through the mask onto the wafer. Using several chemicals as developers, the areas of the photoresist on the wafer that were exposed to the light formed protective polymers. The areas of the photoresist that were not exposed were thus undeveloped, and susceptible to removal by the etchant. The wafer was then placed in an etching bath, with the undeveloped regions of the photoresist and the underlying silicon oxide layer removed thereby. The remaining developed photoresist was then *stripped* off, leaving the underling oxide layer intact, by using another set of acids. The result of this photolithographic process was a silicon wafer covered by a patterned oxide layer.[21]

Using diffusion, oxide masking, and photolithography, Fairchild Semiconductor's production staff used the following process sequence to manufacture NPN diffused-silicon mesa transistors. N-type silicon wafers were placed inside a diffusion furnace. An acceptor dopant, boron, was then diffused into the wafer, forming a thin, P-type layer of

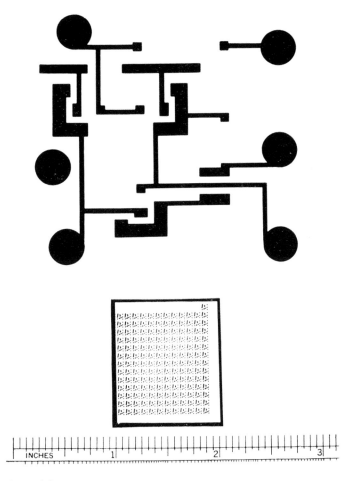

Figure A.8
An illustration of the reduction of pattern design in the production of masks for semiconductor photo-lithography. Courtesy of McGraw-Hill.

silicon across the entire surface of the wafer. This P-type layer would come to form the base regions of the junction transistors that were being created within the wafer. The underlying N-type material in the wafer, not affected by this *base diffusion*, would come to form the collector regions of the junction transistors.[22]

A silicon dioxide layer was grown on the surface of the wafers during the base diffusion by mixing oxygen or water vapor into the furnace. Growing the oxide layer during the base diffusion protected the wafer from damage. After the base diffusion, the wafers were subjected to photolithographic processing to define a pattern of openings in the oxide layer across the entire wafer. These openings through the oxide to the underlying silicon wafer would allow for a donor dopant to be diffused into the wafer, forming a new N-type silicon layer at the surface of the P-type base region. This new diffused N-type layer formed the emitter region of the junction transistor. This *emitter diffusion*

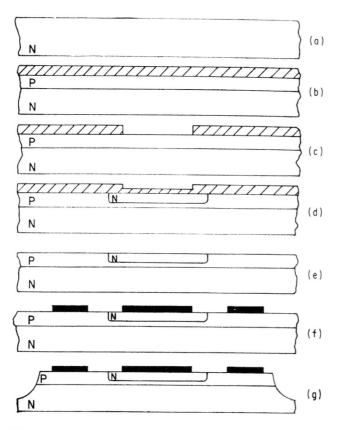

Figure A.9

A diagrammatic representation of the process steps used to create an NPN mesa transistor. Diagram a shows the original wafer of N-type silicon in cross section. Diagram b shows the P-type base region diffused into the wafer, with a covering layer of silicon oxide. Diagram c depicts the windows formed in the oxide layer by photolithography for the diffusion of the emitter regions. Diagram d presents the resulting N-type emitter region, with a covering oxide. Diagram e presents the result of oxide stripping, exposing the silicon surface of the wafer and the emitter-base PN junction. Diagram f shows the result of the photolithographic patterning of the evaporated aluminum film to form the emitter and base contacts. Diagram g shows the final structure of the NPN transistor after mesaing. Courtesy of McGraw-Hill.

took place in a diffusion furnace containing phosphorus vapor as the donor dopant. At this stage, the wafer was covered by multiple NPN transistor structures, having emitter, base, and collector regions separated by two PN junctions.[23]

The next stage of processing was for the formation of ohmic metal contacts to the emitter, base, and collector regions of the transistor structures. The emitter and base contacts were formed using photolithographic processes. After the emitter diffusion, the oxide layer was stripped off the wafer using an etchant. A film of aluminum was then evaporated onto the wafer. A second mask was used at this point in a photolithographic process to etch away the unwanted aluminum, leaving only the emitter and base contacts. An ohmic metal contact to the collector regions of the transistor structures was also formed by plating a layer of metal across the entire back of the wafer. At this stage of processing, the surface of the wafer was free of oxide, covered by a pattern of emitter and base contacts, and the back of the wafer covered by the metal for the collector contact.[24]

With the complete transistor structures and contacts formed, the process of *mesaing* was the final step in forming the many transistors in the same wafer. To define the area and size of the base region and the collector-base PN junction, silicon was etched away around the entire circumference of the transistor structure, down into the bulk of the collector region. The resulting profile of the transistor resembled the shape of the geological mesa formations of the American southwest, hence the appellation *mesa transistor* and the term *mesaing* for this final etching process. Wax was placed onto the surface of the wafer through a glass screen, forming protective dots of wax over the emitter and collector contacts, and defining the circumference of the base region. Another acid etching procedure gave the final mesa form, with the wax preventing etching of the contacts and transistor structures underneath.[25]

Up to this point in manufacturing, the procedures had formed a fully *batch* process. Each step in the processing simultaneously advanced all of the many transistor structures on the single wafer. This batch processing, as opposed to sequential processing, gave the diffusion approach to manufacturing junction transistors, as compared with grown-junction and alloy-junction methods, significant economic advantages. The peril

Figure A.10
A photograph of a single wafer, covered by many transistor structures. The visible rings and dots are the emitter and base contacts of these transistors. Courtesy of McGraw-Hill.

of the batch-production approach was that a problem with a single step in the manu-facturing process could cause catastrophic crashes in yield, wiping out vast numbers of potential transistors. [26]

After the mesaing operation, the manufacturing technology for making the NPN diffused-silicon mesa transistor moved from the batch to the sequential mode. The indi-vidual mesa transistors were cut from the silicon wafer in an operation called *wafer dicing*, with discrete individual devices often referred to as *die* and *dice*. The individual mesa transistor die then moved into a complex and expensive, piece-by-piece process of *assembly*. The transistor die needed to be placed inside a *package*, resembling a small metal can, to protect the transistor and to electrically connect the transistor contacts to the larger metal *leads* of the package, so that the transistor could be easily placed into electrical circuits. Assembly workers first mounted the transistor die to the *header* of the transistor package—a plate to which the die could be soldered, providing also the elec-trical connection between the collector contact and a package lead. Workers then used a delicate process called *thermocompression* to connect the emitter and base contacts to the remaining package leads using minute gold wires. Once these contact-to-lead connec-tions were made, the metal cap of the package was welded onto the header.[27]

Assembly was complete at this point, and the packaged mesa transistor was then sent to final testing. In final testing, a series of electrical measurements were made of the mesa transistor to determine if it met a series of specified values for the product, or *specs*. Other tests were performed across the course of processing the mesa transistors, to gauge the yield of the different process steps, to quickly identify problems, and to discard any defective transistors as soon as possible in the process for reasons of economy.[28]

With the silicon mesa transistor, the emitter-base PN junction was exposed at the top surface to the environment within the sealed package, as the collector-base PN junction was also so exposed around the full edge of the mesa. These exposed junctions proved to be a source of instabilities and failures in mesa transistors. The electrical fields at the exposed junctions could attract loose particles—bits of dust, tiny shards of metal or sol-der, etc.—to them, resulting in failure-producing shorts. These particles could also cause instabilities in or degradations of electrical performance. Exposed junctions were the cause of reliability problems for mesa transistors.[29]

Planar Transistors and Integrated Circuits

The solution to these reliability problems with mesa transistors came in the form of a new type of diffused junction silicon transistor developed at Fairchild Semiconductor in the late 1950s: the *silicon planar transistor*. The planar transistor was based on a new way of using oxide layers on silicon wafers. Previously, oxide layers that had been exposed to diffusion processes were widely considered to be "dirty"—loaded with dopants and other potential contaminants that could ruin the transistor if left in place. For this rea-son, the oxide layer was regularly removed at the end of wafer processing, leaving the

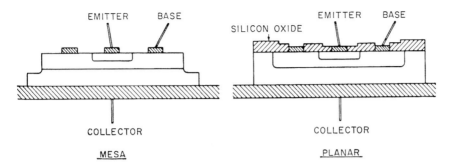

Figure A.11
Cross-sectional comparison of the mesa and planar transistor. Courtesy of McGraw-Hill.

silicon surface largely exposed. Nevertheless, researchers did know that oxide layers served to protect the silicon, as well as making it more electrically stable by neutralizing *surface states*, charged electrical states often found on clean silicon surfaces. The *planar process* developed at Fairchild Semiconductor went against the conventional wisdom concerning "dirty" oxides, leaving them in place during and after processing.[30]

The junction transistors made with the planar process differed from the mesa transistor in that both PN junctions within it—the emitter-base junction and the collector-base junction—were covered by protective oxide. This made planar transistors much more reliable than mesa transistors. Further, all the transistor contacts—those for the emitter, base, and collector—could be made at the surface of the transistor. Because the circumference of the base region was defined by an oxide-masked diffusion operation, no mesaing operation was required, giving the transistor its relatively flat—*planar*—form. The planar process was similar to the process for producing mesa transistors in many respects, and may be reviewed quickly.[31]

Taking the example of an NPN silicon planar transistor, wafers of N-type silicon were prepared from grown crystals as described previously. An oxide layer was then formed over the surface of the entire wafer. A first mask was used with photolithographic processing to open a series of windows in the oxide layer, through which an acceptor dopant would be diffused to form P-type base regions in the wafer crystal. Because it was susceptible to oxide masking, the chemical element boron was used as this acceptor dopant. During this base diffusion step, the boron atoms would diffuse both vertically and laterally in the silicon crystal. Thus, the collector-base PN junction came to the surface of the silicon wafer *underneath* the oxide layer, protected by it. This oxide layer was left in place, and additional oxide was then formed over the entire surface of the wafer, covering both the existing oxide and also the surface of the diffused base region.[32]

A second mask was used with photolithographic processing to open a series of windows in the new oxide layer over the diffused base regions. These windows would allow the diffusion of phosphorus into the base region to form a N-type emitter region and the emitter-base PN junction. These windows were smaller than those used for the base

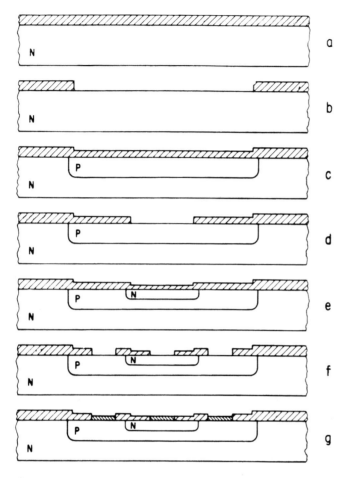

Figure A.12

Schematic representation of the planar process for fabricating an NPN planar transistor. (a) The starting N-type silicon wafer with a covering oxide layer, shown in cross section. (b) The wafer after photolithography to open windows in the oxide for base diffusion. (c) The wafer after P-type base region formed by diffusion, with covering oxide layer. (d) The structure after photolithography to open windows in oxide layer for emitter diffusion. (e) The transistor structure after emitter diffusion, again covered by an oxide layer. (f) The wafer after photolithography to open windows in oxide to allow contact of evaporated aluminum contacts to emitter and base regions. (g) The final structure after photolithographic patterning of the aluminum film, with protective oxide layer remaining in place. Courtesy of McGraw-Hill.

diffusion for several reasons: so the emitter would fit into the base region, so the emitter-base junction would reach the wafer surface underneath the new oxide, and so that a wide enough ring of the base region would exist at the wafer surface for making a metal contact to it. Again, the oxide layer was left in place on the surface of the wafer following the emitter diffusion, and additional oxide was again formed over the entire wafer surface.[33]

The third mask was employed with photolithography to create a more complex series of openings in the oxide layer through which aluminum would be evaporated to form the emitter and base contacts, at minimum. If desired, openings to allow aluminum to form contacts to the collector region could be made as well. If not, metal contacts could be made to the collectors by metal plated on the back of the wafer. Another round of masking and photolithography removed unwanted aluminum, leaving only the transistor contacts behind. At the end of processing, most of the transistor surface was covered by the protective oxide, covering all the regions where the PN junctions came to the wafer surface. The remaining areas were covered by the aluminum contacts. As with the mesa transistor process, the production of planar transistors was, to this point, entirely a batch process. Many planar transistors were formed on a single wafer. After wafer dicing, the planar transistors were assembled and tested in the same manner as mesa transistors.[34]

The reliability of electronic components such as silicon mesa transistors was of primary concern in the years covered by this documentary history. The primary market for silicon transistors was for military electronic systems, particularly aerospace computers. The more common junction transistors of the late 1950s were formed from the semiconductor element germanium. Germanium transistors, however, would routinely fail at the high temperatures involved in aerospace systems. Silicon transistors, on the other hand, could perform at these elevated temperatures. By the late 1950s, the U.S. military was acutely interested in the reliability of transistors and other electronic components. The failure of components was a major reason that vital electronic systems were often non-functional, requiring expensive maintenance.[35]

The U.S. military also began to emphasize the miniaturization of electronic systems along with reliability for these aerospace applications. The size and weight of electronic systems added an enormous cost to aerospace projects. Consider the case of an airborne computer, used in an aircraft for navigation and bombing guidance. Not only did the size and weight of the computer itself added great costs in terms of the propulsion power required to keep it airborne, but also added were the costs of the systems required to provide electrical power to the computer and to cool it. The total costs of such aerospace electronic systems would be greatly reduced if they were smaller, lighter, consumed less power, and operated at higher temperatures. The U.S. military's strong interests in this direction led many in the semiconductor industry to investigate several approaches to *microcircuitry* (alternatively known as *microelectronics* and *microminiaturization*) at the end of the 1950s.[36]

Electronic components firms pursued a number of very different approaches to micro-circuitry: hybrid circuits, thin films, 2D and 3D packaging modules, functional devices, and semiconductor integrated circuits. Hybrid circuits combined miniaturized components with techniques from the printed circuit board industry to reduce the size of circuits. Thin-film approaches sought to form components from patterned layers of thinly deposited material. Thin-film and hybrid-circuit approaches were often closely related. 2D and 3D packaging modules aimed at circuit miniaturization through new forms of circuit packaging that more closely packed discrete components, often stacking them instead of relying only on the then-common large, flat printed circuit boards. Functional devices, a more radical departure, sought to create the electronic function of a circuit in a novel material without reproducing individual circuit components. That is, the functional device would recreate the function of a circuit containing (for example) a transistor, a resistor, and a capacitor without having regions within the functional device that corresponded to these discrete components.[37]

The approach of semiconductor integrated circuits was pursued at Texas Instruments and Fairchild Semiconductor and is reviewed below. The concept for semiconductor integrated circuits, developed in the 1950s, looked to create all the components for an electronic circuit—resistors, capacitors, diodes, transistors—in a unitary piece of semiconductor crystal. How this might be accomplished was an open issue in the late 1950s, as were the issues of how such integrated components could be electrically isolated from one another in the semiconductor crystal and how these integrated components could be electrically interconnected to form a circuit. Perhaps the largest question facing the concept of semiconductor integrated circuits was if they could be made practically and economically.[38]

After Texas Instruments developed a semiconductor integrated circuit structure containing resistors, capacitors, and transistors in a single bar of germanium in 1958, Fairchild Semiconductor's managers initiated two efforts in microcircuitry in 1959. First, hybrid circuits were developed, placing several individual transistors along with resistors in a single transistor-size package. Second, a development project was launched to create a semiconductor integrated circuit based on the planar process: the *planar integrated circuit*. The process that Fairchild Semiconductor's engineers developed for producing the planar integrated circuit was very similar to the process for making planar transistors, indeed that was the point. The planar integrated circuit was very much an outgrowth of the planar process, and was thus closely linked to Fairchild Semiconductor's existing manufacturing technology.[39]

Resistor, capacitor, diode, and transistor structures were all formed in silicon wafers using oxide making, diffusion, and photolithography. Resistor structures were defined in diffused regions. Capacitors and diodes were both built around single PN junctions between diffused regions. Planar transistors were built as previously described, around two PN junctions produced by diffusions. Interconnecting these structures required only a modification of the process used to form the aluminum contacts to planar transistors.

The oxide layer covering a planar structure was not only protective but also electrically insulating. Thus, a patterned film of aluminum lines could run across the oxide layer, electrically isolated from the integrated components below in the wafer, and interconnecting the integrated components through windows formed in the oxide layer by photolithography.[40]

The challenge that Fairchild Semiconductor faced was finding a process to electrically isolate the integrated components from one another in the wafer. The firm's engineers initially developed an approach that they termed *physical isolation*, in which moats were etched away from the back of the silicon wafer through to the oxide layer. These moats, surrounding the integrated components, were then filled with an insulating epoxy material. In this way, the integrated components were isolated from one another by the epoxy-filled moats and electrically connected to one another by the aluminum interconnection lines deposited atop the oxide layer. An alternative approach, which would eventually come to predominate, was termed *electrical isolation* by the firm. In this approach, wells of P-type material were formed across the width of the silicon wafer, diffusing boron in from both the surface and the back of the wafer. These diffused wells provided extra PN junctions between the integrated components, which could be biased so as to electrically isolate the components from each other. In the physical isolation process and also in the diffused, electrical isolation process, the planar integrated circuits were formed in a batch process up to the step of wafer dicing. Assembly and testing of the planar integrated circuits proceeded in much the same manner as for mesa and planar transistors. Both the planar process and the planar integrated circuit would quickly grow to dominate both the semiconductor industry and then electronics more broadly in the 1960s.[41]

Digital Computers

The mesa transistors, planar transistors, and planar integrated circuits produced by Fairchild Semiconductor in the late 1950s and the early 1960s were used in military digital computers, often in aerospace systems. In the digital computers of the 1950s and the 1960s, information was represented in a binary form—as a series of values of bits, each having only a possible value of 0 or 1. Calculations and other operations were performed on such information in *logic circuits*. These circuits were called logic circuits because the mathematical and other operations that the computer performed were based on a system of formal logic that had been developed by George Boole in the nineteenth century. In the 1930s, Claude Shannon had shown that electrical circuits could be seen as models of the logic operations of Boole's system. In this way, an electronic system—built from a set of basic types of logic circuits—could perform mathematical and other operations on information.[42]

Logic circuits were built from basic building blocks called *logic gates*. In the 1940s and the early 1950s, vacuum tubes, functioning as electronic switches, were used to construct

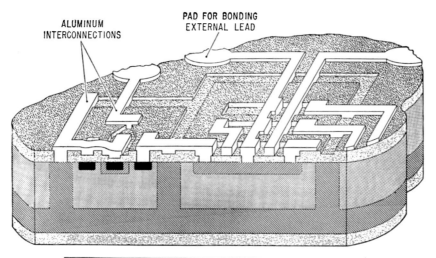

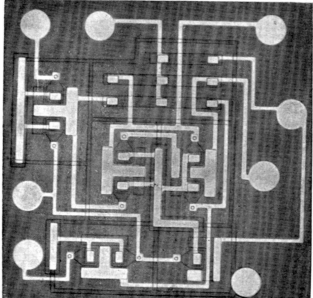

Figure A.13
A cross-sectional diagram and a photograph of a planar integrated circuit in Fairchild Semiconductor's Micrologic line. Courtesy of McGraw-Hill.

these logic gates. With the advent of semiconductor electronics, diodes and transistors also became possibilities for creating logic gates and other circuits for digital computers. The changing costs and capabilities of diodes and transistors in the 1950s led to the development of a variety of new *logic forms*, distinct approaches to the design of digital logic circuits that were based on the types of components that were used and how they were interconnected. In the 1950s and the 1960s, there were all-diode, diode-transistor, resistor-transistor, and all-transistor logic forms. Transistor manufacturers created products especially for these different logic forms. Integrated circuits for digital computers were logic circuits and as such the choice of logic form was a major decision, connected to the fundamental design of the computer system they would go into. Fairchild Semiconductor chose direct-coupled transistor logic (DCTL), a resistor-transistor logic form that was in vogue in advanced military computing, for its Micrologic line of planar integrated circuits and hybrid circuits.

In addition to logic, memory was the other primary function in digital computing—the storage and retrieval of information. In the 1950s and the 1960s, magnetic drums provided a means for storing data, as did magnetic tapes. For fast, readily accessible memory, large numbers of magnetic ceramic rings, also known as *cores*, were strung at the interstices of arrays of wires, forming *magnetic core memory*. Electrical pulses running through the wires could read the magnetic state of a core (magnetized or not representing the binary values of 1 and 0), or change the magnetic state. To read and write to the core memory, transistors—*core drivers*—were needed in circuits to control these pulses of electrical current. The DCTL logic form and the use of core memory were the signatures of military digital computers.[43]

Notes

Introduction

1. Works treating the dynamics and consequences of the spread of digital electronics are too numerous to review. The work of the sociologist Manuel Castells can, however, be highlighted for its explorations of the dynamics of digitalization and its simultaneous economic and cultural consequences. A fine introduction to his work is Manuel Castells, *The Internet Galaxy: Reflections on the Internet, Business, and Society* (Oxford University Press, 2001).

2. Christophe Lécuyer, *Making Silicon Valley: Innovation and the Growth of High Tech, 1930–1970* (MIT Press, 2006); David C. Brock, ed., *Understanding Moore's Law: Four Decades of Innovation* (Chemical Heritage Press, 2006); Chong-Moon Lee, William Miller, Marguerite Hancock, and Henry Rowen, eds., *The Silicon Valley Edge: A Habitat for Innovation and Entrepreneurship* (Stanford University Press, 2000); AnnaLee Saxenian, *Regional Advantage: Culture and Competition in Silicon Valley and Route 128* (Harvard University Press, 1994).

3. Recent works by the historians Christophe Lécuyer, Ross Bassett, Leslie Berlin, and Michael Riordan and recent historical accounts by Gordon Moore and Jay Last examined the place of Fairchild Semiconductor in the history of semiconductor electronics and in the history of Silicon Valley. The narratives and arguments presented in this volume build on the work of these authors, especially *Making Silicon Valley* by Lécuyer. See Lécuyer, *Making Silicon Valley: Innovation and the Growth of High Tech, 1930–1970*; Ross Bassett, *To the Digital Age: Research Labs, Start-up Companies, and the Rise of MOS Technology* (Johns Hopkins University Press, 2002); Leslie Berlin, *The Man Behind the Microchip: Robert Noyce and the Invention of Silicon Valley* (Oxford University Press, 2005); Michael Riordan, "The Silicon Dioxide Solution," *IEEE Spectrum* 44:12 (2007), 50–56; Michael Riordan, "From Bell Labs to Silicon Valley: A Saga of Semiconductor Technology Transfer, 1955–61," *The Electrochemical Society Interface* 16, no. 3 (2007), 36–41; Jay Last, "Two Communications Revolutions," *Proceedings of the IEEE* 86, no. 1 (1998), 170–175; Gordon Moore, "The Role of Fairchild in Silicon Technology in the Early Days of 'Silicon Valley'," *Proceedings of the IEEE* 86, no. 1 (1998), 53–62.

4. Peter Shaw, "The American Heritage and Its Guardians," *American Scholar* 45 (1976), 175–182; Constance B. Schulz, "'From Generation unto Generation': Transitions in Modern Documentary History Editing" (Review Essay), *Reviews in American History* 16, no. 3 (1988), 337–350; Mary Jo Kline, *A Guide to Documentary Editing*, second edition (Johns Hopkins University Press, 1998).

5. Candice Falk, Barry Paterman, and Jessica Moran, eds., *Emma Goldman: A Documentary History of the American Years, Volume 1: Made for America, 1890–1901* (University of Illinois Press, 2008); Robert D. Wood, *Life in Laredo: A Documentary History from the Laredo Archives* (University of North Texas Press, 2004); Ava F. Kahn, *Jewish Voices of the California Gold Rush: A Documentary History, 1849–1880* (Wayne

State University Press, 2002); David Gellman and David Quigley, eds., *Jim Crow New York: A Documentary History of Race and Citizenship, 1777–1877* (NYU Press, 2003); Carroll W. Pursell, *A Hammer in Their Hands: A Documentary History of Technology and the African-American Experience* (MIT Press, 2006).

6. Shaw, "The American Heritage and Its Guardians"; Schultz, "From Generation unto Generation"; Lester Cappon, "A Rationale for Historical Editing, Past and Present," *William and Mary Quarterly* 3, no. 23 (1966), 56–75.

7. See, for example, the six volumes of the *Papers of Thomas A. Edison* published by the Rutgers University Press.

8. Phil Scott, *The Pioneers of Flight: A Documentary History* (Princeton University Press, 2003); Robert C. Williams and Philip L. Cantelon, eds., *American Atom: A Documentary History of Nuclear Policies from the Discovery of Fission to the Present, 1939–1984* (University of Pennsylvania Press, 1984); Thomas Shannon, *Genetic Engineering: A Documentary History* (Greenwood, 1999); Pursell, *A Hammer in Their Hands*.

9. Another important repository of documents on Fairchild Semiconductor is the Computer History Museum. Former employees of Fairchild Semiconductor have supplied these materials for the Museum's Information Technology Corporate Histories collection.

10. For an introduction to the work of Frederic L. Holmes, see Holmes, "Laboratory Notebooks: Can the Daily Record Illuminate the Broader Picture?" *Proceedings of the American Philosophical Society* 134, no. 4 (1990), 349–366 and "Scientific Writing and Scientific Discovery," *Isis* 78, no. 2 (1987), 220–235; W. Bernard Carlson and Michael E. Gorman, "Understanding Invention as a Cognitive Process: The Case of Thomas Edison and Early Motion Pictures, 1888–91," *Social Studies of Science* 20 (1990), 387–430. For Andrew Pickering's viewpoint, see "The Mangle of Practice: Agency and Emergence in the Sociology of Science," *American Journal of Sociology* 99 (1993), 559–589; Pickering, *The Mangle of Practice* (University of Chicago Press, 1995); Pickering, "Decentering Sociology: Synthetic Dyes and Social Theory," *Perspectives on Science* 13 (2005), 352–405.

11. Holmes, "Laboratory Notebooks: Can the Daily Record Illuminate the Broader Picture?" *Proceedings of the American Philosophical Society* 134, no. 4 (1990), 365–366.

12. Pickering "The Mangle of Practice: Agency and Emergence in the Sociology of Science," *American Journal of Sociology* 99 (1993), 559–589; Pickering, *The Mangle of Practice*; Pickering, "Decentering Sociology."

13. This volume is directly applicable to a variety of instructional purposes, beyond its clear relevance to readers with a particular interest in the history of electronics, modern computing, and Silicon Valley. Within the disciplines of science and technology studies and the history of science, it could be used in advanced undergraduate and graduate courses on the history of electronics, computing, and science and technology in the twentieth century. The documents reproduced herein and the interpretive essays could also prove of use in graduate courses on methodology, historical methods, and the practice of documentary and archival research. This use in methodological instruction could also be highly relevant for the field of business history. Instructors of advanced undergraduate and graduate courses in business history covering Silicon Valley, high-technology industries, and the relationships between social and technical innovations may find this volume useful. It might also be directly relevant to instruction in engineering schools. The volume's provision of a fine-grain case study of the dynamics of innovation makes it valuable for graduate courses in management science, technology management, and innovation studies.

Chapter 1

1. For a discussion of the founders' backgrounds, see Christophe Lécuyer, *Making Silicon Valley: Innovation and the Growth of High Tech, 1930–1970* (MIT Press, 2006). Details of these backgrounds are found in Jay Last, oral history interview by Lécuyer, 1 April 1996; Last, oral history interview by Brock, 21 June 2004; Gordon Moore, oral history interview by Ross Bassett and Lécuyer, 18 February 1997; Moore, oral history interview by Arnold Thackray and Brock, Interview sessions from 2001 to 2007; Jean Hoerni, oral history interview by Lécuyer, 4 February 1996; C. Sheldon Roberts, oral history interview by Lécuyer, 6 July 1996; Victor Grinich, oral history interview by Lécuyer, 7 February 1996; Julius Blank, oral history interview by Lécuyer, 20 June 1996; Blank, oral history interview by Brock, 20 March 2006; Eugene Kleiner, oral history interview by Lécuyer, 21 May 1996.

2. Christophe Lécuyer and David C. Brock, "The Materiality of Microelectronics," *History and Technology* 22 (2006), 301–325; Michael Riordan and Lillian Hoddeson, *Crystal Fire: The Birth of the Information Age* (Norton, 1997).

3. Riordan and Hoddeson, *Crystal Fire*. On the early history of digital computing and the increasing transistorization of systems, see Arthur Norberg, *Computers and Commerce: A Study of Technology and Management at Eckert–Mauchly Computer Company, Engineering Research Associates, and Remington Rand, 1946–1957* (MIT Press, 2005); Paul Ceruzzi, *A History of Modern Computing* (MIT Press, 1998); Martin Campbell-Kelly and William Aspray, *Computer: A History of the Information Machine* (Basic Books, 1996).

4. Riordan and Hoddeson, *Crystal Fire*; Riordan, "From Bell Labs to Silicon Valley: A Saga of Semiconductor Technology Transfer, 1955–1961," *Interface*, Fall 2007, 36–41; Lécuyer and Brock, "The Materiality of Microelectronics"; Bo Lojek, *History of Semiconductor Engineering* (Springer, 2007); Morris Tanenbaum, oral history interview by Brock and Lécuyer, 3 May 2004 and 26 July 2004.

5. Gordon Teal, "Technical Highlights of TI, 1952–1962," Texas Instruments Incorporated folder, Internal History Collection, Center for the History of Physics, American Institute of Physics; Caleb Pirtle, *Engineering the World: Stories from the First 75 Years of Texas Instruments* (Southern Methodist University Press, 2005); Lécuyer and Brock, "The Materiality of Microelectronics"; Riordan and Hoddeson, *Crystal Fire*.

6. Teal, "Technical Highlights of TI"; John McDonald, "Where Texas Instruments Goes from Here," *Fortune*, December 1961; Pirtle, *Engineering the World*; Lécuyer and Brock, "The Materiality of Microelectronics"; Riordan and Hoddeson, *Crystal Fire*.

7. Lécuyer, *Making Silicon Valley*.

8. Lécuyer, *Making Silicon Valley*; Riordan and Hoddeson, *Crystal Fire*. A wealth of information about the state of silicon manufacturing technology development at Shockley Semiconductor directed at diffused silicon mesa transistors, field effect transistors, and PNPN diodes can be found in lengthy internal project and "special" reports that Shockley and many of Fairchild's eventual founders wrote in May 1957. These reports are in the William Shockley Papers, SC222, Department of Special Collections, Stanford University Libraries. See in particular William Shockley et al. "Project Report 7: Field Effect,"15 May 1957 and G. Smoot Horsley et al., "Special Report 5: NPNP Development," 3 May 1957.

9. One can speculate that William Shockley reoriented his firm toward PNPN diodes for a number of reasons. For one thing, the reorientation may have been a response to TI's announcement in March 1956 that it was manufacturing silicon transistors with grown junction and diffusion techniques. Another reason might have been that the Bell System was interested in this device and would constitute a ready market for the PNPN diode. It may also have been the case that Shockley conceived the transistor as an intermediate step to more interesting and promising functional devices, such as PNPN diodes.

10. Robert and Betty Noyce to parents, 28 May 1957, Leslie Berlin Papers, M 1491, series 3, box 6, folder 5, Stanford Archives and Special Collections; Lécuyer, *Making Silicon Valley*; Riordan and Hoddeson, *Crystal Fire*.

11. Jay Last to Vic Jones, 20 September 1957, courtesy of Jay Last; William Shockley, personal notebook, William Shockley papers, SC222 95–153, box B4, Stanford Archives and Special Collections; Noyce, interview by Herb Kleinman, 18 November 1965, Herb Kleinman collection, M827, Stanford Archives and Special Collections; Lécuyer, *Making Silicon Valley.*.

12. Eugene Kleiner, letter to Hayden Stone & Company, June 1957, courtesy of Jay Last; Last to parents, 7 July 1957; A. Coyle to *New York Times*, 26 April 1998, courtesy of Jay Last; Hayden, Stone & Company, *Fairchild Camera and Instrument*, February 1958, courtesy of Jay Last; Fairchild Camera and Instrument, *Annual Reports* for 1955–57; Nelson Stone, oral history interview by Lécuyer, 21 April 1995; Lécuyer, *Making Silicon Valley.*.

13. Noyce to parents, 4 September 1957, Leslie Berlin Papers, M 1491, series 3, box 6, folder 5, Stanford Archives and Special Collections.

14. Minutes of the Fairchild Camera and Instrument Corporation Board Meeting, 15 August 1957, National Semiconductor Corporation.

15. "8 Leave Shockley to Form Coast Semiconductor Firm," *Electronic News*, 20 October 1957; contract among the California group, Parkhurst (Hayden Stone), Fairchild Controls, and Fairchild Camera and Instrument, 23 September 1957, William Shockley Papers, SC 222 95–153, box B4, Stanford Archives and Special Collections.

16. Last, personal notebook, courtesy of Last; Gordon Moore and Jay Last, oral history interview by Brock and Lécuyer, 20 January 2006; Kleiner, oral history interview by Lécuyer; Blank, oral history interview by Lécuyer.

17. Last, personal notebook, courtesy of Last; "New Palo Alto Company Plans to Produce Transistors," *Palo Alto Times*, 17 October 1957, collection of Lécuyer; Victor Grinich, oral history interview by Lécuyer, 7 February 1996; Leslie Berlin, *The Man Behind the Microchip: Robert Noyce and the Invention of Silicon Valley* (Oxford University Press, 2005).

18. Thomas Bay, oral history interview by Lécuyer, 2 July 1996; interview with Robert Noyce, no date, Intel Museum; Lécuyer, *Making Silicon Valley*.

19. James Bridges, "Progress in the Reliability of Military Electronics Equipment during 1956," *IRE Transactions on Reliability and Quality Control* 11 (1957), 1–7; "USAF Reliability Emphasis Grows," *Aviation Week*, 1 April 1957, 28; Jacob Neufeld, *Ballistic Missiles in the United States Air Force, 1945–1960* (Office of Air Force History, 1990); Paul Ceruzzi, *Beyond the Limits: Flight Enters the Computer Age* (MIT Press, 1989); Samuel Fishbein, *Flight Management Systems: The Evolution of Avionics and Navigation Technology* (Praeger, 1995).

20. Noyce, interview by Kleinman; Last, interview by Lécuyer; Lécuyer, *Making Silicon Valley.*.

21. Interestingly, in diodes Pacific Semiconductors pursued the military computing and avionics market. The firm supplied microdiodes to Autonetics for the guidance and control system of the Minuteman missile. Joseph Ross, oral history interview by Craig Addison, SEMI; Sanford Barnes, oral history interview by Jack Ward, 2003, Semiconductor Museum; Thompson Ramo Wooldridge Incorporated Annual Report, 1958, Baker Library, Harvard University; Davis Dyer, *TRW: Pioneering Technology and Innovation since 1900* (Harvard Business School Press, 1998).

22. Last to parents, 6 October 1957, courtesy of Jay Last; William Hester, "Dr. E. M. Baldwin," *Solid State Journal*, March 1961, 19–19; Bay, oral history interview by Lécuyer; Gordon Moore and Last, oral history interview by Brock and Lécuyer.

23. Bay, oral history interview by Lécuyer; Orville Baker, oral history interview by Lécuyer, 15 December 2000.

24. Last, personal notebook; Bay, oral history interview by Lécuyer.

25. Last, personal notebook. Reportedly, obtaining this order required a visit by Hodgson and Sherman Fairchild, Fairchild Camera's chairman, to Thomas Watson, IBM's chief executive. Because the purchasing officers of IBM's Military Systems division were reluctant to buy from an untried firm, Sherman Fairchild, who was IBM's largest individual shareholder and the head of the executive committee of IBM's board of directors, asked Watson to buy the core drivers from his new venture. Watson acquiesced.

26. L. E. Miller, "The Design and Characteristics of a Diffused Silicon Logic Amplifier Transistor," *Proceedings of Wescon*, 1958, part 2, 132–140; Grinich, oral history interview by Lécuyer; Last, oral history interview by Lécuyer; David Allison, oral history interview by Lécuyer, 23 June 2000.

27. Carl Frosch and Lincoln Derick, "The Oxidation of Silicon to Prevent Surface Erosion During High Temperature Heating Operations—Case 38139-20," 14 June 1955, courtesy of Nick Holonyak; Derick and Frosch, "Oxidation of Semiconductor Surfaces for Controlled Diffusion," U.S. patent 2,802,760 submitted on 2 December 1955 and granted on 13 August 1957; Frosch and Derick, "Surface Protection and Selective Masking during Diffusion," *Journal of the Electrochemical Society* 104 (1957), 547–552; Michael Riordan, "From Bell Labs to Silicon Valley: A Saga of Semiconductor Technology Transfer, 1955–61," *The Electrochemical Society Interface* 16, no. 3 (2007), 36–41.

28. Lojek, *History of Semiconductor Engineering*; Jules Andrus, "Fabrication of Semiconductor Devices," U.S. Patent 3,122,817, filed 15 August 1957 and granted 3 March 1964; Harry Sello, oral history interview by Brock and Lécuyer, 4 November 2004, 7 January 2005, and 16 March 2005; James Gibbons, oral history interview by Lécuyer, 18 December 2001 and 30 May 2002.

29. Phillip Scranton has written extensively on batch manufacturing and flexible production. See Scranton, *Endless Novelty: Specialty Production and American Industrialization, 1865–1925* (Princeton University Press, 2000). Scranton details how batch production was used for a variety of products at the core of industrial activities and consumer culture. Silicon manufacturing technology of the kind pursued at Fairchild Semiconductor revived this batch approach in the context of postwar high technology.

30. Last, personal notebook; Last, oral history interview by Lécuyer; Grinich, oral history interview by Lécuyer.

31. Moore, "The Role of Fairchild in Silicon Technology in the Early Days of Silicon Valley," *Proceedings of the IEEE* 86 (1998), 53–62; Moore and Last, oral history interview by Brock and Lécuyer; Last, oral history interview by Lécuyer.

32. Hoerni, oral history interview by Lécuyer; Allison, oral history interview by Lécuyer; Moore, oral history interview by Bassett and Lécuyer.

33. Moore and Noyce, "Method for Fabricating Transistors," U.S. Patent 3,108,359, filed 30 June 1959, issued 29 October 1963; Moore, "progress report," 1 April 1958 and "progress report," 1 May 1958, courtesy of Gordon Moore; Moore and Last, oral history interview by Brock and Lécuyer.

34. Moore, "progress report," 1 May 1958, courtesy of Gordon Moore; Last, personal notebook; Moore and Last, oral history interview by Brock and Lécuyer; Hoerni, oral history interview by Lécuyer.

35. Moore and Last, oral history interview by Brock and Lécuyer; Kleiner, oral history interview by Lécuyer; Last, oral history interview by Lécuyer.

36. Last, personal notebook; Blank, oral history interview by Lécuyer; Robert Robson, oral history interview by Brock and Lécuyer, 16 December 2005; Grinich, oral history interview by Lécuyer; Lécuyer, *Making Silicon Valley*.

37. Last, personal notebook; Gordon Teal, "Technical Highlights of TI, 1952–1962," Texas Instruments Incorporated folder, Internal History Collection, Center for the History of Physics, American Institute of Physics.

38. Last, personal notebook. The group of Fairchild Semiconductor founders had designed their NPN mesa transistor to meet IBM's requirements for a core driver—a middle-of-the-road device in terms of specifications that could also handle medium powers. After introducing this transistor to the market, the group discovered that they had been lucky in their decision and that circuit engineers were interested in using their device in many other circuits than those employed to drive core memories. See Last, oral history interview by Lécuyer; Bay, oral history interview by Lécuyer.

39. Last, personal notebook; Bay, interview by George Rotsky, circa 1988, George Rotsky collection, M851, Stanford Archives and Special Collections; Bay, oral history interview by Lécuyer; J. M. Wuerth, "The Evolution of Minuteman Guidance and Control," *Navigation* 23 (1976): 64–75; Donald MacKenzie, *Inventing Accuracy* (MIT Press, 1990).

40. Grinich, oral history interview by Lécuyer; communication of Richard Hodgson to Lécuyer, 10 October 1998; Lécuyer, *Making Silicon Valley*.

41. Last, personal notebook; Hoerni, oral history interview by Lécuyer.

42. Last, personal notebook; Hoerni, oral history interview by Lécuyer; Hoerni, oral history interview by Charles Sporck, no date, Stanford Archives and Special Collections; Moore, oral history interview by Brock; Allison, oral history interview by Lécuyer.

43. Last, personal notebook; "New \$1 Million Plant Set for Mountain View," *The Register Leader*, 12 November 1958, courtesy of Jay Last; *Leadwire*, August 1958–March 1959, courtesy of Jay Last; Fairchild Camera and Instrument, *Prospectus*, 25 January 1960, courtesy of Eugene Kleiner; Moore and Last, oral history interview by Brock and Lécuyer.

44. Hoerni, oral history interview by Lécuyer; Hoerni, oral history interview by Sporck; on nickel "gettering," see Moore, oral history interview by Thackray and Brock.

45. Wuerth, "The Evolution of Minuteman Guidance and Control"; Moore and Last, oral history interview by Brock and Lécuyer; Grinich, oral history interview by Lécuyer; Bay, oral history interview by Lécuyer; Lécuyer, *Making Silicon Valley*.

46. Moore, "The Role of Fairchild in Silicon Technology in the Early Days of Silicon Valley," *Proceedings of the IEEE* 86 (1998), 53–62; "New Company to Build Tiny Electronic Devices in Plant Here," *The Register Leader*, 12 November 1958, courtesy of Jay Last; Hoerni, oral history interview by Lécuyer; Last, oral history interview by Lécuyer; Lécuyer, *Making Silicon Valley*.

47. Hoerni, oral history interview by Lécuyer. On the historical significance of the planar process, see Lécuyer, *Making Silicon Valley*; Riordan, "The Silicon Dioxide Solution."

48. Hoerni, patent notebook, National Semiconductor; Hoerni, oral history interview by Lécuyer; Hoerni, oral history interview by Sporck. For an example of the gold doping of silicon diodes at the Bell

Labs, see E.G. Rupprecht, H.J. Patterson, and P. Miller, "Hyperfast Diffused-Silicon Diode and Transistor for Logic Circuits," *International Solid State Circuits Conference, Digest of Technical Papers* 2 (1959), 72–73.

49. Hoerni, patent notebook; Hoerni, "Patent Manufacturing Process," U.S. Patent 3,108,914, filed 30 June 1959 and granted 29 October 1963; Moore, oral history interview by Brock; Hoerni, oral history interview by Lécuyer; Hoerni, oral history interview by Sporck.

50. Hoerni, patent notebook; Moore, "The Role of Fairchild in Silicon Technology in the Early Days of Silicon Valley."

51. Hoerni, patent notebook. Hoerni, "Semiconductor Device," U.S. Patent 3,064,167, filed May 1, 1959; patent issued November 13, 1962; Hoerni, "Method of Manufacturing Semiconductor Devices," U.S. patent 3,025,589, filed May 1, 1959; patent issued March 20, 1962.

52. L. Arthur D'Asaro, interview by Lécuyer, 7 May 2008; D'Asaro, oral history interview by Brock, 21 July 2009; James Goldey, communication to Brock, October 2008; Hoerni, oral history interview by Lécuyer; Moore, oral history interview by Brock. For oxide regrowth at the Bell Labs, see Derick and Frosch, "Oxidation of Semiconductor Surfaces for Controlled Diffusion," U.S. patent 2,802,760 submitted on 2 December 1955 and granted on 13 August 1957; and Andrus, "Fabrication of Semiconductor Devices," U.S. Patent 3,122,817, filed 15 August 1957 and granted 3 March 1964.

53. Hoerni, "Multiple Elastic Scattering in Electron Diffraction by Crystals," *Physical Review* 102, no. 6 (1956), 1534–1542. It is possible that Hoerni's familiarity with diffusion processes may have led him to assess that the "dirty" nature of the silicon dioxide layers after several steps of diffusion processing would, nevertheless, pose no threat to the performance of transistors if it was left in place.

54. Last, personal notebook, entries for 7 May 1958 and 15 September 1958; M. M. Atalla, E. Tannenbaum, and E. Scheibner, "Stabilization of Silicon Surfaces by Thermally Grown Oxides," *Bell System Technical Journal* (May 1959), 749–783; Moore and Last, oral history interview by Brock and Lécuyer.

55. Hoerni, patent notebook, National Semiconductor; Hoerni, oral history interview by Lécuyer; Hoerni, oral history interview by Sporck; Moore and Last, oral history interview by Brock and Lécuyer; Last, oral history interview by Lécuyer.

56. Hoerni, "Planar Silicon Transistors and Diodes," paper presented at the 1960 Electron Devices Meeting, Washington, Bruce Deal Papers, 88–333, Stanford Archives and Special Collections; Hoerni, patent notebook, National Semiconductor; Hoerni, oral history interview by Lécuyer; Hoerni, oral history interview by Sporck.

57. Hoerni, patent notebook, National Semiconductor; Hoerni, oral history interview by Lécuyer; Hoerni, oral history interview by Sporck; Sello, oral history interview by Brock and Lécuyer.

58. Moore, oral history interview by Arnold Thackray and Brock. See also L. N. Duryea, "Fairchild Investigation," 28 May 1959, William Shockley Papers, SC 222 05–153, box B4, folder Fairchild info 3 July 1959, Stanford Archives and Special Collections..

59. Moore and Last, oral history interview by Brock and Lécuyer; William Hester, "Dr. E. M. Baldwin," *Solid State Journal*, March 1961, 18–19; Grinich, oral history interview by Lécuyer; Lécuyer, *Making Silicon Valley*.

60. Moore, oral history interview by Brock; Moore and Last, oral history interview by Brock and Lécuyer.

61. Hoerni, oral history interview by Lécuyer.

62. Hoerni, oral history interview by Lécuyer; Hoerni, oral history interview by Sporck; Sello, oral history interview by Brock and Lécuyer; David James, oral history interview by Lécuyer, 14 December 2000; Moore, oral history interview by Ross Bassett and Lécuyer; Moore and Last, oral history interview by Brock and Lécuyer.

63. Just as oxide masking and diffusion had been prominent research topics in the semiconductor community when Hoerni first conceived the planar process at the end of 1957, the community continued to pursue these avenues in 1959 as Hoerni and his Fairchild Semiconductor colleagues moved the planar process into production. In 1959, two engineers in Bell Labs' branch organization in Allentown, Pennsylvania, K. E. Daburlos and H. J. Patterson, pursued a research line very close to the planar process. Allentown was the site of Western Electric's manufacture of semiconductor devices, and Bell Labs had an active organization in Allentown connected to semiconductor manufacturing. While Daburlos and Patterson created diffused silicon transistors using many of the same steps as Hoerni's planar process, they nevertheless appear to have followed the standard Bell Labs approach of always removing the "dirty" oxide layer, thereby consistently missing the essence of Hoerni's process. Hoerni, progress reports, 1 February 1960, 1 March 1960, 1 April 1960, and 1 October 1960, Technical Reports and Progress Reports, M 1055, box 5, Stanford Archives and Special Collections; Lojek, *History of Semiconductor Engineering*; Hoerni, oral history interview by Lécuyer; Hoerni, oral history interview by Sporck; James, oral history interview by Lécuyer; K. E. Daburlos and H. J. Patterson, "Oxide Masking," *Bell Laboratories Record* 38 (November 1960): 417–420.

64. Hoerni also explored other ways in which he could use the planar process. He investigated especially the ways in which the new process could be used to make a new kind of transistor: the unipolar transistor, later called the metal oxide semiconductor (MOS) transistor. See Hoerni patent notebook, National Semiconductor.

65. *Leadwire*, November 1959; Hoerni, oral history interview by Lécuyer.

66. *Leadwire*, November 1959; Fairchild Camera, "Prospectus"; Moore and Last, oral history interview by Brock and Lécuyer.

67. *Leadwire*, November 1959; "Fairchild Camera—Portrait of a Growth Company," *Financial World*, 12 September 1962.

68. Moore, memorandum, 5 November 1959, Moore papers, courtesy of Gordon Moore.

69. Moore, memorandum, 5 November 1959; Moore and Last, oral history interview by Brock and Lécuyer.

70. "Planar Transistor Offers Wide Beta," *Electronic Daily*, 23 March 1960, courtesy of Jay Last; R. Painter, "Across-Board Competency New Transistor Field Need," *Electronic News*, 25 July 1960; Painter, " Transistor Entry Tightens," *Electronic News*, 1 August 1960; John Tilton, *International Diffusion of Technology: The Case of Semiconductors* (Brookings Institution, 1971); Ernest Braun and Stuart McDonald, *Revolution in Miniature* (Cambridge University Press, 1982).

71. Braun and Stuart McDonald, *Revolution in Miniature*; John Linvill and C. Lester Hogan, "Intellectual and Economic Fuel for the Electronics Revolution," *Science* 195, no. 4283 (March 1977): 1107–1113; George Ebel, "Reliability Physics in Electronics: A Historical View," *IEEE Transactions on Reliability* 47, no. 3-SP (September 1998): SP-379–SP-389; William Denson, "The History of Reliability Prediction," *IEEE Transactions on Reliability* 47, no. 3-SP (September 1998): SP-321–SP-328; J. H. Saleh and K. Marais, "Highlights from the early (and pre-) history of reliability engineering," *Reliability Engineering and System Safety* 91 (2006): 249–256.

72. Braun and Stuart McDonald, *Revolution in Miniature*; Hyungsub Choi and Cyrus Mody, "The Long History of Molecular Electronics," *Social Studies of Science* 39 (2009), 11–50; Jack Kilby, "Invention of the Integrated Circuit," *IEEE Transactions on Electron Devices* 23 (July 1976): 648–654; R. Warner and B. Grung, *Transistors: Fundamentals for the Integrated-Circuit Engineer* (Wiley, 1990). For early work on hybrid circuits, see T. Prugh, J. Nall, and N. Doctor, "The DOFL Microelectronics Program," *Proceedings of the IRE*, May 1959, 882–894; Thomas O. Stanley, oral history interview with Brock, 30 March 2009.

73. Ian Ross and Eugene Reed, "Functional Devices," in Edward Keonjian, ed., *Microelectronics: Theory, Design, and Fabrication* (McGraw-Hill, 1963).

74. In 1959, Jack Morton, who directed semiconductor research at the Bell Labs decided to abandon this line of research and Arthur D'Asaro was reassigned to another project. Morton took a much more conservative approach to the miniaturization problem and focused the Bell Labs' resources on the making of hybrid circuits. For D'Asaro's stepping element, see Ross and Reed, "Functional Devices"; L. A. D'Asaro, "A Stepping Transistor Element," *IRE Wescon Convention Record*, 1959, part 3, 37–42; D'Asaro, interview by Lécuyer; D'Asaro, oral history interview by Brock. For the shift register work at RCA, see J. Torkel Wallmark, "Design Considerations for Integrated Devices," *Proceedings of the IRE* 48 (1960), 293–300; Stanley, oral history interview by Brock. Interestingly, an engineer at Texas Instruments also worked on functional devices in the late 1950s. In a patent filed in early 1959, Richard Stewart proposed a transistor-based functional device. See Richard F. Stewart, "Integrated Semiconductor Circuit Device," U.S. Patent 3,138,747, filed 12 February 1959 and granted 23 June 1964.

75. Last, "Some comments on the development of the first integrated circuits," 26 November 2000; Last, "Development of the Integrated Circuit, August 1959–June 1960," 2000.

76. Kilby, "Invention of the Integrated Circuit"; Kilby, "Semiconductor Solid Circuits," *Electronics*, 7 August 1959, 110–111.

77. Kilby, "Invention of the Integrated Circuit"; T. R. Reid, *The Chip: How Two Americans Invented the Microchip and Launched a Revolution* (Simon and Schuster, 1984).

78. Kurt Lehovec, "Multiple Semiconductor Assembly," U.S. Patent 3,029,366, filed 22 April 1959, granted 10 April 1962; Lehovec, "Invention of p-n Junction Isolation in Integrated Circuits," *Transactions on Electron Devices*, ED-25, no. 4 (1978), 495–496; Lehovec, oral history interview by Brock, 21 and 31 August 2007.

79. Noyce, patent notebook, National Semiconductor; Last, personal notebook; James, oral history interview by Lécuyer.

80. Robert Noyce, "Semiconductor Circuit Complex Having Isolation Means," U.S. Patent 3,150,299, filed 11 September 1959 and granted 22 September 1964 and "Semiconductor Circuit Complexes," U.S. patent 3,117,260, filed 11 September 1959 and granted 7 January 1964; Lehovec, "Multiple Semiconductor Assembly," U.S. Patent 3,029,366, filed 22 April 1959, granted 10 April 1962.

81. Noyce, "Semiconductor Device and Lead Structure," U.S. Patent 2,981,877, filed July 30, 1959; patent issued April 25, 1961.

82. "New Products Steal the Show," *Leadwire*, September 1959, courtesy of Jay Last; Isy Haas, Jay Last, Lionel Kattner, and Bob Norman, oral history of panel on the Development and Promotion of Fairchild Micrologic Integrated Circuits, moderated by David Laws, 6 October 2007, Computer History Museum; Moore and Last, oral history interview by Brock and Lécuyer; Last, oral history interview by Lécuyer; Last, oral history interview by Brock.

83. Oral history of panel on the Development and Promotion of Fairchild Micrologic Integrated Circuits; Last, oral history interview by Lécuyer; Last, oral history interview by Brock.

84. Last, patent notebook, National Semiconductor; Last, "Solid-state Circuitry Having Discrete Regions of Semi-conductor Material Isolated by an Insulating Material," U.S. patent 3,158,788, filed 15 August 1960, granted 24 November 1964; Last, "Method of Making Solid-State Circuitry," U.S. patent 3,313,013, filed 15 August 1960, granted 11 April 1967; Last, oral history interview by Lécuyer, 1 April 1996; Last, oral history interview by Brock; oral history of panel on the Development and Promotion of Fairchild Micrologic Integrated Circuits.

85. "Jim Nall Wins Highest Prize," *Leadwire*, November 1959, courtesy of Jay Last; Lionel Kattner, oral history interview by Lécuyer, 13 October 2000; oral history of panel on the Development and Promotion of Fairchild Micrologic Integrated Circuits.

86. Kattner, patent notebooks, National Semiconductor; Last, "Solid-State Circuitry Having Discrete Regions of Semiconductor Material Isolated by an Insulating Material," U.S. patent 3,158,788, filed August 15, 1960 and granted November 24, 1964; Last, "Method of Making Solid-State Circuitry," U.S. patent 3,313,013, filed August 15, 1960 and granted April 11, 1967; Kattner, oral history interview by Lécuyer.

87. Isy Haas, patent notebook, National Semiconductor; Kattner, patent notebooks; Last, progress reports, 1 August 1960, 1 October 1960, and 1 December 1960, Technical Reports and Progress Reports, M1055, box 5, Stanford Archives and Special Collections; Kattner, oral history interview by Lécuyer; Oral history of panel on the Development and Promotion of Fairchild Micrologic Integrated Circuits.

88. Kattner, oral history interview by Lécuyer; oral history of panel on the Development and Promotion of Fairchild Micrologic Integrated Circuits.

89. Kattner, oral history interview by Lécuyer; oral history of panel on the Development and Promotion of Fairchild Micrologic Integrated Circuits; Last, oral history interview by Lécuyer.

90. According to Allison, in 1959 the group of Fairchild Semiconductor founders debated and voted on whether they would share their financial gains as a group with top employees. Some pressed for it, but the majority chose not to do so. Allison, oral history interview by Lécuyer; Hoerni, oral history interview by Lécuyer; Last, oral history interview by Lécuyer; oral history of panel on the Development and Promotion of Fairchild Micrologic Integrated Circuits.

91. Kattner, oral history interview by Lécuyer; Allison, oral history interview by Lécuyer; James, oral history interview by Lécuyer; Last, oral history interview by Brock; Last, oral history interview by Lécuyer; Hoerni, oral history interview by Lécuyer; Norman, oral history interview by Brock; Lécuyer, *Making Silicon Valley*.

Chapter 2

1. Eugene and Rose Kleiner's letter is in Jay Last's personal collection of papers on the history of Fairchild Semiconductor. Permission to reproduce this letter was granted by Jay Last.

2. Eugene Kleiner, oral history interview by Christophe Lécuyer, 21 May 1996. "Rose Kleiner," *Palo Alto Times*, 6 May 1998.

3. Kleiner, oral history interview, 21 May 1996; Julius Blank interview by Lécuyer, 20 June 1960; Lécuyer and David Brock, "The Materiality of Microelectronics," *History and Technology* 22 (2006), 301–325.

4. Lécuyer, *Making Silicon Valley*.

5. Kleiner, oral history interview by Lécuyer; Lécuyer, *Making Silicon Valley*.

6. Arthur Rock, oral history interview by Brock, 9 October 2002; Gordon Moore, oral history interview by Arnold Thackray and Brock, 2001–2007; Jay Last, oral history interview by Lécuyer, 1 April 1996; Sheldon Roberts, oral history interview by Lécuyer, 6 July 1996; Lécuyer, *Making Silicon Valley*.

7. The original copy of Jay Last's personal notebook is in his private collection of papers on the history of Fairchild Semiconductor and other semiconductor firms in Silicon Valley. Permission to reproduce extracts of his notebook was given by Jay Last.

8. Last, foreword to this volume; Last and Moore, oral history interview by Brock and Lécuyer.

9. Last, oral history interview by Lécuyer, 1 April 1996; Last, oral history interview by Brock, 21 June 2004.

10. Gordon Moore and Last, oral history interview by Brock and Lécuyer, 20 January 2006; Last, oral history interview by Brock; Last, oral history interview by Lécuyer.

11. Contract among the California group, Parkhurst (Hayden Stone), Fairchild Controls, and Fairchild Camera and Instrument, 23 September 1957, William Shockley Papers, SC 222 95–153, box B4, Stanford Archives and Special Collections; Last, oral history interview by Brock; Last, oral history interview by Lécuyer; Gordon Moore and Last, oral history interview by Brock and Lécuyer.

12. Gordon Moore and Last, oral history interview by Brock and Lécuyer. "Photoetching" (more commonly known as photolithography) was pioneered by Jules Andrus at the Bell Telephone Laboratories and Jay Lathrop and James Nall at the Diamond Ordnance Fuze Laboratory.

13. Moore and Last, oral history interview by Brock and Lécuyer.

14. Ian M. Ross, interview with David Brock, 21 September 2007.

15. Victor Grinich, oral history interview by Lécuyer, 7 February 1996; Robert Norman, interview by Brock, 8 August 2007; Saul Rosen, "Recollections of the Philco Transac S-2000," *IEEE Annals of the History of Computing* (April-June 2004), 34–47; James McKenney and Amy Weaver Fisher, "Manufacturing the ERMA Banking System: Lessons from History," *IEEE Annals of the History of Computing* 15, no. 4 (1993), 7–26; Louis Brown, "Flyable TRADIC: The First Airborne Transistorized Digital Computer," *IEEE Annals of the History of Computing* 21, no. 4 (1999), 55–61; M. M. Irvine, "Early Digital Computers at Bell Telephone Laboratories," *IEEE Annals of the History of Computing* (July September 2001), 23–42; Samuel Snyder, "Computer Advances Pioneered by Cryptologic Organizations," *IEEE Annals of the History of Computing* 2, no. 1 (1980), 60–70.

16. Julius Blank, oral history interview with David Brock, 20 March 2006; Blank, oral history interview by Lécuyer, 20 June 1996.

17. Jean Hoerni's patent notebook is at National Semiconductor. Permission to reproduce this entry was granted by Dick Schubert of National Semiconductor.

18. Jean Hoerni, oral history interview by Christophe Lécuyer, 4 February 1996; Hoerni, oral history interview by Charles Sporck, no date, Stanford Archives and Special Collections. Hoerni and James Ibers, "Complex Amplitudes for Electron Scattering by Atoms," *Physical Review* 91, no. 5 (1953), 1182–1185; Hoerni, "Multiple Elastic Scattering in Electron Diffraction by Molecules," *Physical Review* 102, no. 6 (1956), 1530–1533; Hoerni, "Multiple Elastic Scattering in Electron Diffraction by Crystals," *Physical Review* 102, no. 6 (1956), 1534–1542.

19. Hoerni, oral history interview by Lécuyer; Hoerni, oral history interview by Sporck.

20. Carl Frosch and Lincoln Derick, "The Oxidation of Silicon to Prevent Surface Erosion During High Temperature Heating Operations—Case 38139-20," 14 June 1955, courtesy of Nick Holonyak; Lincoln Derick and Carl Frosch, "Oxidation of Semiconductor Surfaces for Controlled Diffusion," U.S. patent 2,802,760 submitted on 2 December 1955 and granted on 13 August 1957. See also Holonyak, "The Origins of Diffused-Silicon Technology at Bell Labs, 1954–55," *Interface*, fall 2007, 30–34; Michael Riordan, "From Bell Labs to Silicon Valley: A Saga of Semiconductor Technology Transfer, 1955–1961," *Interface*, fall 2007, 36–41.

21. Frosch and Derick, "Surface Protection and Selective Masking during Diffusion," *Journal of the Electrochemical Society* 104 (1957), 547–552. Gordon Moore and Jay Last, oral history interview by Brock and Lécuyer, 20 January 2006; Lécuyer, *Making Silicon Valley*; Michael Riordan, "The Silicon Dioxide Solution," *IEEE Spectrum* 44, no. 12 (2007), 50–56.

22. In their June 1955 memorandum, Frosch and Derick had stated that "the protective quartz envelope" grown through oxidation (quartz is formed of silicon dioxide) "may be useful for protecting an electrical device from atmospheric conditions. For example, the device might prove more stable if left enclosed in such a quartz envelope." But they do not seem to have followed up on these ideas. Frosch and Derick, "The Oxidation of Silicon to Prevent Surface Erosion During High Temperature Heating Operations—Case 38139-20," 14 June 1955, courtesy of Holonyak.

23. Moore and Last, oral history interview by Brock and Lécuyer.

24. Lincoln Derick and Carl Frosch, "Oxidation of Semiconductor Surfaces for Controlled Diffusion," U.S. patent 2,802,760 submitted on 2 December 1955 and granted on 13 August 1957. L. Arthur D'Asaro, communication to Christophe Lécuyer, 7 May 2008; James Goldey, communication to David Brock, October 2008. Not all semiconductor researchers, however, thought that the silicon oxide layer had to be removed after processing. In November 1955—two years before Hoerni's conception of the planar transistor—Herbert Henkels of Westinghouse filed a patent on a power transistor that incorporated a layer of silicon oxide. In Henkels' scheme, the silicon oxide layer insulated the transistor from large films of silver or other conductive material that acted as a heat sink and also formed the transistor electrodes. In contrast, Hoerni viewed the oxide layer as a way to protect the transistor junctions. See Herbert Henkels, "Power Transistor," U.S. patent 2,858,489, filed 4 November 1955 and granted 28 October 1958.

25. Moore and Last, oral history interview by Brock and Lécuyer. According to Roger Borovoy, who worked as Fairchild Semiconductor's patent lawyer in the 1960s, Gordon Moore had described something similar to a planar device in his Shockley Semiconductor patent notebook. When Borovoy attempted to collect royalties on Fairchild's planar patent from Clevite, the transistor manufacturer that had bought Shockley Semiconductor, Clevite's lawyers showed him this entry in Moore's notebook. As a result, Borovoy abandoned his attempt to collect royalties from Clevite. In recent recollections, Borovoy noted that Shockley Semiconductor or Clevite would have lost any patent interference litigation had they claimed rights to the planar process. He stated "there was a glib statement in [Moore's notebook], but the planar process was a hard thing to build. This statement did not amount to anything. They would have lost an interference." When asked in 1996 whether he remembered such a patent notebook entry, Moore stated that he did not recollect having had such an idea at Shockley Semiconductor. Moore's patent notebook at Shockley Semiconductor seems to have been lost. Roger Borovoy, oral history interview by Ross Bassett and Lécuyer, 14 June 1996; Leslie Berlin, "Roger Borovoy, November 7, 2003," Leslie Berlin papers, M 1491, series 3, box 5, folder 7, Stanford Archives and Special Collections; Moore, oral history interview by Lécuyer and Bassett, 18 February 1996.

26. Moore and Last, oral history interview by Brock and Lécuyer; Hoerni, oral history interview by Lécuyer; Hoerni, oral history interview by Sporck.

27. Moore and Last, oral history interview by Brock and Lécuyer.

28. Hoerni, patent disclosure, 14 January 1959. See facsimile and essay in this volume.

29. Gordon Teal, "Technical Highlights of TI, 1952–1962," Texas Instruments Incorporated folder, Internal History Collection, Center for the History of Physics, American Institute of Physics; Caleb Pirtle, *Engineering the World: Stories from the First 75 Years of Texas Instruments* (Dallas: Southern Methodist University Press, 2005); Robert Gray, "Learning from History: Case Studies of the Weapons Acquisition Process" (Review Essay), *World Politics* 31, no. 3 (1979), 457–470; William Denson, "The History of Reliability Prediction," *IEEE Transactions on Reliability* 47, no. 3-SP (1998), SP-321–SP-328; George Ebel, "Reliability Physics in Electronics: A Historical View," *IEEE Transactions on Reliability* 47, no. 3-SP (1998), SP-379–SP-389; John Linvill and C. Lester Hogan, "Intellectual and Economic Fuel for the Electronics Revolution," *Science*, NS 195, no. 4283 (1977), 1107–1113.

30. Lécuyer, *Making Silicon Valley*.

31. Fairchild Camera and Instrument, annual reports, 1955–58, National Semiconductor.

32. Julius Blank, oral history interview with David Brock, 20 March 2006; Blank, oral history interview by Lécuyer; 20 June 1996.

33. "Fairchild Semiconductor Corporation Has Opening for Vice President and General Manager," *Wall Street Journal*, 8 December 1957; William Hester, "Dr. E. M. Baldwin," *Solid State Journal*, March 1961, 18–19.

34. Leslie Berlin, *The Man Behind the Microchip: Robert Noyce and the Invention of Silicon Valley* (Oxford University Press, 2005).

35. Berlin, *Man Behind the Microchip*; C. Sheldon Roberts, oral history interview by Lécuyer, 6 July 1996; Louis Brown, "Flyable TRADIC: The First Airborne Transistorized Digital Computer," *IEEE Annals of the History of Computing* 21, no. 4 (1999), 55–61; M. M. Irvine, "Early Digital Computers at Bell Telephone Laboratories," *IEEE Annals of the History of Computing*, July September 2001, 23–42; Samuel Snyder, "Computer Advances Pioneered by Cryptologic Organizations," *IEEE Annals of the History of Computing* 2, no. 1 (1980), 60–70; Saul Rosen, "Recollections of the Philco Transac S-2000," *IEEE Annals of the History of Computing* (April-June 2004), 34–47.

36. P. F. Olsen and R. J. Orrange, "Real-Time Systems for Federal Applications: A Review of Significant Technological Developments," *IBM Journal of Research and Development* 25, no. 5, September 1981, 405–416.

37. Gary Beatovich, A Case Study of Manned Strategic Bomber Acquisition: The B-70 Valkyrie, master's thesis, Air Force Institute of Technology, School of Systems and Logistics, Wright-Patterson Air Force Base, 1990; Orville Baker, oral history interview by Christophe Lécuyer, 15 December 2000.

38. T. B. Lewis, "Digital Computer Equipment for an Advanced Bombing, Navigation and Missile Guidance Subsystem for the B-70 Air Vehicle," *Proceedings of the IRE* 49, no. 1, January 1961, 313–318.

39. Robert Gray, "Learning from History: Case Studies of the Weapons Acquisition Process," *World Politics* 31, no. 3 (1979), 457–470; William Denson, "The History of Reliability Prediction," *IEEE Transactions on Reliability* 47, no. 3-SP (1998), SP-321–SP-328; George Ebel, "Reliability Physics in Electronics: A Historical View," *IEEE Transactions on Reliability* 47, no. 3-SP (1998), SP-379–SP-389; John Linvill and

C. Lester Hogan, "Intellectual and Economic Fuel for the Electronics Revolution," *Science*, NS 195, no. 4283 (1977), 1107–1113; Lécuyer, *Making Silicon Valley*.

40. William Hester, "Dr. E. M. Baldwin," *Solid State Journal*, March 1961, 18–19.

41. Thomas Bay, oral history interview by Lécuyer, 2 July 1996; Allen J. Scott, "The aerospace-electronics industrial complex of Southern California: The formative years, 1940–1960," *Research Policy* 20 (1991), 439–456.

42. Gordon Moore and Jay Last, oral history interview by Brock and Lécuyer; Lécuyer, *Making Silicon Valley*.

43. Victor Grinich, oral history interview by Lécuyer, 7 February 1996.

44. Grinich, oral history interview by Lécuyer.

45. Gordon Moore and Jay Last, oral history interview by Brock and Lécuyer.

46. Moore and Jay Last, oral history interview by Brock and Lécuyer.

47. Allen J. Scott, "The aerospace-electronics industrial complex of Southern California: The formative years, 1940–1960," *Research Policy* 20 (1991), 439–456.

48. Lécuyer and Brock, "Gordon Earle Moore," *Annals of the History of Computing* (July September 2006) 2–8; Moore, oral history interview by Arnold Thackray and Brock, 2001–2007; Moore, oral history interview by Ross Bassett and Lécuyer, 18 February 1997.

49. P. F. Olsen and R. J. Orrange, "Real-Time Systems for Federal Applications: A Review of Significant Technological Developments," *IBM Journal of Research and Development* 25, no. 5, September 1981, 405–416; Richard Hodgson, interview by Lécuyer, 10 October 1998; Jean Hoerni, oral history interview by Lécuyer, 4 February 1996; Thomas Bay, oral history interview by Lécuyer, 2 July 1996; Lawrence E. Davies "IBM to Expand Computer Output," *New York Times*, 28 April 1965.

50. Bay, oral history interview by Lécuyer.

51. Bay, oral history interview by Lécuyer.

52. Eugene Kleiner, oral history interview by Lécuyer, 21 May 1996; Lécuyer, *Making Silicon Valley*.

53. Kleiner, oral history interview by Lécuyer; Jay Last, oral history interview by Lécuyer, 1 April 1996; Lécuyer, *Making Silicon Valley*.

54. Roberts, oral history interview by Lécuyer, 6 July 1996.

55. David Allison, oral history interview by Christophe Lécuyer, 23 June 2000.

56. Allison, oral history interview by Lécuyer; Moore, oral history interview by Brock.

57. For development work at Fairchild Semiconductor on photolithography, see Robert Noyce, "Progress Report of Photoetching," 1 February 1958 and "Progress Report," 1 March 1958, Gordon Moore Papers; Moore and Last, oral history interview by Brock and Lécuyer.

58. Last, oral history interview by Lécuyer.

59. This document is in the personal collection of Gordon Moore. Permission to reproduce it was granted by Gordon Moore.

60. Gordon Moore, "Progress Report," 1 April 1958, Moore personal papers collection, Intel; Moore, oral history interview by Arnold Thackray and Brock, 2001–2007; Moore, oral history interview by Ross Bassett and Lécuyer, 18 February 1997.

61. Moore and Robert Noyce, "Method for Fabricating Transistors," U.S. Patent 3,108,359, filed 30 June 1959, issued 29 October 1963.

62. At first, Moore proposed to set up an elaborate process for comparing the two transistors. In this process, engineers would have processed batches of NPN and PNP transistors in parallel and used various tests and criteria to compare the two devices. A committee composed of Moore, Noyce, Last, Hoerni, Grinich, and Allison would then have chosen the transistors to produce first. Moore later abandoned this idea and made the decision on his own. See Moore, "Decision between NPN and PNP for first preproduction device," March 1958, Moore papers, Intel; David Allison, oral history interview by Lécuyer, 23 June 2000.

63. To solve these problems, Hoerni lapped off the back of the transistor and did a back-side diffusion of the collector. He also used aluminum for the emitter and base contacts. Hoerni, oral history interview by Sporck; Hoerni, oral history interview by Lécuyer.

64. Moore and Last, oral history interview by Brock and Lécuyer, 20 January 2006.

65. Lécuyer, *Making Silicon Valley*.

66. Moore, oral history interview by Arnold Thackray and David Brock; Moore, oral history interview by Lécuyer and Ross Bassett, 18 February 1997; Moore and Last, oral history interview by Brock and Lécuyer, 20 January 2006.

67. Gordon Moore and Jay Last, oral history interview by Brock and Lécuyer.

68. Atalla soon published his talk as M.M. Atalla, E. Tanenbaum, and E.J. Scheibner, "Stabilization of Silicon Surfaces by Thermally Grown Oxides," *Bell System Technical Journal* (May 1959), 749–783.

69. The Hughes presentation was published as B. Schwartz, "The Use of Organo-Substituted Hydrolyzable Silanes on Silicon Devices," *Journal of the Electrochemical Society* (October 1959), 371–373. Other groups also experimented with silicone coatings to protect and electrically stabilize diffused transistors. Among these were engineers at General Electric and a group at the American Bosch Arma Corporation, a maker of military avionics systems. See Harry Sello, oral history interview by Brock and Lécuyer, 7 January 2005 and Edward Keonjian, "Microminiaturizing a Space Vehicle Computer," *Electronics*, 29 April 1960. Additionally, at the end of 1957 Jay Lathrop and James Nall from the Diamond Ordnance Fuze Laboratory had reported at a meeting of the Institute of Radio Engineers about their efforts using photolithography to create a miniaturized hybrid circuit that combined thin-film components with diffused germanium transistors for proximity fuzes. For size considerations, Lathrop and Nall had encapsulated their unpackaged diffused germanium transistors in a protective resin along with the passive components of the hybrid circuit. Fairchild Semiconductor's founders were closely following developments in photolithography, and may have also have picked up on Lathrop's and Nall's use of resin to protect the surfaces of their germanium transistors. J. R. Nall and J. W. Lathrop, "Photolithographic fabrication techniques for transistors which are an integral part of a printed circuit," *IRE Transactions on Electron Devices* 5, no. 2 (April 1958), 117; Jay W. Lathrop and James R. Nall, "Semiconductor Construction," U.S. Patent 2,890,395, filed 31 October 1957, granted 9 June 1959.

70. "New $1 Million Plant Set for Mountain View" and "New Mountain View Company to Build Tiny Electronic Devices Plant here," *The Register Leader*, 12 November 1958, courtesy of Jay Last.

71. Fairchild Camera's plant in Long Island was unionized. Long Island was a major center of military aircraft production in the 1950s. "New $1 Million Plant Set for Mountain View" and "New Mountain

View Company to Build Tiny Electronic Devices Plant here," *The Register Leader*, 12 November 1958, courtesy of Jay Last.

72. Jay Last, oral history interview by Lécuyer, 1 April 1996.

73. Gordon Moore and Jay Last, oral history interview by Brock and Lécuyer, 20 January 2006.

74. Julius Blank, oral history interview with Brock; Lécuyer and Brock, "The Materiality of Microelectronics," *History and Technology* 22 (2006), 301–325.

75. Gordon Moore, oral history interview by Brock, 2009.

76. Gordon Moore and Jay Last, oral history interview by Brock and Lécuyer, 20 January 2006.

77. These part numbers followed a naming convention for electronic components promulgated by the Electronic Industries Association, a trade group. The advertisement appeared in several trade publications. It is reproduced in this volume with permission from Fairchild Semiconductor. The 2N697 had slightly different amplifying characteristics than the 2N696. Both transistors were made with the same manufacturing process. They were sorted out from one another during testing.

78. Thomas Bay, oral history interview by Lécuyer, 2 July 1996.

79. Last notebook, entry for 25 August 1958; Fairchild Camera and Instrument, "Prospectus," January 25, 1960, courtesy of Eugene Kleiner; Bay, oral history interview by Lécuyer.

80. L. E. Miller, "The Design and Characteristics of a Diffused Silicon Logic Amplifier Transistor," *Proceedings of Wescon* 2 (1958) 132–140.

81. Moore and Last, oral history interview with Brock and Lécuyer; Roger Borovoy, oral history interview by David Brock, 2007; Borovoy, oral history interview by Ross Bassett and Christophe Lécuyer, 14 June 1996.

82. Moore and Last, oral history interview with Brock and Lécuyer; Borovoy, oral history interview by Brock, 2007; Borovoy, oral history interview by Bassett and Lécuyer.

83. Moore and Last, oral history interview with Brock and Lécuyer; Borovoy, oral history interview by Brock, 2007; Borovoy, oral history interview by Bassett and Lécuyer.

84. Jean Hoerni, patent notebook, National Semiconductor.

85. Jean Hoerni's patent disclosure is in Jay Last's personal collection of papers on the history of Fairchild Semiconductor. It is reproduced here with the permission of Jay Last.

86. Jean Hoerni, oral history interview by Christophe Lécuyer, 4 February 1996; Gordon Moore, oral history interview by Arnold Thackray and David Brock; Moore and Jay Last, oral history interview by Brock and Lécuyer, 20 January 2006; Sheldon Roberts, oral history interview by Lécuyer, 6 July 1996; Robert Robson, oral history interview by Brock and Lécuyer, 16 December 2005. For a treatment of the planar process, see Lécuyer, *Making Silicon Valley: Innovation and the Growth of High Tech, 1930–1970* (MIT Press, 2006) and Michael Riordan, "The Silicon Dioxide Solution," *IEEE Spectrum*, December 2007, 44–50. Arjun Saxena discusses the effort to make half-planar structures, but mistakenly claims that this effort inspired Hoerni's ideas for the planar process, rather than resulted from them. Arjun Saxena, *Invention of Integrated Circuits: Untold Important Facts* (World Scientific, 2009), 97–99.

87. Gordon Moore, "The Role of Fairchild in Silicon Technology in the Early Days of Silicon Valley," *Proceedings of the IEEE* 86 (1998), 53–62; Hoerni, oral history interview by Lécuyer; Hoerni, oral history

interview by Charles Sporck, no date, Stanford Archives and Special Collections; Robson, oral history interview by Brock and Lécuyer; Victor Grinich, oral history interview by Lécuyer, 7 February 1996.

88. Moore, "The Role of Fairchild in the Early Days of Silicon Valley"; Moore, oral history interview by Thackray and Brock.

89. Hoerni, oral history interview by Lécuyer; Hoerni, oral history interview by Sporck; Moore, oral history interview by Ross Bassett and Lécuyer; Moore, oral history interview by Thackray and Brock; Grinich, oral history interview by Lécuyer; Emerson Pugh, Lyle Johnson, and John Palmer, *IBM's 360 and Early 370 Systems* (MIT Press, 1991), 70. Hoerni's interest in his planar process as a solution to the mesa reliability problems may have been reinforced by reports from a variety of research organizations on the use of glass, epoxy, and resin to encapsulate and protect transistor chips. Researchers at Bell Labs, Motorola, General Electric, Hughes, and the Diamond Ordnance Fuze Laboratory had all made public announcements of such efforts by the end of 1958. Emerson Pugh, Lyle Johnson, John Palmer, *IBM's 360 and Early 370 Systems* (MIT Press, 1991); see also note 69.

90. Hoerni, "Semiconductor Device," U.S. Patent 3,064,167, filed May 1, 1959 and issued November 13, 1962; Hoerni, "Method of Manufacturing Semiconductor Devices," U.S. patent 3,025,589, filed May 1, 1959 and issued March 20, 1962; Hoerni, oral history interview by Lécuyer; Hoerni, oral history interview by Sporck; David Allison, oral history interview by Lécuyer, 23 June 2000.

91. Jules Andrus, "Fabrication of Semiconductor Devices," U.S. Patent 3,122,817, filed on 15 August 1957 and granted 3 March 1964; "Planar Patent Rights Upheld for Fairchild," *Electronic News*, 14 November 1964; Roger Borovoy, oral history interview by Ross Bassett and Lécuyer, 14 June 1996.

92. "Planar Patent Rights Upheld for Fairchild," *Electronic News*, 14 November 1964; Borovoy, oral history interview by Bassett and Lécuyer. Texas Instruments also argued, unsuccessfully, that Hoerni's planar patents were invalid. See Jack Robertson, "Silicon Planar Plot Thickens: TI Assigned Fabrication Patent," *Electronic News*, 31 May 1965.

93. Jean Hoerni's patent disclosure is in Jay Last's personal collection of papers on the history of Fairchild Semiconductor. It is reproduced with permission from Jay Last.

94. Hoerni, patent notebook.

95. Jean Hoerni, oral history interview by Charles Sporck, no date, Stanford Archives and Special Collections.

96. Hoerni, oral history interview by Lécuyer; Hoerni, oral history interview by Charles Sporck, Stanford Archives and Special Collections; Gordon Moore, oral history interview by Arnold Thackray and David Brock; Moore and Jay Last, oral history interview by Brock and Lécuyer, 20 January 2006.

97. Hoerni, oral history interview by Lécuyer; Hoerni, oral history interview by Sporck. For an example of the gold doping of silicon diodes at Bell Labs, see E. G. Rupprecht, H. J. Patterson, and P. Miller, "Hyperfast Diffused-Silicon Diode and Transistor for Logic Circuits," *International Solid State Circuits Conference, Digest of Technical Papers* 2 (1959), 72–73.

98. Hoerni, patent notebook, 5 November 1958, 3 December 1958, and 1 January 1959, National Semiconductor.

99. The first version of the 2N706, introduced in August 1959, did not rely on gold doping, but Fairchild Semiconductor's engineers soon developed a gold-doped version of this transistor. Communication from Gordon Moore.

100. Hoerni, "Selective Control of Electron and Gold Lifetime in Transistors," U.S. patent 3,184,347, issued 18 May 1965; Gordon Moore and Jay Last, oral history interview by Brock and Lécuyer, 20 January 2006. Following up on his gold doping studies, Hoerni looked for an equivalent for use in PNP transistors—without success. Later, in the early 1960s, the speed of PNP transistors was greatly improved by the use of epitaxy.

101. Robert Noyce's patent notebook is held at National Semiconductor. Permission to reproduce this document was granted by Dick Schubert of National Semiconductor.

102. Geoffrey Dummer, "Electronic Components in Great Britain," *Proceedings of the Components Symposium*, Washington, May 6, 1952, 15–20; Harwick Johnson, "Semiconductor Phase Shift Oscillator and Device," U.S. Patent 2,816,228, filed 21 May 1953, issued 10 December 1957.

103. Jack Kilby, "Semiconductor Solid Circuits," *Electronics*, 7 August 1959, 110–111; Kilby, "Invention of the Integrated Circuit," *IEEE Transactions on Electron Devices* 23 (July 1976): 648–654; Edward Keonjian, "Microminiaturizing a Space Vehicle Computer," *Electronics*, 29 April 1960; Jack Kilby and Edward Keonjian, "Design of a Semiconductor Solid-Circuit Adder," *1959 International Electron Devices Meeting* 5 (1959), 76–78; J. T. Wallmark and S. M. Marcus, "An Integrated Semiconductor Shift Register," *IEEE Transactions on Electron Devices* (September 1961), 350–361; J. T. Wallmark, "Design Considerations for Integrated Electronic Devices," *Proceedings of the IRE* (March 1960), 293–300; J. T. Wallmark and S. M. Marcus, "Semiconductor Devices for Microminiaturization," *Electronics* (26 June 1959), 35–37.

104. Ernest Braun and Stuart McDonald, *Revolution in Miniature* (Cambridge University Press, 1982).

105. T. Prugh, J. Nall, and N. Doctor, "The DOFL Microelectronics Program," *Proceedings of the IRE*, May 1959, 882–894; L. Arthur D'Asaro, "A Stepping Transistor Element," *IRE Wescon Convention Record*, 1959, part 3, 37–42; D'Asaro, interview by Lécuyer, 7 May 2008; Ian Ross and Eugene Reed, "Functional Devices," in Edward Keonjian, ed., *Microelectronics: Theory, Design, and Fabrication* (McGraw-Hill, 1963); Jack A. Morton, "Strategy and tactics for integrated electronics," *IEEE Spectrum*, June 1969, 26–33; Jack A. Morton, "Foreword," in Edward Keonjian, ed., *Microelectronics: Theory, Design, and Fabrication* (McGraw-Hill, 1963).

106. Hyungsub Choi and Cyrus Mody, "The Long History of Molecular Electronics," *Social Studies of Science* 39 (2009), 11–50; Bassett, *To the Digital Age*; Thomas O. Stanley, oral history interview with David Brock and Gardner Hendrie, 30 March 2009; Samuel Snyder, "Computer Advances Pioneered by Cryptologic Organizations," *IEEE Annals of the History of Computing* 2, no. 1 (1980), 60–70; C. Harry Knowles, oral history interviews with David Brock, 18 September 2007 and 19 November 2007.

107. David James, oral history interview by Christophe Lécuyer, 14 December 2000.

108. Jay Last, personal notebook, entry for 20 January 1959, courtesy of Jay Last; Edward Keonjian, "Miniaturizing a Space Vehicle Computer," *Electronics*, 29 April 1960, 95–98; Keonjian, *Survived to Tell: The Autobiography of Edward Keonjian* (Sunstone, 1996). Keonjian's meeting with Fairchild Semiconductor's founders appears to have been influential. Keonjian's project showed that there was a military market for advanced, silicon-based microcircuitry for use in digital computers in the American ICBM program. At the meeting, Keonjian and Fairchild Semiconductor's founders discussed "surface protection ideas." For the hybrid circuits he designed for the Atlas guidance computer, Keonjian had experimented with coating the surfaces of diffused transistors with a protective varnish made of silicone (just as Hughes had recently disclosed). In his article on the Atlas computer, Keonjian noted that "attempts to coat circuit components with a suitable protective substance have not given entirely satisfactory results. A special treatment (pacification) of semiconductor surfaces, to make them invulnerable to their environment, is still experimental." In Keonjian's discussion with the Fairchild's founders about the importance

of surface protection, and the partial successes achieved to date, Noyce may have seen a unique opportunity in microcircuitry for exploiting the protection conferred by the silicon oxide layer in Hoerni's planar process.

109. Jean Hoerni, oral history interview by Christophe Lécuyer, 4 February 1996; Last, personal notebook, entry for 20 January 1959.

110. Kurt Lehovec, "Multiple Semiconductor Assembly," U.S. Patent 3,029,366, filed 22 April 1959, granted 10 April 1962; Lehovec, "Invention of p-n Junction Isolation in Integrated Circuits," *Transactions on Electron Devices*, ED-25, no. 4 (1978), 495–496; Lehovec, oral history interview by Brock, 21 and 31 August 2007.

111. Jack Kilby, "Miniaturized Electronic Circuits and Method of Making," typescript of patent application of 6 February 1959, reproduced in Arjun N. Saxena, *Invention of Integrated Circuits: Untold Important Facts* (World Scientific, 2009): 190–211; Lehovec, "Multiple Semiconductor Assembly," U.S. Patent 3,029,366, filed 22 April 1959, granted 10 April 1962. Both Kilby and Lehovec did mention alternative interconnection schemes in their patents. In Kilby's case he did mention that interconnecting wires could be laid on top of an insulating layer on the semiconductor piece. Whether Kilby had in fact envisioned depositing metal films that were adherent to such an insulating layer was a major issue in the patent litigation between Texas Instruments and Fairchild Semiconductor over the Kilby and Noyce patents in the mid 1960s. In his patent, Lehovec mentioned a possible process in which conductive inks could be used to print interconnection pathways atop an insulating layer of quartz. While Lehovec's suggestion derived from printed circuit board practices, it was very far from the mainstream in silicon device manufacturing technology.

112. M. M. Irvine, "Early Digital Computers at Bell Telephone Laboratories," *IEEE Annals of the History of Computing* (July-September 2001), 23–42; Louis Brown, "Flyable TRADIC: The First Airborne Transistorized Digital Computer," *IEEE Annals of the History of Computing* 21, no. 4 (1999), 55–61.

113. The hand and pen used on the last page and a half of the 23 January 1959 entry in Robert Noyce's patent notebook are significantly different from those used at the beginning of the entry. It is possible that Noyce drew the circuit diagrams at a later date than the earlier portions of the entry.

114. M. Irvine, "Early Digital Computers at Bell Telephone Laboratories," *IEEE Annals of the History of Computing* (2001), 42; Jay Last, November 1957 personal notebook entry, in this volume.

115. Noyce, "Semiconductor Device and Lead Structure," U.S. Patent 2,981,877, filed July 30, 1959; patent issued April 25, 1961.

116. The disallowed claim was, in essence, a succinct description of Hoerni's planar process with the novel addition of the metal interconnection: "The method of fabricating unitary semiconductor device-and-lead structures, which comprises oxidizing a surface of a semiconductor body containing a P-N junction extending to said surface, thereby forming on said surface an insulating oxide layer congenitally united with said body, removing said oxide layer from a contact area on said surface, leaving a portion of said layer extending across said junction, forming a metal contact adherent to said contact area, and depositing an adherent metal strip on said layer extending from said contact across said junction." In March 1960, the Patent Office informed Fairchild Semiconductor's lawyers that this claim had been disallowed because of its "method" character. Later that month, John Ralls, the lead attorney on Noyce's patents, wrote to Noyce, advocating that they attempt to get the claim re-instated, but that as a fallback position they would file a separate methods-focused patent application if unsuccessful. Noyce concurred with the strategy in a letter to Ralls in April 1960. Stunningly, in August 1960, Ralls' firm wrote Noyce to tell him that they had reversed course and abandoned the methods claim, and had modestly rewritten

the structure claims in light of two existing patents that they had uncovered: "Inasmuch as we have discovered several references that would anticipate the method claim, number 11 in this application, this claim has been canceled in lieu of the action indicated [previously]. . . . We have also voluntarily amended the structure claim so as to differentiate it from several references which we uncovered independently. . . . We believe that these references do not now anticipate the amended claims in case the Patent Office should discover and cite them." One of these references was U.S. patent 2,858,489. The patent, filed in 1955 and granted in 1958, covered the invention by Herbert Henkels of Westinghouse of a new form of silicon power transistor. Henkels patent bears a strong family resemblance to Hoerni's planar process, including, for example, maintaining a silicon oxide layer in place atop the transistor structure after diffusion operations, with the oxide layer covering junctions at the surface of the device. Keeping Henkels' patent in low profile may have been of particular importance to the firm's lawyers, not just for Noyce's patent application but also for the planar patent applications filed by Hoerni. Hoerni's planar patent applications were both filed after Henkels' patent had issued, and Hoerni's patents had not yet issued. Typescript of original patent application "Semiconductor Device-and-Lead Structure," 23 March 1960 letter from Ralls to Noyce, 13 April 1960 letter from Noyce to Ralls, 8 August 1960 letter of Hanger to Noyce, Robert Noyce Papers, Collection M1490, Series 1, Oversized Box 1, Folders 8, 9 and 10, Department of Special Collections, Stanford University Libraries.

117. T. R. Reid, *The Chip: How Two Americans Invented the Microchip and Launched a Revolution* (Simon and Schuster, 1984); Roger Borovoy, oral history interview by Ross Bassett and Lécuyer, 14 June 1996.

118. Noyce, "Semiconductor Circuit Complex Having Isolation Means," U.S. Patent 3,150,299, filed 11 September 1959 and granted 22 September 1964 and "Semiconductor Circuit Complexes," U.S. patent 3,117,260, filed 11 September 1959 and granted 7 January 1964.

119. Arjun Saxena does cite Noyce's two isolation patents in his recent highly detailed study of early patenting on integrated circuits, but mistakenly claims that they are on subjects outside of integrated circuits and do not have to do with his original conceptions of the planar integrated circuit. Arjun Saxena, *Invention of Integrated Circuits: Untold Important Facts* (World Scientific, 2009), 237, 31.

120. Kurt Lehovec, "Multiple Semiconductor Assembly," U.S. Patent 3,029,366, filed 22 April 1959, granted 10 April 1962; Lehovec, "Invention of p-n Junction Isolation in Integrated Circuits," *Transactions on Electron Devices*, ED-25, no. 4 (1978), 495–496; Lehovec, oral history interview by Brock, 21 and 31 August 2007.

121. Typescript patent application, Robert Noyce, "Improved Semiconductor Circuit Complex," Internal reference D-924, Robert Noyce Papers, M1490, Series 1, Oversized Box 1, Folder 8, Department of Special Collections, Stanford University Libraries; Typescript patent application, Robert Noyce, "Semiconductor Circuit Complexes," Internal reference D-922, Robert Noyce Papers, M1490, Series 1, Oversized Box 1, Folder 8, Department of Special Collections, Stanford University Libraries; See also correspondence between Noyce and patent attorneys in Folders 8, 9, and 10.

122. Typescript patent application, Robert Noyce, "Improved Semiconductor Circuit Complex," Internal reference D-924, Robert Noyce Papers, M1490, Series 1, Oversized Box 1, Folder 8, Department of Special Collections, Stanford University Libraries; Typescript patent application, Robert Noyce, "Semiconductor Circuit Complexes," Internal reference D-922, Robert Noyce Papers, M1490, Series 1, Oversized Box 1, Folder 8, Department of Special Collections, Stanford University Libraries; See also correspondence between Noyce and patent attorneys in Folders 8, 9, and 10; Reid, *The Chip*; Borovoy, oral history interview by Ross Bassett and Lécuyer; Borovoy interview by Brock.

123. Gordon Moore and Jay Last, oral history interview by Brock and Lécuyer, 20 January 2006; Lécuyer, *Making Silicon Valley*.

124. Rheem Semiconductor failed to become a major competitor in silicon transistors. It was sold to Raytheon and incorporated into the military contractor's internal semiconductor operations. Lécuyer, *Making Silicon Valley*; Berlin, *Man Behind the Microchip*; Charles Sporck, *Spin-off: A Personal History of the Industry that Changed the World* (Saranac Lake, 2001).

125. Lécuyer, *Making Silicon Valley*.

126. Moore and Last, oral history interview by Brock and Lécuyer.

127. This copy of *Leadwire* comes from Jay Last's personal collection. It is reproduced with his permission and the permission of Fairchild Semiconductor.

128. The group did not make any major changes to diffusion.

129. David Allison, oral history interview by Christophe Lécuyer, 23 June 2000; Thomas Bay, oral history interview by Lécuyer, 2 July 1996; Gordon Moore, oral history interview by Thackray and Brock; Moore and Jay Last, oral history interview by Brock and Lécuyer, 20 January 2006.

130. Noyce later claimed that he had conceived the tunnel diode earlier than Esaki. While working at Shockley Semiconductor, Noyce made entries in his patent notebook that he believed anticipated Esaki's tunnel diode. William Shockley dissuaded Noyce from pursuing his ideas, and the matter was dropped. Nevertheless, Noyce's familiarity with ideas around the tunnel diode may have played a role in Fairchild Semiconductor's rapid entry into this area. Leslie Berlin, *The Man behind the Microchip* (Oxford University Press, 2005), p. 66; Leslie Berlin and H. Craig Casey Jr., "Robert Noyce and the Tunnel Diode," *IEEE Spectrum*. May 2005.

131. Jay Last, patent notebook, entries for 15 August 1958, 2 November 1958, 13 November 1958, 24 June 1959 and 25 June 1959, National Semiconductor; Communication from Jay Last, 6 November 2008.

132. Leo Esaki, "Solid State Physics in Electronics and Telecommunications," in *Proceedings of the International Conference on Solid State Physics*, volume 1 (Academic Press, 1960), 514; Jay Last, "Development of the Integrated Circuit, August 1959–January 1961," unpublished manuscript, circa 2002. Jack Kilby published an article on integrated circuits in *Electronics* in the first week of August 1959. This article may have given new impetus to the microelectronics program at Fairchild. See Jack Kilby, "Semiconductor Solid Circuits," *Electronics*, 7 August 1959, 110–111.

133. Moore and Last, oral history interview by Brock and Lécuyer.

134. This document comes from Gordon Moore's personal collection. It is reproduced in this volume with his permission.

135. There is a large literature treating postwar industrial R&D. For a good introduction to this literature and the issues involved, see Phillip Scranton, "Technology, Science and American Innovation," *Business History* 48, no. 3 (July 2006): 311–331.

136. Gordon Moore, oral history interviews with Thackray and Brock, 2001–2007.

137. In January 1959, Gordon Moore and Victor Grinich had written a memorandum advocating the building of a family of mesa transistors. With the advent of the planar process, Moore promoted a similar family of planar transistors. See Moore and Grinich, "Device Planning," January 23, 1959, Moore collection.

138. This project was abandoned in late 1960. It had become clear that the way to reduce the cost of planar silicon transistors was to lower the costs of producing existing transistors rather than to design entirely new transistors.

139. Jean Hoerni, oral history interview by Christophe Lécuyer, 4 February 1996; Hoerni, oral history interview by Charles Sporck, no date, Stanford Archives and Special Collections.

140. Isy Haas, Jay Last, Lionel Kattner, and Bob Norman, oral history of panel on the Development and Promotion of Fairchild Micrologic Integrated Circuits, moderated by David Laws, 6 October 2007, Computer History Museum; communication from L. Arthur D'Asaro, 7 May 2007; communication from Gordon Moore, November 2008; R. Warner and B. Grung, *Transistors: Fundamentals for the Integrated-Circuit Engineer* (Wiley, 1990); Raymond Warner, "Microelectronics: Its Unusual Origin and Personality," *IEEE Transactions on Electron Devices* 48, no. 11 (2001), 2457–2467; Jack A. Morton, "Strategy and Tactics for Integrated Electronics," *IEEE Spectrum*, June 1969, 26–33; J. Goldey, J. Forster, and B. Murphy, "Silicon Integrated Circuits," in F. M. Smits, ed., *A History of Engineering and Science in the Bell System: Electronics Technology (1925–1975)* (AT&T Bell Laboratories, 1995).

141. Jay Last, interview with Brock and Lécuyer; Gordon Moore, oral history interviews with Thackray and Brock, 2001–2007.

142. Oral history of panel on the Development and Promotion of Fairchild Micrologic Integrated Circuits, moderated by David Laws, 6 October 2007, Computer History Museum.

143. Gordon Moore, oral history interviews with Thackray and Brock, 2001–2007.

144. See Fairchild Semiconductor R&D monthly reports for 1960, Technical Reports and Progress Reports, M1055, box 5, Stanford Archives and Special Collections.

145. Ross Bassett, *To the Digital Age: Research Labs, Start-Up Companies, and the Rise of MOS Technology* (Johns Hopkins University Press, 2002).

146. This copy of *Leadwire* comes from Jay Last's personal collection. It is reproduced with his permission and the permission of Fairchild Semiconductor.

147. Lécuyer, *Making Silicon Valley*; Berlin, *The Man Behind the Microchip*, 110–113.

148. Bassett, *To the Digital Age*, 50.

149. Last, personal notebook.

150. Lécuyer, "Silicon for Industry: Component Design, Mass Production, and the Move to Commercial Markets at Fairchild Semiconductor, 1960–1967," *History and Technology* 16 (1999), 179–216; Lécuyer, *Making Silicon Valley*.

151. Lécuyer, "Silicon for Industry"; Lécuyer, *Making Silicon Valley*.

152. Last, oral history interview by Lécuyer; Bay, oral history interview by Lécuyer.

153. "Fairchild Camera—Portrait of a Growth Company," *Financial World*, 12 September 1962. Stock prices for FCI in the second half of the 1950s were drawn from data on the American Stock Exchange published in the *Wall Street Journal*.

154. Lécuyer, *Making Silicon Valley*. For the financial community's coining of "high technology," see Lécuyer and Brock, "High Tech Manufacturing," *History and Technology*, 25, no. 3 (September 2009), 165–171.

155. Allison, oral history interview by Lécuyer; Richard Hodgson, oral history interview by Leslie Berlin; Last, oral history interview by Lécuyer.

156. Lécuyer, *Making Silicon Valley*.

157. Ibid.

158. This drawing comes from the personal collection of Lionel Kattner. It is reproduced with his permission.

159. Lionel Kattner, oral history interview by Christophe Lécuyer, 13 October 2000.

160. Last, oral interviews by Lécuyer; Last, oral history interview by Brock; Moore and Last interview by Brock and Lécuyer; Norman interview by Brock; Kattner interview by Lécuyer; Isy Haas, Jay Last, Lionel Kattner, and Bob Norman, oral history of panel on the Development and Promotion of Fairchild Micrologic Integrated Circuits, moderated by David Laws, 6 October 2007, Computer History Museum.

161. Victor Grinich, oral history interview by Lécuyer, 7 February 1996; Kattner, oral history interview; Isy Haas, Jay Last, Lionel Kattner, and Bob Norman, oral history of panel on the Development and Promotion of Fairchild Micrologic Integrated Circuits, moderated by David Laws, 6 October 2007, Computer History Museum. For a discussion of James Nall's work at DOFL, see Bo Lojek, *History of Semiconductor Engineering* (Springer, 2007).

162. It was only in 1962 that experts in the semiconductor industry were able to make triple diffused integrated circuits in a reproducible fashion.

163. Robert Noyce, "Semiconductor Circuit Complex Having Isolation Means," U.S. Patent 3,150,299, filed 11 September 1959 and granted 22 September 1964 and "Semiconductor Circuit Complexes," U.S. patent 3,117,260, filed 11 September 1959 and granted 7 January 1964; Last, oral history interview by Brock; Last, oral history interview by Lécuyer.

164. Jay Last, oral history interview by Christophe Lécuyer, 1 April 1996; Kattner, oral history interview; oral history of panel on the Development and Promotion of Fairchild Micrologic Integrated Circuits.

165. Last, oral history interview by Brock; Last, oral history interview by Lécuyer; Kattner, oral history interview by Lécuyer; oral history of panel on the Development and Promotion of Fairchild Micrologic Integrated Circuits.

166. Last, "Solid-State Circuitry Having Discrete Regions of Semiconductor Material Isolated by an Insulating Material," U.S. patent 3,158,788, filed August 15, 1960 and granted November 24, 1964; Last, "Method of Making Solid-State Circuitry," U.S. patent 3,313,013, filed August 15, 1960 and granted April 11, 1967; Last, oral history interview by Lécuyer; Kattner, oral history interview by Lécuyer; communication from Kattner to Lécuyer, 22 November 2008; oral history of panel on the Development and Promotion of Fairchild Micrologic Integrated Circuits.

167. The collector regions in each transistor pair were electrically joined.

168. When Kattner later worked on the diffused isolation version of the flip-flop circuit in the summer and fall of 1960, he devised a new interconnect pattern. With the diffusion isolated circuit, he worked with a solid piece of material and as a result did not need as much metal on top of the silicon oxide to interconnect the five components in the circuit. Communication from Kattner to Lécuyer, 22 November 2008.

169. Communication from Kattner to Lécuyer, 22 November 2008.

170. Last, oral history interview by Lécuyer; Kattner, oral history interview by Lécuyer; oral history of panel on the Development and Promotion of Fairchild Micrologic Integrated Circuits; communication from Kattner.

171. Jay Last's patent notebook is held at National Semiconductor. This notebook entry is reproduced with permission from National Semiconductor.

172. Last, "Some comments on the development of the first integrated circuits," 26 November 2000, courtesy of Jay Last. Roger Borovoy, oral history interview by Ross Bassett and Lécuyer, 14 June 1996.

173. Last, "Solid-State Circuitry Having Discrete Regions of Semiconductor Material Isolated by an Insulating Material," U.S. patent 3,158,788, filed August 15, 1960 and granted November 24, 1964 and "Method of Making Solid-State Circuitry," U.S. patent 3,313,013, filed August 15, 1960 and granted April 11, 1967.

174. Lionel Kattner's notebook is held at National Semiconductor. This notebook entry is reproduced with permission from National Semiconductor.

175. This entry appears in a slightly different form in Kattner's other patent notebook (10 June 1960). The later entry was witnessed by Isy Haas and Samuel Fok. FF-105 was Kattner's fifth trial run for making physically isolated flip-flops. A run is a batch of silicon wafers processed at the same time.

176. For prior attempts to make a physically isolated flip-flop circuit, see Kattner, notebooks, entries for 4 March, 7 March, 30 March, and 1 April 1960.

177. For a discussion of these processes, see Jay Last, "Solid-State Circuitry Having Discrete Regions of Semiconductor Material Isolated by an Insulating Material," U.S. patent 3,158,788, filed August 15, 1960 and granted November 24, 1964 and "Method of Making Solid-State Circuitry," U.S. patent 3,313,013, filed August 15, 1960 and granted April 11, 1967.

178. Isy Haas' patent notebook is held at National Semiconductor. These notebook entries are reproduced with permission from National Semiconductor.

179. Lionel Kattner, oral history interview by Christophe Lécuyer, 13 October 2000; Isy Haas, Jay Last, Lionel Kattner, and Bob Norman, oral history of panel on the Development and Promotion of Fairchild Micrologic Integrated Circuits, moderated by David Laws, 6 October 2007, Computer History Museum.

180. Jay Last, "Some comments on the development of the first integrated circuits," 26 November 2000, courtesy of Jay Last; oral history of panel on the development and promotion of Fairchild micrologic integrated circuits; Robert Noyce, "Semiconductor Circuit Complex Having Isolation Means," U.S. Patent 3,150,299, filed 11 September 1959 and granted 22 September 1964 and "Semiconductor Circuit Complexes," U.S. patent 3,117,260, filed 11 September 1959 and granted 7 January 1964.

181. Although Last supported Haas and Kattner's attempt to diffuse these isolation wells, both recall that others in the R&D leadership were extremely skeptical. Kattner recalls that Gordon Moore was particularly dubious that the attempt was worthwhile. Last, "Some comments on the development of the first integrated circuits"; oral history of panel on the Development and Promotion of Fairchild Micrologic Integrated Circuits Laws; Lionel Kattner, oral history interview by Christophe Lécuyer, 13 October 2000; Last, oral history interview by Lécuyer, 1 April 1996.

182. Last, "Some comments on the development of the first integrated circuits"; oral history of panel on the Development and Promotion of Fairchild Micrologic Integrated Circuits Laws; Lionel Kattner, oral history interview by Christophe Lécuyer, 13 October 2000; Last, oral history interview by Lécuyer, 1 April 1996. For Kattner's work on physically isolated flip-flops in August 1960, see Kattner, patent notebook,

26 August 1960 and Kattner, Micrologic process development notebook, 30 August 1960, National Semiconductor Corporation.

183. The grid-like isolation pattern separating islands into which planar devices would be formed that Haas drew in his entry is nearly identical to figures and descriptions in Noyce's patent application of September 1959 which issued as patent 3,117,260 in 1964.

184. Isy Haas, patent notebook, entry for 29 September 1960, courtesy of National Semiconductor Corporation; Last, "Some comments on the development of the first integrated circuits"; oral history of panel on the Development and Promotion of Fairchild Micrologic Integrated Circuits Laws; Kattner, oral history interview by Lécuyer, 13 October 2000.

185. This document is in Jay Last's personal collection of papers. It is reproduced with Jay Last's permission.

186. Robert Norman, interview by Brock, 8 August 2007; oral history of panel on the Development and Promotion of Fairchild Micrologic Integrated Circuits.

187. Robert Norman, interview by Brock, 8 August 2007; Jay Last, communication with David Brock, 8 May 2009; oral history of panel on the Development and Promotion of Fairchild Micrologic Integrated Circuits. In his interview with Brock and on the Micrologic panel, Norman consistently maintained that his presentations did not lead R&D results by too great a distance, but rather that the required proofs of concept were in place. In fact, Norman did cite reliability and lifetime tests in several of his presentations in 1960. In these tests, individual transistors and hybrid circuits were evaluated as proxies for the envisioned planar integrated circuits. On the basis of these evaluations, Norman and his colleagues made claims about the eventual performance and reliability of planar integrated circuits. Nevertheless, these claims largely preceded the actual fabrication of these circuits. Norman, Last, and Haas, "Solid State Micrologic Elements," presented at the Solid State Circuits Conference, February 1960, Fairchild Semiconductor Technical Paper TP-7 and Norman, "Status Report on Micrologic Elements," Presented at the 51st Guidance Panel, June 1960, Fairchild Semiconductor Technical Paper TP-10, Bruce Deal Papers, box 1, M1051, Stanford Archives and Special Collections.

188. Last, oral history interview by Lécuyer; Moore, oral history interview by Ross Bassett and Last, oral history interview by Lécuyer; Brock, ed., *Understanding Moore's Law: Four Decades of Innovation* (Chemical Heritage Press, 2006); Lécuyer, *Making Silicon Valley*.

189. Robert Norman, oral history interview with David Brock, 8 August 2007; Gordon Moore, oral history interviews with Thackray and Brock, 2001–2007; Motorola 68000 oral history panel, 23 July 2007, Computer History Museum; Zilog Z8000 Microprocessor oral history panel, 27 April 2007, Computer History Museum; Lécuyer, *Making Silicon Valley*.

190. Jay Last's lecture notes are in his personal collection of papers on the history of Fairchild Semiconductor. They are reproduced with Jay Last's permission.

191. Jay Last, oral history interview by Christophe Lécuyer 1 April 1996; Lionel Kattner, oral history interview by Lécuyer, 13 October 2000; Isy Haas, Jay Last, Lionel Kattner, and Bob Norman, oral history of panel on the Development and Promotion of Fairchild Micrologic Integrated Circuits, moderated by David Laws, 6 October 2007, Computer History Museum.

192. Bassett, *To the Digital Age*; Thomas O. Stanley, oral history interview with David Brock and Gardner Hendrie, 30 March 2009; L. Epstein, C. Lawrenson, and I. Feinberg, *Microminiaturized Packaging of 2N384 and 2N697: Final Report 1 October 1960–1 February 1962*, U.S. Army Signal Supply Agency.

193. Lécuyer, *Making Silicon Valley*.

194. This article is from the issue of the *Solid State Journal* in the private collection of Jay Last. It is reproduced in this volume with the permission of Horizon House.

195. Fairchild Semiconductor also experienced a surge in yields, which led to a momentary overproduction of transistors. See Robert Freund, *Competition and Innovation in the Transistor Industry*, PhD dissertation, Duke University, 1971; Lécuyer, "Silicon for Industry: Component Design, Mass Production, and the Move to Commercial Markets at Fairchild Semiconductor, 1960–1967," *History and Technology* 16 (1999): 179–216.

196. This document is held at the Stanford Archives and Special Collections (Technical Reports and Progress Reports, M1055, box 5, folder 4). It is reproduced in this volume with permission from the Stanford Archives and Special Collections and from Fairchild Semiconductor.

197. Communication from Jay Last to Lécuyer; Robert Robson, oral history interview by Brock and Lécuyer, 16 December 2005.

198. Lionel Kattner, patent notebook, entry for 26 August 1960 and Micrologic process development notebook, entry for 30 August 1960, courtesy of National Semiconductor Corporation.

199. Lionel Kattner, electrical isolation notebook, entry for 27 September 1960, courtesy of National Semiconductor; Jay Last, "Fairchild Micrologic History, January 1959–1961," unpublished chronology, courtesy of Jay Last.

200. Jay Last, "Some comments on the development of the first integrated circuits," 26 November 2000, courtesy of Jay Last.

201. This memorandum is in Jay Last's personal collection of papers. It is reproduced in this volume with his permission.

202. Jay Last, oral history interview by Christophe Lécuyer, 1 April 1996; Lionel Kattner, oral history interview by Lécuyer, 13 October 2000.

203. Robson, oral history interview by Brock and Lécuyer.

204. Donald Farina, who had worked with Norman on circuit designs for the Micrologic program, was leading the effort on the "kit," the customizable circuit. The customizable circuit described by Graham and pursued by Farina prefigured the "standard cell" approach in which a set of basic circuit modules could be combined in various ways to create custom or application-specific integrated circuits. Indeed, across the 1960s in a series of connected start-ups, Farina and Norman conducted very early work in standard cells and in the "fabless" as well as "foundry" business models. Donald Farina, oral history interview with David Brock, 24 July 2007; Robert Norman, oral history interview with David Brock, 8 August 2007.

205. E. North to Thomas Bay, "Microcircuit Sales," 30 July 1965, Computer History Museum; Isy Haas, Jay Last, Lionel Kattner, and Bob Norman, oral history of panel on the Development and Promotion of Fairchild Micrologic Integrated Circuits, moderated by David Laws, 6 October 2007, Computer History Museum; Eldon Hall, *Journey to the Moon: The History of the Apollo Guidance Computer* (American Institute of Aeronautics and Astronautics, Inc, 1996); A. Faulkner, F. Gurzi, and E. Hughes, "Magic: An Advanced Computer for Spaceborne Guidance Systems," no date, Computer History Museum.

206. Jay Last, communication with David Brock, 8 May 2009; "Keynote Panel Discussion: Hybrid versus Silicon Monolithic Circuits," *IEEE International Solid State Circuits Conference 1965 Digest of Technical Papers*, 30; E. M. Davis, "The Case for Hybrid Circuits," *IEEE International Solid State Circuits Conference 1965 Digest of Technical Papers*, 32–33; E. A. Sack, "Monolithic Circuits: Mass Produced for a Broad Market," *IEEE International Solid State Circuits Conference 1965 Digest of Technical Papers*, 31.

207. Brock, *Understanding Moore's Law*; Lécuyer, *Making Silicon Valley*.

208. DCTL circuits had low noise immunity. In other words, external electrical signals interfered with their functioning and affected their overall reliability.

209. Orville Baker, oral history interview by Lécuyer; Last, oral history interview by Lécuyer; Lécuyer, *Making Silicon Valley*.

210. E. North to Thomas Bay, "Microcircuit Sales," 30 July 1965, Computer History Museum; oral history of panel on the Development and Promotion of Fairchild Micrologic Integrated Circuits; John Linvill and C. Lester Hogan, "Intellectual and Economic Fuel for the Electronics Revolution," *Science* 195, no. 4283 (March 1977): 1107–1113.

211. Lécuyer, *Making Silicon Valley*; Berlin, *The Man Behind the Microchip*.

Conclusion

1. On the interplay of materials and human intentions, see Andrew Pickering, "The Mangle of Practice: Agency and Emergence in the Sociology of Science," *American Journal of Sociology* 99 (1993), 559–589; Pickering, *The Mangle of Practice* (University of Chicago Press, 1995).

2. Lécuyer, *Making Silicon Valley*.

3. Ross Bassett. *To the Digital Age: Research Labs, Start-Up Companies, and the Rise of MOS Technology* (Johns Hopkins University Press, 2002); Lécuyer, *Making Silicon Valley*; Lécuyer and Brock, "Gordon Earle Moore," *IEEE Annals of the History of Computing* 28, no. 3 (2006), 89–95.

4. Lécuyer, *Making Silicon Valley*; Lécuyer, "Silicon for Industry: Component Design, Mass Production, and the Move to Commercial Markets at Fairchild Semiconductor, 1960–1967," *History and Technology* 16 (1999), 179–216; Leslie Berlin, *The Man Behind the Microchip: Robert Noyce and the Invention of Silicon Valley* (Oxford University Press, 2005).

5. Lécuyer, *Making Silicon Valley*; Lécuyer, "Silicon for Industry"; Berlin, *The Man Behind the Microchip*.

6. Caleb Pirtle, *Engineering the World: Stories from the First 75 Years of Texas Instruments* (Southern Methodist University Press, 2005); Wilfred Corrigan, oral history interview by Jack Ward, 2006, Semiconductor Museum; Jack Haenichen, oral history interview by Ward, 2007, Semiconductor Museum.

7. Lécuyer, *Making Silicon Valley*.

8. Ibid.; Berlin, *The Man Behind the Microchip*.

9. "Davis and Rock," 13 July 1961, courtesy of Jay Last; John Wilson, *The New Venturers: Inside the High-Stakes World of Venture Capital*. (Addison-Wesley, 1985); Lécuyer, *Making Silicon Valley*; Martin Kenney, *Understanding Silicon Valley: The Anatomy of an Entrepreneurial Region* (Stanford University Press, 2000).

10. David C. Brock, ed., *Understanding Moore's Law: Four Decades of Innovation* (Chemical Heritage Press, 2006).

11. Stanley Mazor, communication to Lécuyer; Mazor, "Moore's Law, Computers, and Me," *IEEE Solid-State Circuits Magazine*, Winter 2009, 29–38; Mazor, oral history interview by Rob Walker, 9 June 2000, http://silicongenesis.stanford.edu; Albert Yu, *Creating the Digital Future* (Free Press, 1998); Les Vadasz, oral history interviews by Brock and Lécuyer, 15 March, 19 April 2005, and 7 June 2005; William Davidow, oral history interview by Brock, 8 May 2007; Gordon Moore, oral history interviews by Thackray and Brock, 2001–2007.

12. Brock, *Understanding Moore's Law*; David C. Brock and Hyungsub Choi, "Semiconductor Roadmapping: Origins, Functions, and Exemplary Status," unpublished manuscript.

13. Brock, *Understanding Moore's Law*.

14. Brock and Lécuyer, "Digital Foundations: The Making of Silicon Gate Manufacturing Technology; Part I: Emergence" and "Digital Foundations: The Making of Silicon Gate Manufacturing Technology; Part II: Establishment," unpublished manuscripts; Lécuyer and Brock, "From Nuclear Physics to Semiconductor Manufacturing: The Making of Ion Implantation," *History and Technology*, 25, no. 3 (September 2009), 193–217.

15. Ashutosh Mauskar, "Analog Tools Must Catch Up," *EE Times*, 26 March 2008; Tekla Perry, "Donald Pederson," *IEEE Spectrum*, June 1998, 22–27.

16. David Hodges, oral history interview by Lécuyer, 24 September 2008; Carver Mead, oral history interview by Brock and Arnold Thackray, 30 September 2004, 8 December 2004, 15 August 2005. Donald Pederson, "An Historical Overview of Circuit Simulation," *IEEE Transactions on Circuits and Systems*, 31, no. 1, January 1984, 103–111; Perry, "Donald Pederson"; Albert Sangiovanni-Vincentelli, "The Tides of EDA," *IEEE Design and Test of Computers*, November-December 2003, 59–75.

17. Udayan Gupta, *Done Deals: Venture Capitalists Tell Their Stories* (Harvard Business School Press, 2000).

18. Paul Freiberger and Michael Swaine, *Fire in the Valley: The Making of the Personal Computer* (Osborne–McGraw-Hill, 1984); Paul Ceruzzi, *A History of Modern Computing* (MIT Press, 1998).

19. Lécuyer, "What Do Universities Really Owe Industry? The Case of Solid State Electronics at Stanford," *Minerva* 43 (2005), 51–71; Arthur Norberg and Judy O'Neill, *Transforming Computer Technology: Information Processing for the Pentagon, 1962–1986* (Johns Hopkins University Press, 1996); Thierry Bardini, *Bootstrapping: Douglas Engelbart, Coevolution, and the Origins of Personal Computing* (Stanford University Press, 2000); Michael Lewis, *The New New Thing: A Silicon Valley Story* (Norton, 1999); Michael Hiltzik, *Dealers of Lightning: Xerox PARC and the Dawn of the Computer Age* (Harper Business, 1999).

20. Hodges, oral history interview by Lécuyer; Manuel Castells, *The Internet Galaxy: Reflections on the Internet, Business, and Society* (Oxford University Press, 2001); Janet Abbate, *Inventing the Internet* (MIT Press, 2000).

Appendix

1. See e.g., Roy H. Mattson, *Basic Junction Devices and Circuits* (Wiley, 1963); Lloyd P. Hunter, ed., *Handbook of Semiconductor Electronics*, second edition (McGraw-Hill, 1962).

2. G. W. A. Dummer, *Electronic Components, Tubes and Transistors* (Pergamon, 1965).

3. Michael Riordan and Lillian Hoddeson, *Crystal Fire: The Invention of the Transistor and the Birth of the Information Age* (Norton, 1997).

4. Hunter, *Handbook of Semiconductor Electronics*; William Shockley, *Electrons and Holes in Semiconductors* (Van Nostrand, 1950); U.S. Department of the Army, *Technical Manual TM11–690: Basic Theory and Application of Transistors* (U.S. Department of the Army, 1959); Riordan and Hoddeson, *Crystal Fire*; H. E. Bridgers, J. H. Scaff, and J. N. Shive, eds., *Transistor Technology*, volume 1 (Van Nostrand, 1958).

5. Shockley, *Electrons and Holes in Semiconductors*, 77–110; Bridgers, Scaff, and Shive, *Transistor Technology*, volume 1.

6. Shockley, *Electrons and Holes in Semiconductors*, 77–110; U.S. Army, *Basic Theory and Application of Transistors*, p. 36; Bridgers, Scaff, and Shive, *Transistor Technology*, volume 1.

7. See Ross Knox Bassett, *To the Digital Age: Research Labs, Start-up Companies, and the Rise of MOS Technology* (Johns Hopkins University Press, 2002); Christophe Lécuyer, *Making Silicon Valley: Innovation and the Growth of High Tech, 1930–1970* (MIT Press, 2006); David C. Brock, ed., *Understanding Moore's Law* (Chemical Heritage Press, 2006).

8. Shockley, *Electrons and Holes in Semiconductors*, 2–26; U.S. Army, *Basic Theory and Application of Transistors*, 5–42; Gordon Moore, "Semiconductor Integrated Circuits," in Edward Keonjian, ed., *Microelectronics: Theory, Design, and Fabrication* (McGraw-Hill, 1963), 262–359.

9. Shockley, *Electrons and Holes in Semiconductors*, 2–26; U.S. Army, *Basic Theory and Application of Transistors*, 5–42; Moore, "Semiconductor Integrated Circuits," 262–359.

10. Mattson, *Basic Junction Devices and Circuits*, 25–118, 160–215; Shockley, *Electrons and Holes in Semiconductors*, 2–26, 77–118.

11. Mattson, *Basic Junction Devices and Circuits*, 25–118, 160–215; Shockley, *Electrons and Holes in Semiconductors*, 2–26, 77–118; U.S. Army, *Basic Theory and Application of Transistors*, 5–42.

12. Mattson, *Basic Junction Devices and Circuits*, 25–118, 160–215; Shockley, *Electrons and Holes in Semiconductors*, 2–26, 77–118; U.S. Army, *Basic Theory and Application of Transistors*, 5–42; Hunter, *Handbook of Semiconductor Electronics*, 3–1 to 4–45.

13. Mattson, *Basic Junction Devices and Circuits*, 25–118, 160–215; Shockley, *Electrons and Holes in Semiconductors*, 2–26, 77–118; U.S. Army, *Basic Theory and Application of Transistors*, 5–42; Hunter, *Handbook of Semiconductor Electronics*, 3–1 to 4–45.

14. Mattson, *Basic Junction Devices and Circuits*, 25–118, 160–215; Hunter, *Handbook of Semiconductor Electronics*, 3–1 to 4–45.

15. Mattson, *Basic Junction Devices and Circuits*, 25–118, 160–215; Hunter, *Handbook of Semiconductor Electronics*, 3–1 to 4–45; Frank J. Biondi, ed., *Transistor Technology*, volume 2 (Van Nostrand, 1958).

16. Lécuyer, *Making Silicon Valley*, 129–167; Bassett, *To the Digital Age*, 12–56; Frank J. Biondi, ed., *Transistor Technology*, volume 3 (Van Nostrand, 1958); Bo Lojek, *History of Semiconductor Engineering* (Springer, 2007).

17. Moore, "Semiconductor Integrated Circuits," 262–359; Lojek, *History of Semiconductor Engineering*, 41–66, 103–154.

18. Moore, "Semiconductor Integrated Circuits," 262–359; Lojek, *History of Semiconductor Engineering*, 41–66, 103–154.

19. Moore, "Semiconductor Integrated Circuits," 262–359; Lojek, *History of Semiconductor Engineering*, 41–66, 103–154; Biondi, *Transistor Technology*, volume 3.

20. Moore, "Semiconductor Integrated Circuits," 262–359; Lojek, *History of Semiconductor Engineering*, 41–66, 103–154.

21. Moore, "Semiconductor Integrated Circuits," 262–359; Lojek, *History of Semiconductor Engineering*, 41–66, 103–154.

22. Moore, "Semiconductor Integrated Circuits," 262–359; Lojek, *History of Semiconductor Engineering*, 41–66, 103–154.

23. Moore, "Semiconductor Integrated Circuits," 262–359; Lojek, *History of Semiconductor Engineering*, 41–66, 103–154.

24. Moore, "Semiconductor Integrated Circuits," 262–359; Lojek, *History of Semiconductor Engineering*, 41–66, 103–154.

25. Moore, "Semiconductor Integrated Circuits," 262–359; Lojek, *History of Semiconductor Engineering*, 41–66, 103–154; Hunter, *Handbook of Semiconductor Electronics*, 1-9–1-10.

26. Lécuyer, *Making Silicon Valley*, 129–167; Bassett, *To the Digital Age*, 12–56; Biondi, ed., *Transistor Technology*, volume 3; Lojek, *History of Semiconductor Engineering*, 41–66, 103–154; Brock, *Understanding Moore's Law*.

27. Moore, "Semiconductor Integrated Circuits," 262–359; Lojek, *History of Semiconductor Engineering*, 41–66, 103–154.

28. Lécuyer, *Making Silicon Valley*, 129–167.

29. Ibid., 129–167; Bassett, *To the Digital Age*, 12–56.

30. Lécuyer, *Making Silicon Valley*, 129–167; Bassett, *To the Digital Age*, 12–56; Michael Riordan, "The Silicon Dioxide Solution," *IEEE Spectrum*, December 2007, 51–56.

31. Lécuyer, *Making Silicon Valley*, 129–167; Bassett, *To the Digital Age*, 12–56; Riordan, "The Silicon Dioxide Solution," 51–56.

32. Moore, "Semiconductor Integrated Circuits," 262–359; Lojek, *History of Semiconductor Engineering*, 41–66, 103–154.

33. Moore, "Semiconductor Integrated Circuits," 262–359; Lojek, *History of Semiconductor Engineering*, 41–66, 103–154.

34. Moore, "Semiconductor Integrated Circuits," 262–359; Lojek, *History of Semiconductor Engineering*, 41–66, 103–154.

35. Lécuyer, *Making Silicon Valley*, 129–167.

36. Ibid., 129–167; Bassett, *To the Digital Age*, 12–56.

37. Keonjian, *Microelectronics*.

38. Bassett, *To the Digital Age*, 12–56.

39. Moore, "Semiconductor Integrated Circuits," 262–359; Lécuyer, *Making Silicon Valley*, 129–167; Bassett, *To the Digital Age*, 12–56; Leslie Berlin, *The Man Behind the Microchip: Robert Noyce and the Invention of Silicon Valley* (Oxford University Press, 2005), 97–127.

40. Moore, "Semiconductor Integrated Circuits," 262–359.

41. Ibid., 262–359.

42. J. N. Harris, P. E. Gray, and C. L. Searle, *Digital Electronic Circuits* (Wiley, 1966); Martin Campbell-Kelly and William Aspray, *Computer: A History of the Information Machine*, second edition (Westview, 2004); Paul E. Ceruzzi, *A History of Modern Computing* (MIT Press, 1998).

43. Lécuyer, *Making Silicon Valley*, 129–167; Harris, Gray, and Seale, *Digital Electronic Circuits*; Campbell-Kelly and Aspray, *Computer*; Ceruzzi, *History of Modern Computing*.

Bibliography

Abbate, J. *Inventing the Internet*. MIT Press, 2000.

Aspray, W., ed. *Technological Competitiveness: Contemporary and Historical Perspectives on the Electrical, Electronics, and Computer Industries*. IEEE Press, 1993.

Atalla, M. M., E. Tannenbaum, and E. Scheibner. "Stabilization of Silicon Surfaces by Thermally Grown Oxides." Bell System Technical Journal 38 (May 1959): 749–783.

Bardini, T. *Bootstrapping: Douglas Engelbart, Coevolution, and the Origins of Personal Computing*. Stanford University Press, 2000.

Barling, G. "The Changing World of Avionics." *Measurement and Control* 24 (1991): 78–95.

Bassett, R. New Technology, New People, New Organization: The Rise of the MOS Transistor, 1945–1975. Ph.D. dissertation, Princeton University, 1998.

Bassett, R. *To the Digital Age: Research Labs, Start-Up Companies, and the Rise of MOS Technology*. Johns Hopkins University Press, 2002.

Beard, E. *Developing the ICBM*. Columbia University Press, 1976.

Berlin, L. Entrepreneurship and the Rise of Silicon Valley: The Career of Robert Noyce, 1956–1990. Ph.D. dissertation, Stanford University, 2001.

Berlin, L. "Robert Noyce and Fairchild Semiconductor, 1957–1968." *Business History Review* 75 (1) (2001): 63–102.

Berlin, L. *The Man Behind the Microchip: Robert Noyce and the Invention of Silicon Valley*. Oxford University Press, 2005.

Berlin, L., and H. C. Casey Jr. "Robert Noyce and the Tunnel Diode." *IEEE Spectrum*, May 2005.

Bondyopadhayay, P. K. "Moore's Law Governs the Silicon Revolution." *Proceedings of the IEEE* 86 (1) (1998): 78–81.

Braun, Ernest, and S. McDonald. *Revolution in Miniature*. Cambridge University Press, 1982.

Bridgers, H. E., J. H. Scaff, and J. N. Shive, eds. *Transistor Technology*, volume 1. Van Nostrand, 1958.

Bridges, J. "Progress in the Reliability of Military Electronics Equipment during 1956." *IRE Transactions on Reliability and Quality Control* 11 (1957): 1–7.

Brock, D. C. *Understanding Moore's Law: Four Decades of Innovation*. Chemical Heritage Press, 2006.

Brock, D. C., and H. Choi. "Semiconductor Roadmapping: Origins, Functions, and Exemplary Status." Unpublished manuscript, 2009.

Brock, D. C., and C. Lécuyer. "Digital Foundations: The Making of Silicon Gate Manufacturing Technology; Part I: Emergence." Unpublished manuscript, 2009.

Brock, D. C., and C. Lécuyer. "Digital Foundations: The Making of Silicon Gate Manufacturing Technology; Part II: Establishment." Unpublished manuscript, 2009.

Brown, J. E. "Integrated Circuits in Consumer Products." *IEEE Spectrum* 1 (6) (June 1964): 75.

Brown, L. "Flyable TRADIC: The First Airborne Transistorized Digital Computer." *IEEE Annals of the History of Computing* 21 (1999): 55–61.

Campbell-Kelly, M., and W. Aspray. *Computer: A History of the Information Machine*. Basic Books, 1996.

Cappon, L. "A Rationale for Historical Editing, Past and Present." *William and Mary Quarterly* 23 (1) (1966): 56–75.

Carlson, W. B., and M. E. Gorman. "Understanding Invention as a Cognitive Process: The Case of Thomas Edison and Early Motion Pictures, 1888–91." *Social Studies of Science* 20 (1990): 387–430.

Castells, M. *The Rise of the Network Society*. Blackwell, 1996.

Castells, M. *The Internet Galaxy: Reflections on the Internet, Business, and Society*. Oxford University Press, 2001.

Ceruzzi, P. *Beyond the Limits: Flight Enters the Computer Age*. MIT Press, 1989.

Ceruzzi, P. *A History of Modern Computing*. MIT Press, 1998.

Choi, H., and C. Mody. "The Long History of Molecular Electronics." *Social Studies of Science* 39 (2009): 11–50.

Daburlos, K. E., and H. J. Patterson. "Oxide Masking." *Bell Laboratories Record* 38 (November 1960): 417–420.

Danhof, C. *Government Contracting and Technological Change*. Brookings Institution, 1968.

Danko, S. F. "Printed Circuits and Microelectronics." *Proceedings of the IRE* 50 (1962): 937–945.

D'Asaro, L. A. "A Stepping Transistor Element." *IRE Wescon Convention Record*, 1959, part 3, 37–42.

Davies, L. "IBM to Expand Computer Output." *New York Times*, 28 April 1965.

Davis, E. M. "The Case for Hybrid Circuits." *IEEE International Solid State Circuits Conference 1965 Digest of Technical Papers*, 32–33.

Deal, B., and J. Early. "The Evolution of Silicon Semiconductor Technology: 1952–1977." *Journal of the Electrochemical Society* 126 (1979): 20C–32C.

DeGrasse, R. "The Military and Semiconductors." In *The Militarization of High Technology*, ed. J. Tirman. Ballinger, 1984.

Denson, W. "The History of Reliability Prediction." *IEEE Transactions on Reliability* 47: 3-SP (1998): SP-321–SP-328.

Dummer, G. "Electronic Components in Great Britain." *Proceedings of the Components Symposium*, Washington, May 6, 1952, 15–20.

Dummer, G. *Electronic Components, Tubes and Transistors*. Pergamon, 1965.

Dummer, G. "Integrated Electronics: A Historical Introduction." *Electronics and Power* 13 (1967): 71–77.

Dummer, G. *Electronic Inventions and Discoveries: Electronics from Its Earliest Beginnings to the Present Day*. Pergamon, 1983.

Dyer, D. *TRW: Pioneering Technology and Innovation since 1900*. Harvard Business School Press, 1998.

Ebel, G. "Reliability Physics in Electronics: A Historical View." *IEEE Transactions on Reliability* 47: 3-SP (1998): SP-379–SP-389.

Eckert, M., and H. Schubert. *Crystals, Electrons, Transistors: From Scholar's Study to Industrial Research*. American Institute of Physics, 1986.

Engelbart, D. "Microelectronics and the Art of Similitude." *IEEE International Solid State Circuit Conference Digest of Technical Papers* 3 (February 1960), 76.

English-Lueck, J. A. *Cultures@SiliconValley*. Stanford University Press, 2002.

Esaki, L. "Solid State Physics in Electronics and Telecommunications." *Proceedings of the International Conference on Solid State Physics, Brussels, 1958*, vol. 1, ed. M. Desirant and J. L. Michels. Academic Press, 1960.

Falk, C., B. Paterman, and J. Moran. *Made for America, 1890–1901*. vol. 1. *Emma Goldman: A Documentary History of the American Years*. University of Illinois Press, 2008.

Fishbein, S. *Flight Management Systems: The Evolution of Avionics and Navigation Technology*. Praeger, 1995.

Flamm, K. *Creating the Computer: Government, Industry, and High Technology*. Brookings Institution, 1988.

Flamm, K. *Mismanaged Trade? Strategic Policy and the Semiconductor Industry*. Brookings Institution, 1996.

Forester, T., ed. *The Microelectronics Revolution*. MIT Press, 1980.

Freiberger, P., and M. Swaine. *Fire in the Valley: The Making of the Personal Computer*. Osborne–McGraw-Hill, 1984.

Freund, R. Competition and Innovation in the Transistor Industry. Ph.D. dissertation, Duke University, 1971.

Friedrichs, G., and A. Schaff. *Microelectronics and Society*. Pergamon, 1982.

Frosch, C., and L. Derick. "Surface Protection and Selective Masking during Diffusion." *Journal of the Electrochemical Society* 104 (1957): 547–552.

Fuller, C., and J. A. Ditzenberger. "Diffusion of Boron and Phosphorus into Silicon." *Journal of Applied Physics* 25 (November 1954): 1439–1440.

Gellman, D., and D. Quigley, eds. *Jim Crow New York: A Documentary History of Race and Citizenship, 1777–1877*. New York University Press, 2003.

Goldey, J., J. Forster, and B. Murphy. "Silicon Integrated Circuits." In *A History of Engineering and Science in the Bell System: Electronics Technology (1925–1975)*, ed. F. M. Smits. AT&T Bell Laboratories, 1995.

Golding, A. The Semiconductor Industry in Britain and the United States: A Case Study in Innovation, Growth, and the Diffusion of Technology. D. Phil. Thesis, University of Sussex, 1971.

Goldstein, A. "Finding the Right Material: Gordon Teal as Inventor and Manager." In *Sparks of Genius: Portraits of Engineering Excellence*, ed. F. Nebeker. IEEE Press, 1993.

Goldstein, A., and W. Aspray, eds. *Facets: New Perspectives on the History of Semiconductors*. IEEE Press, 1997.

Gorgol, J., and I. Kleinfeld. *The Military-Industrial Firm*. Praeger, 1972.

Gray, R. "Learning from History: Case Studies of the Weapons Acquisition Process." *World Politics* 31 (3) (1979): 457–470.

Grove, A. *Physics and Technology of Semiconductor Devices*. Wiley, 1967.

Gupta, U, ed. *Done Deals: Venture Capitalists Tell Their Stories*. Harvard Business School Press, 2000.

Hall, E. *Journey to the Moon: The History of the Apollo Guidance Computer*. American Institute of Aeronautics and Astronautics, 1996.

Hayes, D. *Behind the Silicon Curtain: The Seduction of Work in a Lonely Era*. South End, 1989.

Heinrich, T. "Cold War Armory: Military Contracting in Silicon Valley." *Enterprise and Society* 3 (2002): 247–284.

Henriksen, P. "Solid State Physics Research at Purdue." *Osiris* 3 (1987): 237–260.

Hester, W. "Dr. E. M. Baldwin." *Solid State Journal*. March (1961): 18–19.

Hiltzik, M. *Dealers of Lightning: Xerox PARC and the Dawn of the Computer Age*. Harper Business, 1999.

Hoddeson, L. "The Entry of Quantum Theory of Solids into the Bell Telephone Laboratories, 1925–1940." *Minerva* 18 (1980): 422–447.

Hoddeson, L. "The Discovery of the Point-Contact Transistor." *Historical Studies in the Physical Sciences* 12 (1981): 41–76.

Hoddeson, L., E. Braun, J. Teichmann, and S. Weart, eds. *Out of the Crystal Maze*. Oxford University Press, 1992.

Hoddeson, L. "Research on Crystal Amplifiers during World War II and the Invention of the Transistor." *History and Technology* 11 (1994): 121–130.

Hoerni, J., and J. Ibers. "Complex Amplitudes for Electron Scattering by Atoms." *Physical Review* 91 (5) (1953): 1182–1185.

Hoerni, J. "Multiple Elastic Scattering in Electron Diffraction by Molecules." *Physical Review* 102 (6) (1956): 1530–1533.

Hoerni, J. "Multiple Elastic Scattering in Electron Diffraction by Crystals." *Physical Review* 102 (6) (1956): 1534–1542.

Hogan, C. "Lester. "Types of Integrated Circuits." *IEEE Spectrum* 1 (6) (June 1964): 63–71.

Holbrook, D. "Government Support of the Semiconductor Industry: Diverse Approaches and Information Flows." *Business and Economic History* 24 (2) (1995): 133–165.

Holbrook, D. Technical Diversity and Technological Change in the American Semiconductor Industry, 1952–1965. Ph.D. dissertation, Carnegie Mellon University, 1999.

Holbrook, D., W. Cohen, D. Hounshell, and S. Klepper. "The Nature, Sources, and Consequences of Firm Differences in the Early History of Semiconductor Industry." *Strategic Management Journal* 21 (2000): 1017–1041.

Holmes, F. "Laboratory Notebooks: Can the Daily Record Illuminate the Broader Picture?" *Proceedings of the American Philosophical Society* 134 (4) (1990): 349–366.

Holmes, F. "Scientific Writing and Scientific Discovery." *Isis* 78 (2) (1987): 220–235.

Hunter, L. *Handbook of Semiconductor Electronics*. McGraw-Hill, 1970.

Irvine, M. "Early Digital Computers at Bell Telephone Laboratories." *IEEE Annals of the History of Computing* (2001), 22–42.

Kahn, A. *Jewish Voices of the California Gold Rush: A Documentary History, 1849–1880*. Wayne State University Press, 2002.

Kargon, R., S. Leslie, and E. Schoenberger. "Far Beyond Big Science: Science Regions and the Organization of Research and Development." In *Big Science: The Growth of Large-Scale Research*, ed. P. Galison and B. Hevly. Stanford University Press, 1992.

Kenney, M., ed. *Understanding Silicon Valley: The Anatomy of an Entrepreneurial Region*. Stanford University Press, 2000.

Keonjian, E. "Microminiaturizing a Space Vehicle Computer." *Electronics*, 29 April 1960.

Keonjian, E. *Survived to Tell: The Autobiography of Edward Keonjian*. Sunstone, 1996.

Kilby, J. "Semiconductor Solid Circuits." *Electronics*, August 7, 1959, 110–111.

Kilby, J. "Invention of the Integrated Circuit." *IEEE Transactions on Electron Devices* 23 (July 1976): 648–654.

Kilby, J., and E. Keonjian. "Design of a Semiconductor Solid-Circuit Adder." *1959 International Electron Devices Meeting*, 5 (1959), 76–78.

Kleinman, H. The Integrated Circuit: A Case Study of Production Innovations in the Electronics Industry. Ph.D. dissertation, George Washington University, 1966.

Kline, M. J. *A Guide to Documentary Editing*. Johns Hopkins University Press, 1998.

Knowles, C. "Harry. "Research and Development in Integrated Circuits." *IEEE Spectrum* 1 (6) (June 1964): 76–79.

Last, J. "Two Communications Revolutions." *Proceedings of the IEEE* 86 (1) (1998): 170–175.

Lécuyer, C. Making Silicon Valley: Engineering Culture, Innovation, and Industrial Growth, 1930–1970. Ph.D. dissertation, Stanford University, August 1999.

Lécuyer, C. "Silicon for Industry: Component Design, Mass Production, and the Move to Commercial Markets at Fairchild Semiconductor, 1960–1967." *History and Technology* 16 (1999): 179–216.

Lécuyer, C. "Fairchild Semiconductor and Its Influence." In *The Silicon Valley Edge: A Habitat for Innovation and Entrepreneurship*, ed. C.-M. Lee, W. Miller, M. Hancock, and H. Rowen. Stanford University Press, 2000.

Lécuyer, C. "Making Silicon Valley: Engineering Culture, Innovation, and Industrial Growth, 1930–1970." *Enterprise and Society* 2 (2001): 666–672.

Lécuyer, C. "High Tech Corporatism: Management-Employee Relations in U.S. Electronics Firms, 1920s-1960s." *Enterprise and Society* 4 (2003): 502–520.

Lécuyer, C. "What Do Universities Really Owe Industry? The Case of Solid State Electronics at Stanford." *Minerva* 43 (2005): 51–71.

Lécuyer, C. *Making Silicon Valley: Innovation and the Growth of High Tech, 1930–1970*. MIT Press, 2006.

Lécuyer, C., and D. C. Brock. "Gordon Earle Moore." *IEEE Annals of the History of Computing* 28 (3) (2006): 89–95.

Lécuyer, C., and D. C. Brock. "The Materiality of Microelectronics." *History and Technology* 22 (2006): 301–325.

Lécuyer, C., and D. C. Brock. "From Nuclear Physics to Semiconductor Manufacturing: The Making of Ion Implantation." *History and Technology* 25 (2009): 193–217.

Lécuyer, C., and D. C. Brock. "High Tech Manufacturing." *History and Technology* 25 (2009): 165–171.

Lee, C.-M., W. Miller, M. Hancock, and H. Rowen, eds. *The Silicon Valley Edge: A Habitat for Innovation and Entrepreneurship*. Stanford University Press, 2000.

Leslie, S. *The Cold War and American Science: The Military-Industrial-Academic Complex at MIT and Stanford*. Columbia University Press, 1992.

Leslie, S. "How the West Was Won: The Military and the Making of Silicon Valley." In *Technological Competitiveness: Contemporary and Historical Perspectives on the Electrical, Electronics, and Computer Industries*, ed. W. Aspray. IEEE Press, 1993.

Leslie, S. "Regional Disadvantage: Replicating Silicon Valley in New York's Capital Region." *Technology and Culture* 42 (2001): 236–264.

Leslie, S. "Blue Collar Science: Bringing the Transistor to Life in the Lehigh Valley." *Historical Studies in the Physical and Biological Sciences* 42 (2001): 71–113.

Leslie, S., and R. Kargon. "Electronics and the Geography of Innovation in Post-War America." *History and Technology* 11 (1994): 217–231.

Leslie, S., and R. Kargon. "Selling Silicon Valley: Frederick Terman's Model for Regional Advantage." *Business History Review* 70 (1996): 435–472.

Levin, R. "The Semiconductor Industry." In *Government and Technical Progress: A Cross Industry Analysis*, ed. R. Nelson. Pergamon, 1982.

Lewis, M. *The New New Thing: A Silicon Valley Story*. Norton, 1999.

Lewis, T. B. "Digital Computer Equipment for an Advanced Bombing, Navigation and Missile Guidance Subsystem for the B-70 Air Vehicle." *Proceedings of the IRE* 49 (1) (January 1961): 313–318.

Linzmayer, O. *Apple Confidential 2.0: The Definitive History of the World's Most Colorful Company*. No Starch, 2004.

Linvill, J., and C. L. Hogan. "Intellectual and Economic Fuel for the Electronics Revolution." *Science*, NS 195: 4283 (1977): 1107–1113.

Lojek, B. *History of Semiconductor Engineering*. Springer, 2007.

Lowen, R. *Creating the Cold War University: The Transformation of Stanford*. University of California Press, 1997.

MacKenzie, D. *Inventing Accuracy*. MIT Press, 1990.

Malone, M. *The Big Score: The Billion Dollar Story of Silicon Valley*. Doubleday, 1985.

Malone, M. *The Microprocessor: A Biography*. Springer-Verlag, 1995.

Matthews, G. *Silicon Valley, Women, and the California Dream: Gender, Class, and Opportunity in the Twentieth Century*. Stanford University Press, 2003.

Mattson, R. H. *Basic Junction Devices and Circuits*. Wiley, 1963.

Mauskar, A. "Analog Tools Must Catch Up." *EE Times*, 26 March 2008.

Mazor, S. "Moore's Law, Computers, and Me." *IEEE Solid-State Circuits Magazine*, winter 2009: 29–38.

McKenney, J., and A. Weaver Fisher. "Manufacturing the ERMA Banking System: Lessons from History." *IEEE Annals of the History of Computing* 15 (4) (1993): 7–26.

Merrill, A. *Investing in the Scientific Revolution: A Serious Search for Growth Stocks in Advanced Technology*. Doubleday, 1962.

Miller, L. E. "The Design and Characteristics of a Diffused Silicon Logic Amplifier Transistor." *Proceedings of Wescon* 2 (1958).

Millman, S., ed. *A History of Engineering and Science in the Bell System: Communications Sciences (1925–1980)*. AT&T Bell Laboratories, 1984.

Misa, T. "Military Needs, Commercial Realities, and the Development of the Transistor, 1948–1958." In *Military Enterprise and Technological Change: Perspectives on the American Experience*, ed. M. R. Smith. MIT Press, 1985.

Moll, J. "William Bradford Shockley: 1910–1989." Biographical Memoirs, National Academy of Sciences (U.S.) 68 (1995): 305–323.

Moore, G. "Semiconductor Integrated Circuits." In *Microelectronics: Theory, Design, and Fabrication*, ed. E. Keonjian. McGraw-Hill, 1963.

Moore, G. "Cramming More Components onto Integrated Circuits." *Electronics* 19 (April) (1965): 114–117.

Moore, G. "Progress in Digital Integrated Electronics." *Technical Digest—IEEE International Electron Devices Meeting* (1975), 11–13.

Moore, G. "The Accidental Entrepreneur." *Engineering and Science*, summer 1994: 27.

Moore, G. "Some Personal Perspectives on Research in the Semiconductor Industry." In *Engines of Innovation: US Industrial Research at the End of an Era*, ed. R. Rosenbloom and W. Spencer. Harvard Business School Press, 1996.

Moore, G. "The Role of Fairchild in Silicon Technology in the Early Days of 'Silicon Valley.'" *Proceedings of the IEEE* 86 (1998): 53–62.

Morgan, J. *Electronics in the West: The First Fifty Years*. National Press Books, 1967.

Morris, P. R. *A History of the World Semiconductor Industry*. Peregrinus, 1990.

Morton, J. "Foreword." In *Microelectronics: Theory, Design, and Fabrication*, ed. E. Keonjian. McGraw-Hill, 1963.

Morton, J. "Strategy and Tactics for Integrated Electronics." *IEEE Spectrum*, June 1969: 26–33.

Nall, J. R., and J. W. Lathrop. "Photolithographic Fabrication Techniques for Transistors which are an Integral Part of a Printed Circuit." *IRE Transactions on Electron Devices* 5 (2) (April 1958): 117.

Nelson, C. *Missile and Aircraft Procurement Management*. Vantage, 1961.

Neufeld, J. *Ballistic Missiles in the United States Air Force, 1945–1960*. Office of Air Force History, 1990.

Norberg, A. "The Origins of the Electronics Industry on the Pacific Coast." *Proceedings of the IEEE* 64 (1976): 1314–1322.

Norberg, A., and J. O'Neill. *Transforming Computer Technology: Information Processing for the Pentagon, 1962–1986*. Johns Hopkins University Press, 1996.

Norberg, A. *Computers and Commerce: A Study of Technology and Management at Eckert-Mauchly Computer Company, Engineering Research Associates, and Remington Rand, 1946–1957*. MIT Press, 2005.

Norman, R., J. Last, and I. Haas. "Solid-State Micrologic Elements." *IEEE International Solid State Circuits Conference Digest of Technical Papers* 3 (February 1960), 83.

Noyce, R. "Microelectronics." *Scientific American* 23 (3) (1977): 63–69.

Olsen, P. F., and R. J. Orrange. "Real-Time Systems for Federal Applications: A Review of Significant Technological Developments." *IBM Journal of Research and Development* 25 (5) (September 1981): 405–416.

O'Mara, P. M. *Cities of Knowledge: Cold War Science and the Search for the Next Silicon Valley*. Princeton University Press, 2004.

Peck, M., and F. M. Scherer. *The Weapons Acquisition Process: An Economic Analysis*. Graduate School of Business Administration, Harvard University, 1962.

Perry, T. "Donald Pederson." *IEEE Spectrum* 35 (1998): 22–27.

Pickering, A. "The Mangle of Practice: Agency and Emergence in the Sociology of Science." *American Journal of Sociology* 99 (1993): 559–589.

Pickering, A. *Mangle of Practice*. University of Chicago Press, 1995.

Pickering, A. "Decentering Sociology: Synthetic Dyes and Social Theory." *Perspectives on Science* 13 (2005): 352–405.

Pirtle, C. *Engineering the World: Stories from the First 75 Years of Texas Instruments*. Southern Methodist University Press, 2005.

Prugh, T., J. Nall, and N. Doctor. "The DOFL Microelectronics Program." *Proceedings of the IRE*, May 1959, 882–894.

Pugh, E. *Building IBM; Shaping an Industry and Its Technology*. MIT Press, 1995.

Pugh, E., L. Johnson, and J. Palmer. *IBM's 360 and Early 370 Systems*. MIT Press, 1991.

Pursell, C. W. *A Hammer in Their Hands: A Documentary History of Technology and the African-American Experience*. MIT Press, 2006.

Queisser, H. *The Conquest of the Microchip*. Harvard University Press, 1988.

Ramo, S. "The Impact of Missiles and Space on Electronics." *Proceedings of the IRE* 50 (1962): 1237–1241.

Reid, T. R. *The Chip: How Two American Companies Invented the Microchip and Launched a Revolution*. Simon and Schuster, 1984.

Riordan, M. "From Bell Labs to Silicon Valley: A Saga of Semiconductor Technology Transfer, 1955–61." *The Electrochemical Society Interface* 16:3 (2007), 36–41.

Riordan, M. "The Silicon Dioxide Solution." *IEEE Spectrum* 44 (12) (2007): 50–56.

Riordan, M., and L. Hoddeson. *Crystal Fire: The Birth of the Information Age*. Norton, 1997.

Rosen, S. "Recollections of the Philco Transac S-2000." *IEEE Annals of the History of Computing* 26 (April-June 2004): 34–47.

Rosenberg, N. *Perspectives on Technology*. Cambridge University Press, 1976.

Rosenberg, N. *Inside the Black Box*. Cambridge University Press, 1982.

Rosenberg, N. *Exploring the Black Box: Technology, Economics, and History*. Cambridge University Press, 1994.

Ross, I., and E. Reed. "Functional Devices." In *Microelectronics: Theory, Design, and Fabrication*, ed. E. Keonjian. McGraw-Hill, 1963.

Rupprecht, E. G., H. J. Patterson, and P. Miller. "Hyperfast Diffused-Silicon Diode and Transistor for Logic Circuits." *International Solid State Circuits Conference, Digest of Technical Papers*, 2 (1959), 72–73.

Ryerson, C. "The Reliability and Quality Control Field from Its Inception to the Present." *Proceedings of the IRE* 50 (1962): 1321–1338.

Sack, E. A. "Monolithic Circuits: Mass Produced for a Broad Market." *IEEE International Solid State Circuits Conference 1965 Digest of Technical Papers*, 31.

Sah, C.-T. "Evolution of the MOS Transistor—From Conception to VLSI." *Proceedings of the IEEE* 76 (1988): 1280–1326.

Saleh, J. H., and K. Marais. "Highlights from the early (and pre-) history of reliability engineering." *Reliability Engineering & System Safety* 91 (2006): 249–256.

Sangiovanni-Vincentelli, A. "The Tides of EDA." *IEEE Design & Test of Computers* 20 (6) (2003): 59–75.

Saxena, A. *Invention of Integrated Circuits: Untold Important Facts*. World Scientific, 2009.

Saxenian, A. *Regional Advantage: Culture and Competition in Silicon Valley and Route 128*. Harvard University Press, 1994.

Scherer, F. *The Weapons Acquisition Process: Economic Incentives*. Harvard Business School, 1964.

Schulz, C. "'From Generation unto Generation': Transitions in Modern Documentary History Editing." (Review Essay)." *Reviews in American History* 16 (3) (1988): 337–350.

Schwartz, B. "The Use of Organo-Substituted Hydrolyzable Silanes on Silicon Devices." *Journal of the Electrochemical Society*, October 1959: 371–373.

Schwop, J., and H. Sullivan, eds. *Semiconductor Reliability*. Engineering Publishers, 1961.

Scott, A. "The Aerospace-Electronics Industrial Complex of Southern California: The Formative Years, 1940–1960." *Research Policy* 20 (1991): 439–456.

Scott, P. *The Pioneers of Flight: A Documentary History*. Princeton University Press, 2003.

Scranton, P. *Endless Novely: Specialty Production and American Industrialization, 1865–1925*. Princeton University Press, 1997.

Scranton, P. "Technology, Science and American Innovation." *Business History* 48 (3) (July 2006): 311–331.

Seidenberg, P. "From Germanium to Silicon: A History of Change in the Technology of Semiconductors." In *Facets: New Perspectives on the History of Semiconductors*, ed. A. Goldstein and W. Aspray. IEEE Press, 1997.

Seitz, F. *On the Frontier: My Life in Science*. American Institute of Physics, 1994.

Shannon, T. *Genetic Engineering: A Documentary History*. Greenwood, 1999.

Shaw, P. "The American Heritage and Its Guardians." *American Scholar* 45 (1976): 175–182.

Shockley, W. "The Path to the Conception of the Junction Transistor." *IEEE Transactions on Electron Devices* 23 (1976): 597–620.

Shockley, W. *Electrons and Holes in Semiconductors*. Van Nostrand, 1950.

Siegel, L., and J. Markoff. *The High Cost of High Tech*. Harper & Row, 1985.

Slater, R. *Portraits in Silicon*. MIT Press, 1987.

Smits, F. M. *A History of Engineering and Science in the Bell System: Electronics Technology (1925–1975)*. AT&T Bell Laboratories, 1985.

Snyder, S. "Computer Advances Pioneered by Cryptologic Organizations." *IEEE Annals of the History of Computing* 2 (1) (1980): 60–70.

Spiegel, J., and E. M. Bennett. "Military System Reliability." *IRE Transactions on Reliability and Quality Control*. 10 (1961): 1–8, 53–63.

Sporck, C. *Spin-off: A Personal History of the Industry that Changed the World*. Saranac Lake, 2001.

Steinmueller, E. Microeconomics and Microelectronics: Economic Studies of Integrated Circuit Technology. Ph.D. dissertation, Stanford University, 1987.

Sturgeon, T. "How Silicon Valley Came to Be." In *Understanding Silicon Valley: The Anatomy of an Entrepreneurial Region*, ed. M. Kenney. Stanford University Press, 2000.

Tilton, J. *International Diffusion of Technology: The Case of Semiconductors*. Brookings Institution, 1971.

Tirman, J., ed. *The Militarization of High Tech*. Ballinger, 1984.

U.S. Department of the Army. *Technical Manual TM11–690: Basic Theory and Application of Transistors*. U.S. Department of the Army, 1959.

Usselman, S. "IBM and Its Imitators: Organizational Capabilities and the Emergence of the International Computer Industry." *Business and Economic History* 22 (1993): 1–35.

Usselman, S. "Fostering a Capacity for Compromise: Business, Government, and the Stages of Innovation in American Computing." *Annals of the History of Computing* 18 (2) (1996): 30–39.

von Halven, W., ed. *Semiconductor Reliability*. Engineering Publishers, 1962.

Wallmark, J. T. and S. M. Marcus. "Semiconductor Devices for Microminiaturization." *Electronics* (26 June 1959): 35–37.

Wallmark, J. T. "Design Considerations for Integrated Electronic Devices." *Proceedings of the IRE*, March 1960: 293–300.

Wallmark, J. T., and S. M. Marcus. "An Integrated Semiconductor Shift Register." *IRE Transactions on Electron Devices* 8 (5): 350–361.

Warner, R., and B. Grung. *Transistors: Fundamentals for the Integrated-Circuit Engineer*. Wiley, 1990.

Warner, R. "Microelectronics: Its Unusual Origin and Personality." *IEEE Transactions on Electron Devices* 48 (11) (2001): 2457–2467.

Weston, J. F., ed. *Procurement and Profit Renegotiation*. Wadsworth, 1960.

Williams, R., and P. L. Cantelon, eds. *American Atom: A Documentary History of Nuclear Policies from the Discovery of Fission to the Present, 1939–1984*. University of Pennsylvania Press, 1984.

Wilson, J. *The New Venturers: Inside the High-Stakes World of Venture Capital*. Addison-Wesley, 1985.

Wilson, R., P. Ashton, and T. Egan. *Innovation, Competition, and Government Policy in the Semiconductor Industry*. Lexington Books, 1980.

Wolfe, T. "The Tinkerings of Robert Noyce." *Esquire*, December 1983: 346–373.

Wolff, M. "The Genesis of the Integrated Circuit." *IEEE Spectrum* 13 (1976): 45–53.

Wood, R. *Life in Laredo: A Documentary History from the Laredo Archives*. University of North Texas Press, 2004.

Wuerth, J. M. "The Impact of Guidance Technology on Automated Navigation." *Navigation* 14 (1967): 328–339.

Wuerth, J. M. "The Evolution of Minuteman Guidance and Control." *Navigation* 23 (1976): 64–75.

Yu, A. *Creating the Digital Future*. Free Press, 1998.

Index

Staff meeting 11/11/57. Thos + Max.

hourly vs monthly   Green wax

[Requisitions - Project leads to $1000
        "   "   + Bob 5000
             >5000 Policy committee

Cardex files ??

Tool list

Receiving and/or stockroom clerk.

procedures will be written up by Max

write up

- Patent Attorney - ÷

Staff Meeting 11/18/57

                                    Finished by
→ power: transformers here: 2 weeks. to go   12/2/57
→ ceiling: started today 2 weeks -   12/2/57

(this is only main power - no bench power)

→ plumbing, sewers etc } laid out
      gas, air

→   air handling - blowers, pressure : laid out.

→   small rooms :   12/15/57.

→ benches & lab : finished by Dec 1.
   cabinets: arrive this Thursday - also 6 Hoods.

   furnace benches: arrive today

→ phones : no estimate 2-3 weeks   DA6-6695 in 2 weeks
        4 trunks

   two estimates to J.B today

   6 up to 12/31/57